Aug 1995   9-95

THE
GODHEAD

THE
GODHEAD

Devotional Studies
on the
Three Persons of the Trinity

LEHMAN STRAUSS

LOIZEAUX BROTHERS
Neptune, New Jersey

The Godhead
© 1990 by Lehman Strauss. All rights reserved.
A publication of Loizeaux Brothers, Inc.
A nonprofit organization devoted to the Lord's work
and to the spread of His truth.

Formerly published in three volumes:
The First Person, 1967
The Second Person, 1951
The Third Person, 1954

Library of Congress Cataloging-in-Publication Data
Strauss, Lehman.
The Godhead : devotional studies on the Three Persons of the
Trinity / Lehman Strauss.
p.   cm.
"Formerly published in three volumes: The First Person, 1967;
The Second Person, 1951; and The Third Person, 1954"—
Includes bibliographical references and index.
ISBN 0-87213-824-0
1. Trinity—Meditations. 2. God—Meditations. I. Title.
BT113.S82 1990
231′.044—dc20   90-45993

Printed in the United States of America
10 9 8 7 6 5 4 3 2 1

DEDICATION

To Elsie Marie

whose love for God and His Word
and whose loyalty to me at all times
proved her to be a true servant of Jesus Christ
and a most faithful and loving helpmeet

and

To my two sons
Richard and John

whose love and faithfulness have been a fountain of joy

this volume is affectionately and gratefully dedicated
by the Author.

PUBLISHER'S PREFACE

One of a publisher's delights is seeing consistent demand for a book over a long period of time. It is confirmation that the decision to publish was a wise one—that the author chose his subject well and communicated effectively the truths of God's Word for the blessing of His people. This is the case with Lehman Strauss's studies on the Godhead.

Originally published in three volumes—*The First Person* (1967), *The Second Person* (1951) and *The Third Person* (1954)—these devotional studies on the Trinity have blessed thousands around the world. It is therefore a special joy to present this combined edition of all three works. It is our hope that this convenient format will ensure its distribution to and use by new generations of Bible students.

LOIZEAUX BROTHERS, INC.

Neptune, New Jersey
November 1990

TABLE OF CONTENTS

THE FIRST PERSON

THE SECOND PERSON

THE THIRD PERSON

THE
FIRST
PERSON

PART I

THE NECESSITY FOR GOD

A NEED IN THIS PRESENT HOUR
THE TESTIMONY OF GOD IN CREATION
THE ANTHROPOLOGICAL ARGUMENT

A NEED IN THIS PRESENT HOUR

A feeling of awe well-nigh staggers me as I lift my pen to write this book. The most difficult question ever asked of me was propounded by my eldest son when he was still a lad. It happened one day after we returned home from the morning preaching service. Richard was only seven at that time. Now he is a father instructing his own children. But his question continues to engage all of my thinking powers. Little did he know how profound his question was when he asked me what God was like.

My reader will have to forgive me for trying to answer my son's question. I know that the greatest word in the vocabulary of any language or dialect is God; the loftiest thought that any mind can entertain is the thought of God. Any person attempting to explain God must be gripped with something of the thoughts of the hymn writer who wrote: "How shall my tongue describe Him?"

Trying to show the necessity for God is made still more difficult when we recall that God Himself makes no attempt to prove His existence. The Bible, God's written revelation of Himself, and of His plans and purposes, does not argue for the existence of God. This Book of all books commences with the declarative statement, "In the beginning God," [1] and lets it go at that. This

[1] Genesis 1:1

17

characteristic pervades the whole of Scripture. The writers of both the Old and New Testament books took the existence of God for granted. They never sought to prove Him who already is. When Moses, divinely chosen, and under the inspiration and guidance of the Holy Spirit, penned those first words of our Holy Bible, he doubtless pursued a wise course, and I do not question that theologians and preachers would do well to copy his example.

A study of the Gospel narratives on the teachings of Jesus about God shows no sustained argument for His Father's existence. He assumed that existence in all of His discourses when referring to God. He spoke of God as an eternal, conscious Being. Moreover, He taught clearly that God is knowable, saying: "And this is life eternal, that they might know Thee the only true God." [2] He taught that God is revealed, and therefore can be known.

Now without attempting to be "wise above what is written," which would be sheer folly, I am constrained to pursue my quest. What is God like? Possibly some of you are wondering if my attempt to answer the question is wise and necessary. I feel that my reasons justify my search after truth about God. Surely in such a pursuit there are depths unfathomable and heights unattainable. A fool indeed is he who believes that the finite can measure the infinite. "Canst thou by searching find out God? canst thou find out the Almighty unto perfection?" [3] Our answer to this question is an emphatic "No," at least not in this life. But even though we cannot find out the Almighty unto perfection, we should strive to know that which is knowable. True, "now I know in part," [4] but a

[2] John 17:3   [3] Job 11:7   [4] 1 Corinthians 13:12

bigger fool is he who neglects that "part" he can and should know.

Man should know the knowable because of the rise of a new conception about God which contradicts the *true* conception of God. When a group of scientists from all over the world meet to exchange ideas about the latest discoveries, new theories, and future outlooks, and then wind up with a "new" conception of God that denounces the *true* conception of God, there is need for a restatement, with emphasis, of the fundamental, basal teaching of Him who is the infinite, eternal Creator of all things.

When a certain college professor, addressing the American Association for the Advancement of Science, declares that "Man is only a temporary chemical episode in an insignificant planet, and since this is clearly proved by modern science, we must furnish ourselves with an entirely new conception of God," there is need for a restatement of the Christian view of God.

When an historian tells us that "the conception of God is not the same to the man of today as it was to the man of 1775, and it will not be the same to the man of 2075 as it is today," there is need for a restatement of the Christian view of God.

When a man like Robert Blatchford, an influential journalist in England a generation ago, writes: "I claim that the heavenly Father is a myth; that in face of a knowledge of life and the world, we cannot reasonably believe in Him. There is no heavenly Father watching tenderly over us, His children. He is the baseless shadow of a wistful human dream. I do not believe in God. The belief in God is still generally accepted. . . . But, in the light of scientific discoveries and demonstrations, such a belief is unfounded and utterly untenable today," there is a need for a restatement of the Christian view of God.

When the American Association for the Advancement of Atheism publishes in its catechism of unbelief questions and answers like the following—

Q: "What is God?"
A: "God is an imaginary character—a myth—a creation of fiction believed by idolaters to be a real being that created and governs all things."
Q: "Is there a real God?"
A: "The universe contains no real God."

—there is need for a restatement of the Christian view of God.

When some American colleges and universities saturate their students with the philosophy of Friedrich Nietzsche who wrote; "What distinguishes us is not that we do not rediscover any God either in nature or behind nature, but that we recognize what was worshiped as God, not as divine—but as pitiable, as absurd, as injurious—not only an error but a crime against life. We deny God as God," there is need for a restatement of the Christian view of God.

When the returns from a widespread questionnaire, sent out by Dr. James H. Leuba of Bryn Mawr College, were received, and hundreds of professors and students replied to produce the following percentage of avowed atheists—

Psychologists 86%
Biologists 82%
Sociologists 81%
Historians 68%
Physicists 66%

—there is need for a restatement of the Christian view of God.

When an internationally recognized astronomer says, "I have swept the entire heavens with my telescope and I have found no God; there is no such being," there is need for a restatement of the Christian view of God.

When Mormonism, the Latter Day Saints, go from door to door and say, "There are many gods, and Adam is our God," there is need for a restatement of the Christian view of God.

Such a hodgepodge of doubts, distortions, and denials about God are in themselves a challenge to any minister of Jesus Christ. To know that our youth are exposed to this false propaganda makes one want to restate from the housetop the old faith which was once delivered unto the saints. God does exist, the only eternal, personal, conscious Being, the Cause and Creator of the universe and man, and the all-wise, loving Redeemer. The doctrine of God is essential to real scientific progress and to knowledge about man's well-being and destiny.

Ignorance concerning God has had telling effect upon mankind. Who can say without fear of contradiction that the ills of the human race are not traceable to wrong ideas about God? The Apostle Paul, at two different stages in his life, stood on both sides of the issue. After his conversion to Jesus Christ he wrote: "Because that, when they knew God, they glorified Him not as God, neither were thankful; but became vain in their imaginations, and their foolish heart was darkened." [5] Here it is stated that man had a knowledge of the existence of God and of those attributes essential to His Being. Man began with knowledge, not ignorance, of God. When man doubted God, then he descended from the light of wisdom into moral and mental darkness. I would say that every ill of mankind—physical, mental, moral, and otherwise—is the result of man's refusing to retain God in his affections. Men departing from the primitive knowledge of God, followed the downward pull of a fallen, sensuous nature, and, while "Professing themselves to be wise, they became fools." [6]

[5] Romans 1:21   [6] Romans 1:22

THE TESTIMONY OF GOD
IN CREATION

In Psalms 14:1 and 53:1 we read: "The fool hath said in his heart, There is no God." The man who convinces himself that there is no personal God does not do so because he has proof that God does not exist. I am told that our word *fool*, as used in these two verses in the Psalms, is the Hebrew word *nabal*, and that it denotes moral perversity rather than mere weakness or ignorance. Nabal seems to have been just such a person.[1] He does not deny theoretically that God exists, but "in his heart" he shuts God out of his reckoning, and orders his life to suit himself as though there were no God. Such practical atheism does not begin in the head, but in the heart. When the proud heart of man refuses to bow in submission to God, it will ultimately deny Him. Godlessness is utter folly. It is the acme of imbecility to try to push God out of one's thoughts. It is the height of sin and idiocy even to wish there were no God. He is a madman who, by denying the existence of fire, believes that fire will not burn him merely because he denies its existence.

I read of a rich Chinese, "who visited England, and who took great delight in a beautiful microscope which was shown him. Having purchased one for himself, he

[1] 1 Samuel 25:25-38

23

took it back to China, and enjoyed its use there. But one day he chanced to examine a tiny bit of his dinner rice. To his horror he discovered that there were actually tiny living creatures in it! Now, it was part of his creed not to eat anything that had had animal life. What was to be done now? He was not only particularly fond of rice, but it was the staple item of his daily food. He thought that he saw only one way out of it. Accordingly, he dashed in pieces the offending microscope.

"You will say, 'What foolishness!' Yet, the attitude of that Chinese toward his microscope is exactly like the attitude of some men toward the existence of God. They do not want to face the realities of the existence of God, and the horrible possibilities of a coming judgment where they will have to answer for their sins. Therefore, they push away from them the great fact of GOD, and call themselves atheists. When the Chinese man destroyed the microscope, he did not do away with the bacteria in his rice. Neither does atheism destroy the fact of God, or the reality of a coming judgment when men must give an account of their deeds done before a holy and righteous God." (*The Fools of the Bible*, by Robert W. Lancaster)

Look carefully at the following passage of Scripture from the inspired pen of David: "The heavens declare the glory of God; and the firmament sheweth His handywork. Day unto day uttereth speech, and night unto night sheweth knowledge. There is no speech nor language, where their voice is not heard. Their line is gone out through all the earth, and their words to the end of the world. In them hath He set a tabernacle for the sun,

Which is as a bridegroom coming out of his chamber, and rejoiceth as a strong man to run a race. His going forth is from the end of the heaven, and his circuit unto the ends of it: and there is nothing hid from the heat thereof." [2] The theme of this psalm, at least the first six verses, is *the revelation of God.* The atmospheric space, the vast expanse into which one might look night and day, literally writes its silent testimony to the fact of God. "Day unto day uttereth speech." This is simply stating that each passing day sends forth repeatedly and abundantly its own peculiar message that there is a God. This testimony is called "speech." Though silent, it is as real as audible speech in its public declaration of certain truths about God. Human language, oral or written, is not necessary to convey divine truth. Each new day demonstrates clearly and effectively, without obscurity, the personality and power of God. Likewise night, when the day has passed, takes up the intermittent instruction about the Creator of the universe. Only once did I see the aurora borealis, but that one glimpse was sufficient to tell me that no man nor beast was at the controls. Every magnificent flash of those northern lights addressed itself to my intelligence.

But whether it be the instruction of the aurora borealis, the borealis australis, the sun, moon, milky way, or a spot anywhere in the solar system, human lives are influenced world-wide by what creation has to say: "There is no speech nor language, where their voice is not heard. Their line is gone out through all the earth." No nation or language is beyond the reach of this inarticulate in-

[2] Psalm 19:1-6

struction. It speaks to all men everywhere. "But I say, Have they not heard? Yes verily, their sound went into all the earth, and their words unto the ends of the world." [3] The only language creation speaks is that its Creator is Lord of Heaven and earth, and that He is so near, the very earth on which we stand is holy. Think it over!

The New Testament likewise speaks of creation's testimony to the fact of God's existence. "For the invisible things of Him from the creation of the world are clearly seen, being understood by the things that are made, even His eternal power and Godhead; so that they are without excuse." [4] This verse echoes the testimony of the Psalmist. God's character and attributes, which are the "invisible things," are "clearly seen" in what He has done, just as human character is manifest in a man's actions.

Can we actually see the invisible? Most certainly! While we cannot actually see the nature and character of a man's heart as it is concealed within the man, we can know something of that inner man as we observe his words and actions. Even so the invisible God is seen in the outward manifestations of His power and wisdom. Creation is God's *Poima,* or poem, written in a meter that clearly manifests God's eternal and perpetual omnipotence and deity. Those manifestations of God in creation are not merely *relative* in degree but *absolute,* and together they spell out ideal personality.

There is, then, a measure of common or universal knowledge about God. While the natural revelation of

[3] Romans 10:18   [4] Romans 1:20

God is not complete, it has always existed outside of Christianity. Certainly, Paul is not even alluding to any idea that the natural man has the ability to find his way to God, but he is stating that the natural man has a natural knowledge of the fact of God's existence. The Christian view of God is much more inclusive than that of any natural theology, but what we do conclude from Paul's statement is that natural theology does assume a deistic, or theistic, view. I might add here a comment from David Brown: "Two things are thus said to be clearly discovered to the reflecting intelligence by the things which are made—*first,* that *there is an Eternal Power;* and, *secondly,* that this is neither a blind physical *'force'* nor a pantheistic 'spirit of nature,' but a living, conscious *Divine Person,* whose out-going energy is beheld in the external universe."

There are two statements in the eleventh chapter of the Epistle to the Hebrews which add to the foregoing. "Through faith we understand that the worlds were framed by the word of God, so that things which are seen were not made of things which do appear." [5] Those heroes of faith, whose names occupy the major portion of this chapter in Hebrews, had no Bible to tell them that God created the heavens and the earth, and yet it is stated that those antediluvians and patriarchs, through faith, saw God's superscription on every part of His handiwork. Whenever the trials and tests of life closed in upon them, tempting them to doubt, or if prosperity and good fortune smiled upon them, tending to shut out God from their view, their faith was stirred to action by the visible world.

[5] Hebrews 11:3

The physical universe is never a hindrance to the man of faith, but it can be to the doubter and the skeptic. He possesses great wealth and has been delivered from many a pitfall, whose faith looks out upon the vast universe and lays hold upon God. His is a shriveled mind indeed who can look at a world that was planned, created, reduced to form and order, and sustained, and still refuses to believe in God. Let the skeptic and the doubter and the intelligent mind look more closely at the text, and he will see that the ancients were not the victims of blind faith, but the possessors of a measure of understanding, for "Through faith we *understand* that the worlds were framed by the word of God." Anyone reading the Book of Job will certainly be convinced of the extensive knowledge about God and creation that some men had.

Now look at another verse which, speaking of Moses, says, "By faith he forsook Egypt, not fearing the wrath of the king: for he endured, as seeing Him who is invisible." [6] "Seeing Him who is invisible." A strange paradox this! But not altogether so to the honest inquiring mind. The statement may be seemingly, but is not necessarily, absurd. By faith Moses saw Him who is invisible. There are certain things in Christianity that can be understood, in part at least, from the outside, that is, by those outside of the Christian faith. Then there are those things, and they are many, which cannot be understood until after one becomes a Christian. Here is one amazing seeming absurdity, which millions have found to be a blessed and satisfying reality, both within and without the Christian faith, and that is the fact of God's existence.

[6] Hebrews 11:27

Moses is not the only man who has seen Him who is invisible. His distinct apprehension of God has been, and is being, shared by an innumerable host. On everything in creation on which the eye of faith looks, it sees what doubt and skepticism can never see: it sees God. I like to believe that our verse is telling us that Moses, in defiance of Pharaoh's injunctions, was encouraged to quit Egypt because he believed there was a God who created the physical world about him and that that God loved and cared for him.

THE ORDERLINESS OF THE UNIVERSE

It has been stated frequently by others that the highest discovery of science is the orderliness of the universe. The newest and most advanced scientific researches repeatedly confirm this fact.

To illustrate simply, consider the earth's relation to the sun. The greatest distance of the earth from the sun is 94,500,000 miles, or 152,200,000 kilometers, and is called *aphelion*. The least distance of the earth from the sun is 91,500,000 miles, or 146,900,000 kilometers, and is called *perihelion*. The mean, or average, distance of the earth from the sun is 92,870,000 miles. Now the diameter of the sun is over one hundred times greater than that of the earth, and it radiates each second as much heat as would be given out by the burning of 11,000,000,000,000,000 tons of high-grade coal. We know that our small earth is constantly in motion, while it does seem that the sun and the other heavenly bodies appear to move. We are not aware of the earth's motion because, when the earth moves, everything on the earth moves with it. But consider the possibility of the catastrophic climax of the earth and the utter destruction of all life on it if the earth in its orbital motion around the sun were to deviate away from its orbit. Were the earth to move too close to the sun, all life would be consumed by the heat; and were it to drift too far away, we would all freeze in short time. The orderliness of these two objects in the universe is astounding to the finite mind, to say the least.

But as tremendous in size and power as the sun is, it is by no means the greatest object in the universe. The solar system is composed of the Sun as the central body around which revolve nine planets, namely, Mercury, Venus, Earth, Mars, Jupiter, Saturn, Uranus, Neptune, and Pluto. These are accompanied by twenty-eight moons, several thousand tiny planets, called planetoids, some comets, and a great number of meteors, to make up this one family. Each of the planets in the solar system is in motion, each rotating and revolving around the sun in an elliptical orbit. Jupiter, the greatest of the planets in this system, more than 1,300 times as large as the earth and larger than the composite of all the rest of the members in the solar system, has an equatorial speed of nearly thirty thousand miles per hour. How long these planets have been in existence, no man can tell. The marvel of them is their precision-like function in perfect orderliness.

Gigantic as Jupiter is, it becomes dwarfed alongside the giant star Betelgeuse. This bright red prominent star of the winter sky is estimated to be almost four hundred and fifty times as big as the sun. Our earth, compared with Betelgeuse, would look like a grain of sand alongside a huge pumpkin. In fact, if the Sun were to be put at its center, the orbit of the Earth and Mars would still be within the outer surface of Betelgeuse.

In the southern heavens is to be seen another tremendous star, the remarkable star, Antares, with a diameter of nearly 300,000,000 miles. Antares is so far removed from us in distance, that the rays we see today left their source about two hundred and fifty years ago. And these worlds have never collided! How amazing that they conform to some established rule of order!

Now exercise your mind a bit more about the galaxies. We all at some time have watched with wonder the Milky Way. This one galaxy consists of many billions of stars; "the host of heaven cannot be numbered." [7] Viewed from the earth the individual stars appear to be relatively very close together, when actually, even in the very heart of this dense cluster of stars, the distance between them would be millions of miles. Think of it, there are millions of these galaxies in the vast outerspace of the universe! Scientists tell us that these stars are all "restlessly swarming about among one another under the spell of their own inertia and the complex pull of their neighbors on every side," some rushing at a velocity of 200 miles per second. Our sun, dragging its planets with it, lumbering along leisurely at about the rate of 12 miles per second (43,200 miles per hour), is moving at a snail's pace compared with the stars in outer space. And yet there are no

[7] Jeremiah 33:22

cosmic collisions to set off a chain reaction that might explode the universe. No man can question the orderliness of the vast universe about us.

But how are we to account for this orderliness in creation? Personally, I feel that the *origin* and *orderliness* of the universe are inseparably linked together. How did it all come into existence and how is it all sustained? I wax bold to declare that no scientist who denies the Bible's account of creation, namely, "In the beginning God created the heaven and the earth," [8] can intelligently account for these facts. Now I am not trying to prove God by any intellectual process, for, as far as I am able to determine, this has never been done, and never can be done. The finite can never prove the infinite. What I am saying is that here is a universe, upheld and sustained in perfect order. Account for it all, apart from the Christian view, if you can. I have searched books of science until my head swam, and all that I can find is theory after theory, conjecture and disagreement. But when I read the first verse in the Bible, I am satisfied that here is a declarative, an affirmative, that has no parallel for comprehensiveness and majesty. "In the beginning God created the heaven and the earth."

The primary importance of the Bible is its record of facts. In the Bible there is that which satisfies the inquiring mind of the average intelligent and honest person. "Who hath measured the waters in the hollow of His hand, and meted out heaven with the span, and comprehended the dust of the earth in a measure, and weighed the mountains in scales, and the hills in a balance?" [9]

[8] Genesis 1:1   [9] Isaiah 40:12

Let the atheist, the infidel, the skeptic answer these questions if he can. The God of whom the prophet wrote is Jehovah, the one and only true God, eternal, omnipotent, omniscient, and omnipresent, not only creating all things but upholding them as well. Dr. Lee Chestnut has said: "Let no one believe that science, even modern science, has a full explanation of the origin of the universe, including our earth. True there are many hypotheses based upon various analyses of physical phenomena. But, in the end, none of these adequately explains the beginnings."

Yes, "All things were made by Him; and without Him was not any thing made that was made." [10] "For ly Him were all things created, that are in heaven, and that are in earth. . . . And He is before all things, and by Him all things consist." [11] Our eternal God and Saviour preceded all things, and all things were made by Him and for Him, that is, for His purposes. They were not only created by Him, but by Him they cohere, they hang together. We are not finding fault with the scientist who emphasizes the discovery of the "colossal binding force now known to be within the nucleus of the atom." We are insisting, however, that the atom does not answer the all-important question which deals with the origin and orderliness of the universe, but that we must go beyond the atom to the God of the atom. Both worlds, the seen and the unseen, the material and the spiritual, are held together by their Creator. I am not going to give a second thought to some man-made unproven theory of the forces that keep our earth, and other planets, suspended in space,

[10] John 1:3   [11] Colossians 1:16-17

so long as I know that God put them where they are. The Bible says: "He . . . hangeth the earth upon nothing," [12] and He who put it there can keep it there. God is both the Law and the Lord of creation and gravitation. Our God and Saviour is "upholding all things by the word of His power." [13]

THE COSMOLOGICAL ARGUMENT

Most theologians, when writing on Christian theism, include in their evidences for the divine existence the cosmological argument, or the argument based on the law of causality. The principle states simply that every event and effect must have an adequate cause. That the universe is here no one will deny. Its parts are finite and the inhabitants dwelling on the earth are finite; therefore it is dependent on some force outside of itself. The orderliness of the universe rules out any possibility of its coming into existence by chance.

In any great feat of engineering, such as a huge bridge spanning a chasm or body of water, the careful planning of highly specialized architects, engineers, and workmen is an absolute essential. A large modern building cannot be erected unless there is proper planning to the minutest detail. Likewise, in building a universe there must first be some detailed plans by an all-wise Intelligence, a supreme Architect and Builder whose wisdom is flawless. It is not difficult to think that back of the creation of the universe is God. I find no adequate cause, apart from God, sufficient to explain the world with its miracles and

[12] Job 26:7   [13] Hebrews 1:3

mysteries. Certainly atheistic evolution and infidelity have no scholarly explanation for the existence of the universe. The world bears the marks of design and dependence, hence of mind and management. All its forms and forces indicate plan and purpose. No scientific quest into these matters has ever brought to light anything irregular or irrational, but always there are the evidences of origin and order. The universe is truly a great effect. It must have had an original cause sufficient to produce it.

Clarence Edward Macartney writes of James Beattie, a Scottish poet of considerable merit, "He had a gifted son, James Hay, who died at the age of twenty-two, leaving behind him a collection of poems which the father afterward published. In the exquisite memoirs in this volume the father tells of the religious education of his son. He desired to see how far his own reason could go in tracing out the first principle in all religion, the being of God. The boy at five years of age could read a little, but had received no particular instruction with respect to God. One day his father planted the three initial letters of the boy's name in the mold of the garden with seeds of garden cresses. Ten days later the boy came running, asking his father to come and see. The father smiled at the report and seemed inclined to disregard it. But the child insisted, and when he came to the place the father said, 'Yes, I see it, but there is nothing in this worth noting; it is a mere chance,' and turned to go away. But the boy followed him, and, taking hold of his coat, said with great earnestness that it could not be mere chance, that somebody must have arranged it so. Then the father said to him, 'So you think that what appears so regular as the letters of your name cannot be by chance?'

" 'Yes,' the child said with firmness, 'I think so.'

" 'Then look at yourself,' his father replied, 'and consider your hands and fingers, your legs and feet, and other limbs. Are they not regular in their appearance and useful to you?'

"Here the boy answered that they were indeed. 'Came you then hither by chance?' the father asked.

" 'No,' the boy answered, 'that cannot be. Something must have made me.'

" 'And who is that something?' his father asked.

"Beattie had now gained the point that he had in mind; and seeing the child's reason taught him that what begins to be must have a cause, and that what is formed with regularity must have an intelligent cause, he gave him the name of the great Being (God) who made him and all the world."

The Bible says: "For every house is builded by some man; but He that built all things is God." [14] Saint Thomas Aquinas believed this verse sufficient on which to build the axiom that every effect supposes a cause. He argued that all motion in the universe implies a prime unmoved mover, and that one is God. Scientists are agreed that atoms must either be self-moved or moved by a prime mover.

Handrich states it as follows: "The universe could not have been eternal, but must have had a beginning, because to be eternal the universe must be a gigantic per-

[14] Hebrews 3:4

petual-motion machine, one which theoretically operates by an amount of energy circulating in an enclosed system, without the addition of any energy from the outside. But we know of no perpetual-motion machine of man's making. Every mechanical device of man's fashioning must finally come to a standstill because of the loss of energy due to friction. The many motions of the planets in the universe could not have been going on forever, hence the existence of the eternal Creator dismisses the difficulty. A creatorless universe leaves an unsolved problem with the unbeliever, and while we would not advocate anyone laying aside his scientific studies, we would urge upon every man to consider the revelation of God, and when one accepts what God has written in His Word, he will become one of those who, 'Through faith . . . understand that the worlds were framed by the word of God, so that things which are seen were not made of things which do appear.' [15] It is certain that something has existed from eternity, but matter is not that something. Since matter cannot spontaneously move, we have arrived, in our thinking, to a point where an eternal Being, independent of the universe, created and sustains it."

[15] Hebrews 11:3

THE ANTHROPOLOGICAL ARGUMENT

Anthropology is a word that has long been used as a name for the science of man in general. Permit me to state my premise and then proceed with my subject. The premise is this; namely, a study of both the psychical and physical aspects of man will lead any student with an open mind to a belief in the existence of God.

BELIEF IN GOD'S EXISTENCE IS INTUITIVE

We understand that which is intuitive to be perceived by the mind at once without the intervention of any thought process. But when is a belief intuitive? Immanuel Kant, in *The Critique of Pure Reason*, says: "Necessity and universality are infallible tests for distinguishing pure and empirical knowledge, and are inseparably connected with each other." Now if belief in God is universal and necessarily a part of man, it can be said to be intuitive.

Samuel M. Zwemer, in *The Origin of Religion*, wrote: "On two great conceptions modern scientists are agreed: namely, on the unity of the race and on the essential religious nature of man. . . . Man is very much alike everywhere from China to Peru. . . . He always has been and is incurably religious. . . . Humanity itself finds its roots in God. . . ." Belief in God is as old as the oldest records and remains of man, not merely of civilized man, but of man the farthest removed from today. The idea of God is among the most primitive tribes in remotest areas, and it is marked by a spontaneity. Low savages are as theistic as some professing Christians, and these heathen people ascribe attributes of deity to their god which are assigned to no other being. The supreme Being is called by various names in widely separated areas, but missionaries who have visited the remote tribes of the earth tell us that men everywhere, however savage, believe in a Creator of the world and of men. We fail to find a hint anywhere as to a time or manner, when or how, the idea of God originated with man. The most ancient traditions of the human race indicate that mankind commenced existence in harmony with the supreme Being.

This writer has listened to missionaries from many parts of our world, and they all testify that the heathen everywhere have the knowledge of God, not merely as an abstract idea, but such knowledge as to render their immorality inexcusable. The most depraved know that those who live in sin are punishable by God.

Now we are not intimating that every child has a conception of God formed in his mind. We contend, contrariwise, that the human mind, when developed under the best conditions most conducive to learning, can never attain to a full conception of God. We are saying, however, that the idea of God is self-manifested universally as is the light of day. A man may have eyes and never see so long as he is shut up in a dark cave. So a man may possess the intuitive idea of God, and still be incapable within himself of any analysis or apprehension of God.

Someone may argue that if the idea of God is intuitively recognized by all human beings under normal conditions, then what is the value of a bóok which argues to prove that God exists? I would be the first to appreciate such a question. Let me testify to the value of these studies in my own life. They have done two things for me. First, they have sent me on a diligent search to know more about Him who created me and sustains me, and to whom I muɔt answer for the way I live my life. Secondly, they have strengthened me when the forces of evil would have closed in upon me to make me a critic and a skeptic. My intuitive recognition of God has been greatly expanded and strengthened. I distinguish between my innate knowledge of God and my acquired knowledge of God. The idea of God is certainly in man, but man is unable to know about his Creator and Provider until God is studied in His Word and works. The intuitive knowledge of God is given without constraint or compulsion, but the greater knowledge about God is acquired as the result of study, reflection, prayer, and the exercise of the learning processes. The fact that I know there is a God does not satisfy me. I desire to know experientially, to know why I believe what I believe, to *know* that I know.

MAN'S ADAPTABILITY TO THE EARTH

Theodore L. Handrich, in *The Creation—Facts, Theories, and Faith,* says, "An adaptation is the way in which a living thing, or any of its parts, is fitted to live in its surroundings. The gills of a fish permit it to obtain oxygen from water. The lightweight, hollow bones of a bird adapt it for flying through the air. The chlorophyll-containing leaves of a plant adapt it for utilizing the energy of sunlight in manufacturing food. The padded feet of a camel permit it to walk across the hot sands and bare rocks of the desert. The short, heavy bill of a grosbeak enables it to crack seeds and thus to live on them. The eyes, ears, hands, feet, lungs, teeth, sweat glands, brain, digestive system, and the many other parts of man are all adaptations to his particular environment."

J. M. Pendelton wrote, "We see evidences of adaptation all around us. The earth seems to be adapted to man and to other animals, and they seem to be suited to the earth. The soil is adapted to such productions as are necessary to the support of physical life. The lungs and the air are adapted to each other. Birds are fitted for the air, and fishes for the sea. There is adaptation everywhere and in everything; and adaptation, so far as we are capable of judging, indicates intelligence and design. Intelligence and design are not properties of matter, but attributes of spirit. Where there is intelligence there is mind, and where there is design it must be the result of intelligence, and there must be a Designer. If, then, the many instances of adaptation visible everywhere are suggestive of design, the question arises, 'Who is the Designer?' and the only answer is, 'God, the Creator and Ruler of all things.' "

The Christian idea of the origin of man is found in

the Bible. "And the LORD God formed man of the dust of the ground." [1] While I have never seen an experiment which chemically analyzed the human body, I am told that the basic chemicals of which man's body is formed are in the physical earth. The fact then that man is adaptable to the earth only, should not take us by surprise. Someone has well said, "The oustanding reason for contending that the earth is the theatre of life is the conclusive scientific and scriptural evidence that of all celestial bodies it is the only planet capable of sustaining life as we know it. Man cannot live in the bowels of the earth, nor can he venture many miles above its surface."

The sun and moon have attracted the chief interest of scientists above that of other heavenly bodies. Less than two hundred years ago no less an authority than Sir William Herschel, a noted English astronomer, seriously suggested that the sun might be inhabited. Today such a suggestion would be preposterous. The moon, on the other hand, might offer to some a greater possibility of man's inhabiting it, but the findings of the most careful observers would rule out any probability, the reason being the difference in pressure. Both the mass and volume of the moon are only a fraction of that of the earth. The surface gravity is much smaller than the earth's, so that an object would weigh only one-sixth as much on the moon as it does on the earth. A man taking a brisk walk on the moon would bound from fifteen to eighteen feet in one step. How unnatural! On the other hand, how naturally man is adapted to the earth!

[1] Genesis 2:7

FEARFULLY AND WONDERFULLY MADE

David wrote in one of the most majestic and mighty of the Psalms, "I will praise Thee; for *I am fearfully and wonderfully made*." [2] The science of anatomy, or anthropotomy, was largely unknown in David's day, yet his description of man, in stages of both prenatal and postnatal development, is at once astounding. Perhaps his most significant declaration is that the design, dawn, and development of a human life is the work of God. He does not separate the material from the spiritual, nor the scientific from the theological. The Psalmist gives to us, through divine revelation, what evolution can never produce. He takes up where evolution leaves off. The evolutionist may trace life back to protoplasm, but there he must stop. Divine revelation keeps on going beyond that point into a realm where science and philosophy cannot penetrate.

J. A. Alexander, in his translation and explanation of the Psalms, makes the verse to read as follows: "I thank Thee because fearfully I am distinguished." [2] He sees the Psalmist making it a subject of grateful acknowledgment that God has distinguished him, or made him, to differ from inferior creatures, both in constitution and in destiny.

Assuming that Alexander is correct in his translation, we can say that we are extraordinarily and superlatively made *mentally*, that is, we are endowed with capacities

[2] Psalm 139:14

of reason far superior to all other forms of life. Neither a dog, nor a monkey, nor a horse, nor an elephant can add, subtract, multiply, or divide. Man, above all other creatures on the earth, has the mental numerical concept to design equations, apply calculus, or to fix geometrical relationships. "Here is an area where the beast of the field, the fowl of the air, or the fish of the sea do not come."

Man is extraordinarily and superlatively made *linguistically*. He is the only creature on the earth that can express his thoughts in words, and convey his ideas in intelligible sentences. No creature in the animal world can interchange with man information, thoughts, and opinions by the use of spoken language. The dog may bark, the cat may "meow," the horse may neigh, the bird may chirp, the dove may coo, the monkey may chatter, but not one of them can read or write a book.

Again it is Christianity that has given to us the outstanding example of man's remarkable faculty to express himself in spoken language. It is quite likely that no man living today will ever know how many languages and dialects are spoken in the earth. Still we do know that missionaries of the gospel of Jesus Christ have translated portions of the Bible into more than eleven hundred languages. How can such a seeming impossibility be achieved? The answer lies in the fact that the functions of the human mind and the fundamental vehicle of expressing one's thoughts are common to the whole of humanity. These endowments of the savage are equal to those of the civilized. The faculty of speech is man's distinctive inheritance from God. This one point in itself has left the evolutionist somewhat abashed. Man has God to thank for this remarkable distinction.

Man is extraordinarily and superlatively made *physically*. While I am not qualified to discuss this subject at length, I have discovered sufficient in my reading and daily observation to convince me that evidence abounds in support of plan and design. No one can deny nor even doubt the wonder and mystery of the human body.

Let us give some thought to the eye. A proverb says: "The hearing ear, and the seeing *eye,* the LORD hath made even both of them." [3] Now, quite frankly this writer needs no course on the subject of ophthalmology to convince him that the eye, which is one small organ in the vast network of mechanisms that make up the human body, has God for its Designer and Creator. He believes it because the Bible states it is so. Of all the organs of the human body, not absolutely essential to our existence, the eye is possibly the most desirable since it opens the way to most of the pleasures and privileges of life.

Now the subject immediately before us is the necessity for God, and here we are looking at the marvelous mechanism of the human body in our endeavor to show sufficient evidence for the existence of the God of the Bible. Dr. A. Rendle Short, the late professor of surgery in the University of Bristol, England, in his book, *Wonderfully Made,* in which he shows the reasonableness of the Biblical account of man's creation, says, "The eye furnishes a good test case if only for the reason that many of its functions are so understandable."

In order to function properly the eye must be suited to

[3]Proverbs 20:12

discern objects at distances varying from inches to miles. The same eye that views a landscape covering five miles can read a book at a distance of a few inches. The eye is adapted to different degrees of light far exceeding the distinction of light from darkness. The two eyes must focus and function together and be capable of moving around so as to avoid the constant turning of the head. Even when the eye is kept still, a wide range of vision is possible. A normal human being can see not merely black and white, but seven colors in addition to the many mixtures. This gift not only adds immensely to the pleasures of life, but it keeps us from danger. In possessing this rare gift man has something which is not found in lower forms of animal life. Everything about the human eye is designed for man's pleasure, protection, and progress. How can we account for this? "The seeing *eye,* the Lord hath made."

No further attempt will be made at this point in our study to press the subject. I have had no training whatever in medical science, but I would consider myself to be a fool if I failed to recognize that the intricate and delicate mechanisms of the human body could not have come into existence apart from a supernatural Being who both designed and created that body. I could not deny, much less doubt, the existence of a personal God.

PART II

THE NATURE OF GOD

INTRODUCTION

In this section which treats of the nature of God, it is my intention to look into the subject in a rather general way. In his *Body of Divinity*, Dr. John Gill treats the attributes of God as being separate and distinct from the nature of God. We shall combine them here. I somehow feel that the word "attributes" is not an ideal term when used in connection with God, since it might convey to some the idea that something is being ascribed or imputed to God. But whenever we use the term, we have in mind those excellencies or virtues that are considered as belonging to God, inherent in Him, characteristic of Him, and without which He could not be God.

The nature of God is not fully comprehensible by the human, finite mind; however, we must pursue that which is apprehensible and which God Himself has been pleased to reveal. "Canst thou by searching find out God? canst thou find out the Almighty unto perfection?" [1] The answer is an emphatic "No." But then this does not forbid us to search and inquire after God. There is a clear self-revelation of God in the Scriptures, hence the Bible must be the starting point of our investigation. Man can not learn God through human experience alone, nor can he find out the nature of God inductively by scientific meth-

[1] Job 11:7

ods. God's special revelation is the only means by which we can obtain a real knowledge of Him. Christianity rests upon a revelation that is both real and vital. This revelation is made known to us through the Holy Scriptures. Among other things, it consists of a self-disclosure of God, and it is accurate and final.

Whenever men theorize, as did ancient philosophers who were deprived of the Bible and those who through prejudice or unbelief will not accept the testimony of Scripture, there arises various systems of philosophy such as *polytheism*, with its many gods; *pantheism*, with its claims that matter is God and God is therefore impersonal; and *materialism*, which contends that all matter is self-functioning, and which tends toward evolution.

In this little volume, we are making every effort to avoid human rationalizing and theorizing, but rather to discover God as He only can reveal Himself.

THE PERSONALITY OF GOD

God is a personal Being. This is the Christian view of God in contrast to the error of pantheism. Many religious people, so called, are pantheists. Pantheism is the belief that all things in the aggregate constitute God, that God is everything, and everything is God. To the pantheist, God is identified with nature, not independent and separate from it, thus a mere unconscious force working in the world. Pantheism differs from atheism with its positive denial of God, and from agnosticism with its dogmatic doubt about the existence of God, but it is neither Christian nor truly religious.

Religion has been defined as a belief in an invisible superhuman power on whom man regards himself as dependent, and to whom he thinks himself to some degree responsible. Religion includes the idea of communion between God and man, therefore if God were not a personal Being, there could be no communion. There can be no real communion between man and a mere influence. It is absolutely essential to the true definition of religion that both God and man be personal beings.

The unerring language of Scripture states clearly that there is a similarity to be traced between God and man which makes possible communion between the two. "And God said, Let Us make man in Our image, after Our likeness. . . . So God created man in His own image, in the image of God created He him; male and female created He them." [1] The faculties and constituent elements belonging to personality—namely, intelligence, emotion, and will—belong to God and man. God asserts that there is a correspondency between Himself and man, therefore man is justified in tracing the characteristics of God from the pattern of his own personality, even though man is, in his fallen state, imperfect.

Because of the limitations of human thought and language to know and explain God, the Holy Scriptures use anthropomorphisms, which are the ascriptions of human attributes, feelings, and conduct to God who is a spiritual Being. [2] Thus we read of God's "face," [3] His "arms," [4] "eyes," [5] "mouth," [6] "hand" and "ear." [7] Such anthropomorphisms are many in the Bible. When these members of the physical body are ascribed to God, such ascriptions do not assert that God actually possesses a body with its many members, but rather that He is capable of performing those things which are the functions of those members mentioned. "He that planted the ear, shall He not hear? He that formed the eye, shall He not see?" [8] We can understand anthropomorphic expressions, therefore God descends to our capacities and uses language we can comprehend.

There is a vast difference between divine personality and human personality. The original "likeness" and "image" of God in Adam and Eve were perfect. After the

---

[1] Genesis 1:26-27   [2] John 4:24   [3] Exodus 33:11,20
[4] Deuteronomy 33:27   [5] 2 Chronicles 16:9   [6] Isaiah 58:14
[7] Isaiah 59:1   [8] Psalm 94:9

Fall man's personality was imperfect, so that it must be stated clearly that only God possesses perfect personality. Still, there is a certain likeness between the fallen person with his finite personality, and the Infinite God who is perfect. Man as a personal being needs a personal God. Both are alike in that they possess the constituent elements of personality: intelligence, sensibility, and will.

In a creative sense man is related to God, but the only way he can speak of God is in a human manner. How else can we conceive of God and express our thoughts of Him? "For in Him we live, and move, and have our being. . . . For we are also His offspring." [9] Certainly there are attributes and characteristics in God which man cannot express in terms of human life and language, but God has condescended to us in order that we might know Him and find the way back to Him. Since God has stated that He made man in His image and likeness, we can do nothing other than accept His declaration and act upon it.

The God of the Bible, who is the God of creation and the God and Father of our Lord Jesus Christ, differs from gods of man's fashioning in His expressions of intelligence, sensibility, and will. As to His *intelligence* we accept the testimony that "His understanding is infinite." [10] "Hast thou not known? hast thou not heard, that the everlasting God, the LORD, the Creator of the ends of the earth, fainteth not, neither is weary? there is no searching of His understanding." [11] "Known unto God are all His works from the beginning of the world." [12]

In like manner, the Scriptures declare that God pos-

[9] Acts 17:28   [10] Psalm 147:5   [11] Isaiah 40:28
[12] Acts 15:18

sesses *sensibility* by those properties of personality they ascribe to Him, such as grief,[13] anger,[14] jealousy,[15] love,[16] hatred.[17]

Then, too, the element and exercise of *will* is said to be manifest in God. The Psalmist testified of Him, "He hath done whatsoever He hath pleased." [18] Isaiah quotes God as saying, "I will do all My pleasure." [19] Daniel adds, "He doeth according to His will in the army of heaven, and among the inhabitants of the earth." [20] The next time you open your Bible to read, watch for the personal pronouns used of God, such as "Thee," "Thou," "He," "Him." The pronouns used of God are not neuter, as though God were a mere force or principle, but rather personal pronouns in the masculine gender, thus representing Him as a person.

In His unique personality, the God of the Bible differs from the false gods of man's making. He only is a living personality, therefore He is above all else, and never should we put Him on the level of another god of man's fashioning. He will take second place to no thing or person. The devotees of idolatry will gladly admit Christ into their temples as one of their million gods, but the sovereign eternal God will not be one of them. The world has countless religions, but Christianity is not one of them. The world lays claim to many saviors, but Jesus Christ is not one of them. When the ark of Jehovah is placed in a pagan temple beside Dagon, that god, made by men's hands, must be demolished.[21] If the prophets of Baal

[13] Genesis 6:6　　　[14] I Kings 11:9　　　[15] Deuteronomy 6:15
[16] I John 4:8-9　　　[17] Proverbs 6:16　　　[18] Psalm 115:3
[19] Isaiah 46:10　　　[20] Daniel 4:35　　　[21] I Samuel 5

choose to challenge the God of the Bible, they must learn to their own hurt that their gods are impersonal and therefore cannot hear nor speak in response to their pleadings.[22]

The advent of the gospel is as dynamite to blast the foundations of the world's religions, and this is the reason why leaders of idolatry strive to banish Christianity from their presence. Wherever Romanism constitutes a minority group its leaders welcome religious freedom. But in Spain, Latin America, and Quebec, the Roman Catholic hierarchy seems unwilling to tolerate Protestantism as a minority group. They prefer their idols and images to the God of the Bible. They refuse to accept the words of our Lord that, "God is . . . Spirit: and they that worship Him must worship Him in spirit and in truth," [23] and that true worship of the one true God must be through Jesus Christ.[24]

[22] 1 Kings 18   [23] John 4:24   [24] John 14:6

THE ETERNALNESS OF GOD

By the eternalness of God is meant the state or quality of being eternal. That which is eternal is infinite in existence, that is, having no beginning nor end of existence. God is both timeless and perpetual. We exclude from Him all possibility of beginning and ending, of flux and change. The essence of God cannot be bounded by space nor time. God always was and always will be, and He will no more have an end than He had a beginning. Being the cause of time He is free from all succession of time. Time has in it past, present, and future; eternity has not. So when we think of God as being eternal, we think of Him as existing in an eternal present without past or future, an eternal today without a yesterday or a tomorrow. Though God is the author of time, He is in no way conditioned by it.

The Bible begins with the statement, "In the beginning God created the heaven and the earth." [1] This tells us that all space, matter, energy, and time had a beginning, but that God was before all these. Everything marked by time must have a beginning and may have an end. A created thing or being has no guarantee of itself that it will exist endlessly, the extent of its existence being dependent upon its Creator. But this One who created all

[1] Genesis 1:1

things is not in the chain of causes and effects. He Himself is the prime cause, and from Him has issued every lesser cause and every effect. God is not in time, neither is He subject to the law of time. He gave time its start, but the causes of His existence are in Himself.

God is the author, thus the source of all life. Men propound their theories as to the origin of life, some arguing for the evolutionary hypothesis, and others for spontaneous generation. But the Bible declares that all life comes from God. Time, space, matter, and energy commenced with Him. Life in all of its forms owes its existence to Him, and of course this includes man.[2] If there were no other form of life in the universe, nor even a universe, their nonexistence would not affect the existence of God. Before there was life anywhere else God existed as the very essence of life. Our Lord taught that, "the Father hath life in Himself."[3] All other life depends upon Him for existence, but His self-existence makes Him independent. "He giveth to all life, and breath, and all things. . . . For in Him we live, and move, and have our being."[4] But no one ever gave Him life. He is life. The attribute of eternalism is peculiarly God's.

Let us look now at some Scriptures which bear upon the fact that God is eternal. At the burning bush Moses said to God, "Behold, when I come unto the children of Israel, and shall say unto them, The God of your fathers hath sent me unto you; and they shall say to me, What is His name? what shall I say unto them? And God said unto Moses, I AM THAT I AM: and He said, Thus shalt thou say unto the children of Israel, I AM hath sent me

[2] Genesis 2:7   [3] John 5:26   [4] Acts 17:25,28

unto you." [5] Hardly a person has not been baffled by this passage when reading it for the first time in the English Bible. Exactly what did God mean? He simply wanted to be known by His name, "I AM." In the divine vocabulary there is no past or future tense. With God there is no "was" or "will be," but always the "now," the present. "I AM" is God's name and indicates His absolute and essential being, His self-existence and eternalness. The *New Standard Dictionary* defines the word "am" to mean "present, permanent existence." Testifying to His own eternalism, our Lord said, "Before Abraham was, I am." [6] Because He claimed eternalism, "they took up stones to stone Him." [7] At least they understood that He claimed to be the One who met Moses at the burning bush. And indeed it was He, for He said, "He that hath seen Me hath seen the Father. . . . Believe Me that I am in the Father, and the Father in Me." [8]

Another testimony to the fact that God is eternal is found in a psalm of Moses. "Before the mountains were brought forth, or ever Thou hadst formed the earth and the world, even from everlasting to everlasting, Thou art God." [9] In verses one to six of Psalm 90 we have a contrast between God and man. God is seen to be eternal while man is frail and finite. In fact the entire psalm is the prayer of a mortal man to the eternal God. Verse two reminds us that before ever God gave birth to the earth and the universe, and brought the ancient mountains into existence, He was there as the pre-existent, eternally-existent One. We often hear the expression, "as old as

---

[5] Exodus 3:13-14   [6] John 8:58   [7] John 8:59
[8] John 14:9,11   [9] Psalm 90:2

the hills," and some of them are old, billions of years they tell us. But the One who put them there predates them, for there never was a period when He was not. God is a timeless Being. The psalm teaches the *infinity* of God and the *infirmity* of man. Man counts the years by time, but time no more exists with God than it does for the unconscious sleeping ones.[10] Such a God is a safe dwelling place for His people and a suitable refuge for every succeeding generation. Let Heaven and earth pass away; we have a God greater than all the world.[11]

This same truth in substance is found in Psalm 102. This is a psalm of sorrow, one of the seven "penitential psalms." [12] It seems to have been written sometime after the Holy City lay in ruins.[13] The writer recognized that the sufferings of the people are the chastisements of the Lord. But the psalm concludes in the form of a prayer as it rises to a song of hope in the majestic thought that God is eternal: "I said, O my God, take me not away in the midst of my days: Thy years are throughout all generations. Of old hast Thou laid the foundation of the earth: and the heavens are the work of Thy hands. They shall perish, but Thou shalt endure: yea, all of them shall wax old like a garment; as a vesture shalt Thou change them, and they shall be changed: But Thou art the same, and Thy years shall have no end." [14]

This is both a solemn and satisfying truth to the child of God. It is *solemn* in that it feeds the mind a new sense of God's greatness and majesty. It is *satisfying* to know that the God of all creation, the Eternal Now, the I AM,

[10] Psalm 90:4   [11] I John 2:15-17   [12] Psalms 6,32,38,51,102,130,143
[13] Psalm 102:13-14   [14] Psalm 102:24-27

is the One who stooped to become my Saviour. And since eternalism and immutability are closely associated, my eternal salvation is already assured. He is without change, thus what He has done for my soul stands. By imparting His life to me, I am assured of living eternally with Him. Eternal life had a beginning in me but it shall have no end, and all because the One who imparted His life to me is both eternal and immutable.[15]

Man had a beginning. This means that man is a creature of time, that is, he is not from eternity past. However, he is created by God to endless existence, therefore he is destined to have an eternity future. He will live on endlessly in Heaven or hell, and the place in which he spends his future eternity is determined by his own choice. All men will be raised from the dead, though not all at the same time. There is a first and a second resurrection. The saved shall be raised to the resurrection of life and the unsaved to the resurrection of damnation.[16] But in each case it is to endless existence: either we will spend eternity in the presence of the eternal God, or else be banished from His presence eternally.

[15] Hebrews 6:17; James 1:17   [16] John 5:28-29

THE SOVEREIGNTY OF GOD

By the sovereignty of God we mean that God possesses and exercises supreme authority in all creation, including man. Modern political science and modern religion hold to the theory that sovereignty resides in the individual and that any form of government is merely the agency by which man exercises his sovereignty. Roman Catholicism teaches, though denied by some Roman Catholics, that sovereignty resides in the Roman Catholic Church. The "god" of modern religious thought no more resembles the Supreme Sovereign of the Bible than does the dim light of a 15-watt light bulb the glory of the noonday sun. The absolute and universal sovereignty of God is plainly and positively affirmed in Holy Writ.

When we say that God is sovereign we are merely affirming that which God Himself has already stated: namely, His right to govern the universe which He created. Jehoshaphat in his great prayer asked God, "O LORD God of our fathers, art not Thou God in heaven? and rulest not Thou over all the kingdoms of the heathen? and in Thine hand is there not power and might, so that none is able to withstand Thee?" [1] Answers to this question are found in many passages in Scripture, but none are more clear and concise and positive than the follow-

[1] 2 Chronicles 20:6

61

ing, "Thine, O Lord, is the greatness, and the power, and
the glory, and the victory, and the majesty: for all that
is in the heaven and in the earth is Thine; Thine is the
kingdom, O Lord, and Thou art exalted as head above
all." [2] God does as He pleases, only as He pleases, always as He pleases, "according to the purpose of Him
who worketh all things after the counsel of His own
will." [3] His own Word expressly declares, "Remember the
former things of old: for I am God, and there is none
else; I am God, and there is none like Me, Declaring the
end from the beginning, and from ancient times the
things that are not yet done, saying, My counsel shall
stand, and I will do all My pleasure: Calling a ravenous
bird from the east, the man that executeth My counsel
from a far country: yea, I have spoken it, I will also
bring it to pass; I have purposed it, I will also do it." [4]

In the Book of Daniel we have a remarkable prophetic
foreview of the Times of the Gentiles. All of the kingdoms, empires, and dynasties of men from Daniel's time
to the Second Coming of Christ to the earth to establish
His kingdom are named. God sets up kings and rulers
and puts them down as He chooses. In all of His dealings
with men He would teach them, among other things, "that
the most High ruleth in the kingdom of men, and giveth
it to whomsoever He will." [5] "He doeth according to His
will in the army of heaven, and among the inhabitants of
the earth: and none can stay His hand, or say unto Him,
What doest Thou?" [6] "But our God is in the heavens: He
hath done whatsoever He hath pleased." [7] "Whatsoever

[2] 1 Chronicles 29:11
[5] Daniel 4:25,32
[3] Ephesians 1:11
[6] Daniel 4:35
[4] Isaiah 46:9-11
[7] Psalm 115:3

the LORD pleased, that did He in heaven, and in earth, in the seas, and all deep places." [8] Such is the imperial, sovereign God, unrivaled in Himself, unaffected by anything outside of Himself.

If you ask wherein the sovereignty of God is founded, I would begin with the answer that He is entitled to sovereignty on the ground that Heaven and earth and all creatures are His by creative right. Being the Almighty Creator of all things, He is naturally the absolute and sovereign Lord over that which He created. God Himself defends His sovereignty on this ground. Read Job 38:1-40:5, and if you have been tempted to question God's moral right to act as He pleases, you will at once be brought to silence as was Job. "For the LORD is a great God, and a great King above all gods. In His hand are the deep places of the earth: the strength of the hills is His also. The sea is His, and He made it: and His hands formed the dry land. O come, let us worship and bow down: let us kneel before the LORD our maker." [9] He only can lay claim to sovereignty since He is "the LORD, the most high God, . . . possessor of heaven and earth." [10] Omnipotence is His power whereby He is able to create all things; sovereignty is the exercise of His moral power whereby it is lawful for Him to do what He will with His own creation.

God is entitled to sovereignty on the ground that He administrates His creation. And do not think for one moment that the universe does not need to be governed. If God were to withdraw, leaving the world to its own fate or fortune, we have no guaranty that the earth would

[8] Psalm 135:6   [9] Psalm 95:3-6   [10] Genesis 14:22

not be destroyed by another flood. If there is no personal God in control, and we have nothing more than the "laws of nature" to depend upon, we have no assurance that cloudbursts and flash floods will not one day destroy both life and property. If we cannot depend upon a personal God and Creator to govern His creation, we have no assurance that the great subterranean fires burning beneath the thin crust of the earth will not convulse and suddenly consume us. If the God of the Bible is not controlling His universe, we have no guaranty that a mighty tornado will not arise with such velocity and violence as to sweep all life on earth to destruction. Man is helpless to hold back or harness the winds. The wind blows where He (God) pleases.[11] The storms stir when and where He commands, and they are never without purpose.[12] Light and darkness are controlled by Him.[13] The heavenly bodies move at His bidding.[14] I submit to you that the alterations and variations of the elements are under God's sovereign control,[15] and for the reason that He is "upholding all things by the word of His power," [16] we must bow to His sovereignty. "It is of the LORD's mercies that we are not consumed, because His compassions fail not. They are new every morning: great is Thy faithfulness." [17]

God displays His sovereignty in the control He exercises over the irrational creatures.[18] This is further illustrated in the case of the ass God made to speak;[19] the ravens that fed Elijah;[20] the crowing cock;[21] the

[11] Mark 4:39   [12] Exodus 9:23-26   [13] Exodus 10:21-23
[14] Matthew 2:9   [15] Amos 4:7-10; Psalm 147:15-18
[16] Hebrews 1:3   [17] Lamentations 3:22-23
[18] Genesis 2:19; 6:19,20; Exodus 8:1-4, 16-18, 20-24; 10:12-14
[19] Numbers 22:28-30   [20] I Kings 17:1-6   [21] Matthew 26:34,74

catch of fishes;[22] and other instances similar to these.

What should be our attitude toward the sovereign God? We should bow before Him in holy awe as did Job;[23] Isaiah,[24] and Daniel.[25] Our attitude should be one of godly fear, reverence, obedience, and certainly one of complete submission and surrender, as is illustrated by Eli[26] and Job.[27] We should say with our blessed Lord, "Even so, Father: for so it seemed good in Thy sight." [28] "Not My will, but Thine, be done." [29]

[22] John 21:6
[25] Daniel 10:6-9
[28] Matthew 11:26
[23] Job 42:5-6
[26] I Samuel 3:18
[29] Luke 22:42
[24] Isaiah 6:1-5
[27] Job 1:21; 13:15

THE OMNIPOTENCE OF GOD

Omnipotence is an essential attribute of God, a peculiar right of His in which none of His creatures can share. The word *omnipotent* means "all power," so that the omnipotence of God is that ability and strength whereby He can bring to pass whatsoever He pleases. It appears once in the Bible and is used of God only.[1] His power is as great as His will, so that only He can say, "I will do all My pleasure. . . . I have spoken it, I will also bring it to pass; I have purposed it, I will also do it." [2] His power to perform is as great as His capacity to think and will. Anything He should will, He is able to perform without resistance or restraint. "None can stay His hand." [3] The hand that spelled out the doom of Babylon on the wall of Belshazzar's palace brought to nought the kingdom of Babylon.[4]

The nature of God's power should not be confused with the nature of His authority. Sometimes the word "power" is used when "authority" is meant. One may have the power of authority, that is, the right to exercise power, but not possess the strength and ability to demonstrate his authority. The Cuban revolt is an example of authority without power on the one hand, and power without

[1] Revelation 19:6   [2] Isaiah 46:10-11   [3] Daniel 4:35
[4] Daniel 5

66

authority on the other. Batista had authority without power; Castro had power without authority. The power of God is not to be understood as His authority, but rather His strength and might to do all His pleasure. The apostles were given authority of the Lord,[5] but men in the local churches did not always submit to that authority. God possesses sovereign authority and He also possesses the power to exercise His authority.

God's power is originally and essentially in Himself. We derive our strength from God, but His power is essentially in His own nature. If at any time He would not be all-powerful, then He would cease to be God. "Power belongeth unto God." [6] Omnipotence is God's peculiar prerogative, thus to be omnipotent is to be essentially God. If you believe in God, then believe Him for who He is and for what He can do. Never question His ability to do anything. Millions stand every week to recite the words, "I believe in God the Father Almighty," but I am sure some of them do not speak the truth. They need to have their faith confirmed in the belief that "power belongeth unto the Lord." God has declared this tremendous truth once, and we should hear it twice, once with each ear. We need to be reminded again and again of this elementary but essential truth. God is not sitting in Heaven as an idle and unconcerned viewer of passing events, as some men believe. If I believed this I would collapse under every provocation and pressure with no sense of security whatever. But I do believe that power belongs to God, my God and my Father.

Infinite power as pertains to the nature of God is ex-

<hr>

[5] 2 Corinthians 10:8; 13:10   [6] Psalm 62:11

pressed in His works. The Psalmist called upon all of
God's works to praise Him, and then gave as his reason,
"For He commanded, and they were created." [7] God's
power is absolute so that He needs to speak only once in
order to carry out His will. "God hath spoken once; twice
have I heard this; that power belongeth unto God." [8]
"For He spake, and it was done; He commanded, and
it stood fast." [9] "And God said . . . and there was." [10]
"And God said . . . and it was so." [11] All creation might
well join in praise of the mighty Creator who became our
Redeemer, and shout in unison, "By the word of the
LORD were the heavens made; and all the host of them
by the breath of His mouth." [12]

We see divine omnipotence expressed in God's preserv-
ing and providential power. The apostle speaks of God's
power as "eternal power." [13] Since His power has neither
beginning nor end, the believer has no fear about his future provision in this life nor in the life to come.[14] The
truth of God's omnipotence was a source of comfort and
hope to Jeremiah,[15] and to the apostles.[16] Even so it
should provide the same comfort and hope for every
Christian! God created me, therefore He is able to sustain and support me, "For in Him we live, and move,
and have our being." [17] "By Him all things consist." [18]
He is "upholding all things by the word of His power." [19]
The manner in which the world is preserved and con-

---

[7] Psalm 148:1-5   [8] Psalm 62:11   [9] Psalm 33:9
[10] Genesis 1:3   [11] Genesis 1:6-7, 11, 14-15, 24, 29-30
[12] Psalm 33:6   [13] Romans 1:20   [14] Isaiah 45:11-13; 46:4
[15] Jeremiah 32:17   [16] Acts 4:24-32   [17] Acts 17:28
[18] Colossians 1:17 [19] Hebrews 1:3

tinues cannot be accounted for apart from divine omnipotence.

We see divine omnipotence expressed in the redemption of man. Think of all that led up to our redemption. There is the miraculous conception in the virgin, inexplicable apart from divine omnipotence. "The *power* of the Highest shall overshadow thee. . . . For with God nothing shall be impossible." [20] Modern theology rejects the whole idea of the virgin birth, thereby showing how weak its god is. But the God of the Bible, Divine Omnipotence, brought the Clean out of the unclean.[21] Divine power preserved Christ from the attacks of Satan;[22] brought Him forth from death and the grave;[23] and set Him at the right hand of the Majesty on high.[24]

When He comes again in the clouds of Heaven with power and great glory,[25] we shall see the Redeemer, the living demonstration of divine omnipotence, God and Man in one Person. The union of the two natures, divine and human, is as great a display of God's power as has ever been witnessed. It is marked by mystery and miracle.[26] The death of the Redeemer was the death of the God-Man, the same Person who poured forth His Spirit as God and who was pierced as man.[27]

There is no more comforting truth than that the Almighty Creator became my Saviour. Well may every believer trust such a God! His ability knows no inability. Satan would take away the gift of our salvation if he

[20] Luke 1:35,37
[21] Job 14:4
[22] Matthew 4:1-11
[23] Romans 1:4
[24] Ephesians 1:20
[25] Matthew 24:30
[26] 1 Timothy 3:16
[27] Zechariah 12:10

could, but the Saviour "is *able* to save them to the utter-most that come unto God by Him." [28] Yes, He is *able to save!*

The temptations and trials of life would drive the believer to defeat and distraction, but "He is *able* to succour [help] them that are tempted." [29] Yes, He is *able to succour!*

In our human weakness we would stumble and fall and lose our way, but He "is *able* to keep [guard] you from falling, and to present you faultless before the presence of His glory with exceeding joy." [30] Yes, He is *able to sustain!*

As newborn babes we all needed nourishment, and still do, in order that we might grow and be stablished in the faith. And how blessed to know that the Word that saved us,[31] is the same Word that stablishes us.[32] "The word of His grace . . . is *able* to build you up." [33] "Now to Him that is of power to stablish you." [34] Yes, He is *able to stablish!*

Sometimes we wonder if there will be a sufficient supply of grace when we are in need. Especially is this true when we have sacrificed to help others. But we need never doubt, because "God is *able* to make all grace abound toward you; that ye, always having all sufficiency in all things, may abound to every good work." [35] Yes, He is *able to supply!*

Finally, no believer ever need fear about his future after death. We need not question whether or not we shall be raised from death and be transformed into the image

---

[28] Hebrews 7:25   [29] Hebrews 2:18   [30] Jude 24

[31] Romans 10:17; 1 Peter 1:23   [32] 1 Peter 2:2

[33] Acts 20:32   [34] Romans 16:25   [35] 2 Corinthians 9:8

of Christ. He "shall change our vile body, that it may be fashioned like unto His glorious body, according to the working whereby He is able even to subdue all things unto Himself." [36] One day God asked Abraham, "Is any thing too hard for the LORD?" [37] The question was a challenge to Abraham's faith in "Almighty God," for it was to Abraham that God first revealed Himself by this name.[38] After this revelation of Himself to His child, Abraham was willing to sacrifice Isaac, "Accounting that God was *able* to raise him up, even from the dead." [39] Yes, He is *able to subdue* all things, even death!

At all times and under every circumstance the child of God should be able to say, "The LORD is the strength of my life; of whom shall I be afraid?" [40] "Now unto Him that is able to do exceeding abundantly above all that we ask or think, according to the power that worketh in us, Unto Him be glory in the church by Christ Jesus throughout all ages, world without end. Amen." [41]

Now there are some things which God cannot do. This statement in no way contradicts all that has gone before in this chapter. God is able to do whatsoever He wills, but since His will is limited by His nature, He can do only those things that are in harmony with His perfect Being. Anything contrary to His nature He cannot do.

First, *God cannot deny Himself*.[42] He cannot renounce Himself. He is not like man who swerves and changes his views because of circumstances. We are faithless and disown Him, but He abideth faithful. One of God's dear children, who had been ill for many years and who

[36] Philippians 3:21   [37] Genesis 18:14   [38] Genesis 17:1
[39] Hebrews 11:19   [40] Psalm 27:1   [41] Ephesians 3:20-21
[42] 2 Timothy 2:13

trusted in Him thoughout her trial, was asked, "What if after all these years of faith and trust God should fail you in the end?" She replied, "He would lose more than I would. I would lose only my poor soul, but He would lose His good name." Though we are untrue to the Lord, He remains true to His own nature. He must complete that which He has begun.[43] "He cannot unsay His own plighted word."

Secondly, *God cannot deceive*.[44] The text says it is "impossible for God to lie." Whatever God promised to come to pass must come to pass, and this is the foundation of faith. The Word of God can no more fail than He Himself can fail. This is the anchor of hope to which we have fled and upon which we have laid hold. God's Word offers a strong fortress against doubt and discouragement. This is a mighty safe refuge to which to flee. Actually God has pledged His own existence on the fulfillment of His promise. Oh, cling to His promises!

[43] Philippians 1:6   [44] Hebrews 6:18

THE OMNIPRESENCE OF GOD

The word "omnipresence" comes from two Latin words, *omnis,* meaning "all," and *praesens,* meaning "to be at hand or present." Sometimes the word "immensity" is applied to God and used synonymously with "omnipresence." I prefer the word "omnipresence." It denotes that perfection of the divine Being by which He transcends all spacial limitations, and yet He is present in every part of space with His whole being. Because He is immense, He is omnipresent. He is everywhere present and everywhere active. His presence has no dependence on space or matter. The manifestations of His glory may vary at different times and places, but He Himself is present at every spot of His vast creation.

In connection with God's omnipresence we must avoid the error of pantheism which teaches that God is everything and everything is God. Pantheism recognizes an omnipresent activity of God, but denies His personality. Many persons who believe that the Being of God is the substance of all things will not believe in His personality and transcendence. I once heard a lecture by an educated pantheist whose oratory and philosophic ability held his audience. I sincerely believe he belongs in that category of which God says, "Professing themselves to be wise, they became fools." [1] The Bible teaches that God is a

[1] Romans 1:22

personal Being, and that His whole essence is here, there, and everywhere.

The omnipresence of God is clearly taught in Scripture. "Can any hide himself in secret places that I shall not see him? saith the LORD. Do not I fill heaven and earth? saith the LORD." [2] By filling Heaven and earth God does not mean merely that He fills them with His knowledge or His power. While it is true that God knows all that takes place in His universe and controls all activities and all action, by filling Heaven and earth is meant that every place is filled with His essence. No place can be imagined that is deprived of the presence of God. Having neither bounds nor limitation, God is essentially everywhere present in Heaven and earth. As God is eternal and is therefore not measured by time, even so He is omnipresent and is therefore not limited by place or space. It is just as natural for me to think that God is everywhere, as to think that God is.

Read carefully the following verses: "Whither shall I go from Thy spirit? or whither shall I flee from Thy presence? If I ascend up into heaven, Thou art there: if I make my bed in hell, behold, Thou art there. If I take the wings of the morning, and dwell in the uttermost parts of the sea; Even there shall Thy hand lead me, and Thy right hand shall hold me. If I say, Surely the darkness shall cover me; even the night shall be light about me. Yea, the darkness hideth not from Thee; but the night shineth as the day: the darkness and the light are both alike to Thee." [3] This Psalm 139 is one of the most glorious on the nature of God and His relation to

[2] Jeremiah 23:24   [3] Psalm 139:7-12

man. Its division by verses brings out the fine poetic
style of the psalm. The twenty-four verses are divided
into four stanzas with six verses in each stanza: God is
omniscient, God is omnipresent, God is omnipotent, and
God is omnirighteous.[4] It is the second stanza that is to
occupy us here.

We dare not conclude in our minds that the Psalmist
had a desire to run away from God. The point is that if
he wished to he could not. God is in Heaven and in hell,
in the seas and on the land. If one were to attempt to take
refuge from God in darkness, he would find Him there,
for to God there is no difference.[5] Man's proximity to God
is altered neither by a change of hemispheres, nor distance, nor darkness. There is no place where one can
escape God. In Heaven there is the presence of His
glory; in hell there is the presence of His wrath. The
wicked could wish to escape His presence, as they will
seek to do, but they cannot.[6]

How different is the God of the Bible from the many
and varied gods of idolaters! The poor unbeliever does
not know where his god is. When the prophets of Baal
called upon their god, there was no reply. Then Elijah
mocked them, saying, "Cry aloud: for he is a god; either
he is talking, or he is pursuing, or he is in a journey, or
peradventure he sleepeth, and must be awaked." [7] So they
followed Elijah's advice and cried louder, but still there
was no reply. But this is not like the God of the Christian,
nor is it like the trusting Christian to act as foolishly as
did the prophets of Baal. God is never far from us, for

[4] W. Graham Scroggie   [5] Amos 9:2-6   [6] Revelation 6:16
[7] I Kings 18:27

in Him we live and move and have our being.[8] Augustine
said that God is not partly here and partly there, but
totally present at every point in the universe.

It was so foolish of Jonah to think he could flee from
the presence of the Lord.[9] Is God in the east only and
not in the west? Why would any believer try to run away
from God and refuse to witness the message of salvation?
There are two cardinal truths in the Jonah incident: God
can and does speak to men; and no man can escape from
God. Certainly Jonah must have encountered the truth of
God's omnipresence in the religious heritage of his people.
At any rate, Jonah attempted to do the impossible. He
tried to escape from God by fleeing to a particular locale.
Actually I feel that Jonah knew better but his disobedience had warped his better judgment. Here is a
solemn lesson for every servant of God. Let not one of
us think for a moment that we can escape from the call
of God.

The omnipresence of God is the strength of His servants. It is that objective presence known and experienced
by those who love and serve Him. It was this very presence that our Lord promised to His own.[10] It is His
presence in His Church that believers enjoy and experience,[11] even though their number be few.[12] His presence
is the strength and stay of the dying.[13]

Psalm 121 is a psalm of comfort, assuring safety and
protection from evil for all who put their trust in God.
In it we are reminded that God neither slumbers nor
sleeps,[14] so that we may be sure of His presence through

---

[8] Acts 17:27-28   [9] Jonah 1:3   [10] John 14:23; Matthew 28:19-20
[11] Ephesians 4:6; Revelation 1:12-20
[12] Matthew 18:20   [13] Psalm 23:4   [14] Psalm 121:3-4

all our sleeping hours, and say in the morning, "When I awake, I am still with Thee." [15] My own personal testimony is that the presence of God is evident to my reason and consciousness. It is a presence I feel and know by experience. Since God is essentially in every part of the world, I am conscious of His presence wherever I go. He has said, "Fear thou not; for I am with thee." [16] If fear prevails and takes hold of me, it is not because God is not where I am, but rather because I am forgetful of His presence. We need to cultivate the practice of God's presence, for it is more valuable than money, property, or earthly friends. By cultivating His presence I mean living a separated life, for it is then only that we can enjoy His provision and protection. "Be ye not unequally yoked together with unbelievers. . . . Come out from among them, and be ye separate, saith the Lord, and touch not the unclean thing; and I will receive you. . . . *I will dwell in them.*" [17] A separated man will never feel forsaken and alone. When David's soldiers mutinied and the people spoke of stoning him, he "encouraged himself in the LORD his God." [18] So may we!

The last of the names of God in the order of their appearance in the Old Testament is in the Book of Ezekiel: "And the name of the city from that day shall be, *The Lord is there.*" [19] The phrase, "The LORD is there," is the translation of a Hebrew name for God, "Jehovah-Shammah." It is the name whereby God promised His presence in the midst of His people. He dwelt among them in a tent and a tabernacle,[20] then in a temple.[21]

[15] Psalm 139:18
[16] Isaiah 41:10
[17] 2 Corinthians 6:14-18
[18] 1 Samuel 30:6
[19] Ezekiel 48:35
[20] 2 Samuel 7:5-7
[21] 2 Chronicles 7:1-3

In the new dispensation Jehovah has been present in the Person of the Lord Jesus Christ in whom the whole fullness of God was pleased to dwell,[22] for Christ was the effulgence of God's glory and the very image of His substance.[23] The Word became flesh and tabernacled among us,[24] so we can say that Christ is "God with us." [25]

And now that the Son is in Heaven, God's presence is in believers as living temples.[26] The true Church is now the "habitation of God through the Spirit." [27] Wherever a child of God is, *Jehovah-Shammah*—The LORD is there.

> I know not where His islands lift
>   Their fronded palms in air;
> I only know I cannot drift
>   Beyond His love and care.

[22] Colossians 1:19　　[23] Hebrews 1:3　　[24] John 1:14
[25] Isaiah 7:14; 9:6　　[26] 1 Corinthians 3:16; 6:19
[27] Ephesians 2:22

THE OMNISCIENCE OF GOD

The word "omniscience" comes from two Latin words, meaning "all" and "knowledge." The omniscience of God is that attribute whereby He knows all things, actualities, and possibilities—past, present, and future. God has complete and perfect knowledge of all things that ever have been, all things that could have been, all things that are, and all things that are going to be. There never has been a time when there was anything God did not know, nor will there ever be such a time.

The fact of God's omniscience is stated clearly in Scripture. "The LORD is a God of knowledge." [1] "His understanding is infinite." [2] "God . . . knoweth all things." [3] God's knowledge is not to be compared with man's knowledge. Man's knowledge is as a grain of dust compared with God's knowledge. Before the Fall man would readily acknowledge the omniscience of God. Even today among savages men know they are not dealing with an ignorant deity. If man thought his God was limited in knowledge, he would not bother to offer a sacrifice, recite a prayer, or so much as lift up his hands heavenward or bow his head. No man would attempt to worship an ignorant deity.

There is an innate consciousness in man which tells

[1] 1 Samuel 2:3   [2] Psalm 147:5   [3] 1 John 3:20

him that God knows more than he does. It commenced with Adam and has grown up with all rational and intelligent creatures. Zophar recognized this fact;[4] Isaiah wrote of it;[5] Paul stated it.[6] The universe and man are the expression of knowledge far beyond the comprehension of the small, finite mind of God's creatures.

Take a moment to look at Paul's statement in Romans 11:33: "O the depth of the riches both of the wisdom and knowledge of God! how unsearchable are His judgments, and His ways past finding out!" The depth of God's wisdom and knowledge is inexhaustible and inconceivable. No man is capable of investigating the grounds or reasons for God's providential dispensations, decisions, and decrees. As a bloodhound who finds it impossible to trace out and track down the scent of an escaped criminal, even so man cannot search out the mind and ways of the Lord. They are "unsearchable . . . past finding out," that is, they cannot be traced out or tracked down. As we contemplate God's "mercy upon all," [7] we are carried to new heights, only to discover that while we have arrived at another and higher plateau in pursuit of knowledge, we are unable to sound the depths with the plummet of the human mind and words. We can only wonder and adore our great God, who is infinite in His Being, incomprehensible in His judgments, and inexhaustible in knowledge; and then exclaim, "Who hath known the mind of the Lord?" [8] We need direction, counsel, and teaching, but He needed no one to direct, counsel, or instruct Him.[9]

Any departure on our part from these two contrasting

[4] Job 11:7-9   [5] Isaiah 40:28
[6] Romans 11:33; 1 Corinthians 2:10-11
[7] Romans 11:32   [8] Romans 11:34   [9] Isaiah 40:13

conceptions of God's knowledge and man's knowledge will result in disaster for man. Satan knows this, for it was that very weapon he used in his attack against our first parents. He said, "For God doth know that in the day ye eat thereof, then your eyes shall be opened, and ye shall be as gods, knowing good and evil." [10] Satan was telling Eve that the fruit of the tree of knowledge was the very thing she needed, and that God did not want her to have it lest she might become like God. It was because the desire for knowledge is inherent in man that Satan used this device. Our first parents knew what good was like but evil they did not know, because they had no personal experience in the doing of evil or in suffering for it. Man aspired to an experiential and experimental knowledge of evil.

Now man could not possibly know evil as God knows evil. God knows evil only because He is omniscient, thus He only can know evil, and yet hate it, and remain holy. Satan convinced Eve that she would be as God in respect of His knowledge. She was deceived.[11] No man dare aspire to equality with God. The whole scheme was satanic.[12] One of the vain imaginations of mankind since the Fall is that he can rise up to parity with the Creator. But God is unique in His omniscience. He has given to man a revelation of knowledge, and that revelation is in His Word. "Beware lest any man spoil you through philosophy and vain deceit, after the tradition of men, after the rudiments of the world, and not after Christ." [13]

"Intellect in man is hardly more than the capacity or readiness to acquire knowledge, which knowledge, when

[10] Genesis 3:5   [11] 1 Timothy 2:14   [12] Isaiah 14:12-14
[13] Colossians 2:8

acquired, as compared with omniscience, is even less than elementary, while the understanding of God is all-inclusive and infinite." [14] Any knowledge which man attains must be by the gradual process of acquiring it through God-given means, "For precept must be upon precept, precept upon precept; line upon line, line upon line; here a little, and there a little." [15] In this men do not differ. "For who maketh thee to differ from another? and what hast thou that thou didst not receive? now if thou didst receive it, why dost thou glory, as if thou hadst not received it?" [16] Omniscience is not the mere ability to acquire knowledge, but rather it is the actual possession of all knowledge. It is even as Peter testified, "Lord, Thou knowest all things." [17]

Man's acquisition of knowledge is as one watching a parade. He sees each unit as it passes before his view, and then at best he can take in only part. But God creates the marchers, lines up the parade, plans the course of march, and then directs every movement. He says, "I am God, and there is none like Me, Declaring the end from the beginning, and from ancient times the things that are not yet done, saying, My counsel shall stand, and I will do all My pleasure." [18] From the divine vantage point God sees the entire parade even before it starts. Omniscience includes prescience or foreknowledge. If God were wanting in knowledge of anything, past, present, or future, He would not be perfect and therefore could not be God.

This leads me to say a few words about prophecy. All prophecy is founded on God's omniscience, that is, it is

[14] Lewis Sperry Chafer   [15] Isaiah 28:9-10   [16] I Corinthians 4:7
[17] John 21:17   [18] Isaiah 46:9-10

the result of His foreknowledge and predetermination of things. Here is an area of study to which one could devote a lifetime. Take for example God's prediction that the Israelites would be in a strange land and be afflicted four hundred years;[19] or that the same people would be in captivity in Babylon for seventy years, and then be delivered at the end of that time;[20] or the prophecy of the Times of the Gentiles as seen in Daniel 2; or the manner and place of Messiah's birth.[21] All prophecy is God's foreknowledge of future events, decreed and determined by Him, so that with Him nothing is casual or contingent. Yes, God knows the whole plan of the ages because He planned the ages.[22]

God knows every creature and every created thing, animate and inanimate.[23] "He telleth the number of the stars; He calleth them all by their names."[24] He knows the ravens and their young ones,[25] He knows every sparrow.[26] He said, "I know all the fowls of the mountains: and the wild beasts of the field are Mine."[27]

God knows every thought and action of all men. We cannot probe the depths of another's heart, but nothing is impenetrable to God. "All things are naked and opened unto the eyes of Him with whom we have to do."[28] We can discern others by their exterior, but God knows the condition of the heart. He has said, "I the LORD search the heart, I try the reins, even to give every man according to his ways, and according to the fruit of his doings."[29] He only can see and know the heart.[30] He only

[19] Genesis 15:13   [20] Jeremiah 29:10, cf. 2 Chronicles 36:14-21
[21] Isaiah 7:14; Micah 5:2   [22] Ephesians 1:9-12; 3:4-9
[23] Hebrews 4:13   [24] Psalm 147:4, cf. Isaiah 40:26
[25] Job 38:41   [26] Matthew 10:29   [27] Psalm 50:11
[28] Hebrews 4:13   [29] Jeremiah 17:10   [30] 1 Samuel 16:7

knows the vanity in man's heart.[31] David prayed,
"Cleanse Thou me from secret faults." [32] Secret to whom?
Certainly not to God! [33]

Omniscience is necessary in order for God to deal
justly with sinners. He could neither cleanse nor condemn sins He knows nothing about. If my thoughts and
actions are concealed from Him, He cannot be a righteous
judge. Now, no man is competent fully to know and
judge himself, but he must wait until Christ comes, who
will bring to light the hidden things of darkness.[34] But
God knows all things perpetually and infallibly, even to
every thought, every word in my tongue,[35] and every
imagination.[36] "He knoweth what is in the darkness." [37]
Little wonder men would strip God of His omniscience
if they could. The sinner hates this divine perfection, for
by it he must be judged. What a practical appeal God's
omniscience should make to every sinner!

The contemplation of God's perfect knowledge is food
for the souls of the saints. If I am perplexed at times,
"He knoweth the way that I take." [38] In times of weari-
ness and weakness, "He knoweth our frame; He remembereth that we are dust." [39] In times of sorrow and
affliction, I hear Him say, "I have surely seen the affliction of My people which are in Egypt, and have heard
their cry by reason of their taskmasters; for I know their
sorrows." [40] Hallelujah, He is "the only wise God." [41]

The wonder of it all is that the omniscient God became
incarnate in the Person of Jesus Christ in order to save

[31] Job 11:11   [32] Psalm 19:12   [33] Psalm 90:8
[34] 1 Corinthians 4:1-5 [35] Psalm 139:1-4   [36] 1 Chronicles 28:9
[37] Daniel 2:22   [38] Job 23:10   [39] Psalm 103:14
[40] Exodus 3:7   [41] 1 Timothy 1:17; Jude 25

us. Of Christ it is written that He knows men's thoughts;[42] He only knows the Father;[43] He knows what is in man;[44] He knows those who trust Him and those who do not.[45] Here is a strong proof for the essential deity of Christ. The contemplation of His omniscience should fill the soul with holy awe and wonder.

[42] Luke 6:8   [43] Matthew 11:27   [44] John 2:24-25
[45] John 6:64

THE HOLINESS OF GOD

Holiness is that natural and essential attribute of God whereby He is absolutely and essentially perfect and righteous. He is necessarily holy because He is holiness in the highest degree. He is infinitely and eternally holy, and in this He is unique, different from all creatures, men and angels. God's holiness is not an acquired perfection; it is essentially God Himself. As He was God from eternity, so He was holy from eternity, therefore He is as necessarily holy as He is necessarily God. He cannot be God and not be holy. His nature could not subsist without holiness.

God only is absolutely holy. Moses, in his song of redemption, makes Jehovah the theme of his praises, and asks "Who is like unto Thee, O Lord, among the gods? who is like Thee, *glorious in holiness*?" [1] Hannah answered this question in her prayer when she said, "There is none holy as the Lord." [2] God Himself assumes the title of "the Holy One," [3] and in this He distinguishes Himself from man, saying, "I am God, and not man; the Holy One in the midst of thee." [4] No man or angel can be essentially and infinitely holy. Holiness is not the peculiar glory of God's creatures, but only of God Him-

[1] Exodus 15:11   [2] 1 Samuel 2:2   [3] Isaiah 40:25
[4] Hosea 11:9

self. Any holiness in God's creatures is imparted to them by God. When the song of Moses shall be combined with the song of the Lamb, the saints shall sing of the Lord, "For Thou only art holy." [5]

Whenever God pledged Himself to man, He sware of His holiness. When He made a promise to Abraham, the inspired writers tell us that, "He sware by Himself." [6] Since God is holiness, to say that He sware by Himself is synonymous with saying that He sware by His holiness, "whose name is Holy." [7] God Himself says, "My covenant will I not break, nor alter the thing that is gone out of My lips. *Once have I sworn by My holiness.*" [8] Amos wrote, "The Lord GOD hath sworn by His holiness." [9] These passages show that the holiness of God is essentially God Himself. Thus when He would draw out the confidence of man, and allay all suspicion and unbelief, giving to man the fullest guarantee possible that He would not fail him, He would sware by His holiness.

Now, no man could pledge himself by his own holiness, simply because man is mutable; he changes. On one occasion we might hate a particular sin, and speak out against it with all earnestness, sincerity, and indignation; then at some later date we might indulge in that very sin. But God is always the same. He is immutable in His essence, "with whom is no variableness." [10] He says, "I am the LORD, I change not." [11] In all of His attributes He is immutable. Whatever He was before the universe was brought into existence, He is the same now, and will re-

---

[5] Revelation 15:4 [6] Genesis 22:16, cf. Hebrews 6:13
[7] Isaiah 57:15 [8] Psalm 89:34-35 [9] Amos 4:2; 6:8
[10] James 1:17 [11] Malachi 3:6

main so forever. But fallen man is inconstant, inconsistent, "Unstable as water," [12] and not to be depended upon.[13]

This attribute of God, as none other, is announced with a thrice-repeated emphasis by the seraphim: *"Holy, holy, holy,* is the LORD of hosts." [14] Most commentators say the emphasis suggests the realization of the Trinity, the three Persons in the one Godhead. I do not object to this as a suggestion; however, I believe this passage to be a rather weak text to prove the Trinity. The thrice-uttered "holy" by the seraphim is intended to exalt and magnify before men this sublimest of God's attributes. Stephen Charnock said, "The threefold repetition of a word notes the certainty or absoluteness of the thing, or the irreversibleness of the resolve." What Charnock probably meant was that God repeated a thing three times to impress man with the certainty or absoluteness of the thing. Actually God needs to say a thing only once and then it is certain and absolute. At any rate, He wants man to be impressed with this all-important perfection of His nature.

Other instances of a threefold repetition to emphasize certainty, absoluteness, and importance are found in the striking prophecy where God foretells the setting aside of the royal house of David, because of the wickedness of the leaders, until Messiah should come and set up His kingdom.[15] God said, "I will *overturn, overturn, overturn,* it," and by this He means that there shall not be a man of David's line sitting on the throne of David until David's greater Son should appear in power and glory.[16]

[12] Genesis 49:4   [13] Psalm 146:3   [14] Isaiah 6:3
[15] Ezekiel 21:24-27   [16] Luke 1:32

And then there is the threefold cry of woe in which God announces the certainty and absoluteness of the coming judgments of the Great Tribulation. The messenger cried, "*Woe, woe, woe,* to the inhabiters of the earth." [17] Again God is emphasizing to man the magnitude of His pronouncement.

God's holiness is seen in His hatred for sin and in His judgment of both sin and sinners. Man can find pleasure in wickedness, but God never! "For Thou art not a God that hath pleasure in wickedness." [18] Holiness can neither take part in sin nor approve it in others, but must necessarily hate everything contrary to it. Charnock says, "The vehemency of this hatred is expressed variously in Scripture; He loathes it so, that He is impatient of beholding it; the very sight of it affects Him with detestation. [19] He hates the first spark of it in the imagination. [20] With what variety of expressions He doth repeat His indignation at their polluted services: 'I hate . . . I despise . . . I will not smell . . . I will not accept . . . I will not regard.' [21] He abhors it so, that His hatred redounds upon the person that commits it." [22] This fact was never revealed more clearly than at the Cross where Christ became sin for us. In that dark hour, when the Holy Father blotted out all the view of His Son, Christ cried, "My God, My God, why hast Thou forsaken Me?" Then, answering His own question, He says, "Thou art holy." [23] There at Calvary we are permitted to view the divine abhorrence of sin.

Unlike man, God is impartial in His hatred and judg-

[17] Revelation 8:13   [18] Psalm 5:4   [19] Habakkuk 1:13
[20] Zechariah 8:17   [21] Amos 5:21-22   [22] Psalm 5:5
[23] Psalm 22:1,3

ment of sin. We are prone to minimize the sins of our own children, of those nearest and dearest to us, while we discuss freely with indignation the sins of others. But it is not so with God. He will put to death a Nadab and an Abihu, punish a David, pursue a Jonah, prevent a Moses from entering Canaan, or pronounce an anathema upon a Peter as when Jesus called him Satan. A man will never loathe cancer so much until that dread and filthy disease causes the loss of his own eyes, arms, or legs, or else the life of one of his own precious loved ones. But God's hatred for sin is necessarily universal and perpetual. The fountain of holiness can never issue forth the slightest approval of sin at any time or place, or in any person. No fountain can send forth at the same place both sweet water and bitter, salt water and fresh.[24]

The holiness of God is evidenced in all of His laws. Whether they be moral laws, natural laws, or ceremonial laws, they are all the outgrowth of His holiness. Moreover, the law in all its aspects was designed to impress upon Israel the idea of the holiness of God, and to urge upon the people the divine demands for leading a holy life. God's eternal and unalterable law demands only good and forbids all evil. In this His law never changes. "Wherefore the law is holy, and the commandment holy, and just, and good. . . . For we know . . . the law is spiritual." [25] The law partakes of the nature and character of the Lawgiver. Its specific commandments are intrinsically good as well as beneficial in their effects. The word "spiritual" sums up the three qualities: holy, just, and good. "The law of the Lord is perfect. . . . The

[24] James 3:11-12   [25] Romans 7:12,14

statutes of the LORD are right . . . the commandment of the LORD is pure. . . . The judgments of the LORD are true." [26]

One of the greater sins against God's holiness is the vain imagination, or false representation, of God. Most men know little or nothing about the holiness of God, or else they do not really believe in His holiness. All men who believe in God believe in His mercy, love, and grace, but such a view of God, while true as far as it goes, is a lopsided one. They think only of the kind of a God that suits their fancy, thus they rule out of their thinking a God who hates and judges sin. The gods of man's inventions since the fall of Adam are the very reverse of the Holy God of the Bible.[27] Here are solemn and fearful words, among them God's own appraisal of man's view of Him: "Thou thoughtest that I was altogether such an one as thyself." The God which the vast majority of people accept is like a kindly, generous, lenient old man, who winks at our "minor infractions of laws" and the "insignificant indiscretion of youth." But the Bible says, "God is angry with the wicked every day." [28]

Because God is holy, our desire should be to be holy. "But as He which hath called you is holy, so be ye holy in all manner of conversation; Because it is written, Be ye holy; for I am holy." [29] I know of no finer way of honoring Him. He does not ask us to know everything, nor to be able to do everything, but He does require holiness. "Exalt ye the LORD our God, and worship at His footstool; for He is holy." [30]

[26] Psalm 19:7-9
[29] I Peter 1:15-16
[27] Psalm 50:16-22
[30] Psalm 99:5
[28] Psalm 7:11

THE GOODNESS OF GOD

The goodness of God is that essential perfection of
the divine nature which inclines Him to deal bountifully
with His creatures. It is that benevolence of God which
issues forth from His nature, and aims to promote the
happiness and well-being of the creature. Of all God's
attributes, His goodness is doubtless the most pleasant
and desirable to man, inasmuch as it provides the necessities and conveniences and natural pleasures of life.

God only is originally, essentially, eternally, infinitely,
and inherently good in Himself. Any goodness in His
creation issued forth from Him. Man's goodness is not
within himself; he acquired it from the Creator, but "the
goodness of God endureth continually." [1] When the rich
man came running to Jesus, he asked Him, "Good
Master, what shall I do that I may inherit eternal life?
And Jesus said unto him, Why callest thou Me good?
there is none good but one, that is, God." [2] Our Lord's
reply did not disclaim that He Himself was good. On
the contrary, He is claiming absolute goodness, which is
deity. Actually our Lord rebuked the man for using the
word "good" lightly. Since the epithet is applicable to God
only, Christ wanted this man to use the term carefully
and correctly. The young man regarded Christ as a hu-

[1] Psalm 52:1   [2] Mark 10:17-18

man teacher only, thus to attach the word "good" to a mere man is a superficial view of the term. The inquirer had moral and spiritual needs, but with a distorted view of goodness, those needs could not be met. He needed to see that God only is good and that all men are not good.[3] As regards Christ Himself, He either claimed goodness and Godhead; or He denied goodness and Godhead. If Christ meant that He was not God, then He meant that He was not good. By issuing a command to the young man,[4] Christ claimed deity, else He would have been asking him to violate the Second Commandment.[5] The important point is that none is good save One, and that One is God.

Some able teachers of the Scriptures speak of the goodness of God as being synonymous with God's mercy, His love, or His grace. I understand these attributes to differ in some respects, therefore I would suggest that we consider each of them separately.

As an example, goodness and mercy differ in that God's goodness reaches out to more persons than does His mercy. His goodness extends to all. "The LORD is good to all."[6] God's inclination to deal bountifully with man is not confined to those who obey Him, "For He maketh His sun to rise on the evil and on the good, and sendeth rain on the just and on the unjust."[7] "He is kind unto the unthankful and to the evil."[8] God is not good to people more because they are good, nor less because they are evil. Parents are never more wrong than when they tell their little ones, "God won't be good to you if you

[3] Psalm 14:1, cf. Romans 3:12   [4] Mark 10:21
[5] Exodus 20:4-5   [6] Psalm 145:9   [7] Matthew 5:45
[8] Luke 6:35

are naughty!" Our Lord taught that the sunshine and the rain are proof of God's goodness to all men. Divine goodness is not conditioned by the attitude of those to whom it flows. Paul emphasizes this point in Romans 5:6-8. God is dealing with all men on the principle of divine goodness. Augustine said, "Good for good, evil for evil: that is natural. Evil for good: that is devilish. Good for evil: that is divine."

All that emanates from God is of necessity good, therefore every act of creation was an impartation of His goodness. I know of no demands upon God which made it necessary for Him to create the world, but when He chose to create a world, it was necessary that He should create it good. Thus the goodness of God is emphasized first in creation. Read once again that famous first chapter of Genesis, note verses 4,10,12,18,21,25,31. They all tell us the same story, "And God saw that it was *good*." The chapter then closes with this statement, "And God saw every thing that He had made, and, behold, *it was very good*." The goodness of God is the first attribute describing His creation, thus it seems that one of the divine motives in creation was to display His goodness. "The earth is full of the goodness of the LORD." [9]

In connection with the thought that all creation is good, Paul wrote, "For every creature [created thing] of God is good, and nothing to be refused, if it be received with thanksgiving." [10] The Spirit of God had just warned the believer against those who forbid marriage and the eating of meats. Now there doubtless have been instances where it was better for a person to remain unmarried, or

[9] Psalm 33:5   [10] I Timothy 4:4

to refrain from certain foods. But God instituted marriage and He is the Giver of all food.[11] Both are for the propagation and sustenance of human life. We should thank Him daily for all of these good things of life and enjoy them in moderation. But are we as earnest and regular as we should be in giving thanks to God for them? Food is good because God created it, and its use is sanctified to us for good through prayer and faith. When we humbly and gratefully offer thanks to God at the table for the food He provides, it acquires a holy quality by our acknowledgment that it is His gift to us. It is only right and proper that we do this.[12] First, God created these good things, then He created us in order that He might impart His goodness to us.[13] Indeed the Lord is good! What a variety of natural pleasures He has provided for His creatures! The first recorded lie of the devil was his casting aspersions upon the goodness of God.[14]

It has always been a problem with some persons to see certain individuals enjoying more of God's goodness than do others. As we have seen in Matthew 5:45 and Luke 6:35, God is impartial in His benevolences to man. However, not all persons have the same capacities of reception of good and of usefulness. God does never withhold the necessities of life from any one who trusts Him for them, but I can believe that He might bestow a greater measure of His goodness upon those who in turn use it to bless others. And I can believe that He might withhold some things from those who treat Him with impunity through despising His goodness. Read Romans 2:4-5, and there

---

[11] Genesis 1:28-29
[12] 1 Samuel 9:13; Matthew 14:19; 15:36; Acts 27:35
[13] James 1:17-18   [14] Genesis 3:1-5

you will see the man who looks down his nose at the kindness, the benignity of God. For all such there will come
a payday for this contempt of God's goodness. Men sometimes form their own opinions about how they study and
work to succeed in life and provide for themselves and
their families, making light of God's goodness. But all
who form in their minds a low estimate of the goodness
of the Lord must expect divine retribution sooner or later.
Most persons have not learned that to comprehend the
goodness of God will lead them to repent and forsake
their sins, which in turn will cause them to trust God for
the daily supply of His goodness. Oh, let us say from our
hearts, "Thou art good, and doest good." [15]

Take a good look at Psalm 107. The psalm opens with
the statement, "O give thanks unto the LORD, for *He is
good.*" We are presented with four figures of speech, each
depicting human need in some form. The plight of a man
on his journey by land;[16] the plight of a prisoner enslaved;[17] the plight of one who is sick;[18] the plight of
the sea voyager in a storm.[19] In each instance we see the
goodness of God in deliverance.

The goodness which He manifests here is no ordinary,
common, run-of-the-mill goodness. Here is divine goodness shown toward the tired and bewildered traveler, the
enslaved captive, the sick and the dying, the seamen
being buffeted and tossed about on the sea of life. The
entire Old Testament resounds with the praiseful refrain,
"He is good." [20] And rightly so! Who is there among us
who can deny that God has been good? Then let us not

[15] Psalm 119:68   [16] Psalm 107:4-9   [17] Psalm 107:10-16
[18] Psalm 107:17-22   [19] Psalm 107:23-32
[20] 1 Chronicles 16:34; 2 Chronicles 5:13; 7:3; Ezra 3:11

delay to praise Him for His goodness. But it would seem, from reading the psalm, that right here is where we fail God. Each display of God's goodness calls forth from the recipient a word of thanks. "Oh that men would praise the LORD for His goodness." [21]

[21] Psalm 107:8,15,21,31

THE MERCY OF GOD

God's mercy may be defined as an outward manifestation of His pity and compassion by which He relieves the misery of the sinful and suffering in their distress. Mercy presupposes misery. Mercy is as natural and essential to God as are all His attributes. Since the fall of man there has not been a second when God did not have man's misery at heart. "The Latin word *Misericordia* signifies having another's misery at heart, but not his miserable heart." [1]

The mercy of God may be said to arise from His goodness, though goodness and mercy are not synonymous terms.[2] The unfallen angels are the objects of God's grace and goodness, but He has never exercised mercy toward them, simply because they know no misery and suffering, and therefore need no mercy. Sin brought with it misery and suffering, and this in turn moved God in the exercise of His pity and compassion.

The terms in Scripture which describe the characteristics of God's mercy are worth noting. His mercy is said to be "great" [3] and "plenteous," [4] or, full and abundant; "from everlasting to everlasting," [5] or eternal; "tender," [6] as emanating from the innermost, the tenderest part of

---

[1] John Gill [2] Psalm 23:6 [3] 1 Kings 3:6
[4] Psalm 86:5 [5] Psalm 103:17 [6] Luke 1:78

98

one's being;[7] "abundant,"[8] meaning an exceeding or overflowing measure. God is said to be rich in "goodness,"[9] "grace,"[10] "glory,"[11] and "mercy."[12] Not one of us could measure the mercy of God, "For as the heaven is high above the earth, so great is His *mercy* toward them that fear Him."[13]

The Puritan writers made the distinction between the *general* mercy of God and His *special* mercy. There is a sense in which God's mercy is extended to the entire earth and all creation in it. "The LORD is good to all: and His tender *mercies* are over all His works."[14] "God has pity upon the brute creation in their needs, and supplies them with suitable provision."[15] "The earth, O LORD, is full of Thy *mercy*."[16] This does in no way contradict what is written in the second paragraph of this chapter, when we remember that the whole creation is under the curse as a result of the Fall.[17]

The *special* mercy of God is that pity and compassion which He extends to those who trust Him. They are called "vessels of mercy" to whom He shall make known the riches of His glory.[18] His special mercy is seen in the regeneration of the lost. Regeneration may be defined as that act of God in which He imparts spiritual life to believing sinners dead in trespasses and sins. This life is His own life, so that the believer is said to become a partaker of the divine nature.[19] All who have been born

---

[7] Philippians 1:8; 2:1; Colossians 3:12
[8] I Peter 1:3
[9] Romans 2:4
[10] Ephesians 1:7; 2:7
[11] Ephesians 3:16
[12] Ephesians 2:4
[13] Psalm 103:11
[14] Psalm 145:9
[15] A. W. Pink
[16] Psalm 119:64
[17] Genesis 3:14,17-19; Romans 8:21-22
[18] Romans 9:23
[19] 2 Peter 1:4

again will surely testify that salvation has come to them because of the abundant mercy of God.[20]

The Apostle Paul testified of himself, "Who was before a blasphemer, and a persecutor, and injurious: but *I obtained mercy,* because I did it ignorantly in unbelief." [21] Paul is not excusing himself, nor is he suggesting that he was saved because he did certain things in ignorance. What he is saying is that God in mercy arrested him and saved him in his frenzy of blind zeal. Paul never forgot that display of divine mercy that rescued him from the judgment and hell. He was humbled at the recollection of his sordid past, and he attributed his present status in Christ to the pity and compassion of God. Surely we would join with Paul in praising God for His mercy which granted us the opportunity to hear the gospel of salvation, and the larger opportunity of serving Him. It was an interesting observation on my part to see how Paul placed *mercy* alongside of *grace* and *peace* in the three Pastoral Epistles.[22]

While God's mercy is available to all, it is not wanted by all. Some hearts are too proud to receive mercy. It is written that "His *mercy* is on them that fear Him from generation to generation." [23] But how many there are who have no fear of God whatever! A man once told me that he didn't want mercy from anyone but that he could stand on his own two feet. Unfortunately for him, and others like him, he will not stand at all in the judgment. Let me say again that it is "Not by works of righteous-

---

[20] Ephesians 2:1-5; Titus 3:5; 1 Peter 1:3
[22] 1 Timothy 1:2; 2 Timothy 1:2; Titus 1:4
[21] 1 Timothy 1:13
[23] Luke 1:50

ness . . . but according to His *mercy* He saved us." [24]
"So then it is not of him that willeth, nor of him that
runneth, but of God that sheweth *mercy*." [25] There is no
hope for the person who is too proud to receive divine
pity.

It is God's sovereign right to exercise mercy upon
whom He will. "For He saith to Moses, I will have *mercy*
on whom I will have *mercy,* and I will have compassion
on whom I will have compassion. . . . Therefore hath
He *mercy* on whom He will have *mercy,* and whom He
will He hardeneth." [26] The fact that Pharaoh did not
receive divine mercy was no capricious or arbitrary act
on God's part. God knew beforehand that Pharaoh was
going to reject His mercy,[27] therefore any action on God's
part thereafter was based on Pharaoh's conduct.[28] It is
clear that Pharaoh was responsible for hardening his
own heart.[29] Whenever God hardens a man's heart the
divine procedure is a judicial one and therefore it cannot be questioned by any. The man who receives salvation cannot boast in any way for possessing it, but he
must attribute it to the mercy of God. On the other hand,
the man who comes short of divine mercy, and is lost, can
never charge God with injustice. God did not make
Pharaoh wicked, nor does He make any one wicked.
Neither can Pharaoh, or anyone else, accuse God of par-
tiality or of being unrighteous in His dealings with the
children of men. God has the same feeling of compassion
toward all sinners and He desires to help all. God exer-

[24] Titus 3:5
[27] Exodus 3:19
[25] Romans 9:16
[28] Exodus 4:21
[26] Romans 9:15, 18
[29] Exodus 5:2; 8:15

cises His sovereign will in the destiny of each individual, and He does so always in justice. I do not consider myself to be any better than Pharaoh, for in some respects I am probably not as good as he. Nor do I know why I did not harden my heart against God. I only know that I have been saved because of God's great heart of compassion, and I shall praise Him now and throughout eternity for it.

This leads me to say a few words about the relationship of God's mercy to His plan of redemption. Mercy has no saving merit apart from the death of Christ. It was God's mercy that sent Him to earth, as Zacharias spoke in his prophecy.[30] But it is only on the merits of Christ's sacrificial death that God can show mercy toward sinners and save them. The sinner who attempts to cast himself on the mercy of God, out of Christ, does so in vain. This is brought out clearly in the New Testament usage of the word "propitiation." [31] In Romans 3:25 it is used to designate the place of propitiation, while in 1 John 2:2 and 4:10 it is that which appeases or propitiates. The word is translated "mercy seat."

The mercy seat was the lid or covering of the ark of the covenant. It was ordered of God and became the place where God met and communed with Moses.[32] It was on the mercy seat that the high priest put the blood once a year on the great Day of Atonement,[33] thus its meaning is always associated with the covering or removal of sin.[34] When Christ is said to be the propitiation for our sins, it means that through His blood God extends the mercy

---

[30] Luke 1:78   [31] Romans 3:25; 1 John 2:2; 4:10
[32] Exodus 25:17-22   [33] Hebrews 9:25   [34] Psalm 32:1

of His justifying grace to the believing sinner. The blood on the mercy seat of the ark was a type of the blood of Christ shed for sinners. Thus the One who shed His blood became the mercy seat where God meets the sinner and extends mercy to him. Where Christ is described as "the propitiation . . . for the sins of the whole world" [35] the indication is that provision has been made for all men, so that no one is excluded from the scope of God's mercy, not even Pharaoh. The efficacy of the propitiation affects those only who believe. It was on this basis the Publican was justified.[36] And it is on this ground that believers have access to God's throne of grace.[37]

This glorious truth, when appreciated and appropriated by Christians, will teach us that we should be merciful to one another. This is doubtless what Christ taught in Matthew 9:10-13; 12:7 and 23:23. Since God is the "Father of mercies," [38] it follows that His children should feel and manifest mercy to each other.[39]

Now in conclusion, turn with me to Psalm 136. Here is a song of the age-abiding mercy of the Lord. It commences and concludes on the same note: "O give thanks." It is a call to praise God for His mercy. It is a liturgical psalm in an antiphonal arrangement, being sung by two choirs. It is possible that the high priest sang the first line of each verse, and a choir of priests and Levites sang the refrain. Or it could be that a choir sang the first line, and the congregation responded with the refrain. At any rate, it was a call to thanksgiving for the enduring mercy of Jehovah. "It seems like an interleaved Bible, and

---

[35] I John 2:2 [36] Luke 18:13 [37] Hebrews 4:16
[38] 2 Corinthians 1:3 [39] Philippians 2:1; Colossians 3:12

teaches us to interleave all things with the thought of the mercy of God." [40] The following outline is suggested with the hope that it might serve as an aid to our appreciation of God's mercy:

> Manifested in His Person[41]
> Manifested in His Power[42]
> Manifested in the Past [43]
> Manifested in His Providence[44]

"O give thanks . . . for His *mercy* endureth for ever." [45]

> There's a wideness in God's mercy,
>   Like the wideness of the sea:
> There's a kindness in His justice,
>   Which is more than liberty.
>
> There is welcome for the sinner,
>   And more graces for the good;
> There is mercy with the Saviour;
>   There is healing in His blood.

[40] F. B. Meyer
[42] Psalm 136:4-9
[45] Psalm 136:1,26
[41] Psalm 136:1-3 (See The Names of God)
[43] Psalm 136:10-24   [44] Psalm 136:25

THE LOVE OF GOD

The Bible is the only source of any and all accurate descriptions of God. Some of these descriptions are unique in that they are used of God only. We usually describe persons by the use of adjectives such as gracious, merciful, good, loving, etc. But in several instances in Scripture a noun is used to depict the nature of God. Thus we read that God is Spirit,[1] God is Light,[2] God is Love,[3] and God is Life.[4] In John 4:24 the King James Version reads, "God is a Spirit." There is no indefinite article in Greek, so that the statement should read, "God is Spirit," which simply means that God in His essence is Spirit. Likewise God in His essence is Light, Life, and Love.

The love of God is one of the most misunderstood subjects in the field of religion. Men who deny the inspiration of the Scriptures speak freely about the love of God, and yet there is no accurate verbal description of God's love apart from that which appears in the Bible. If the Bible is not the Word of God, how do we know that God is Love? You cannot find this great fact in nature. It is not a part of man's intuitive knowledge. Missionaries returning from all parts of the pagan world tell us the heathen know nothing of a God of love. The heathen have

[1] John 4:24
[4] John 5:26
[2] I John 1:5
[3] I John 4:8,16

105

their gods, but they are angry gods, constantly demanding appeasement. Christianity is unique in that it is the only religion that claims a supreme Being of love.

Definitions of the love of God are many and varied so that one is almost restrained from attempting another. But we must try to understand our subject, therefore an effort must be put forth. I think of the love of God as that eternal and essential attribute, that principle of God's nature, whereby He is moved to communicate Himself to man regardless of any sacrifice on His part. Divine love is in no way to be compared with human love. There is a love that has its basis in *passion* seeking gratification, such as sex love. There is a love that has its basis in *pleasurableness,* a love that is called out of one heart to another, a sort of philanthropy, a communication which affords pleasure. But God's love has its basis in *preciousness,* a love flowing from God's heart because He prizes those whom He loves.

There never has been a man in all the world who ever knew anything experientially about the love of God apart from the sacrifice of Jesus Christ at Calvary. There is no word in all of human language for that kind of love. The soul of man is so precious to God He could not stop at any cost to have it for Himself, going even to the extent of self-sacrifice. Man may hate God, curse Him, deny Him, and defy Him; still He pursues the vilest enemy in order that He might do him good. This is God. This is Love. He is "the God of love." [5]

But only as we behold the Cross and God's sacrifice thereon can we perceive His love. "Hereby perceive we

[5] 2 Corinthians 13:11

the love of God, because He laid down His life for us." [6]
To know God in Christ on the Cross is to know intuitively
divine love in its greatest and highest expression. God in
Christ, reconciling the world to Himself [7] is the acme, the
highest expression and exhibition of love. Actually God
laid down His own life for us,[8] and this He did in the
Person of His Son. Since God is Spirit,[9] and a Spirit does
not have flesh and bones,[10] God prepared Himself a
body,[11] and it was that body He sacrificed for unworthy
sinners.[12] When God the Holy One bare our sins in His
own body on the tree,[13] men, angels, and demons witnessed for the first time a full demonstration of His love.
"Herein is love." [14] Read once again the scriptural record
of the trial and torture of Christ; see Him suffering for
those very ones who tortured Him; hear Him pray for
them; and you will never say God does not love you.
Indeed it was "great love." [15]

There is still a further exhibition of God's love for us
when we come to know the fact that God had a special
love from all eternity for the Son He sacrificed. The
Father loved the Son before the foundation of the world.[16]
He testified of that love at Christ's baptism,[17] and on the
Mount of Transfiguration.[18] It is repeated for emphasis
that "the Father loveth the Son." [19] God gave me two
sons, and I love them dearly, but I sincerely believe they
are strangers to me compared with God's love for His
Son Jesus Christ. We give up our sons to the service of

[6] I John 3:16
[7] 2 Corinthians 5:19
[8] Acts 20:28
[9] John 4:24
[10] Luke 24:39
[11] I Timothy 3:16
[12] Romans 5:8
[13] I Peter 2:24
[14] I John 4:10
[15] Ephesians 2:4
[16] John 17:24
[17] Matthew 3:17
[18] Matthew 17:5
[19] John 3:35; 5:20; Colossians 1:13

our country, when they leave home for college or business careers or marriage, but God gave up His Son into the hands of vile and vicious persecutors who maltreated Him, and all because He loved the persecutors. "For God so loved the world, that He gave His only begotten Son." [20] Oh, what love!

Then God has a peculiar love for His children, a special love for those who love the Lord Jesus Christ. Christ said, "For the Father Himself loveth you, because ye have loved Me," [21] and again, "That the world may know that Thou hast sent Me, and hast loved them, as Thou hast loved Me." [22] "He that loveth Me shall be loved of My Father." [23] "If a man love Me, he will keep My words: and My Father will love him." [24] In John 14:21 and 23 the special love of the Father is extended to the obedient Christian. Just as the Father is said to love the Son because of His obedience,[25] so He is said to love the believer for the same reason. You see, love and obedience go together.[26] When we are obedient to Christ's commandments we prove our love for Him, and it is then that the Father's special love becomes a precious experience to us. The Father is well pleased with His Son, and He is well pleased with those who honor His Son. I know God loved me when I was yet in my sins; I experienced His love as my heavenly Father when I became saved; but then I have known at times His special love which was the reward of loving obedience.

All mankind is loved by God,[27] but not all men are the "beloved of God." The term "beloved of God" is used

[20] John 3:16   [21] John 16:27   [22] John 17:23
[23] John 14:21   [24] John 14:23   [25] John 10:17-18
[26] John 14:15; 15:10   [27] John 3:16

only of His children,[28] because they are "accepted in the beloved [Christ]." [29] I am commanded by God to love everyone, but I have a special love for my own sons. They are my own flesh and blood, the objects of a special love I cannot manifest in someone else's children. The Apostle John wrote, "Behold, what manner of love the Father hath bestowed upon us, that we should be called the sons of God." [30] If you ask me what then is the manner of this love, I can only say that it "passeth knowledge," [31] and that it is a bestowment.

Then, too, God manifests His love to His children in chastening them.[32] We need divine discipline and training for our blessing and benefit, and when we receive it from our heavenly Father it is for our good. Chastening may not be pleasant but it is profitable. When believers are chastened of the Lord, it is in order that they might not be condemned with the world.[33] God's goal for His children is to make them like His Son.[34] We have this thought brought out in the word "afterward." [35] Some of life's trials, testings, and tribulations are difficult to explain in this life; but in the "afterward," when we see Him and are like Him, we will fully comprehend His love for us. God's goal in saving us is more than deliverance from hell and providing a home for us in Heaven. He wants us to be like His only well-beloved Son. To that end we have been "chosen" [36] and "predestinated." [37] To that glorious end Christ gave Himself for us.[38] In the conforming process God applies His own chastening methods

[28] Romans 1:7
[29] Ephesians 1:6
[30] 1 John 3:1
[31] Ephesians 3:19
[32] Hebrews 12:6-11
[33] 1 Corinthians 11:32
[34] 1 John 3:2
[35] Hebrews 12:11
[36] Ephesians 1:4
[37] Romans 8:29
[38] Ephesians 5:25-27

to iron out some of the spots and wrinkles from our lives. And all of this is because He loves us.

When I was a boy and needed chastening, my mother would tell me that the chastening she was about to administer was going to hurt her more than it would hurt me. When she would tell me this there would be tears in her eyes. It was something I could never understand in those days. After God gave me my own children I learned in a measure what my mother meant. But now that I have come to know the Lord, I know more fully the meaning of chastening love. It is expressed in these words of the prophet, "In all their affliction He was afflicted, and the angel of His presence saved them: in His love and in His pity He redeemed them; and He bare them, and carried them all the days of old." [39] The prophet of God looks back to the Lord's chastening of His people, and he reminds them that in all their affliction He was afflicted.

There is something in this for us. He not only redeemed us by His own sufferings, but He suffers with us to this very hour. He is touched with the feelings of our infirmities. It grieves God to see our waywardness and it grieves Him when He chastises us. This is the love of God.

[39] Isaiah 63:9

THE GRACE OF GOD

In his *Synonyms of the New Testament,* Archbishop Trench says of the word *grace,* "It is hardly too much to say that the Greek mind has in no word uttered itself and all that was at its heart more distinctly than in this." After reading these words, the late Dr. Kenneth S. Wuest revised Trench's statement so that it reads as follows, "It is hardly too much to say that the mind of God has in no word uttered itself and all that was in His heart more distinctly than in this."

The word itself, whether in English (*grace*) or in Greek (*charis*), is a beautiful word. We sometimes sing Philip Doddridge's hymn,

> Grace! 'tis a charming sound,
>   Harmonious to the ear;
> Heaven with echo shall resound,
>   And all the earth shall hear.
>
> Saved by grace alone!
>   This is all my plea:
> Jesus died for all mankind,
>   And Jesus died for me.

By the grace of God we mean that moral attribute of God which moved Him to assume full responsibility for the guilt and penalty of the ill-deserving and undeserving race of mankind. The exercise of grace is optional with God. As He sovereignly chooses He may or may not stoop to His willfully sinning creatures in order to manifest goodness to them. But the almighty Sovereign did bend from the heights of His majesty to the depths of man's misery—and this is grace! Grace has only one direction it can take; it must flow downward. The grace of God is His unmerited and unmeritable favor by which He bestows every kindness, at no cost, upon wicked sinners who do not deserve anything. When God acted out from Himself His favor toward them that deserved His wrath, He acted in grace. Divine *justice* demands the sinner's death, but divine *grace* intervenes to assume the full penalty of justice and set the sinner free.

In this brief discussion of the grace of God we shall confine our comments to the relation of God's grace to His saving work for sinners, showing that salvation *commences* in grace, *continues* in grace, and will be *completed* through grace. Salvation is in three steps or stages linked with the three tenses of time, past, present, and prospective.

Salvation *commences* in grace. This must be so because salvation commences with God, as does grace. Our heavenly Father is called "the God of all grace." [1] He said, "I am gracious. . . . I will be gracious." [2]

When we say that salvation commences in grace we are not suggesting that God forgives sin and the sinner merely because of greatheartedness on His part. Such a view distorts and perverts the doctrine of pure grace.

[1] 1 Peter 5:10   [2] Exodus 22:27; 33:19

God does not forgive sin as a creditor might cancel a debt, or as the president of the United States might issue a pardon to a condemned criminal. The grace of God in salvation is not a bighearted act on God's part. The salvation accomplished for the sinner is provided by a righteous and just God. God's grace could never cancel the penalty and guilt of our sins. The saving of a sinner is an act of grace, to be sure, but it is likewise a judicial action flowing out of the voluntary and substitutionary death of Jesus Christ on the cross at Calvary. When Christ hung upon the cross, He was "the Lamb of God, which taketh away the sin of the world." [3] While salvation is God's free gift to sinners, do not think for one moment that the sins of all mankind or even the sins of one sinner, can go unpunished. The grace of God in salvation can never be disassociated from the substitutionary death of our Lord Jesus Christ. "In whom we have redemption through His blood, the forgiveness of sins, according to the riches of His *grace*." [4] The redemption of sinners is all of grace and all of God, but at great cost to Himself. [5] "We see Jesus . . . that He by the *grace* of God should taste death for every man." [6] "Being justified freely by His *grace* through the redemption that is in Christ Jesus." [7]

When we say that salvation commences in grace we mean that God takes the initiative and follows through to salvation's completion, totally apart from human effort or human works. "For by *grace* are ye saved through faith; and that not of yourselves: it is the gift of God: Not of works, lest any man should boast." [8] In His deal-

---

[3] John 1:29 [4] Ephesians 1:7 [5] 1 Peter 1:18-19
[6] Hebrews 2:9 [7] Romans 3:24 [8] Ephesians 2:8-9

ing with Adam and Eve, after they had fallen, God took the initiative in the matter of their salvation.[9] "For the *grace* of God that bringeth salvation hath appeared to all men." [10] Some theologians have called this "prevenient grace," by which is meant that God takes the initial step to save man, and restores to the sinner the ability to respond favorably to God.

The only gospel the Church of Christ has to preach is "the gospel of the grace of God." [11] There are numerous satanic perversions of "the gospel of the grace of God," but God pronounces a severe curse upon those who introduce and promote them. "But though we, or an angel from heaven, preach any other gospel unto you than that which we have preached unto you, let him be accursed. As we said before, so say I now again, If any man preach any other gospel unto you than that ye have received, let him be accursed." [12]

In our day the word "grace" is not often heard. We hear about a new morality, civic duties, scientific advancement, human progress, a social gospel, and Christian socialism, but who is proclaiming the gospel of the grace of God? On Sunday, August 12, 1883, C. H. Spurgeon preached, "I am here this morning to sound out that word 'grace' so that those who know its joyful sound shall be glad, and those who despise it shall be cut to the heart. *Grace* is the essence of the Christian gospel. *Grace* is the one hope for this fallen world. *Grace* is the sole comfort of saints looking forward to glory. The gospel of grace is the announcement that God is prepared to deal

[9] Genesis 3:8-9   [10] Titus 2:11   [11] Acts 20:24
[12] Galatians 1:8-9

with guilty men and women on the ground of free favor and pure mercy."

The Apostle Paul wrote concerning Israel's salvation, "Even so then at this present time also there is a remnant according to the election of grace. And if by grace, then is it no more of works: otherwise grace is no more grace. But if it be of works, then is it no more grace: otherwise work is no more work." [13] Before ever God called Abraham, thus before Israel began as a nation, we read that "Noah found *grace* in the eyes of the LORD." [14] After the nation began, God said to her leader, "Thou hast found grace in My sight." [15] So whether before the law was given, or during the administration of the law in Israel, or since the coming of Christ, whenever God has saved anyone He did it in grace.

Salvation *continues* in grace. So far we have been discussing God's free and saving grace to sinners, the grace of God that has appeared offering salvation to all men. [16] If any man dares to take away the grace of God from the Christian gospel, he removes its very lifeblood, and there is nothing left worth preaching. *Grace* is the heart of the gospel, so that without it the gospel is dead. *Grace* is the vocabulary of the gospel, so that without it there is nothing to be said. *Grace* is the music of the gospel, so that without it there is discord. Extract grace from the gospel and you have no gospel at all.

But in addition to saving grace for sinners, the Bible teaches other aspects of grace. The Apostle James wrote, "But He giveth more grace. Wherefore he saith, God

---

[13] Romans 11:5-6   [14] Genesis 6:8   [15] Exodus 33:12-13,16-17
[16] Titus 2:11

resisteth the proud, but giveth grace unto the humble." [17]
Now I do not believe this statement from James means
that God gives more saving grace to one sinner than to
another, so that one might have enough grace to save him
while another might perish unsaved because of any shortage of grace. Perish the thought! I do believe that what
James is teaching here is the fact that God provides His
grace for His children, thereby enabling them to live as
becometh sons of God. Just as He provided saving grace
for sinners,[18] so He provides sanctifying grace for saints,[19]
sufficient grace for sufferers,[20] and strengthening grace for
servants.[21] Grace commences in the sinner and continues
in the saint. God not only saves sinners, but He made
provision to keep them after they become saved. He gives
more grace.

One of God's eternal motives in saving us was to produce in us holiness of life and good works. This is stated
incisively in numerous passages, among them being some
of those verses which state that salvation is by grace.
"For by grace are ye saved through faith; and that not
of yourselves: it is the gift of God: Not of works, lest
any man should boast. For we are His workmanship,
created in Christ Jesus unto good works, which God hath
before ordained that we should walk in them." [22] "For
the grace of God that bringeth salvation hath appeared
to all men, Teaching us that, denying ungodliness and
worldly lusts, we should live soberly, righteously, and
godly, in this present world." [23] "Who His own self bare
our sins in His own body on the tree, that we, being

[17] James 4:6   [18] Ephesians 2:8-9   [19] Titus 2:11-12
[20] 2 Corinthians 12:9   [21] Ephesians 4:7   [22] Ephesians 2:8-10
[23] Titus 2:11-12

dead to sins, should live unto righteousness: by whose stripes ye were healed." [24]

I have known some men of very strong Arminian persuasion who have attacked the doctrine of pure grace on the false premise that it leads to licentiousness or looseness in moral behavior, and laxity in service for Christ. Now I will readily concede that some professing Christians have turned the grace of God into lasciviousness, but not all of them have been outside the ranks of the Arminian school. But let us not throw brickbats at one another. The potentiality and possibility of laxity in morals and service lay within each of us. "Wherefore let him that thinketh he standeth take heed lest he fall." [25]

The leaders of the early Church were able to continue under trial and temptation only by the grace of God and not in human strength. Paul wrote to the Corinthians, "And God is able to make all grace abound toward you; that ye, always having all sufficiency in all things, may abound to every good work." [26] Why were the churches of Macedonia able to remain joyful and generous in great trial and affliction? Paul answers that the grace of God was bestowed upon them.[27] This great apostle to the Gentiles testified often that it was the grace of God that started and sustained him in the ministry. Read his tribute to grace in such passages as Roman 12:3 and 15:15; 1 Corinthians 3:10 and 15:10; Galatians 1:15-16 and 2:9; Ephesians 3:8; 1 Timothy 1:13-14, and then hear him say as regards his entire life, "By the grace of God I am what I am." [28] God is glorified when we Chris-

---

[24] 1 Peter 2:24   [25] 1 Corinthians 10:12   [26] 2 Corinthians 9:8
[27] 2 Corinthians 8:12   [28] 1 Corinthians 15:10

tians extol His grace,[29] so let us "grow in grace, and in the knowledge of our Lord and Saviour Jesus Christ," [30] and let us sing:

> O, to grace how great a debtor
>   Daily I'm constrained to be;
> Let Thy goodness, like a fetter,
>   Bind my wandering heart to Thee.

Salvation is *completed* in grace. Every person who has ever been saved was saved by grace, and the very moment the believing sinner was saved he became the recipient of eternal life. That saving act of God in grace carries the saved one all the way through time and eternity. Every saved person is in possession of eternal life.[31] Now, when the Bible speaks of eternal life it means both the quality and duration of that life. If eternal life could mean to the saved person anything less than eternal, then words are meaningless. Our Lord said, "And I give unto them eternal life; and they shall never perish, neither shall any man pluck them out of My hand. My Father, which gave them Me, is greater than all; and no man is able to pluck them out of My Father's hand." [32] Eternal life is God's gift of grace, and the gifts of God are irrevocable.[33] If God had promised His life to me for twenty years, I would rest in the unalterable fact that I would have it for twenty years and not one day less. It could not be cast aside nor taken from me by men, angels, or demons in nineteen years, three hundred and sixty-four days. And since God has given eternal life to all who

[29] 2 Corinthians 4:15   [30] 2 Peter 3:18   [31] John 3:16; 5:24
[32] John 10:28-29   [33] Romans 11:29

receive the Lord Jesus Christ, the child of God knows that he stands forever in grace. "Therefore being justified by faith, we have peace with God through our Lord Jesus Christ: By whom also we have access by faith into *this grace wherein we stand*." [34] The believer is not only *saved* by grace, but he *stands* in grace.

Now there are those who object to the teaching that Christians are secure in Christ, but hold to the contrary that it is possible for one to be lost after he has been saved by grace. All such fail to understand the doctrine of sovereign grace. Since salvation is all of grace, apart from human effort and works,[35] its continuance and completion are included. To suppose that salvation commences in grace, and then at some point in time and experience, after I have been saved, my continuing as a saved person depends upon any effort on my part, is to pervert the doctrine of God's pure grace. Before I was saved I struggled repeatedly to free myself from the chains of sin, but all to no avail. Then one day I heard the gospel of the grace of God, and my hungry heart believed. Upon receiving Jesus Christ by faith, God in grace set me free from the guilt and penalty of my sins. That day in 1927 salvation commenced in my life. I was sinful and undeserving, yet God did not withhold His grace because of my sin. He justified me on the merit of my Substitute, the Lord Jesus Christ, who died in my place on the cross at Calvary. Since I could not save myself then, how utterly ridiculous to assume that I can, or even need to try to keep myself saved now. His saving grace has proved to be His sustaining grace.

[34] Romans 5:1-2   [35] Ephesians 2:8-9; Titus 3:5

Then there are those who object to the believer's safe-keeping in grace on the ground of Galatians 5:4, which says, "Christ is become of no effect unto you, whosoever of you are justified by the law; ye are fallen from grace." They insist that the one who falls from grace is that person who becomes lost after having been saved. But such a conclusion only shows that the passage has been wrongly interpreted. The words, "ye are fallen from grace," must be interpreted and understood in their context, and when the context is studied the fact will be seen that the statement in question refers not to their justification but to their spiritual lives as Christians. The same meaning is attached to the words, "Christ is become of no effect unto you." The Greek word, *katargeo,* which means "to make ineffectual," is applied to any retarding of growth. The subject is the Galatian Christians. They were related to Christ through grace, but they were putting themselves under the law with its merit system, thereby preventing growth in grace and in the knowledge of the Lord Jesus Christ.[36] The whole point of Galatians 5:4 is that they had been saved by grace (the only way a sinner can be saved) but they were trying to justify themselves by the merit system of the law, and as long as they kept trying to keep themselves saved by attempting to keep the law they were losing the full benefits of their relation to Christ. The Lord Jesus must be everything or nothing to a man. Any divided allegiance between Christ and the law will hinder a Christian's growth in grace, and all believers who have this divided allegiance have fallen from grace.

[36] 2 Peter 3:18

Some years ago I met a Seventh-day Adventist who claimed to have been saved by grace through faith in Jesus Christ. As to whether or not he was truly born again I could not tell nor would I set myself up as a judge; God knows. At an opportune time in our conversation I bore witness for my Lord, testifying how Christ saved me. My acquaintance sharply interrupted me with the question, "Do you keep the Sabbath day?" To this I replied, "Exactly what do you mean by keeping the Sabbath day?" After a brief sputtering spell he referred me to the Fourth Commandment, "Remember the sabbath day, to keep it holy." [37] I promptly proceeded to ask him why he selected this one commandment as a way of life and omitted the other nine, showing him the following verses from God's Word: "For whosoever shall keep the whole law, and yet offend in one point, he is guilty of all." [38] "For the law was given by Moses, but grace and truth came by Jesus Christ." [39] "For Christ is the end of the law for righteousness to every one that believeth." [40]

Now I am going to assume, for the sake of illustration, that this man had been saved, and we all know that if he had been saved he was saved by the grace of God and not through any effort on his part. So that, if he had been saved, like the Galatians he had fallen from grace. By putting himself under the merit system of the law he could not grow in grace and in the knowledge of the Lord Jesus Christ. He claimed to have trusted Christ but now Christ had become of no effect to him. He had fallen into the Galatian error. "O foolish Galatians, who hath be-

[37] Exodus 20:8   [38] James 2:10   [39] John 1:17
[40] Romans 10:4

witched you, that ye should not obey the truth, before whose eyes Jesus Christ hath been evidently set forth, crucified among you? This only would I learn of you, Received ye the Spirit by the works of the law, or by the hearing of faith? Are ye so foolish? having begun in the Spirit, are ye now made perfect by the flesh?" [41]

Any heretical form of the gospel of the grace of God will leave the sinner incomplete and insecure. But the gospel of pure grace brings life and liberty from the penalty and practice of sin. "Stand fast therefore in the liberty wherewith Christ hath made us free, and be not entangled again with the yoke of bondage." [42]

[41] Galatians 3:1-3   [42] Galatians 5:1

THE FATHERHOOD OF GOD

One of the peculiarities of universal religious thought is the way in which the Fatherhood of God is emphasized. World religions have long imbibed and promoted the idea of the universal Fatherhood of God. It follows quite naturally that those who believe and teach this doctrine should attach to it the related idea of the universal brotherhood of man.

Former United States Secretary of Commerce, Henry A. Wallace, once declared, "We cannot understand either this war or the peace to come, unless we have some knowledge of the Bible and the history of the United States. Expressed in the fewest words possible, the meaning of the Bible is: All men are brothers because God is their Father."

The Presbyterian Church, U.S.A., through its General Assembly, declared, "The heart of the gospel is the faith that all men are sons of God." When one member of the assembly moved to strike out this sentence, he was both shouted and voted down.[1]

The International Council of Religious Education went on record with the following statement: "Christian education seeks to develop in growing persons the ability and disposition to participate in and contribute construc-

[1] George A. Brown

123

tively to the building of a social order throughout the world embodying the ideal of the Fatherhood of God and the brotherhood of man."

Religious leaders have advocated the practical application of the doctrine of the universal Fatherhood of God and brotherhood of man as the means to world peace. One committee, in its program, said, "The present evils in the world are due to the failure of nations and people to carry out the laws of God. No permanent peace is possible unless the principles of the Christian religion are made the foundation of national policy and of all social life. This involves regarding all nations as members of one family under the Fatherhood of God. . . . When peace is written it must be founded on the Fatherhood of God and the brotherhood of man."

This teaching is the watchword of modern religious liberalism. Dr. John Horsch wrote, "The thought that there is a kingdom of evil besides the kingdom of God is all wrong. There is only one kingdom and every man is a citizen of it. . . . *All men are God's children.* There is in modern religion no place for individual salvation. What is needed is not individual but social salvation. The social gospel addresses itself to the task of making the world a decent place to live in. This is the business of the church in this new age."

This doctrine is the religion of lodges and secret societies. In a *Quarterly Bulletin* of the Masonic Lodge can be found the following statement: "When the system of speculative Masonry was instituted in London in 1717, Freemasonry became cosmopolitan. Its watchword was Fatherhood of God and the brotherhood of man."

The Odd Fellows insist that their order "was founded on great principles—the Fatherhood of God and the brotherhood of man."

Neither time nor space will permit of further quotations. We have given sufficient of them to show that the trend of thought in modern political, religious, and social organizations is a definite belief in the universal Fatherhood of God and brotherhood of man. Our chief aim here is to examine Holy Writ, the final and authoritative word on the subject.

Henry Wallace said, "The meaning of the Bible is that all men are brothers because God is their Father." Mr. Wallace never read that nor its equivalent in the Bible. In the first place, the concept of fatherhood can neither be appreciated nor appropriated where God is not viewed as personal. Those who refuse to conceive God in essentially personal terms are incorrect when they speak of His Fatherhood. Millions in the earth hold to either a pantheistic or polytheistic view of God, and this, it seems to me, hardly permits a fatherhood at all. A mere theistic faith is not sufficient. The Unitarian view of God is expressed in their own article of faith in the words, "Unitarians recognize a mysterious energy or force in the universe." And yet Unitarians believe in the universal Fatherhood of God and brotherhood of man. The philosophic theisms and the religious theisms, even though embraced in all good conscience, are neither a basis for salvation nor for belief in the universal Fatherhood of God.

Dr. Horsch said, "The thought that there is a kingdom of evil besides the kingdom of God is all wrong." What about this statement? The Bible teaches two kingdoms,[2] each having a head, God and Satan, and the subjects of each being called "children." [3] Satan is called "the prince of this world." [4] The world-system is the devil's kingdom,[5] and it is called "evil." [6] Thus Christ said, "My kingdom is not of this world." [7] The evil powers are called "the *rulers* of the darkness of this world." [8] All those, like Dr. Horsch, who deny the existence of these two kingdoms on the one hand, and claim the universal Fatherhood of God on the other, have been stricken with moral and spiritual color blindness. They may be conscientious in what they believe, but they do not believe right. The only right conception of God is God's revelation of Himself in His own Word, and the Bible nowhere so much as hints at the theories of the universal Fatherhood of God and that there is no kingdom of evil.

In the Old Testament God is mentioned as *a* Father, but never *the* Father of an individual. The Old Testament references to God as Father are used of God's relation to Israel only and always in a national sense.[9] It is true also that Israel is represented as the son of Jehovah,[10] but these references speak of the national sonship of a covenant people, not of individual persons. The Old Testament idea of God as Father falls far short of the proportions it takes on in the New Testament.

The scriptural picture of divine Fatherhood is not a part of the doctrine of creation. There are some who

---

[2] Matthew 8:11-12; Colossians 1:13
[3] Matthew 13:36-39
[4] John 12:31; 14:30; 16:11
[5] 1 John 5:19
[6] Galatians 1:4   [7] John 18:36
[8] Ephesians 6:12
[9] Deuteronomy 32:6; Psalm 89:26; Isaiah 63:16; 64:8; Jeremiah 3:4; 31:9; Malachi 1:6; 2:10   [10] Exodus 4:22; Jeremiah 31:20; Hosea 11:1

tell us that Paul's sermon at Mars' hill supports the doctrine of divine Fatherhood in creation, thus the universal Fatherhood of God. Read the sermon in Acts 17:22-31. Verses 26 and 28 are used to support this doctrine, particularly the statement, "God . . . hath made of one blood all nations . . . for we are also His offspring." Now, it is true that we are the offspring of God in a creative sense, but so also are the birds, the fishes, and the animals. True, all creatures, including man, are the offspring (Greek, *genos*) of God, that is, they had their origin with Him. But these creatures are nowhere said to be the "children" (Greek, *tekna*) of God. No man can be called a child of God by the natural relation he sustains to God in creation. If fatherhood means only the ultimate source of man in creation, then the very heart of the New Testament, with its unique Christian conception, does not make sense.

Take up your Bible and read that arresting passage in John 8:33-59. In this chapter Christ is called "the light of the world," [11] and it is here where He exposes this hidden sin of darkness. The Jews boasted to Him that they were "Abraham's seed." [12] Our Lord answered them with the acknowledgment that they were Abraham's seed, but He added, "But ye seek to kill Me, because My word hath no place in you." [13] Then follows a most penetrating and revealing statement, "I speak that which I have seen with *My Father:* and ye do that which ye have seen with *your father*." [14] In other words He was telling them, "My doctrine and deeds reveal who My Father is, and your

[11] John 8:12   [12] John 8:33   [13] John 8:37
[14] John 8:38

doctrine and deeds reveal who your father is." Obviously they did not have the same father. They could claim neither God nor Abraham as their father. Certainly their prime source in creation was God, and their national identity gave them right to be called "the seed of Abraham," but they were neither Abraham's children,[15] nor God's.[16] Their natural descent from Abraham did not bring them into the family of God. Abraham is the father of them that believe in Jesus Christ.[17]

Who, then, was their father? They said, "We have one Father, even God." [18] Jesus said, "ye do the deeds of your father. . . . Ye are of your father the devil." [19] He proved that neither God nor Abraham was their father. The conclusion of the matter, to which Christ was leading, was that the devil was really their father. Their opposition to Christ and His teachings showed they were the enemies of God and the children of Satan. And such are in the world today active in religion.[20] Our Lord had one among the twelve.[21] Paul contended with one while on the island of Cyprus.[22] Like those Jews whom Jesus called children of the devil, all such are labeled elsewhere "children of disobedience" and "children of wrath." [23]

For many years I was uncertain in my own mind whether there were two or three classifications of sonship in Scripture. I wondered at times if it were possible that one could be a child of Adam, remain unsaved, and still not be a child of the devil. I feel satisfied after further study that there are but two classifications. We are either

[15] John 8:39　　　　[16] John 8:42　　　　[17] Galatians 3:14,29
[18] John 8:41　　　　[19] John 8:41,44
[20] Matthew 13:38; 2 Corinthians 11:13-15　　　[21] John 6:70; 17:12
[22] Acts 13:10　　　　[23] Ephesians 2:2-3; 5:6; Colossians 3:6

children of God or children of the devil (1 John 3:9-10). There are only two distinct fatherhoods and two sets of children.

When our Lord taught the Fatherhood of God in relation to prayer,[24] He was speaking to His own and to them only.[25] The principles in the Sermon on the Mount have no application whatever to unbelievers. Consider as an example the prayer principles Jesus taught in Matthew 6. Millions do not hallow the name of God, nor do they care anything about His coming kingdom or His will being done on earth, nor do they trust Him for daily bread, nor do they have forgiveness in their hearts toward all who have wronged them.[26] The prayer principles taught here are applicable to the children of God's kingdom only. When Christ used the expressions "thy Father," "your Father," "your heavenly Father," He was addressing His apostles. We do not wonder that the people who heard Him speak to His apostles "were astonished at His doctrine." [27] Throughout the world people of many religious faiths regard "the Lord's prayer" as common property and recite it with regularity, but neither the prayer itself nor its common use gives any support to the doctrine of the universal Fatherhood of God. The Father conception of God is not a part of the theistic interpretations of the universe. One can believe in the latter and be a child of the devil. There is a difference between one's belief in God and his relation to God. One may express faith in the fact of God and never experience the Father-child relationship with God.

[24] Matthew 6:9 [25] Matthew 5:1-2 [26] Matthew 6:9,10,11,12
[27] Matthew 7:28

Read the prayers of our Lord; in every one He addresses God as "Father." [28] Praying was, to Him, a warm reality, not calling upon some cold theistic supreme Being. The one exception to this approach to God in prayer is that one cry of His from the cross, "My God, My God, why hast Thou forsaken Me?" [29] The reason for this is obvious. The momentary experience of isolation was caused by sin, not Christ's sin, for He had none of His own, but your sin and mine. He was bearing in His body the sins of the world.[30] But knowing that He paid the price in full, His last words were, "*Father, into Thy hands I commend My spirit.*" [31]

This brings me to the conclusion of the matter: namely, that God in Christ is the only revelation of the Fatherhood of God. The revelation of God as the Father of individuals is not seen until Christ exposed it in His teachings. But more than this, Christ did not expose the Fatherhood of God by what He taught merely; He exposed the Fatherhood of God by what He was. If you reject Jesus Christ as the divine Son, and subtract Him from your conception of God, you have nothing left.[32] It is not possible to know God as Father apart from Jesus Christ.[33] No man has a claim on the Fatherhood of God apart from faith in the Lord Jesus Christ.[34] No man has any claim upon God until the Father relationship has been established. I like those postresurrection words of our Lord to Mary, "Touch Me not; for I am not yet ascended to My Father: but go to My brethren, and

---

[28] Matthew 26:42; Luke 23:34,46; John 11:41; 17:1,5,11,21,24,25
[29] Matthew 27:46; Mark 15:34 [30] Isaiah 53:6; 1 Peter 2:24
[31] Luke 23:46 [32] John 1:14; 5:17-18; 10:29-33
[33] Matthew 11:27; John 14:6 [34] Galatians 3:26

say unto them, I ascend unto My Father, and your Father; and to My God, and your God." [35] There you have the divine order, the "Father" relationship being first. The man who has no heavenly Father through faith in the Lord Jesus Christ has no God.

[35] John 20:17

PART III

THE NAMES OF GOD

THE SIGNIFICANCE OF A NAME

What is in a name? Certainly not much in our modern western world where names have little or no special significance, except to identify or designate a person. Modern names are chosen by parents because the names are pretty, or sound nice, or to commemorate and honor a relative, a close friend, or some celebrity in show business, sports, or politics. Seldom do parents stop to think of the meaning behind a name.

But in the eastern world, especially in Bible times, there was meaning and purpose in the selection of names. There a name was regarded as expressing a deep desire in the hearts of parents, or it might have given a clue to the character of the child, or even, as in some instances, serve as a prophecy of the child's future activity. In the Old Testament there are hundreds of instances of the use of proper names indicating their significance. I have selected one to serve as an illustration. When Jacob and Rachel were journeying from Bethel, Rachel gave birth to a son. The child lived, but the mother died in childbirth. Her dying words uttered her choice of a name for the child. She called him "Benoni," which means, "the son of my sorrow." When Rachel departed this life, Jacob realized that his helpmate had been taken from him, so he called the child "Benjamin," meaning, "the son of my right hand." [1] The purpose in each choice is obvious.

The casual reader of the Bible recognizes the many names and titles given to God in Scripture. Through an understanding of these names we are given clearer insight into God's nature and character. This is but one of several ways whereby we may study God in order to learn more about Him. G. P. Pardington said, "New crises and peculiar needs among His people called forth fresh names; and there can be no emergency among believers to which some name of God does not apply." While we shall never have a full revelation of God in this life, we may be certain that God is knowable,[2] thus Christ prayed to the Father "that they might know Thee the only true God, and Jesus Christ, whom Thou hast sent." [3] True, we can know God only in part while we are in the flesh, but it behooves us to know the knowable until we know even as we are known.[4]

In his excellent volume, *Titles of the Triune God*, Herbert F. Stevenson points out the fact that there is significance in the frequent use in Scripture of the phrase, "the name of the LORD." To call on the "name of the LORD" was to worship Him as God;[5] to praise Him;[6] to seek help when in distress;[7] to come to Him for salvation;[8] to be assured of answers to prayer.[9] Inasmuch as the name of Jesus Christ is invested with every attribute that "the name of the LORD" implied in the Old Testament, it was in that name that the apostles went everywhere preaching, and it was that name which unbelievers

[1] Genesis 35:18   [2] Romans 1:19   [3] John 17:3
[4] 1 Corinthians 13:12   [5] Genesis 21:33; 26:25   [6] 2 Samuel 22:4
[7] 2 Samuel 22:7   [8] John 1:12; Romans 10:13
[9] John 14:13-14; 15:16; 16:23-24

feared. The Jewish leaders forbade the apostles to speak or teach in the name of Jesus,[10] and when they were beaten for doing so, they rejoiced in that they were counted worthy to suffer for His name.[11] Thus they continued to preach and perform miracles in the name of Jesus Christ.[12] Christians rejoice at the sound of His blessed name, for it speaks to us all that He is to His people—their regeneration, redemption, justification, sanctification, and glorification.

The names of God can be divided into three classes:

THREE PRIMARY NAMES

God	(Elohim)
Lord	(Adonai)
LORD, GOD	(Jehovah)

THREE SECONDARY NAMES COMPOUNDED WITH EL (God)

Almighty God	(El Shaddai)
Most High God	(El Elyon)
Everlasting God	(El Olam)

NINE NAMES COMPOUNDED WITH JEHOVAH

LORD God
Jehovah-Jireh
Jehovah-Rapha
Jehovah-Nissi
Jehovah-M'Kaddesh
Jehovah-Shalom
Jehovah-Tsidkenu
Jehovah-Shammah
Jehovah-Roi

[10] Acts 4:18; 5:28   [11] Acts 5:41
[12] Acts 9:14,21; 10:43; 16:18; 19:17

It is from the three basic primary names—God, Lord, and Lord—that we receive the rest of the names of God. These three names are given to us in a single passage in Joshua's prayer at Ai. "And Joshua rent his clothes, and fell to the earth upon his face before the ark of the Lord until the eventide, he and the elders of Israel, and put dust upon their heads. And Joshua said, Alas, O Lord God, wherefore hast Thou at all brought this people over Jordan, to deliver us into the hand of the Amorites, to destroy us? would to God we had been content, and dwelt on the other side Jordan! O Lord, what shall I say, when Israel turneth their backs before their enemies!" [13] Lord and God both are translated *Jehovah*. Lord is translated *Adonai*. God is translated *Elohim*.

[13] Joshua 7:6-8

ELOHIM (God)

The first of God's names, in the order of their appearance in Scripture, is *Elohim*, translated "God" in the Authorized Version. It reportedly occurs not less than 2,500 times in the Old Testament and 32 times in the first chapter of Genesis. The name *Elohim* is derived from two roots: *El*, signifying unlimited strength, energy, might, power; *Alah*, signifying to swear, declare or make a covenant. These two roots, when brought together in the name *Elohim*, mean infinite strength and absolute faithfulness. Thus we are introduced to the God of the Bible as the One with whom nothing is impossible and who always keeps His word. Elohim is the strong, faithful One.

We meet this name of God at the very outset of the Bible. "In the beginning God [Elohim] created the heaven and the earth." [1] That which follows in Genesis chapter one makes no attempt to solve scientific problems, but sets forth the power and faithfulness of *Elohim*. We do know that Moses received the information by divine revelation. Such an One as *Elohim* is to be held in reverence and wholesome fear, for this name suggests might and majesty.

It is divine omnipotence, the first and essential attribute

[1] Genesis 1:1

of Deity, that confronts us at the beginning of the divine record. In creation we see God's might; in providence we see His faithfulness. He upholds all things by the word of His power.[2] There are billions of stars, planets, and planetoids, many of them being thousands of times larger than our earth and moving at great speed. Yet no two ever collide. Why? *Elohim* who created them also controls them. He is the strong, faithful One, creation's amazing Architect and Builder. Indeed, "The heavens declare the glory of God [Elohim]."[3]

I am told that there are six trillion atoms in one ounce of uranium. Packing them in at a billion a second, it would take a million years to put them there. But how did they get there, and who prevents them from exploding? *Elohim,* the strong, faithful One.

Elohim is a plural noun. I see in this that within the Godhead there is a plurality of Persons. It is an interesting observation that He speaks of Himself as "Us."[4] This is all consistent with the Christian view of God. God is a Tri-unity, there being three Persons within the one essential Godhead.

Remembering that the name *Elohim* is formed from two words, one of them being *Alah,* meaning "to swear," we see in Him the God who always keeps His covenant with man. The very name *Elohim* means that God has sworn and He will do it.[5]

This is illustrated for us in God's covenant with Noah. Read Genesis 6:15-18, and there you will see God's pronouncement of judgment upon the earth by means of

[2] Hebrews 1:3   [3] Psalm 19:1   [4] Genesis 1:26; 3:22; 11:7
[5] See Numbers 23:19; Hebrews 6:17-18

the flood and His instructions to Noah to build the ark. Then He added these words, "But with thee will I establish My covenant; and thou shalt come into the ark, thou, and thy sons, and thy wife, and thy sons' wives with thee." [6] Seven days after they went into the ark, the rains came and prevailed on the earth for one hundred and fifty days. But Noah had no cause to fear that God had failed and forsaken him, for it was *Elohim*, the strong, faithful One who had made the covenant. And so we read, "And God [*Elohim*] remembered Noah." [7] Because of His infinite might He was able to deliver Noah, and inasmuch as He had sworn by Himself, God had to deliver him.

This is illustrated for us again in God's covenant with Abraham. He said to Abraham, "I am the Almighty God [Elohim-Shaddai]. . . . I will make My covenant between Me and thee, and will multiply thee exceedingly. . . . As for Me, behold, My covenant is with thee, and thou shalt be a father of many nations." [8] Then He added, "And I will establish My covenant between Me and thee and thy seed after thee in their generations for an everlasting covenant, to be a God unto thee, and to thy seed after thee. And I will give unto thee, and to thy seed after thee, the land wherein thou art a stranger, all the land of Canaan, for an everlasting possession; and I will be their God." [9] God had sworn that He would preserve the Jew and the land for his possession. The terms of the covenant are clearly defined, and *Elohim* binds Himself with an oath. There have been feverish

[6] Genesis 6:18; 7:1   [7] Genesis 8:1   [8] Genesis 17:1,2,4
[9] Genesis 17:7-8

attempts on the part of men and nations to annihilate the Jew and take his land, but *Elohim* had sworn, and He will do it. God confirmed the covenant with Jacob,[10] and it was this assurance that kept Jacob steady for the next twenty years." [11]

Not infrequently do we read the phrase, "And God remembered." [12] How refreshing to know *Elohim!* God who kept His promise with Noah, Abraham, Isaac, and Jacob is our strong, faithful Redeemer. With Him all things are possible.[13] Every promise is affirmed by His will and assured by His name.[14] The certainty of their fulfillment is wrapped up in the very character of *Elohim*. Circumstances may prevent man from carrying out his promises, but *Elohim*, never! Every promise that God ever made from the beginning, relative to man's redemption, has found its fulfillment in Jesus Christ.

[10] Genesis 28:10-15   [11] Genesis 31:36-42
[12] Genesis 8:1; 19:29; 30:22; Exodus 2:24; 6:2-8; Leviticus 26:42
[13] Matthew 19:26; Mark 10:27; Luke 18:27
[14] 2 Corinthians 1:20

JEHOVAH (LORD, GOD)

The second of the primary names of God in Scripture is translated LORD in all capital letters to distinguish it from the word translated Lord, which is in the lower case except for the letter "L." Sometimes it is translated GOD in all capital letters to distinguish it from the word translated God, which is in the lower case except for the letter "G." The English form of the Hebrew word is *Jehovah*.

From the most reliable sources, we gather that the original and true pronunciation of this name has been lost. There is a reason for this. The Jews themselves scrupulously avoided every mention of it, believing that it was wrong to pronounce that name. They repeatedly substituted in its stead *Adonai*. Precisely when this practice arose among the Jews we cannot be certain. We do know, however, that the Septuagint, a Greek version of the Old Testament Scriptures, made between 280 and 130 B.C., read *Adonai* for *Jehovah*. The Jews' fear even to pronounce the name grew out of their interpretation, or application, of Leviticus 24:16, "And he that blasphemeth the name of the LORD, he shall surely be put to death, and all the congregation shall certainly stone him: as well the stranger, as he that is born in the land, when he blasphemeth the name of the LORD, shall be put to death." Because of this special reverence for the name *Jehovah,*

143

the name by which God made Himself known to the Hebrews, it was almost entirely lost sight of. We Christians could do with some of this kind of reverence. Hardly a day goes by but that someone is heard speaking the name of God in vain and in blasphemy. The name *Jehovah* is, above every other name of God, the one most sacred and precious to the Jew.

The name *Jehovah* is translated GOD about 300 times, and LORD about 6,000 times. It is mentioned in Scripture more than any other name of God. It is derived from the Hebrew verb *Havah,* meaning "to be" or "being." The idea is, of course, that of existence, self-existence. Thus *Jehovah* is the eternal, self-existent One, without beginning and without end, "the same yesterday, and to day, and for ever." [1] God is now what He always has been and what He will remain forever.[2] There are some Hebrew scholars who see in the word *Havah* part of the verb *to* become. Very well! But a verb of becoming does not necessarily mean "coming into being," but rather becoming something to someone. God is "the becoming One" in the sense that He becomes this or that to His people. The significance of the name *Jehovah* is, in its revelation of God, becoming to His people what they need in order to supply that need.

The name *Jehovah* itself appears only seven times in the Authorized Version of the Bible, four times in its primary use;[3] and three times compounded with other names: Jehovah-Jireh,[4] Jehovah-Nissi,[5] and Jehovah-Shalom.[6]

---

[1] Hebrews 13:8; Revelation 4:8   [2] Isaiah 43:10-11; Psalm 102:27
[3] Exodus 6:3; Psalm 83:18; Isaiah 12:2; 26:4
[4] Genesis 22:14   [5] Exodus 17:15   [6] Judges 6:24

The meaning of the name *Jehovah* is brought out in His discussion with Moses at the burning bush. When Moses asked God for a name whereby he could describe Him to the children of Israel, God said to him, "I AM THAT I AM. . . . Thus shalt thou say unto the children of Israel, I AM hath sent me unto you." [7] Dr. Unger writes, "The root idea is that of *underived existence.* When it is said that God's name is 'He is,' simply being is not all that is affirmed. *He is* in a sense in which no other being *is. He is;* and the cause of His being is in Himself. *He is because He is.* . . . From the idea of *underived* and *independent existence,* follows that of *independent and uncontrolled will and action.*" There was a time when I could not say, "I am," because I was not. But there never was a time when God could not say, "I AM," because He always was. God is a living personality, distinct from all other beings and far above them all, "One God and Father of all, who is above all, and through all, and in you all." [8] *Jehovah* is independent of time. There is no past nor future with Him, no *was,* nor *will be.* "He has nothing to learn, nothing to acquire, nothing to become." "To whom then will ye liken God? or what likeness will ye compare unto Him? To whom then will ye liken Me? . . . saith the Holy One." [9] "I am God, and there is none else; I am God, and there is none like Me." [10]

"And God said moreover unto Moses, Thus shalt thou say unto the children of Israel, the LORD God of your fathers, the God of Abraham, the God of Isaac, and the God of Jacob, hath sent me unto you: this is My name

[7] Exodus 3:14   [8] Ephesians 4:6   [9] Isaiah 40:18,25
[10] Isaiah 46:9

for ever, and this is My memorial unto all generations." [11]
He was giving assurance to Moses and all Israel that He,
Jehovah, was the *Elohim* of Abraham, Isaac, and Jacob.
He was that strong, faithful One who kept His word
with them and fulfilled every promise. He is the LORD
God, *Jehovah Elohim,* the covenant-keeping One. Abraham went down into Egypt[12] and lied to Abimelech,[13]
yet *Elohim* forgave him and remained faithful to His
word. Isaac repeated the sin of his father Abraham when,
at Gerar, he lied in calling Rebekah his sister,[14] yet
Elohim forgave him and remained faithful to His promise.
Jacob lied to his blind father and deceived him,[15] yet
Elohim remained faithful to His covenant. And now He
says to Moses, Tell My people "that the *Jehovah* Elohim
of your fathers, the *Elohim* of Abraham, the *Elohim* of
Isaac, and the *Elohim* of Jacob, hath sent me unto you:
this is My name for ever, and this is My memorial
unto all generations." You see, Jehovah's relation to Israel
is an eternal one,[16] and it is in connection with His own
people that the name is associated.[17] He did not address
Pharaoh by this name.[18] Pharaoh spoke better than he
knew when he said, "I know not the LORD [Jehovah]." [19]
Had he only known *Jehovah* he would have had respect
for Him.

The name *Jehovah* does not appear in Scripture until
after the creation of man.[20] The fact of man's creation
is stated in Genesis 1:27, and details are given later as
to how God formed man. It is in the latter description

---

[11] Exodus 3:15
[12] Genesis 12:10
[13] Genesis 20:2
[14] Genesis 26:1-11
[15] Genesis 27:6-24
[16] Romans 11:2
[17] Exodus 3:18
[18] Exodus 5:3; 7:16; 9:1, 13; 10:3
[19] Exodus 5:2
[20] Genesis 2:4

that we meet *Jehovah:* "And the LORD God [Jehovah Elohim] formed man of the dust of the ground, and breathed into his nostrils the breath of life; and man became a living soul."[21] It was as *Elohim* that He created heaven and earth and all animal life, but as *Jehovah-Elohim* He made man in His own image and likeness.

Very often in Scripture the Holy Spirit uses the name *Elohim* when the physical universe is in view, but when the salvation and protection of His children are in view, He uses the name *Jehovah*. One illustration will suffice. We read, "Thus did Noah; according to all that God [Elohim] commanded him, so did he."[22] Immediately following we read, "And the LORD [Jehovah] said unto Noah, Come thou and all thy house into the ark; for thee have I seen righteous before Me in this genera-tion."[23] "And they . . . went in, went in male and female of all flesh, as God [Elohim] had commanded him: and the LORD [Jehovah] shut him in."[24] Where the animals are included, the name *Elohim* is used, but it was *Jehovah* who shut *him* (Noah) in. God has a special relationship to man which is distinct from the lower creation. The communion He established with the man whom He made in His own image and likeness brings forth this further revelation of His character and attributes in the name *Jehovah-Elohim*. The fact that the two names are joined together makes it unquestionably clear that *Jehovah* is *Elohim*. They are one and the same Person. This fact God emphasized to Moses in Exodus 3:14-15.

Now the fact that there are repeated references to

[21] Genesis 2:7   [22] Genesis 6:22   [23] Genesis 7:1
[24] Genesis 7:16

LORD (Jehovah) in the Book of Genesis perplexes some
students of the Bible when they read Exodus 6:2-3. Let
us examine these verses. "And God spake unto Moses, and
said unto him, I am the LORD: And I appeared unto
Abraham, unto Isaac, and unto Jacob, by the name of
God Almighty, but by My name JEHOVAH was I not
known to them." God is not saying here that this name
was never used before Moses' time, but that now for the
first time He made known to Moses the meaning and
significance of it. Up to this time no explanation had
been given of the name *Jehovah*. The critics of the Bible
have used this passage to argue that Genesis 1 and 2 are
two separate documents written by different men and are
contradictory in the light of God's words to Moses in
Exodus 6:2-3. We have just given what we believe to be
a sound explanation of this alleged discrepancy, therefore
we consider it unnecessary to argue further the unbeliever's viewpoint.

We come now to a consideration of the three outstanding characteristics of *Jehovah*.

JEHOVAH IS HOLY

"For I am the LORD your God: ye shall therefore
sanctify yourselves, and ye shall be holy; for I am holy:
neither shall ye defile yourselves with any manner of
creeping thing that creepeth upon the earth. For I am
the LORD that bringeth you up out of the land of Egypt,
to be your God: ye shall therefore be holy, for I am

holy." [25] In Leviticus 19 we have a repetition of sundry laws and solemn warnings against any violation of them, and not less than eight times God concludes a warning with the words, "I am the LORD [Jehovah]," and eight times, "I am the LORD [Jehovah] your God [Elohim]."

Jehovah only is absolutely holy.[26] He assumes the title of "the Holy One," [27] and in this He distinguishes Himself from man.[28] He is essentially, eternally, infinitely, and absolutely holy. His holiness is not an acquired perfection; it is essentially God Himself. *Jehovah* is holy beyond the possibility of ever being tempted to sin.[29]

JEHOVAH HATES AND JUDGES SIN

It was as *Jehovah-Elohim* that He appeared to Adam, placing him under moral obligation to obey under penalty of death.[30] It is interesting to read the dialogue between Satan and Eve recorded in Genesis 3. Neither Satan nor Eve mention the name *Jehovah,* but always *Elohim.* The very mention of that holy name brought to mind the divine hatred for sin and the fact that *Jehovah* must judge sin and punish the sinner. In their distortions and doubting and denial of God's Word they avoided that name. From verse 7 to the end of the chapter, it is *Jehovah-Elohim* who pronounces judgment upon the sinners. God's names stand for His character, and as *Jehovah* He cannot condone evil. From the entrance of sin into the world in Genesis 3, right on through the rest of the

[25] Leviticus 11:44-45; 19:1-2
[26] Exodus 15:11; 1 Samuel 2:2   [27] Isaiah 40:25
[28] Hosea 11:9   [29] James 1:13   [30] Genesis 2:16-17

Old Testament, it is *Jehovah* who pronounces judgment against sin.

In Genesis 4, where we find the record of the first murder and the first polygamist, the name *Jehovah* is used, for here again God shows His hatred for sin and His judgment upon it. *Jehovah-Elohim* had already shown that a sacrifice was required for sin,[31] thus we are not surprised to read that *"Jehovah* had respect unto Abel and to his offering: But unto Cain and . . . his offering He had not respect." [32] Both boys had received the same instruction, having been raised at the same family altar, thus *Jehovah* had to judge the disobedient one.

In Genesis 5, where we have a record of the generations of Adam, which is a record of the creature-relationship, the name *Elohim* is used throughout until verse 29. There the name *Jehovah* is used in its only appearance in the entire chapter, but it is in connection with the "curse," Jehovah's judgment upon sin.

It is as *Jehovah* that He rained fire and brimstone upon the wicked cities of Sodom and Gomorrah.[33] It was *Jehovah* who said to Moses, "Whosoever hath sinned against Me, him will I blot out of My book." [34] It was *Jehovah* who plagued the people for making the calf.[35] It was *Jehovah* who descended in a cloud to proclaim His name and then to warn that sin would leave its effect upon their children unto the third and fourth generation.[36] *Jehovah* cannot clear the guilty. Men speak foolishly against God, but sinners must all come to see Jehovah's hatred for sin and His judgment of the sinner.

---

[31] Genesis 3:21 [32] Genesis 4:4-5 [33] Genesis 19:23-25
[34] Exodus 32:33 [35] Exodus 32:35 [36] Exodus 34:5-7

JEHOVAH LOVES AND SAVES SINNERS

It is under the name of *Jehovah* that He provides salvation for sinners. It was *Jehovah-Elohim* who came seeking the sinner whom He had judged.[37] Right here the
evolutionary theory collapses. Man cannot grope up
through his moral and spiritual darkness to find GOD,
but rather GOD loves and seeks the sinner. It was
Jehovah who closed the door of the ark in order to save
Noah.[38] It was *Jehovah* who judged Egypt and saved His
people Israel.[39] In the Book of Judges, which records
about four hundred and fifty years of Israel's history, we
have an excellent illustration of Jehovah's judgment of
sin, and at the same time His love and provision for
sinners.[40] And so *Jehovah* does not forsake sinful, fallen
man. He manifests His love, and ever seeks to save him.

JEHOVAH IN THE NEW TESTAMENT

In the New Testament the name *Jehovah* is ascribed to
Jesus Christ. There are many facts there which ascribe
deity to our blessed Lord, but none more clear and con-
vincing than the fact that the majestic name of Jehovah,
the great I AM, is applied to Him.

In Exodus 17:2,7 we are told that the people tempted
Jehovah in Rephidim. In 1 Corinthians 10:9 we learn
that it was Christ whom the Israelites tempted.

In Isaiah 6:1-5 the prophet saw *Jehovah*, yet that

[37] Genesis 3:8,21   [38] Genesis 7:16   [39] Exodus 12
[40] Judges 3:7-11, 12-15; 4:1-4; 6:1-14; 10:6-10; 11:21-23; 1´´1-14:19

vision was actually one of the preincarnate Christ according to John 12:41.

The same prophet, Isaiah, wrote by inspiration, "The voice of him that crieth in the wilderness, Prepare ye the way of the LORD [Jehovah], make straight in the desert a highway for our God." [41] When John the Baptist introduced the Lord Jesus he quoted Isaiah 40:3, thus showing that the *Jehovah-Elohim* of the Old Testament is Jesus Christ of Nazareth.[42]

In Isaiah 45:21-23 *Jehovah* prophesied of a day when every knee should bow to Him and every tongue swear (or confess) Him. In Philippians 2:9-11 that *Jehovah* of Isaiah's prophecy is none other than our Lord Jesus Christ.

In Joel 2:32 we are told that whosoever shall call on the name of the LORD (Jehovah) shall be delivered, or saved. In Romans 10:13 we learn that it is the Lord Jesus who saves.

In Psalm 102 the name *Jehovah* is mentioned not less than eight times.[43] In verses 25-27 He is depicted as the eternal Creator. The Epistle to the Hebrews shows this psalm to be Messianic and Christ to be the eternal Creator.[44]

We have noted earlier in our study that the Old Testament interpretation of *Jehovah* is in the statement, "I AM THAT I AM." [45] Among the New Testament writers, the Apostle John was divinely inspired to set forth our Lord Jesus Christ as the great "I AM." The Gospel ac-

[41] Isaiah 40:3 [42] Matthew 3:1-3
[43] Psalm 102:1,12,15,16,18,19,21,22
[44] Hebrews 1:10-12 [45] Exodus 3:14

cording to John is peculiarly the Gospel of His deity. In this one Book the three great primary names of Deity —Elohim, *Jehovah*, and Adonai—are all ascribed to Jesus Christ. Let us look together at those passages which show Jesus to be the "I AM."

To the Samaritan woman Christ said, "God is a Spirit: and they that worship Him must worship Him in spirit and in truth. The woman saith unto Him, I know that Messias cometh, which is called Christ: when He is come, He will tell us all things. Jesus saith unto her, I that speak unto thee am *He*." [46] Notice that the last word, "*He*," is in italics, meaning it was not in the original, so that our Lord really said, "It is I AM that speaketh unto thee."

When the disciples were crossing the storm-tossed sea toward Capernaum, Christ appeared walking on the water and said, "It is I AM; be not afraid," [47] The "AM" is unfortunately omitted from the Authorized Version.

It was to the Pharisees that Jesus said, "For if ye believe not that I AM [*He* has been added], ye shall die in your sins." [48] "Then said Jesus unto them, When ye have lifted up the Son of man, then shall ye know that I AM [*He* has been added]." [49] "Jesus said unto them, Verily, verily, I say unto you, Before Abraham was, I AM." [50]

If there was any doubt in the mind of any one of the disciples that Christ was the *Jehovah* of the Old Testament, He told them that before the great betrayal they would know this truth. "Now I tell you before it come, that, when it is come to pass, ye may believe that I AM [*He* has been added]." [51]

When Judas led the officers from the chief priests and Pharisees to take Jesus, and our Lord said unto them "I AM [*He* has been added], they went backward, and fell to the ground." [52] Humanity was forced to bow before Deity.

In addition to these passages which show Jesus to be the "I AM," the *Jehovah* of the Old Testament, John records eight sayings of Christ in which He compounded the name "I AM" with other descriptive terms:

> I AM the Bread of Life[53]
> I AM the Light of the world [54]
> I AM the Door[55]
> I AM the Good Shepherd[56]
> I AM the Son of God[57]
> I AM the Resurrection, and the Life[58]
> I AM the Way, the Truth, and the Life[59]
> I AM the True Vine[60]

All that *Jehovah* was to His people in Old Testament times, our Lord Jesus Christ is to His Church in the present dispensation. He is *Jehovah* the Holy One who hates and judges sin, but who loves and saves sinners.

[51] John 13:19
[54] John 8:12; 9:5
[57] John 10:36
[60] John 15:1,5
[52] John 18:6,8
[55] John 10:7,9
[58] John 11:25
[53] John 6:35,48,51
[56] John 10:11,14
[59] John 14:6

ADONAI (Lord)

The name *Adonai* occurs about 300 times in the Old Testament and is always translated "Lord." It is to be distinguished from the name *Jehovah*, translated "Lᴏʀᴅ." Like the name *Elohim*, it is a plural noun meaning "Lords," confirming the idea of the Trinity. The singular form, *Adon*, is also found in the Old Testament. It was the name most familiar to the Jews, and, as we have seen, the name they substituted for *Jehovah*.

Adonai is used of both deity and humanity, and is therefore applied to God and man. However, the marked distinction between the two usages is seen in the spelling. When the word "lord" is used of man it begins with a small "l," but when it is used of God it is printed with a capital "L." The Hebrew root from which this name is derived means to judge, to rule.[1] It answers to the Greek *Kurios*, meaning a master, a lord, or *the* Lord, one who exercises rule and authority. The first occurrence of the name *Adonai* in Scripture is found in Genesis 15:1-2. Let us examine its use in two well-known earthly relationships.

The first relationship is that of a servant to his master. It appears in connection with Abraham's sending his senior servant to get a wife for Isaac.[2] In these verses the word *Adonai* is translated "master." Read them carefully

[1] L. Berkhof   [2] Genesis 24:1-52

and you will see that the relationship of the slave to his lord and master was different from that of a hired servant to his employer. If the hired servant did not like his assignment he could quit or go on strike. But this the slave could not do. He had been purchased and was therefore the possession of his master. He accepted his lord's will and obeyed it fully.

There are two principles which apply to this relationship between the slave and his lord, or master. The first is that the master has a right to absolute obedience from the slave. Moses learned this when God assigned him the task of delivering Israel from the bondage of the Egyptians. In Exodus 3 Moses offered his excuses and there God revealed Himself as Jehovah, the "I AM." [3] In chapter 4 Moses continued with more excuses, and God replied with an assuring word against each excuse. Then Moses said, "O my Lord [*Adonai*], I am not eloquent, neither heretofore, nor since Thou hast spoken unto Thy servant: but I am slow of speech, and of a slow tongue." [4] The moment he used the word "Lord" (*Adonai*), he committed himself. He admitted that his Master had a right to absolute obedience, and thus he could do nothing other than to obey. It is not the slave's right to choose his own task, only to do what his Master assigns to him.

When Moses died, God said to Joshua, "Moses My servant is dead; now therefore arise, go over this Jordan, thou, and all this people, unto the land which I do give to them, even to the children of Israel." [5] Whenever God loses a servant, He looks for another to take his place. But Joshua must know *Adonai* and his relation to Him;

[3] Exodus 3:14   [4] Exodus 4:10   [5] Joshua 1:2

namely, that of a slave to his Master. Now, Joshua was a great general who possessed rare military strategy, as his victories in warfare proved.[6] But he must know that he is Adonai's slave and that he must take every assignment from Him.

Jericho lay before Israel. This walled fortress dare not be bypassed. As Joshua stood without the camp reconnoitering, he saw a Man stand before him with His sword drawn. Knowing that he was appointed to take Moses' place, Joshua challenged the presence of the Man with the drawn sword. "Art Thou for us, or for our adversaries?" inquired Joshua.[7] The reply came, "As captain of the host of the Lord am I now come." [8] Then Joshua fell on his face and worshiped Him. And why did he worship Him? That majestic Person was none other than the Lord Jesus Christ in preincarnate form. It is not necessary to discuss whether it was a substantial body or an outward form. We need only know that Joshua paid divine honor to Him, which belongs to God only. He who appeared to Joshua is the Captain of our salvation.[9] He is our great Commander, the King of kings, and Lord of lords.

Why did our Lord appear to Joshua at this time? God had lost a servant in Moses, and He wanted to impress upon Joshua the fact that He wanted another servant and not merely a leader. When in verse 14 Joshua said, "What saith my lord unto His servant?" he was acknowledging for the first time that his Master (*Adonai*) had a right to absolute obedience from His slave. (Scholars

[6] Exodus 17:8-13   [7] Joshua 5:13   [8] Joshua 5:14
[9] Hebrews 2:10

are agreed that the translators of the Authorized Version have erred in failing to use the capital "L" here.) All of this was no doubt a humiliating experience for Joshua, but he needed to be humbled. He needed to learn, as we all must learn, that we cannot fight spiritual battles with worldly weapons.[10] Nor can we be successful leaders for God until first we have bowed to the Lordship of Christ and have become His bondslaves, for indeed all things have been put under His feet,[11] and we are His purchased possession.[12]

Joshua obeyed *Adonai* at once when He said, "Loose thy shoe from off thy foot; for the place whereon thou standest is holy. And Joshua did so." [13] It was in a similar way that this same Captain spoke to Joshua's predecessor forty years before.[14] The law stated that when an Israelite was incapable of performing a duty enjoined upon him by God, he was to acknowledge his incompetence by removing his shoe.[15] *Adonai* was now showing His servant Joshua that now he must take orders from his Master.

In Joshua, chapter 6, *Adonai* tells His servant His plans for the campaign against Jericho.[16] How was Joshua going to explain this kind of military strategy to his men? No doubt his warriors gathered about him, expecting to hear him say, "I have decided how we should take Jericho." I can imagine the look on their faces when

---

[10] 2 Corinthians 10:4   [11] Ephesians 1:22-23
[12] 1 Peter 1:18-19; 1 Corinthians 6:19-20
[13] Joshua 5:15   [14] Exodus 3:5
[15] Deuteronomy 25:5-10; Ruth 4:8
[16] Joshua 6:1-5

Joshua told them that they were merely going to march around the walls once each day for six days, and seven times around on the seventh day. But *Adonai* had given His orders to His slave, and the slave could do nothing but obey. The first principle in the master-slave relationship is that the master has a right to expect absolute obedience from his slave. When Joshua obeyed Adonai at Jericho he had great success.

But chapter 7 reveals a tragic defeat at Ai soon after the remarkable triumph at Jericho. Confident after a fresh victory, Joshua failed to consult with Adonai and went against Ai in his own strength. He resorted to his own military genius, planning his own attack against Ai. He did not get orders from his Master, and the men of Ai put Israel's army to flight.[17]

Joshua immediately fell on his face before Jehovah, calling Him "Adonai" repeatedly. But He said to Joshua, "Get thee up; wherefore liest thou thus upon thy face?"[18] Joshua was calling Him "Lord," while refusing to do his Master's will.

Here is a solemn lesson for every Christian. Jesus Christ is "Lord of all,"[19] "Lord of heaven and earth,"[20] "Lord both of the dead and living,"[21] "the Lord of glory,"[22] "the Lord from heaven,"[23] and "LORD OF LORDS."[24] Faith in Him as Lord (*Adonai*) is essential to salvation.[25] He Himself solemnly warns us that calling Him "Lord" is in itself not enough for one to enter the kingdom of Heaven. Each individual person must bow

[17] Joshua 7:1-5
[18] Joshua 7:10
[19] Acts 10:36
[20] Acts 17:24
[21] Romans 14:9
[22] 1 Corinthians 2:8
[23] 1 Corinthians 15:47
[24] Revelation 19:16
[25] Romans 10:9

before His Lordship, become His willing slave, and obey Him.[26] "And why call ye Me, Lord, Lord, and do not the things which I say?" [27]

The second principle which applies to this relationship between the slave and his lord, or master, is the fact that the slave has a right to expect provision and direction from his master. A slave need never be bothered about provision, protection, or providential guidance. These things are the responsibility of the master. Man in his fallen nature needs lordship. His judgments and faculties have been impaired by sin. He needs provision and protection outside of himself. If he does not surrender to the Lordship of Jesus Christ and depend upon Him, then he will become the slave of a demonic power. Man needs security, thus he needs lordship. But "No man can serve two masters." [28] Joshua called upon Israel to make a decision as to whom they were going to serve.[29] Paul likewise made it clear that no servant can serve two masters.[30]

Now, as long as a man submits to the Lordship of Jesus Christ he can count on Christ to protect him and provide for him. Joshua learned this at Jericho. So did Paul at his first meeting with the Saviour. At the first sound of his new Master's voice he cried, "Who art Thou Lord. . . . Lord, what wilt Thou have me to do?" [31] And from that moment on Paul knew the blessing of his new Master's provision,[32] and he was content.[33] He always

---

[26] Matthew 7:21-22, cf. 25:11-12; Luke 13:24-25
[27] Luke 6:46   [28] Matthew 6:24; Luke 16:13
[29] Joshua 24:14-15   [30] Romans 6:16   [31] Acts 9:5-6
[32] Philippians 4:19   [33] Philippians 4:11

considered himself to be the bondslave of *Adonai*.[34] Luke said of Paul, "The Lord stood by him." [35] In his last divinely-inspired words Paul testified, "The Lord stood with me, and strengthened me. . . . And the Lord shall deliver me from every evil work, and will preserve me unto His heavenly kingdom: to whom be glory for ever and ever. Amen." [36] The Lordship of Christ was the substance of his preaching,[37] and he was clear in his announcement of its necessity for salvation.[38] Everyone who ever surrendered to Him has been able to testify, "I love my Master." [39] See Isaiah 6.

Here then, in this first relationship, that of the slave to his master, we learn that *Adonai* has a right to absolute obedience from His slave, and the slave has a right to expect His provision and protection.

The second relationship is that of a wife to her husband. The right of lordship was that of the husband, whether the woman became the wife of a man by the power of her own choice, as in the case of Rebecca and Isaac,[40] or if she were given or sold by her father, as in the case of Rachel and Jacob.[41]

The Old Testament abounds in this second relationship, that of a wife to her husband. Sarah called Abraham "lord." [42] Bathsheba called David "lord." [43] This was a common term of respect that a Hebrew woman used for her husband. The term did not imply that she was a slave,

[34] Romans 1:1; Philippians 1:1; Titus 1:1
[35] Acts 23:11
[36] 2 Timothy 4:17-18   [37] 2 Corinthians 4:5
[38] Romans 10:9
[39] Exodus 21:5   [40] Genesis 24:58
[41] Genesis 29:15-28
[42] Genesis 18:12, cf. 1 Peter 3:6
[43] 1 Kings 1:16-18

for the standard of womanhood was high among the Hebrews. It was a term of relationship.

It signified the husband's place of headship. God said to Eve, "Thy desire shall be to thy husband, and he shall rule over thee." [44] Because she acted independently of him in the temptation, she must now depend upon him. Because she usurped authority over him by taking matters into her own hands and by leading Adam into temptation,[45] she must now be under his rule. Woman's relationship to man is now fixed. He is to bear the rule over her. God has neither altered nor abrogated this relationship. It is natural.

In the Old Testament the marriage relationship is used repeatedly by *Jehovah* to call attention to that spiritual relationship that existed between Himself and Israel.[46] As the relationship between husband and wife is close, intimate, and endearing, so it is between God and His people. She belongs to him, and he is her protector and provider. She pledges to be true, clean, and pure, and he pledges to love and care for her.

Paul uses this relationship to illustrate the Church's relationship to Christ.[47] As a wife is faithful and devoted to her husband, so the believer is to Christ. He is our Master; we are His slaves. He is the Bridegroom; we His bride. Let us be faithful and keep ourselves pure for *Adonai!*

[44] Genesis 3:16   [45] 1 Timothy 2:14
[46] Isaiah 54:5; 62:5; Jeremiah 2:2; 3:14; 31:32; Ezekiel 16:7-14
[47] Ephesians 5:25-33

EL SHADDAI (God Almighty)

The first of the compound names of God that we shall study is made up of two words—*El* (the abbreviated form of *Elohim*) and *Almighty* (the English form of the Hebrew word *Shaddai*). The word *Shaddai* occurs forty-eight times in the Old Testament, of which number the Book of Job contains thirty-one instances.

We have seen in the chapter on Elohim that the Hebrew "El" is translated strong, mighty, powerful. *Elohim* is the strong One, the God of power and might.[1] The same word "El" is also translated by such words as *might* and *power* with regard to men.[2]

The word *Shaddai,* while having in it the thought of strength, comes from the Hebrew singular noun *Shad,* meaning "breast." In numerous places in Scripture, *Shad* is translated "breast," [3] implying sustenance, strength, satisfaction, sufficiency. It is invariably used in Scripture for a mother's breast, through which she transmits sustenance and strength and satisfaction to her babe. The hungry, dissatisfied babe is fretful, but when he receives nourishment and is thereby satisfied, he is quieted and

[1] Psalm 18:32; 68:35; 77:14; Isaiah 46:9
[2] Genesis 31:29; Deuteronomy 28:32; Proverbs 3:27
[3] Job 3:12; Psalm 22:9; Song of Solomon 1:13; 4:5; 7:3,7,8; 8:1,8; Isaiah 28:9

restful. The mother's breast is the babe's resource and sufficiency.

All that a mother is to her baby, *El Shaddai* is to His own children. He is the Mighty One, the believer's Sufficiency, Sustenance, Strength, and Satisfaction. As the mother pours her life into the child of her breast, even so *El Shaddai* pours His life into His children.[4] This is one of the most tender titles used of God, and its use is exclusively in relation to His children. Dr. G. Campbell Morgan says, "To gather sustenance and consolation from the bosom of God is to be made strong for the pilgrimage." Canon Girdlestone points out the fact that in the passage in which *Shaddai* occurs, God is designated as a bountiful giver.

The first use of the name in Scripture bears out its meaning. It was to Abraham that God revealed Himself as *El Shaddai*.[5] Sixteen years before the revelation of *El Shaddai*, God promised Abraham a seed.[6] Abraham already was well advanced in years when this promise was first made, but he believed God. The years passed rapidly, and when Sarah did not conceive, both she and Abraham concluded that soon it would be too late for God's promise to be fulfilled in them. Of course their reasoning was merely human calculation. At Sarah's suggestion Abraham took Hagar, the Egyptian handmaid, to be his wife. Now, it was not an uncommon practice, when a wife was barren, for a handmaid to bear children. This common custom was practiced to insure continuance of a family. Then, too, the original promise contained nothing as to

[4] Isaiah 66:10-13   [5] Genesis 17:1   [6] Genesis 15:4-6

Sarah's becoming a mother. At any rate, Hagar conceived and Ishmael was born.[7]

Thirteen years after Ishmael was born,[8] when Abraham was ninety-nine years old, God appeared to him again. Now it was no longer possible, according to known natural law, for Sarah to conceive. Yet God assured Abraham that a son would be born of him and Sarah.[9] Abraham at once questioned the physical possibility of its fulfillment,[10] and suggested to God that He take Ishmael and fulfill His promise through him.[11] But God would have nothing to do with Ishmael. Thus Abraham believed God and was circumcised.[12]

At this point in the Biblical story the New Testament adds further light. Romans 4:19-21 and Hebrews 11:11 refer to the deadness of the bodies of Abraham and Sarah, as well as the fact that Sarah was "past age." It was necessary that the bodies of both of them should die first so that they might realize that the birth of Isaac was all of God. To experience God's sufficiency one must realize his own insufficiency. Thus God said to Abraham, "I am the *Almighty God.*"[13] It is *El Shaddai* who gives and sustains life, who pours divine life into these poor weak lives of ours. It was by this new name that God revealed Himself. It is *El Shaddai's* work to make fruitful and to nourish life. As the babe is born of its mother and sustained at her breast, even so God is the Author and Sustainer of life. As that name fell upon Abraham's ears for the first time, it must have been a most revealing

---

[7] Genesis 16   [8] Genesis 16:16; 17:1   [9] Genesis 17:15-16
[10] Genesis 17:17   [11] Genesis 17:18
[12] Genesis 17:10-12, 24-27   [13] Genesis 17:1

and refreshing word from Heaven. Since God's name in Scripture stands for His nature, He was revealing to Abraham something of Himself. *El Shaddai* was everything to Abraham now.

The spiritual lesson that Abraham learned from the revelation of the name *El Shaddai* remained with him the rest of his natural life. He must have passed it on to his son Isaac, for years later, when Isaac sent his son Jacob away to Padan-aram to find a bride, he dismissed him with the words, "And God Almighty bless thee." [14] This is Jacob's first venture away from home. He had not been an outdoor man, as was his brother Esau. Moreover, the long journey would be beset by wild beasts and robbers, and there would be no human to strengthen, sustain, and succour him. But Isaac assured him that *El Shaddai* can take him to His breast and sustain him throughout the journey. *El Shaddai* can pour His strength into the most barren life and make it fruitful.

> Safe in the arms of Jesus,
> Safe on His gentle breast.

What comfort at that crucial hour of the breakup of a family to know that the departing one is in *El Shaddai's* care!

Jacob must have come to know *El Shaddai* in experience on that journey, for years later he returned to Bethel and there God gave him his new name, Israel, and said to him, "I am God Almighty [El Shaddai]: be fruitful and multiply." [15] This command was backed by the

[14] Genesis 28:1-4   [15] Genesis 35:9-12

Giver and Sustainer of life Himself. It was when Jacob was on his deathbed that he repeated to Joseph *El Shaddai's* promise,[16] and in that same name he pronounced a final blessing upon his son.[17] None save *El Shaddai*, the all-sufficient One, can multiply and make fruitful. But there is a secret to receiving from Him our daily portion. The Psalmist expresses it in the following words, "He that dwelleth in the secret place of the most High shall abide under the shadow of the Almighty." [18] The abiding life is the fruitful life.[19]

A soul-stirring use of the name is found in the Book of Ruth. Since it is *El Shaddai's* great work to make fruitful, there are times when He must chasten in order to do so. Thus it is that the name "Almighty," or *Shaddai*, is used in Ruth 1:20-21. After Naomi's years of sorrowful sojourn in Moab, when her acquaintances of former years saw her, they said "Is this Naomi?" (meaning "pleasant").[20] To this she replied, "Call me not Naomi [pleasant], call me Mara [bitterness]: for the Almighty [*Shaddai*] hath dealt very bitterly with me. . . . The Almighty [*Shaddai*] hath afflicted me." She had lost the fruit of her womb, her own sons, and her husband, the father of her children. She was not willing to trust *El Shaddai* in Moab, but she learned through her failure, and now she can be a help to others. She confesses that she went out "full" and returned "empty."

El Shaddai is concerned with making His people fruitful. If chastening is necessary to accomplish this, then be certain He will chasten. When Naomi returned home

[16] Genesis 48:1-4   [17] Genesis 49:22-26   [18] Psalm 91:1
[19] John 15:4-5   [20] Ruth 1:19

she was a poor desolate widow, crushed in spirit and engulfed in sorrow. She is a picture of one who refuses to allow *El Shaddai* to make fruitful. But as a mother will chasten her child to train him, so *El Shaddai* will child-train His own. If the branches will not bear fruit, He must prune them.[21] If His children will not obey, He chastens them.[22] The Lord has His own way of dealing with His backslidden children. Sometimes He is severe, but He always has our interests at heart.

[21] John 15:1-2   [22] Hebrews 12:5-11

EL ELYON (Most High God)

The name *El Elyon* is translated in the Authorized Version, "the most high God." Its meaning is clearly given in the passage which first introduces the name to us. *El Elyon* is the "Possessor of heaven and earth." [1] He is the sovereign Creator and Owner of both the celestial and terrestrial worlds, "high over all," above all, omnipotent, and supreme.

The Hebrew word *Elyon,* or most high, is sometimes applied to men and material things of this world. Thus it is not confined to a sacred use in connection with God. The word is translated in various ways in the Authorized Version, as "uppermost basket." [2] Israel's position in relation to other nations is described as "high above all nations." [3] In Ezekiel's description of the Temple he speaks of the *"highest"* chamber.[4] Its descriptive use in Scripture always distinguishes the object being described as the *highest* in relation to other objects like it, such as "the *higher* gate," [5] "the *upper* pool," [6] "the *upper* watercourse." [7] Thus the *higher* gate is higher than other gates, the *upper* pool higher than other pools, and the *upper* watercourse higher than other watercourses.

Our study is concerned with the name *Elyon* as it is

---

[1] Genesis 14:18-23   [2] Genesis 40:17   [3] Deuteronomy 26:19
[4] Ezekiel 41:7   [5] 2 Kings 15:35   [6] 2 Kings 18:17
[7] 2 Chronicles 32:30

used in reference to God. As *El Elyon,* the Possessor of
Heaven and earth, He is superior to all creation, animate
and inanimate, visible and invisible, human and otherwise. He is the Highest, above all and over all. He is the
Most High, since there is none as high as He. In our
study of the name *Elohim* we learned that *El* means "The
Strong One." *Elyon* is the superlative, meaning "Strongest," so that in the name *El Elyon* is the idea of "the
Strongest Strong One." None is as great as He in power
or possessions.

The first mention of the *Most High God* was made by
Melchizedek, king of Salem, to Abraham. It was after
Abraham had taken 318 farmers, whom he had instructed, and in the dead of night attacked the confeder-
ated army of enemy kings, who had taken captive his
nephew Lot. Abraham defeated them, liberated the captives, and brought back with him much treasure.[8] Before
any disposition of the spoils had been made God saw to
it that one of His choice servants was on hand to witness
to Abraham. Melchizedek is called "the priest of the
most high God." His greeting to Abraham after the victory was simple and brief. He did not laud nor congratu-
late Abraham. He simply said, "Blessed be Abram of
the most high God, possessor of heaven and earth: And
blessed be the most high God, which hath delivered thine
enemies into thy hand." [9]

By this simple benediction this mighty minister of God
had introduced to Abraham a characteristic of God's nature that he had not known before. He was reminding
Abraham that *El Elyon,* the Strongest Strong One, had

[8] Genesis 14:12-16

won the battle and the spoils were His. There is none
higher that He in power and possessions both in Heaven
and earth. Abraham grasped the truth of this great revelation of God's nature quickly and learned it well. Overcome by a sense of *El Elyon's* greatness, he at once gave
to Melchizedek tithes of everything he had brought back
from the conquest.[10] *El Elyon* was the Possessor of it all.

Immediately the man of the world reacts unfavorably
to all of this. The king of Sodom felt that what Abraham
gave to God was his loss, and so he suggests that Abraham divide the balance of the spoils with him.[11] This was,
no doubt, a great temptation to Abraham. But he had
just met *El Elyon,* and this new vision of God had
fastened itself upon his heart. "And Abram said to the
king of Sodom, I will lift up mine hand unto the LORD,
the most high God, the possessor of heaven and earth,
That I will not take from a thread even to a shoelatchet,
and that I will not take any thing that is thine, lest thou
shouldest say, I have made Abram rich: Save only that
which the young men have eaten, and the portion of the
men which went with me, Aner, Eschol, and Mamre; let
them take their portion." [12]

I have always felt that Abraham started home to
Sarah, after that consecration meeting, just a bit appre-
hensive. Possibly he wondered what the future held, insofar as material things were concerned. But *El Elyon*
sees to it that no obedient child of His will ever be a
loser, for in the next verse we read, "After these things
the word of the LORD came unto Abram in a vision, say-

[10] Genesis 14:20, cf. Hebrews 7:4   [11] Genesis 14:21
[12] Genesis 14:22-24

ing, Fear not, Abram: I am thy shield and thy exceeding great reward." [13] The time element here is significant. God never tells a man to "fear not" unless he is afraid of something. I have an idea that Abraham was wondering if he possibly made a mistake. Certainly the king of Sodom believed Abraham to be a fool. But *El Elyon* is no man's debtor. He is the Possessor of Heaven and earth. Hear Him say, "I am thy . . . exceeding great reward."

The next appearance of this name in Scripture occurs in connection with Balaam. He testified that he "heard the words of God, and knew the knowledge of the most High." [14] But Balaam's life was the tragedy of a man who had knowledge of *El Elyon,* the Possessor of Heaven and earth, and yet failed to heed that knowledge. Unwilling to trust the God he knew, Balaam sinned when he prostituted the truth for gain. He accepted Balak's gold, which Peter calls "the wages of unrighteousness." [15] Jude says that greed was Balaam's downfall.[16] It is sad indeed when a man knows the Most High God, who possesses all things, and yet submits to sinful means in order to acquire a few dollars.

The last appearance of this name in the writings of Moses lays further stress upon its meaning. "When the Most High divided to the nations their inheritance, when He separated the sons of Adam, He set the bounds of the people according to the number of the children of Israel." [17] Since *El Elyon* is the Possessor of Heaven and earth, He only has the authority to divide among the nations their inheritance. It was in the providence of God

[13] Genesis 15:1   [14] Numbers 24:16   [15] 2 Peter 2:15
[16] Jude 11   [17] Deuteronomy 32:8

that the nations came into being and He proportioned to them their needs. When we look at geography from the divine standpoint, we are forced to concede that "The earth is the LORD's, and the fulness thereof." [18] Among the several appearances of this name in the Psalms, one verse is outstanding in setting forth its meaning—"That men may know that Thou, whose name alone is JEHOVAH, art the *most high* over all the earth." [19] Man must recognize divine authority in the earth.

Perhaps the best illustration of the use of this name appears in the Book of Daniel. We meet God, under the name of *El Elyon*, more times in this book than in any other book in the Bible. Daniel wrote this book of prophecy while he was a captive in Babylon. In 606 B.C. Nebuchadnezzar besieged Jerusalem and led the first deportation of prisoners to Babylon. Daniel was among them. All of his people were in captivity, the land in desolation, the city in ruins, and the Temple of God was utterly destroyed. It must have been a great comfort to Daniel to meet *El Elyon* under those conditions, for He is the Possessor of Heaven and earth, and He can restore the land to His people whenever He chooses to do so.

But the chief purpose of the book is not to comfort Daniel; rather it is to show to those Gentile kings that the earth belongs to *El Elyon*, Israel's God and the God of Heaven and earth. When Nebuchadnezzar sacked and looted the holy city, he took the treasures and sacred vessels from the Temple of *Jehovah* and put them in the house of his gods.[20] Warfare between nations in those

[18] Exodus 19:5; Psalm 24:1; 1 Corinthians 10:26,28
[19] Psalm 83:18   [20] Daniel 1:2

days was in reality warfare between the gods of those nations. In the minds of the Babylonians the gods of Babylon had defeated the God of Israel. And to them the proof of all this lay in the fact that they possessed the sacred vessels taken from *Jehovah's* Temple.

But a series of events began which were to prove that *El Elyon,* Israel's God, is the Possessor of Heaven and earth. The first of these events was Nebuchadnezzar's dream. Daniel's interpretation of the dream introduced to the king the fact that the God of Heaven had given him his kingdom.[21] This was the first indication to Nebuchadnezzar that Israel's God was the Most High God. Nebuchadnezzar seemingly accepted that idea and promoted Daniel.[22]

In the third chapter of Daniel Nebuchadnezzar made a statue all of gold. In the light of Daniel's statement, "Thou art this head of gold," [23] it seems as though Nebuchadnezzar was determined that his kingdom would be an everlasting kingdom, that Babylon would not give way to another kingdom.[24] In substance he was saying to himself, "I'll fix that God of Daniel." God answered his challenge by His miraculous preservation of the three Hebrew young men in the fiery furnace. Having never witnessed anything like this, the king released his three prisoners in the name of *El Elyon.*[25]

Nebuchadnezzar's recognition of *El Elyon* was short-lived. In his heart he refused to subordinate himself to Daniel's God. His second dream, which had to do with a great tree, predicted his insanity. In Daniel's interpre-

[21] Daniel 2:37-38   [22] Daniel 2:46-48   [23] Daniel 2:38
[24] Daniel 2:39-44   [25] Daniel 3:26

tation of the dream he mentions *El Elyon* not less than four times.[26] Nebuchadnezzar became a living maniac until he conceded that the Most High God put him on his throne and that his kingdom depended on Him.[27]

Daniel chapter five is the conclusion of the narrative as it relates to Babylon. Belshazzar defied and blasphemed *El Elyon* by drinking out of the sacred vessels which his father Nebuchadnezzar had taken from the Temple of *Jehovah* in Jerusalem. During the drunken feast, the handwriting appeared on the wall, and that night *El Elyon* took the kingdom from Babylon and gave it to Darius the Mede. It was God's answer to Belshazzar's challenge. But the drunken king did not die without receiving a witness. Daniel faithfully told him of *El Elyon*.[28]

Earthly monarchs have learned that the Most High God rules in Heaven and earth. Satan learned this,[29] and still he continues to inspire godless men to defy and dethrone *El Elyon*. Whenever man rules the world it will be under direct orders of the Most High God, and those men will be His saints associated with Christ in His rule over His coming kingdom.[30]

[26] Daniel 4:17,24,25,32   [27] Daniel 4:34   [28] Daniel 5:18
[29] Isaiah 14:12-15   [30] Daniel 7:18,22-27

EL OLAM (The Everlasting God)

The name *El Olam,* though appearing only compara-
tively few times in the Bible, reveals one of the essential
and blessed aspects of God's nature. It is translated in
the Authorized Version, "The Everlasting God." The
Hebrew word *olam* expresses the idea of eternal duration; however, it is translated in several different ways
in the Old Testament, such as "ever," "everlasting,"
"evermore," "forever." But while "The Everlasting God"
conveys something of the meaning of *El Olam,* it does not
fully teach all that the name implies. *Olam* also expresses
the idea of something secret, hidden, or concealed. Now
there is no conflict between the idea of "everlasting" and
"hidden." As far as the human mind is able to conceive,
that which is eternal is concealed, it is hidden beyond
man's ability to fathom. Thus we see in *olam* the double
meaning of "everlasting" and "hidden." God is the "God
of the ages," and to Him only are all things known.

The name *El Olam* was revealed first to Abraham.
"And Abraham planted a grove in Beer-sheba, and called
there on the name of the LORD, *the everlasting God.*" [1]
This was the third time God revealed Himself to Abra-
ham through one of His names. It was to Abraham that
God disclosed Himself as *El Elyon,* [2] and *El Shaddai.* [3]

[1] Genesis 21:33   [2] Genesis 14:22   [3] Genesis 17:1

It follows from this that Abraham was highly privileged in being one of the first persons on earth to receive from Jehovah the revelation of Himself in these names.

There are two important incidents recorded in Genesis 21, namely, the casting out of Hagar and Ishmael and the planting of the grove in Beer-sheba, where Abraham made a covenant with Abimelech. From the standpoint of context one might argue that the use of the name, "The Everlasting God," applies to the latter incident only. While it is true that the name is first mentioned in connection with the covenant between Abraham and Abimelech at Beer-sheba, many Bible expositors see in it a clear application to both incidents recorded in the chapter.

The first incident in the chapter, in which the name *El Olam* appears, is Abraham's obedience to God in dismissing Hagar and Ishmael from his household.[4] Now Genesis 21 should be carefully compared with Galatians 4:21-31. The Holy Spirit uses the recorded historical facts in the former to teach an important spiritual lesson in the latter. Some of the Galatian Christians had been misinformed by Judaizing teachers that they were under obligation to keep the law. Apparently some of them were being convinced, for Paul writes, "Tell me, ye that desire to be under the law, do ye not hear the law? For it is written, that Abraham had two sons, the one by a bondmaid, the other by a freewoman. But he who was of the bondwoman was born after the flesh; but he of the freewoman was by promise. Which things are an allegory: for these are the two covenants; the one from the mount Sinai, which gendereth to bondage, which is Agar [Hagar]. For this

[4] Genesis 21:12-14

Agar is mount Sinai in Arabia, and answereth to Jerusalem which now is, and is in bondage with her children. But Jerusalem which is above is free, which is the mother of us all." [5]

The two mothers, Sarah and Hagar, represent the two ages (or dispensations) of law and grace. Just as Hagar and Ishmael were cast out to give place to Isaac the son of promise, so the dispensation of law gave place to the dispensation of grace. Thus *El Olam*, The Everlasting God, is "the God of the ages." He reveals Himself to men through the different ages and dispensations.

But it was actually in Beer-sheba, where Abraham planted a tree as a token of his agreement with Abimelech, that the name *El Olam* appears. Though Abimelech was himself a well-disposed man, his servants had violently seized one of Abraham's wells. It seems that Abimelech himself was innocent of the whole affair. When Abraham appealed to him, he insisted that he knew nothing about it. Abraham believed him to be sincere in this, for he paid Abimelech the redemption price of sheep, oxen, and seven ewe lambs. Actually he bought back the well which he had originally digged, the redemption price being a proof of his ownership. It was at this point that Abraham called on *El Olam*. The well was not worth fighting over, since "the God of the ages," who is always available and who is immutable, was Abraham's God. Abraham committed his case to *El Olam*, recognizing the fact that He always vindicates His trusting child. He was not certain in his mind that he could trust Abimelech and his men in the future, but Abraham knew that he could depend on "The

[5] Galatians 4:21-26

Everlasting God." *El Olam* has divided all time and eternity into successive ages or dispensations, therefore we can commit all of our tomorrows to Him.

In a psalm that is attributed to Moses, we have a testimony to *El Olam*. "LORD, Thou hast been our dwelling place in all generations. Before the mountains were brought forth, or ever Thou hadst formed the earth and the world, even from everlasting to everlasting, Thou art God." [6] These first two verses of the psalm emphasize the eternity of God, and they answer to a statement in Moses' farewell address to Israel, when he said, "The eternal God is thy refuge, and underneath are the everlasting arms." [7] The psalm is a testimony to the fact that Jehovah has been the sustenance and shelter for His children in generation after generation. Israel's God is *El Olam*, "from everlasting to everlasting," reaching into the infinite past, beyond the horizon of man's knowledge or memory, even from the remotest hidden ages. Both His pre-existence and eternal existence are here seen. The nature of *El Olam* can be measured by the history of His people. Trace the human race backward, from generation to generation, and backward still more to the vanishing point, and He is discovered to be the same immutable God. Time does not alter Him, "For a thousand years in Thy sight are but as yesterday when it is past, and as a watch in the night." [8] Now let your mind travel forward to succeeding generations, projecting your thoughts as far as you dare, even to the vanishing point, and He still is God.

And He is *our* God! He is our dwelling place. God is

[6] Psalm 90:1-2   [7] Deuteronomy 33:27   [8] Psalm 90:4

our home. Because He lives in the eternal ages, He is
above change. In *El Olam's* way of reckoning time, the
longest life span, even the 969 years of Methuselah,
would be a relatively brief period in relation to His
eternal and unchanging nature. Time no more exists for
God than it did for the unconscious sleeper, Rip Van
Winkle of fable fame. "One day is with the Lord as a
thousand years, and a thousand years as one day." [9] As
His strangers and pilgrims here on earth, we need never
fear. Every succeeding generation, from the day of Adam,
to our present day, has produced its children of God who
have proved His faithfulness. And in this Eternal One
every successive generation of mankind, from our own,
will find Him a suitable refuge. H. F. Stevenson wrote,
"In earlier generations, God dealt with His people according to the needs of *their* day; and now, His grace is sufficient for us in this troubled twentieth century. How very
different are our times and circumstances from those of
Abraham, Isaac, and Jacob! But the same Everlasting
God meets our needs as fully and graciously as He did
theirs: and He will do so as long as life shall last."

The Prophet Isaiah adds his testimony to *El Olam.*
"Hast thou not known? hast thou not heard, that *the
everlasting God,* the LORD, the Creator of the ends of the
earth, fainteth not, neither is weary? . . . But they that
wait upon the LORD shall renew their strength; they shall
mount up with wings as eagles; they shall run, and not be
weary; and they shall walk, and not faint." [10] The first
thirty-nine chapters of Isaiah set forth the judgments of
God upon an iniquitous people. But the opening of chap-

[9] 2 Peter 3:8   [10] Isaiah 40:28,31

ter forty strikes the keynote for all that follows in the re-
mainder of the book. The succeeding chapters look forward to the time when the nation will have paid suffi-
ciently for her sins. The promise of deliverance opens
with the message, "Comfort ye, comfort ye My people,
saith your God." [11] God did not want His people under
the false delusion that He had entirely forgotten them.
He would judicially vindicate them. He neither fainted
nor became weary because of their misgivings. He is *El
Olam,* "the God of the ages," and if His people will wait
upon Him in trust and confidence, they shall "renew
their strength" (i.e., go from strength to strength); they
shall "mount up with wings as eagles" (i.e., rise above
the difficulties). The secret of unfailing strength, then,
is unbroken communion with God. Whether in the enthusiasm and vitality of youth, or the waning strength of
old age, *El Olam* remains unchanged and unchanging. He
is sufficient for old age and every age.

W. S. Hottel points out that the word *Olam* is the
Hebrew synonym of the Greek *aion,* age or dispensation.
Both the English words, "eternal" and "everlasting," are
used in the Old Testament to translate the Hebrew word
olam, which is the exact Hebrew equivalent of the Greek
aion. All that *El Olam* was to the Old Testament saints,
Jesus Christ is to the Church. He is "the King of the
ages." [12] By Him the ages were made.[13] He planned and
framed the time periods. He is well acquainted with the
latter times in which we are living. He not only planned
this age, but He entered into it Himself. At the end of the

[11] Isaiah 40:1
[12] I Timothy 1:17, Greek; see also Revelation 15:3,R.V.
[13] Hebrews 1:2,R.V.

law age He appeared in order that He might die for the sins of the people. At the end of the grace age He will appear again to receive His own to Himself. And we may be certain that He will remain the unchanging and everlasting Lord in any successive ages that He has planned.

EL ROI (The God Who Sees)

The name *El Roi* appears early in the Biblical record. It was given first to God by a servant girl who became a fugitive from her master and mistress. When Abram left Ur of the Chaldees, he was given a specific promise that God was going to make him a great nation. Years passed, but no son had been born to Abram and his wife. At the suggestion of Sarai, Abram's wife, the servant girl in their home was chosen to bear a child to Abram. Now it was not uncommon for a wife, who was barren, to give her servant to her husband to bear children in the wife's name, for it was unspeakable for a married woman not to have children. In response to Sarai's suggestion, Abram obeyed, and Hagar conceived. This was the beginning of sorrow for that household, and for the whole world. It made Hagar feel superior, and she began to look with disdain upon her mistress. Such an attitude on Hagar's part brought bitter response from Sarai, so that she began to deal severely with her. When the tension between these two women became unbearable for Hagar, she packed her personal effects and fled.[1]

Alone in the wilderness, homeless and friendless, Hagar sat by a well to contemplate her plight. Where could she go? What would she do when the moment arrived to give

[1] Genesis 16:1-6

birth to her child? She had brought this upon herself through her insolent behavior toward Sarai, but now that she was alone she suddenly became aware that there was no one to whom she could turn. She looked about her, and seeing no person who might offer her some assistance, she resigned herself to her fate.

Suddenly the Angel of the LORD appeared to her, ministered wise counsel and comfort, and cheered her with a promise. Hagar was so impressed with the fact that God had seen her in her difficulty, she was inspired to call Him *El Roi,* the God who sees. "And she called the name of the LORD that spake unto her, Thou God seest me: for she said, Have I also here looked after Him that seeth me? Wherefore the well was called Beer-lahai-roi." [2] The name which Hagar gave the well is as rich in meaning as is that which she gave to God. She would always remember that place where God saw and met her in her need, where He graciously looked upon her in her affliction. *Beer-lahai-roi* means "the well of Him that liveth and seeth me." Yes, He is the God who sees, considers, has regard for, concerns Himself about our needs. A common expression in our day is "look after." To look after something is to see to it, to make certain it gets attention. *El Roi* is the God who looks after us, who sees to it that our needs are met. He is not the God of the glaring eye who goes about spying as a detective. While it is true that He sees every sinful thought, word, and deed of all men,[3] the name *El Roi* was first used by a lonely, friendless girl who, in her distress, learned that God saw her plight and treated her with grace and mercy.

[2] Genesis 16:13-14   [3] Hebrews 4:13

Years later Abraham's grandson Jacob learned that *El Roi* was looking after him. He went to Padan-aram to find a wife. When he met the girl of his dreams, and proposed marriage to her, her father consented to the marriage on the strict terms that Jacob work for him seven years. Love was not to be denied, so Jacob consented. At the end of the seven years, which seemed to Jacob but a few days,[4] the wedding took place. But after the ceremony Jacob learned that he had been tricked, for the veiled woman was not Rachel whom he loved, but her sister Leah. His new father-in-law then told him that the community ruling demanded that the elder be given in marriage before the younger. Everyone recognizes the unfairness of this, for if this really was an ironclad rule, the time for saying so would have been at the time the agreement was first made. Laban's brazen impudence really showed forth when he requested that Jacob serve him seven years more for Rachel.[5] Jacob consented, for he truly loved Rachel. Jacob remained with Laban twenty years, during which time Laban reduced his wages ten times.[6] What a miserable twenty years Jacob suffered for the love of a woman! But one day God appeared to Jacob and said, "I have seen all that Laban doeth unto thee." [7] *El Roi* had witnessed all, and He it was who was looking after Jacob. This was a comforting revelation to God's child.

The years passed. God had kept His promise to Abraham, which He confirmed to Isaac and Jacob, so that by this time the seed of Abraham had become a small na-

[4] Genesis 29:20   [5] Genesis 29:27-28   [6] Genesis 31:7
[7] Genesis 31:12

tion. But they were a captive nation held in slavery by the Egyptians. Then one day God appeared to Moses in a flame of fire. It was eighty years since Moses had been born and was hidden in the bulrushes, and all that time Israel had been in bondage. The people had cried to God, but seemingly God had not done a thing. But that day, by the burning bush, God said to Moses, "I have surely seen the affliction of My people which are in Egypt, and have heard their cry by reason of their taskmasters; for I know their sorrows; And I am come . . . to deliver them out of the hand of the Egyptians, and to bring them . . . out of that land unto a good land and a large, unto a land flowing with milk and honey." [8] *El Roi* said, "I have surely seen the affliction of My people." Never get the idea that you are passing through a hard place, and that God does not see you. He saw that heathen pregnant girl in her plight, He saw Jacob in his trial during those twenty hard years, and He saw the children of Israel through four centuries of bitter bondage. And *El Roi* sees your trial and knows your need. Whenever you are tempted to feel forsaken, remember that your heavenly Father sees.

When our Lord wrote to the church in Smyrna, He said, "I know thy works, and tribulation, and poverty." [9] He knew all about the godless slurs, the hatred, the persecution in their midst. He encouraged them by telling them that, when they would be cast into prison and put to death, He would be watching. Nothing touches the life of any Christian that *El Roi* does not see. There is a profound wealth of comfort in this thought. Whatever

[8] Exodus 3:7-8   [9] Revelation 2:9

your trial, or in whatever place you find yourself, you can say with Hagar, "Thou God seest me," because *El Roi* sees and knows all. "Behold, the eye of the LORD is upon them that fear Him, upon them that hope in His mercy; To deliver their soul from death, and to keep them alive in famine." [10] Though the night be dark, "He that keepeth thee will not slumber." [11]

I have always appreciated God's words to David when He said, "I will instruct thee and teach thee in the way which thou shalt go: I will guide thee with Mine eye." [12] This statement appears in one of the seven so-called "penitential psalms." The promise is addressed to the penitent whose transgressions are forgiven and whose sin is covered. [13] To all such *El Roi* says, "I will guide thee with Mine eye." This means that He will prevent us from pursuing the wrong path. As a good teacher carefully watches his students to observe every move, so that he can quickly correct any error, so *El Roi* watches over His own. He keeps His eye upon us to observe us lest we go astray. And if His eyes upon us keep our eyes upon Him, we will catch the mere glance which is enough to indicate the way He would have us to go.

We have pointed out how the first mention of the name *El Roi* reveals God as seeing the sorrows and trials of the distressed and suffering, rather than the God of the glaring eye who goes about spying as a detective. On the other hand, we dare not overlook the fact that *El Roi* sees sin and sham as well as sorrow and suffering. This is clearly illustrated in the Book of Jeremiah, chapter

[10] Psalm 33:18-19   [11] Psalm 121:3   [12] Psalm 32:8
[13] Psalm 32:1

thirteen. The pride of the people led them away from Jehovah into all sorts of sinful abominations.[14] This was a departure from the real purpose for which God called and saved them.[15] The weeping prophet then called upon the people to humble themselves lest God should punish them.[16] And if they should ever question why these judgments have come upon them,[17] God will say, "*I have seen* thine adulteries." [18] When *El Roi* judges His people, it is only because He has seen their iniquities, and He is "of purer eyes than to behold evil, and canst not look on iniquity." [19] Therefore if we persist in our sins, He will say, "I will cast you out of My sight," [20] and no longer will we have His watchful, guiding eye upon us. What *El Roi* sees in you and me will determine whether He becomes to us a God of comfort or of judgment.

[14] Jeremiah 13:9-10   [15] Jeremiah 13:11   [16] Jeremiah 13:15-21
[17] Jeremiah 13:22   [18] Jeremiah 13:27   [19] Habakkuk 1:13
[20] Jeremiah 7:15

JEHOVAH-JIREH
(The LORD Will Provide)

The name, *Jehovah-jireh,* while occurring only once in the entire Old Testament, is one of the best known of the compound names of the LORD. Like most of the compound names of God, this one in its first usage is associated with some historic incident. Again it is to Abraham that God revealed Himself. This is now the fourth of God's names of which the first mention is linked with a particular experience in the life of Abraham.

Yet, in the strict sense of the word, the text reveals that the name *Jehovah-jireh* is not used as one of God's titles, but rather as the name of a place. "And Abraham called the name of that place *Jehovah-jireh:* as it is said to this day, In the mount of the LORD it shall be seen." [1] Commenting on this Stevenson writes, "But the faith of the people of God has laid hold upon this name, and raised it to the level of a title of God. And truly it is so: for God is *Jehovah-jireh,* and the place so named bore testimony to what He is—and ever will be to those who put their trust in Him."

As to the literal meaning of the word *jireh,* Stone writes that it "is simply a transliteration of a Hebrew word which appears many times throughout the Scriptures and

[1] Genesis 22:14

is translated for what it means. . . . It is simply a form of the verb *to see*. . . . In the great majority of the cases where the word occurs in the Hebrew Bible, it is translated *see* or *appear*." He then goes on to explain why it is translated "provide" by so many students. "Provision, after all, is merely a compound of two Latin words meaning to see beforehand. We may learn from a dictionary that *provide* is simply the verb, and *prevision* the noun of seeing beforehand. Thus to God prevision is necessarily followed by provision, for He certainly will provide for that need which His foreseeing shows Him to exist. With Him prevision and provision are one and the same thing." Indeed the God of vision is the God of provision. Certainly it is not altogether incorrect to translate *Jehovah-jireh,* "The LORD will provide," for it is quite the same as saying, "The LORD will see to it."

The name is mentioned for the first time at the conclusion of Abraham's severest trial. "And it came to pass after these things, that God did tempt Abraham." [2] The word translated "tempt" means *to prove*. All commentators are agreed that this word is used strictly in a good sense. Elsewhere the Bible says, "Let no man say when he is tempted, I am tempted of God: for God cannot be tempted with evil, neither tempteth He any man." [3] In the case of Abraham, God was putting him to the test. This experience was to be the climax of the faith life of Abraham. This time it was the supreme test. God's first command to Abraham marked the commencement of his faith; [4] this final command from God marked the closing of the life of faith. Whenever God brings a child of His

[2] Genesis 22:1   [3] James 1:13   [4] Genesis 12:1

to a severe test, we may be certain of two things; first, the Lord never puts us to the test until we are ready for it, until He has prepared us for it; secondly, He has made preparation for our victory.

Abraham gave quick and ready response to God when he said, "Here I am." There was no rebellion, no restraint. He was wholly submissive, not knowing what it was God wanted of him. Then God said, "Take now thy son, thine only son Isaac, whom thou lovest, and get thee into the land of Moriah, and offer him there for a burnt offering upon one of the mountains which I will tell thee of." [5] Could any command have been more painful to Abraham than this? Was this to be the end of all of Abraham's hopes? God had only recently confirmed His covenant with Abraham saying, "In Isaac shall thy seed be called." [6] Now He is asking Abraham to slay Isaac. This was indeed the supreme test of Abraham's faith.

It may be well at this point to answer a difficulty which disturbs tender hearts. Is God sanctioning human sacrifice? This command from God to Abraham has brought forth a protest from those who misunderstand its meaning. Abraham was familiar with the offering of human sacrifice among pagan tribes,[7] referred to in Scripture as "the abominations of the heathen." [8] Yet it seems here, on the surface at least, that God is asking one of His children to engage in an abominable pagan practice that He Himself condemns. But before passing judgment, we must take the story as a whole, the end as well as the beginning. We dare not allow our minds to raise hypotheti-

[5] Genesis 22:2   [6] Genesis 21:12   [7] 2 Kings 3:27
[8] 2 Kings 16:3

cal questions for which there is no foundation. I do not allow myself to ask what might have happened had the story ended with Abraham slaying Isaac. The fact of the matter is that he didn't sacrifice Isaac. It was not Isaac's life that God wanted; it was Abraham's heart, and He got it. When the pagan tribesmen offered their children to the god of Moloch, it was because they feared and loved their god. The command of Jehovah was a test of Abraham's love, faith, and obedience. Did Abraham love Him as much as those heathen loved their gods? Yes, God's child had passed the test.

Though Abraham did not understand the command still he believed that God would bless the nations of the world through Isaac. The Holy Spirit provides a commentary on this incident through the writer to the Hebrews. "By faith Abraham, when he was tried, offered up Isaac: and he that had received the promises offered up his only begotten son, Of whom it was said, That in Isaac shall thy seed be called: Accounting that God was able to raise him up, even from the dead; from whence also he received him in a figure." [9] As far as Abraham was concerned, when he received the command, he considered Isaac as though he were dead. When he started out early on that morning, three days' journey from Mount Moriah, as far as he knew God meant what He said. Thus for three days he considered Isaac potentially dead. But Abraham believed and knew all the while that God was going to do something miraculous. He did not understand how God would do it, but he believed that He would

[9] Hebrews 11:17-19

raise Isaac from the dead if necessary in order to fulfill His promise.

When they arrived at the divinely appointed site, Abraham said to his servants, "Abide ye here with the ass; and I and the lad will go yonder and worship, and come again to you." [10] He never thought for a minute that he would return alone. His unshakable faith in the promise of God was sublime. To him "God was able." We have in this verse the first appearance of the word "worship" in the Bible. What a significant expression it is in this connection! It reflects the mood of Abraham's heart and gives to us all the true meaning of worship. When the heart is right in God's sight, no sacrifice is too great to offer Him, and this is the only kind of worship He accepts. With such worship God is pleased and the worshiper is assured and comforted.

When Abraham and Isaac reached the place of sacrifice, Isaac said to his father, "Behold the fire and the wood: but where is the lamb for a burnt offering?" [11] As the question stabbed Abraham's heart, it no doubt brought him to the very height of his trial. He loved his son, for Isaac was his own flesh and blood, but he considered him solely as the possession of God. Abraham was merely God's steward, guarding for his Master a sacred trust, which he was ready to give back to Him at any moment. The Lord testified to Abraham, "I know that thou fearest God, seeing thou hast not withheld thy son, thine only son from Me." [12] Isaac was God's property, therefore He had a right to claim His own possession at any time.

[10] Genesis 22:5   [11] Genesis 22:7   [12] Genesis 22:12

Abraham then gave to Isaac the remarkable answer of faith. He said, "My son, God will provide *Himself* a lamb." [13] In that statement he uttered, perhaps unknowingly in its fullest meaning, one of the clearest Old Testament prophecies of God's great plan of redemption. God would provide *Himself* in the Person of His Son. His redeemed ones would make up "the church of God, which He . . . purchased with His own blood." [14] Christ is called "the Lamb of God, which taketh away the sin of the world," [15] but we cannot fully understand this statement until we apprehend the fact that "God was in Christ, reconciling the world unto Himself." [16] It was this mighty truth which Abraham saw. The gospel is the message of God's providing a sacrifice, but a substitute of mere human design must fail. God must provide Himself a Lamb, else there is no forgiveness of sins. Abraham understood the meaning of these things, for we hear Jesus say, "Your father Abraham rejoiced to see My day: and he saw it, and was glad." [17]

The rest of the story is known to us all. After the angel of the LORD called to Abraham out of Heaven to prevent him from slaying Isaac, Abraham discovered a ram caught in a thicket by its horns. God was telling him to slay the ram and let Isaac live. Then we read the great text in which *Jehovah-jireh* appears. "And Abraham called the name of that place Jehovah-jireh: as it is said to this day, In the mount of the LORD it shall be seen." [18] Notice Abraham did not say that Jehovah has provided, nor that Jehovah does now provide, but Jehovah will

---

[13] Genesis 22:8　　[14] Acts 20:28　　[15] John 1:29
[16] 2 Corinthians 5:19　　[17] John 8:56　　[18] Genesis 22:14

provide. "In the mount of the LORD *it shall be seen.*"
When Abraham said this, the fulfillment of it all was
still in the future. But now *Jehovah-jireh* is a precious
name for God, to all who have been saved through
Christ's atoning work at Calvary. Abraham said, "In the
mount of the LORD, He shall see to it." Now we can say,
"In the mount of the LORD, He has seen to it." Hallelujah,
the Lord has provided!

But is there any application of the meaning of this
name in our everyday Christian experience? Yes, there
is! *Jehovah-jireh,* who provided the sacrifice for Abraham
and subsequently for the world, will certainly provide
other things. "He that spared not His own Son, but delivered Him up for us all, how shall He not with Him also
freely give us all things?" [19] But beware lest you neglect
the two requirements necessary before Abraham could
prove *Jehovah-jireh.* They are implicit obedience to the
Word of God and complete abandonment to the will of
God. Abraham could step out on faith and prove God
because he did not try to save himself nor his son. All
had been surrendered to the Lord.

The New Testament text for *Jehovah-jireh* is found in
the Epistle to the Philippians: "But my God shall supply
all your need according to His riches in glory by Christ
Jesus." [20] But such provision is associated with obedience
and sacrifice. The promise in Philippians 4:19 was given
to a people whose lives were marked by those same characteristics typical of Abraham. They had surrendered all
to God, "an odour of a sweet smell, a sacrifice acceptable,
wellpleasing to God." [21] The only other place in the New

[19] Romans 8:32   [20] Philippians 4:19   [21] Philippians 4:18

Testament where the sacrifice of a sweet smell is mentioned is in the Epistle to the Ephesians. There it speaks of Christ's voluntary death as "an offering and a sacrifice to God for a sweetsmelling savour." [22] The sacrificial giving of the Philippians is linked by the Holy Spirit to Christ's sacrificial giving of Himself on the cross.

Complete obedience to God will cost you everything. But whatever it costs, you can count on God to give you manyfold in return. If you compromise and fail to meet His requirements, you cannot expect Him to provide. Live in the total reality of *Jehovah-jireh* and you never will need to fear or worry. If you would know *Jehovah-jireh,* the Lord your Provider, you must let Him have your Isaac. You must come to Mount Moriah, to Calvary, and there in absolute surrender lay all before Him.

[22] Ephesians 5:2

JEHOVAH-NISSI
(The LORD My Banner)

The journey of the children of Israel from Egypt to Canaan is a remarkably fascinating story. It commenced with their flight southward toward the Red Sea. They were seemingly caught between the wilderness on the one side and the Red Sea on the other, with Pharaoh's hosts pursuing them from behind. But they were exactly where God wanted them to be. He had sent them in that direction. Israel's predicament was actually God's providence. Someone has said that man's extremity is God's opportunity. It must be so, for when Moses lifted aloft the rod of God, then Jehovah divided the waters of the sea so that Israel crossed safely on dry ground.[1] The Lord had demonstrated His power in behalf of His children. Moses had assured, "The LORD shall fight for you." [2]

They continued on to Marah, the place where the water was bitter. Again it was a testing time for the people, and again they were exactly where God wanted them. A bitter trial is not necessarily an indication that we are not where God wants us to be. At Marah the LORD made the bitter waters sweet, and there He revealed Himself as Jehovah-Rapha, the LORD that healeth.[3] The Marah ex-

[1] Exodus 14:19-25   [2] Exodus 14:14   [3] Exodus 15:26

197

perience was just one more opportunity for God to prove Himself to His people.

The children of Israel continued their journey from Marah to Elim. It was in Elim that they murmured against Moses and Aaron because of a food shortage. There they expressed their desire to return to the flesh pots in Egypt.[4] But again they were in the place where God wanted them, for at Elim He fed them with the manna sent down from Heaven.[5] Once more their extremity was God's opportunity.

From Elim they came to Rephidim where there was no water, and again the people complained against Moses, charging him with trying to kill them with thirst.[6] But in answer to Moses' prayer, the LORD performed a miracle by sending forth water from the rock. In their doubting, they said, "Is the LORD among us, or not?"[7] But there God proved that He had not forsaken His people. Many centuries later, Paul recorded this very incident, and said, "That Rock was Christ."[8] He had not forsaken them. They doubted Him repeatedly, but He never failed to meet their need.

Then the incident took place which occasioned God's revelation of Himself as *Jehovah-Nissi*. When it seemed to Israel that all their troubles were over, "Then came Amalek, and fought with Israel in Rephidim."[9] Don't miss the significance of the word "then." It is a time word. After God brought them safely across the Red Sea, and made bitter waters sweet, and opened the rock to give

---

[4] Exodus 16:1-3
[5] Exodus 16:4,15
[6] Exodus 17:1-3
[7] Exodus 17:7
[8] 1 Corinthians 10:4
[9] Exodus 17:8

them refreshing streams in the desert, and fed them manna, thereby leaving them with nothing about which to complain, "*then* came Amalek."

We learn from earlier records that Amalek was a grandson of Esau,[10] the man after the flesh who sold his birthright to Jacob for bread and pottage.[11] The Amalekites were a wild, marauding tribe, living off the spoils they captured from caravans. They were "the first of the nations" to oppose Israel after God's people left Egypt.[12] No doubt the Amalekites thought the Israelites would be easy prey, for though they were two million strong, the fighting forces were not many, nor were they too well equipped for war. Then, too, there were hundreds of thousands of women and children to protect. But they were being attacked, so they had to fight or die.

Moses gave the instructions for the battle. Joshua was to lead his chosen men in the conflict, while Moses took the rod of God and went to the top of the hill to pray, with Aaron and Hur as his companions. The Amalekites thought, no doubt, that the Israelites would be no match for them, inasmuch as they were inexperienced in warfare and physically tired from their journey. But the plan of Moses to have Joshua and his men fight, while he, Aaron, and Hur prayed, was to produce results that Amalek did not anticipate. The battle was a prolonged and bitter one, its fortunes swaying now in favor of Israel, then in favor of Amalek. All day long the successes changed from the one to the other, until Moses observed that the tide of battle turned in Israel's favor

---

[10] Genesis 36:12   [11] Genesis 25:29-34   [12] Numbers 24:20

when his hands were raised in prayer as he held the rod of God.[13] But Moses was unable to maintain his position in prayer. "Moses' hands were heavy," so Aaron and Hur put a stone under him and supported him, one on either side. And then God gave the victory. "Joshua discomfited Amalek and his people with the edge of the sword." [14]

"And the LORD said unto Moses, Write this for a memorial in a book, and rehearse it in the ears of Joshua: for I will utterly put out the remembrance of Amalek from under heaven." [15] This is the first time God is said to have commanded anyone to write. But He wanted the record straight; retold, the incident would most likely become garbled. But why should God tell Moses to rehearse it to Joshua? Joshua was the hero in the eyes of the people; his name was on every lip. However, God wanted it to be clear to all, including Joshua, that victory depended upon Himself. If the celebration were left to the people, they would have had a bronze statue made of Joshua and placed in the center of the camp. They might even have worshiped Joshua as the victorious hero.

Instead, "Moses built an altar, and called the name of it *Jehovah-Nissi*." [16] Joshua's name did not so much as appear on the memorial. The word *nissi* means "banner," "emblem," "war flag." It is the emblem of victory which gleams after the battle is fought and won. *Jehovah-Nissi* means "the LORD is my Banner." This name of God is associated with the conflicts of His people. It is a constant reminder to them that all power is with Him and all strength comes from Him. It was *Jehovah-Nissi* who

[13] Exodus 17:11 [14] Exodus 17:12-13 [15] Exodus 17:14
[16] Exodus 17:15

won the battle. It was under His banner they were led
to victory. They needed to know *Jehovah-Nissi,* because
they were not finished with Amalek. Each succeeding generation was going to have its conflict with this enemy.[17]
Israel need not think for one moment that the victory at
Rephidim meant the end of Amalek. They would meet
him again, and only as they did so in the strength of
Jehovah-Nissi could they be assured of victory in the
future.

But the altar which had been erected as a memorial to
Jehovah-Nissi was soon forgotten. The people were slow
to learn that God is indispensable in the battles of life.
After about one year at Sinai, Israel came to the edge
of the Promised Land. Spies were sent into the land, and
when they returned, there were divided opinions in their
reports. Because of the evil report of the majority, God
announced that all those twenty years old and upward
would die in the wilderness,[18] save Joshua and Caleb.
However, early the next morning the people insisted upon
going into the land. Moses warned them that the Amalekites were there and that Israel would be defeated. "But
they presumed to go up. . . . Then the Amalekites came
down . . . and smote them, and discomfited them, even
unto Hormah." [19] They *presumed.* They said, "We defeated them a year ago, and we can do it again." But no
matter how hard they fought, they could not conquer the
Amalekites this time. They were helpless before the
enemy, simply because they were fighting in their own
strength. *Jehovah-Nissi* was not with them. The people
had not learned an important lesson, namely, spiritual

[17] Exodus 17:16   [18] Numbers 14:26-38   [19] Numbers 14:44-45

battles cannot be won with worldly weapons nor in human strength.

It was sometime after Israel was defeated by Amalek that God warned His people never to make peace with the Amalekites. He said, "Remember what Amalek did unto thee by the way, when ye were come forth out of Egypt; How he met thee by the way, and smote the hindmost of thee, even all that were feeble behind thee, when thou wast faint and weary; and he feared not God. Therefore it shall be, when the LORD thy God hath given thee rest from all thine enemies round about, in the land which the LORD thy God hath given thee for an inheritance to possess it, that thou shalt blot out the remembrance of Amalek from under heaven; thou shalt not forget it." [20] Here God is telling them they must never compromise with Amalek, but rather fight against him until he is utterly defeated.

As soon as the kingdom was established, God repeated this order to Saul.[21] Because the Amalekites were a godless and immoral people, they had to be destroyed for the sake of humanity. But Saul failed to carry out God's orders completely, for while he smote the Amalekites, he spared Agag their king.[22] In his pride he brought Agag back from the battle alive to show him off as a trophy of the victory. Because of this sin, God took the kingdom from him,[23] and eventually Saul was slain by an Amalekite.[24] Amalek is no match for *Jehovah-Nissi*. Nor was an Israelite a match for an Amalekite without *Jehovah-Nissi*.

[20] Deuteronomy 25:17-19   [21] 1 Samuel 15:1-3
[22] 1 Samuel 15:7-8   [23] 1 Samuel 15:17-23   [24] 2 Samuel 1:2-8

Now all that we have said thus far finds application in the life of the Christian. Paul wrote, "Now these things were our examples, to the intent we should not lust after evil things, as they also lusted." [25] It was pointed out that Amalek was a grandson of Esau, and Esau was a man without any spiritual insight, who lived after the lust of the flesh, for the satisfaction of earthly desires. He had no appreciation of spiritual values. The New Testament calls him a "profane person." [26] The profane character of Esau manifested itself in treating with contempt his holy privileges. He treated sacred things lightly in order that he might gratify the flesh. So we are not to be surprised at the family's naming a son Amalek. In the home there was no regard for spiritual and eternal values. So Amalek becomes a type of the flesh that is in us and that seeks to gratify its selfish and worldly desires. We need to know *Jehovah-Nissi,* because "the flesh lusteth against the Spirit, and the Spirit against the flesh." [27] There is warfare going on between the Holy Spirit and Amalek, the old carnal nature. Like Israel, we shall have war with Amalek from generation to generation.

God would have His people remember that this old man in the flesh attacks suddenly where we are weakest. He said, "Remember what Amalek did unto thee by the way, when ye were come forth out of Egypt; How he met thee by the way, and smote the hindmost of thee, even all that were feeble behind thee, when thou wast faint and weary; and he feared not God." [28] The flesh does not change. God Himself makes no attempt to im-

---

[25] 1 Corinthians 10:6   [26] Hebrews 12:16   [27] Galatians 5:17
[28] Deuteronomy 25:17-18

prove it. Paul wrote by inspiration: "For I know that in me (that is, in my flesh,) dwelleth no good thing." [29] Beware of Amalek! He will attack you where you are weakest and when you are the least prepared for him. He is your enemy. You will never be able to convert him. Jesus said, "That which is born of the flesh is flesh." [30] You can never change flesh into spirit. When God saved you He gave you a new life; He did not change the old life in you. Thus the temptation to do wrong is always with the Christian. The "old man" and the "new man" are engaged in conflict.[31]

But *Jehovah-Nissi* is associated with the warfare of His people. If, like Moses, we take the battle to Him in prayer, He will lead to victory. Isaiah wrote, "When the enemy shall come in like a flood, the Spirit of the Lord shall lift up a standard against him." [32] The word "standard" is the Hebrew word *nes* from which *nissi* is derived. And the Standard is Christ Himself. Jesus, the Captain of our salvation, is *Jehovah-Nissi*. Of Him the prophet wrote, "And in that day there shall be a root of Jesse, which shall stand for an ensign [*nes*] of the people." [33] As we look to Him moment by moment, we are assured of victory. "In all these things we are more than conquerors through Him that loved us." [34] "Thanks be to God, which giveth us the victory through our Lord Jesus Christ," [35] and "always causeth us to triumph in Christ." [36]

You, too, can have the victory in *Jehovah-Nissi!*

[29] Romans 7:18　　　　[30] John 3:6　　　　　　[31] Ephesians 4:22-24
[32] Isaiah 59:19　　　　[33] Isaiah 11:10　　　　　[34] Romans 8:37
[35] 1 Corinthians 15:57　[36] 2 Corinthians 2:14

JEHOVAH-TSIDKENU
(The LORD Our Righteousness)

Among the essential moral attributes of God is His
righteousness or justice. It is that fundamental phase of
the holiness of God which consistently shows in all His
dealings with His creatures. Righteousness belongs to
God; it is natural and necessary to Him.

The name *Jehovah-Tsidkenu* means "THE LORD
OUR RIGHTEOUSNESS." [1] It appears in a prophecy
of Jeremiah at a time when the kingdom of Judah was
declining toward a total collapse. With the death of
Josiah, the last of the godly kings, Judah's day of grace
had come to an end. Josiah's three sons reigned in succession, none of them measuring up to their father in
godliness. The kingdom had been corrupted. Jeremiah 22
contains the record of God's pronouncement of judgment
through His servant Jeremiah. Like Nathan who preceded him, the prophet went to the royal palace and said,
"Hear the word of the LORD, O king of Judah." [2] He predicted judgment upon the land and its leaders, and then
the chapter concludes with the solemn pronouncement
against Coniah, that "no man of his seed shall prosper,
sitting upon the throne of David, and ruling any more in
Judah." [3]

[1] Jeremiah 23:6   [2] Jeremiah 22:2   [3] Jeremiah 22:30

Chapter twenty-three opens with a review of the failure of those kings whom God calls pastors or shepherds. And then He says, "Behold, the days come, saith the LORD, that I will raise unto David a righteous Branch, and a King shall reign and prosper, and shall execute judgment and justice in the earth. In His days Judah shall be saved, and Israel shall dwell safely: and this is His name whereby He shall be called, THE LORD OUR RIGHT-EOUSNESS." [4] In contrast to those unrighteous kings, God is one day going to put on the throne His righteous King, and He shall be known by the name *Jehovah-Tsidkenu*, the LORD our righteousness.

God always has been known for His righteousness and justice. Wicked Pharaoh testified, "The LORD is righteous." [5] The Psalmist said, "Righteousness and judgment are the habitation of His throne." [6] "The LORD is righteous." [7] "Thy righteousness is an everlasting righteousness." [8] "He is my Rock, and there is no unrighteousness in Him." [9] Paul wrote, "What shall we say then? Is there unrighteousness with God? God forbid." [10] Indeed, "The LORD is righteous in all His ways." [11] Even after judgment had come upon God's people, they say of Him, "Howbeit Thou art just in all that is brought upon us; for Thou hast done right, but we have done wickedly." [12] Our Lord prayed, "O righteous Father, the world hath not known Thee: but I have known Thee, and these have known that Thou hast sent Me" (John 17:25). He is called "the righteous Judge," [13] and "Shall not the Judge

---

[4] Jeremiah 23:5-6
[5] Exodus 9:27
[6] Psalm 97:2
[7] Psalm 129:4
[8] Psalm 119:142
[9] Psalm 92:15
[10] Romans 9:14
[11] Psalm 145:17
[12] Nehemiah 9:33
[13] 2 Timothy 4:8

of all the earth do right?"[14] Even the angels testify, "Thou art righteous, O Lord."[15]

One can hardly examine those passages which deal with God's righteousness without seeing in bold contrast man's unrighteousness. We all need to be reminded of the fact that the Lord's righteousness is not found in ourselves and that all men without exception naturally stand in need of righteousness before God. When every corner of the universe has been searched, the verdict is, "There is none righteous, no, not one."[16] We cannot deny the universal unrighteousness of man, and because man is unrighteous, he cannot be justified on the ground of his own righteousness in the sight of God. Most people are not willing to accept this verdict which God has rendered, but we must first of all accept it before the heart is prepared to receive the righteousness of God. As long as a man believes that there is some righteousness within his heart by nature, he will cling to that and never turn to the Lord Jesus Christ to trust Him alone.

Before the sixteenth century, our word righteousness was written "rightwise," and it meant "one who is as he ought to be." When Adam came from the hand of God, he was as he ought to be and there was no sin in him. But he departed from God when he chose to follow his own will, and from that very second that he fell through sin he was no longer what he ought to be. He was not "rightwise" but he became unrighteous. The stream issued forth from God pure and clean, but man polluted it. Spoiled in himself, he has spoiled all of his posterity.[17] Now, in

[14] Genesis 18:25   [15] Revelation 16:5   [16] Romans 3:10
[17] Romans 5:12

the sight of God only One is righteous, the Lord Jesus Christ. He only is what He ought to be, thus of Him only could the Father say, "This is My beloved Son, in whom I am well pleased." [18] Keep in mind the fact that we dare not view ourselves by the relative standards of human beings, for by such standards we might see many righteous people. The picture in Romans 3:10 is viewed by the absolute and impeccable standard of God's righteousness, and when we view ourselves alongside of Jesus Christ, we know that we are unrighteous.

We look at ourselves and what can we say? "We are all as an unclean thing, and all our righteousnesses are as filthy rags; and we all do fade as a leaf; and our iniquities, like the wind, have taken us away." [19] We consider our thoughts and words and deeds, the very best of them, and we see ourselves as those lepers who had to cry "unclean." [20] Our lives are as the children of Israel of whom it is written, "They defiled it by their own way and by their doings: their way was before Me as the uncleanness of a removed woman." [21]

Isaiah uses the plural form, "righteousnesses," which means that the pollution extended to their thought life as well as to their deeds. Israel's remnant was taking their rightful place in God's presence. There is no self-justification. It is to this very place that each of us must come before we can know *Jehovah-Tsidkenu,* for He cannot overlook the unrighteousness in us. Paul had to regard the righteousness of the law as refuse in order to gain Christ.[22] Then he wrote of those persons who, "being

---

[18] Matthew 3:17   [19] Isaiah 64:6   [20] Leviticus 13:45
[21] Ezekiel 36:17   [22] Philippians 3:6-9

ignorant of God's righteousness, and going about to establish their own righteousness, have not submitted themselves unto the righteousness of God." [23] If only they had known that "their own righteousness" was the substitution of human effort for God's way of salvation, and that it was not acceptable with God, they might have subjected themselves to God's righteousness by laying aside all self-effort.

Now, the righteousness that God requires of His children is not a mere trait of character; it is the righteousness of God Himself. Jesus said, "Blessed are they which do hunger and thirst after righteousness: for they shall be filled." [24] The righteousness for which we hunger and thirst is His righteousness. But it is not until we see the rottenness of our own righteousness on the one hand, and the righteousness of God on the other, that we will hunger and thirst after His righteousness.

The truth that is set before us in Jeremiah's text, as well as in the New Testament, is that *Jehovah-Tsidkenu* is our Lord Jesus Christ and that righteousness before God can be found only in Him. Righteousness for man is a divine provision.

> No hope can on the law be built
>   Of justifying grace;
> The law that shows the sinner's guilt
>   Condemns him to his face.

If we are to be justified, we must find righteousness, not in ourselves, but in another, namely, in Christ. Peter

[23] Romans 10:3   [24] Matthew 5:6

and Stephen and Paul preached Christ as "the Just (or righteous) One." [25] He is the "righteous Branch." [26] Paul wrote, "But of Him are ye in Christ Jesus, who of God is made unto us . . . righteousness." [27] No man outside of Christ has the quality of being right, that is, in himself he is not what he ought to be. But through faith in Christ a believer becomes what God requires him to be, and he stands before God in Christ in a perfect, unchallenged righteousness. "For He [the Father] hath made Him [Christ] to be sin for us, who knew no sin; that we might be made the righteousness of God in Him." [28] Do you see what God has done for our justification? Being without sin and free from sin, Christ took the place of sinners and was made a sin offering for us, that is, in our stead. Notice the antithesis between "sin" and "righteousness."

Our sins were imputed to Christ, and God imputes righteousness to us. Thus righteousness is what we are made, or become, in Christ. How much of our sinfulness was He made? All of it! Therefore God freely imputes righteousness to us, "Because Christ also suffered for sins once, the righteous for the unrighteous, that He might bring us to God." [29]

While it is true that righteousness is God's free gift to man, the divine bestowal of this gift to man makes a practical change in the life of the believer. If we are made righteous, then we are as we ought to be: "Being then made free from sin, ye became the servants of right-

---

[25] Acts 3:14; 7:52; 22:14   [26] Jeremiah 23:5
[27] I Corinthians 1:30   [28] 2 Corinthians 5:21   [29] I Peter 3:18,R.V.

eousness." [30] We have "put on the new man, which after God is created in righteousness and true holiness." [31] "Who His own self bare our sins in His own body on the tree, that we, being dead to sins, should live unto righteousness: by whose stripes ye were healed." [32]

Until the world sees the fulfillment of Jeremiah's prophecy in the appearance of *Jehovah-Tsidkenu,* let us, His righteous ones, show forth His praises.

I once was a stranger to grace and to God;
  I knew not my danger, and felt not my load;
Though friends spoke in rapture of Christ on the tree,
  "Jehovah Tsidkenu" was nothing to me.

Like tears from the daughters of Zion that roll,
  I wept when the waters went over His soul,
Yet though not that my sins had nailed to the tree
  "Jehovah Tsidkenu"—'twas nothing to me.

When free grace awoke me, by light from on high,
  Then legal fears shook me, I trembled to die:
No refuge, no safety, in self could I see;
  "Jehovah Tsidkenu" my Saviour must be.

My terrors all vanished before the sweet name;
  My guilty fears banished, with boldness I came
To drink at the fountain, life-giving and free:
  "Jehovah Tsidkenu" was all things to me.

"Jehovah Tsidkenu!" My treasure and boast;
"Jehovah Tsidkenu!" I ne'er can be lost;
In Thee I shall conquer by flood and by field—
My Cable, my Anchor, my Breastplate and Shield!

[30] Romans 6:18   [31] Ephesians 4:24   [32] I Peter 2:24

E'en treading the valley, the shadow of death,
This watchword shall rally my faltering breath;
For, when from life's fever my God sets me free,
"Jehovah Tsidkenu" my death-song shall be.

—Robert M. McCheyne

JEHOVAH-RA-AH
(The LORD My Shepherd)

In our earlier studies we learned that the name *Jehovah*, translated in the Authorized Version *God* some 300 times, and *Lord* about 6,000 times, means the eternal self-existent One. Jehovah always was, He is, and He always will be. *Jehovah* is the great I AM of whom the heavenly host sang, "Holy, holy, holy, Lord God Almighty, which was, and is, and is to come." [1] He is "Jesus Christ the same yesterday, and to day, and for ever." [2] We learned further that another important significance attached to this name is what *Jehovah* becomes to His people in order to meet their needs.

The word Ra-ah, in its primary meaning, conveys the idea of tending, pasturing, looking after, shepherding, leading, feeding. Thus the name *Jehovah-Ra-ah* means, "Jehovah my Shepherd." As a shepherd leads and feeds his flock, looking after them with a watchful eye, so the Lord tends His own children. We are all His creation, but not until we become His children by means of the regenerating work of the Holy Spirit, are we aware of how utterly dependent we are upon Him for every need. Thus it has been that this name, *The LORD my Shep-*

[1] Revelation 4:8   [2] Hebrews 13:8

herd, has brought more comfort to more saints than any of the other names of God.

The name *Jehovah-Ra-ah,* the LORD my Shepherd, is best known as it appears in the most exquisite of all compositions, the oft tried and treasured Twenty-Third Psalm. This immortal ode begins with the words, "The LORD is my shepherd." [3] Now notice two things. First, the word "LORD" is here printed in capitals, which indicates that the Hebrew word is *Jehovah.* Secondly, the copula "is" appears in the italicized letters, indicating that it does not appear in the original but that it was inserted by the translators. Bible students disagree as to whether or not this insertion should have been made. Without it the words would read, "JEHOVAH, my shepherd!" Here is an exclamation denoting a delightful discovery. It is that discovery which comes to each believer who has received the Lord Jesus Christ as his personal Saviour. After we have looked into the face of the Redeemer and exclaimed, "Jesus, my Saviour!" we learn that He is also our Shepherd who looks after us, and then we exclaim, "Jesus, my Shepherd!"

The name is used in God's relationship to Israel as a nation. Moses sensed that Israel needed someone to lead them and do for them what a shepherd would do for his sheep, and so he prayed, "Let the LORD, the God of the spirits of all flesh, set a man over the congregation, Which may go out before them, and which may go in before them, and which may lead them out, and which may bring them in; that the congregation of the LORD be not as sheep which have no shepherd." [4] The illustra-

[3] Psalm 23:1   [4] Numbers 27:16-17

tion of the shepherd was well known to the Old Testament saints. The history of Joseph as a young man opens with the words, "Joseph, being seventeen years old, was feeding the flock with his brethren." [5] Years later in Egypt, Joseph's brethren, answering Pharaoh's inquiry, said, "Thy servants are shepherds. . . . thy servants have no pasture for their flocks." [6] Therefore when the analogy of the shepherd and his sheep is used in the sacred writings to show the relationship between God and His people, it is a familiar one.

The Psalmist wrote of Jehovah, "He chose David also His servant, and took him from the sheepfolds: From following the ewes great with young He brought him to feed Jacob His people, and Israel His inheritance. So he fed them according to the integrity of his heart; and guided them by the skilfulness of his hands." [7] "Give ear, O Shepherd of Israel, Thou that leadest Joseph like a flock; Thou that dwellest between the cherubims, shine forth." [8] "He shall feed His flock like a shepherd: He shall gather the lambs with His arm, and carry them in His bosom, and shall gently lead those that are with young." [9] The imagery is portrayed by Isaiah even further when he says, "All we like sheep have gone astray; we have turned every one to his own way." [10] As to Israel's future, Jeremiah wrote, "Hear the word of the LORD, O ye nations, and declare it in the isles afar off, and say, He that scattered Israel will gather him, and keep him, as a shepherd doth his flock." [11] Ezekiel added to this, "And I will set up one shepherd over them, and he shall feed

[5] Genesis 37:2
[6] Genesis 47:3-4
[7] Psalm 78:70-72
[8] Psalm 80:1
[9] Isaiah 40:11
[10] Isaiah 53:6
[11] Jeremiah 31:10

them, even My servant David; he shall feed them, and he shall be their shepherd." [12] The prophet describes in greater detail the future manifestation of the Shepherd-sheep relationship in Ezekiel 34:11-19. All Israel could say at one time, "We are His people, and the sheep of His pasture," [13] but because the people went astray, the Prophet Micaiah said to the king, "I saw all Israel scattered upon the hills, as sheep that have not a shepherd." [14] The prophet's vision came to pass, for today Israel's plight is that of sheep without their Shepherd.

Arthur W. Pink, in his *Exposition of the Gospel of John*, has an interesting paragraph. He wrote, "So far as we have been able to trace, there are five individual shepherds who pointed to Christ, and each of them supplies some distinctive line in the typical picture. First, *Abel*, for in Genesis 4:2 we are told that 'Abel was a keeper of sheep.' The distinctive aspect of typical truth which he exemplifies is *the death* of the Shepherd—slain by wicked hands, by his brother according to the flesh. The *second* is *Jacob*, and a prominent thing in connection with him as a shepherd is his care for the sheep—see Genesis 30:31; 38-40; and note particularly 33:13-14. The *third* is *Joseph:* the very first thing recorded in Scripture about this favorite son of Jacob is that he fed the flock.[15] The *fourth* is *Moses*. Three things are told us about him: he *watered, protected,* and *guided* the sheep: 'Now the priest of Midian had seven daughters: and they came and drew water, and filled the troughs to water their father's flock. And the shepherds came and

[12] Ezekiel 34:23   [13] Psalm 100:3   [14] 1 Kings 22:17
[15] Genesis 37:2

drove them away: but Moses stood up and helped them, and *watered* their flock. . . . Now Moses *kept* the flock of Jethro his father in law, the priest of Midian: and he *led* the flock to the backside of the desert, and came to the mountain of God, even to Horeb.'[16] The *fifth* is *David,* and he is presented as *jeopardizing his life* for the sheep: 'And David said unto Saul, Thy servant kept his father's sheep, and there came a lion, and a bear, and took a lamb out of the flock: And I went out after him, and smote him, and delivered it out of his mouth: and when he arose against me, I caught him by his beard, and smote him, and slew him. Thy servant slew . . . the lion and the bear.'[17] There is one other individual 'shepherd' referred to in the Old Testament and that is 'the idol shepherd,'[18] and he is the Antichrist—how significant that *he* is the *sixth!* The only other individual 'shepherd' mentioned is the Lord Jesus, and He is *the seventh!* Seven is the number of perfection, and we do not reach perfection till we come to Christ, the Good Shepherd!"

The practical application of the meaning of this name is to each individual who will trust the divine Shepherd, *Jehovah-Ra-ah*. In the New Testament this figure of speech was often in the mind and vocabulary of our Lord Jesus Christ. Matthew wrote of Him, "But when He saw the multitudes, He was moved with compassion on them, because they fainted, and were scattered abroad, as sheep having no shepherd."[19] The disciples saw a great crowd of people but the Good Shepherd, with His Shepherd-heart, saw a flock of poor, lost helpless sheep. And

---

[16] Exodus 2:16; 3:1   [17] 1 Samuel 17:34-36   [18] Zechariah 11:16-17
[19] Matthew 9:36

with equal compassion, and the same Shepherd-heart, He sees the individual.[20] When our Lord comes again, and before Him shall be gathered all nations, "He shall separate them one from another, as a shepherd divideth his sheep from the goats." [21]

Not only did our Lord use this figure of speech often in His teaching ministry, but He Himself is *Jehovah-Ra-ah*. On one occasion He said, "I am the good shepherd: the good shepherd giveth His life for the sheep." [22] Those who heard Him could not have mistaken His meaning. Nor can we! Again and again Christ assumed the divine title JEHOVAH, the great I AM of Exodus 3:14. He is the eternal One,[23] having life in Himself,[24] who said, "Before Abraham was, I am." [25] In the Gospel according to John alone there are seven compound names of Jehovah assumed by Christ.[26]

As the Good Shepherd He dies for the sheep. Do not miss the full force of our Lord's words, *"Jehovah-Ra-ah* giveth His life for the sheep." His death at Calvary was indeed the death of Deity. He said, "I lay down My life for the sheep. . . . I and My Father are one." [27] On the cross, "God was in Christ, reconciling the world unto Himself." [28] His flock make up "the church of God, which He hath purchased with His own blood." [29] The death of the Good Shepherd for sinners was the death of *Jehovah-Ra-ah*. In the Person of Christ we have the merging of

[20] Matthew 12:10-13; 18:10-14   [21] Matthew 25:31-32
[22] John 10:11   [23] John 1:1   [24] John 5:26
[25] John 8:58
[26] John 6:35; 8:12; 10:9; 10:11; 11:25; 14:6; 15:1
[27] John 10:15,30   [28] 2 Corinthians 5:19   [29] Acts 20:28

deity and humanity, and there can be no attempt to divide or separate between the two in the one Being. The secret of the Incarnation is that "God was manifest in the flesh." [30] When Thomas saw the great Shepherd after the Resurrection, he exclaimed, "My Lord and my God." [31] Christ's words, "I am the good shepherd" are a clear affirmation of His absolute deity. To know the Good Shepherd personally is to know Jehovah as one's own Redeemer and Provider.

Look now at a second great text in which our Lord is seen as the Shepherd. "Now the God of peace, that brought again from the dead our Lord Jesus, that great shepherd of the sheep, through the blood of the everlasting covenant, Make you perfect in every good work to do His will, working in you that which is wellpleasing in His sight, through Jesus Christ; to whom be glory for ever and ever. Amen." [32] Note the language here. It is not "a" great shepherd, nor "the" great shepherd, but *"that"* Great Shepherd. The Holy Spirit has in mind a particular and familiar Shepherd who was known to all those acquainted with the Old Testament. He is the Shepherd of the "sheep," not of the wolves[33] or the goats.[34] The "Great Shepherd" of the sheep calls attention to the fact that *Jehovah-Ra-ah* is our *"great* high priest," [35] who is touched with the infirmities of His sheep. He is "great" (or mighty) in the dignity of His Person and in the display of His Power. Exalted at the Father's right hand He is now the Great Shepherd of His "little flock," [36] guid-

---

[30] 1 Timothy 3:16   [31] John 20:28   [32] Hebrews 13:20-21
[33] Luke 10:3   [34] Matthew 25:31-32   [35] Hebrews 4:14
[36] Luke 12:32

ing them through the wilderness of this world. The Good Shepherd who died and shed His blood is now the Great Shepherd living in Heaven, interceding for us.[37] The trusting child of God can look into His blessed face and exclaim, "Jehovah, my Shepherd."

To the best of my knowledge Hebrews 13:20-21 contains the only direct reference to Christ's Resurrection in the entire Epistle to the Hebrews. Here we are given the secret to a victorious Christian life. The text reminds us that "that great Shepherd" can "make you perfect." Here, to make perfect means to adjust, to set right. His work as the "good Shepherd" *for* us finds a greater fulfillment in His work as the "great Shepherd" *in* us. The Christian's heart is the Great Shepherd's workshop where He delights to work in us that which is well-pleasing in His sight. Saved persons need every disorder in their souls set right in order to be divinely fitted to do every good work well-pleasing in His eyes. Many of us have had the same experience that Paul had when he said, "For to *will* is present with me; but how to *perform* that which is good I find not." [38] Well, here is good news for each of us. The Good Shepherd who died for us is living as our Great Shepherd to enable and empower us that we "might walk worthy of the Lord unto all pleasing." [39]

A third great text in which our Lord is set forth in the role of the Shepherd comes from the inspired pen of Peter. "And when the chief Shepherd shall appear, ye shall receive a crown of glory that fadeth not away." [40] I believe this to be the only place in the New Testament

[37] Hebrews 7:25   [38] Romans 7:18   [39] Colossians 1:10
[40] 1 Peter 5:4

where this word "chief" (Greek, *archipoimen*) is found. The Holy Spirit coined this word especially for the Lord Jesus Christ. There is none His equal. Peter was never called the Chief Shepherd, nor was any pope. This pre-eminent title belongs to Christ alone. Men have presumed to themselves the exalted position that is Christ's, but when He comes again He will be manifested as the Chief Shepherd.

Here is an interesting observation. The word "feed" in 1 Peter 5:2 (Greek, *poimaino*) means to act as a shepherd. Peter is saying to the elders, "*Shepherd* the flock of God which is among you." The Lord not only shepherds His flock, but He calls us into a blessed partnership with Himself whereby we are privileged to share with Him in the shepherding work. And how greatly we are needed in this work! Our Lord warned, "Beware of false prophets, which come to you in sheep's clothing, but inwardly they are ravening wolves." [41] Fake teachers exploit the sheep and feed them on poisonous plants, hence the need for godly undershepherds. Paul instructed the elders at Ephesus along these same lines.[42] Do we love Him? Do we love His flock? If we do, we will feed His lambs and tend His sheep.[43]

Such, then, is the threefold description of the Shepherd character of our Lord. The Good Shepherd died to deliver us from the penalty of sin; the Great Shepherd lives to deliver us from the practice of sin; the Chief Shepherd is coming again to deliver us from the possibility of sin. At His Second Coming He will have His rewards with Him. He said, "Behold, I come quickly; and My reward is with

[41] Matthew 7:15   [42] Acts 20:28-29   [43] John 21:15-17

Me, to give every man . . . as his work shall be." [44] He is the Good Shepherd, the Great Shepherd, and the Chief Shepherd, but can you say, "The LORD is *my* Shepherd"? I trust so! For one day He will gather His flock to Himself, and "They shall hunger no more, neither thirst any more; neither shall the sun strike upon them, nor any heat: For the Lamb which is in the midst of the throne shall be their shepherd." [45]

[44] Revelation 22:12   [45] Revelation 7:16-17,R.V.

JEHOVAH-RAPHA
(The LORD That Healeth)

Soon after the Israelites departed from Egypt they encountered some severe testings. Their escape from Egypt and passage through the Red Sea were nothing short of a miracle. They sang the song of praise and glorified God. However, after a three-days' journey into the wilderness, they were suddenly aware of the fact that they "found no water." [1] The water barrels, which they had filled before they left Egypt, were now empty. They pushed on to the place called Marah where they discovered water. Eagerly the people rushed to the spring to drink, but with great concern and consternation they turned from it when they tasted it and found it bitter.

This, then, was their first experience in the wilderness —"they found no water." Like the Psalmist, they were "in a dry and thirsty land, where no water is." [2] Those who have been redeemed from Egypt are not long in discovering that this world is a wilderness that offers no satisfaction to the children of God. All of its springs produce only bitter water. Concerning those who depart from God, He says, "For My people have committed two evils; they have forsaken Me the fountain of living waters, and hewed them out cisterns, broken cisterns, that

[1] Exodus 15:22   [2] Psalm 63:1

can hold no water." [3] Nothing, nor anyone, but God can satisfy His people. To the woman at the well Jesus said, "Whosoever drinketh of this water shall thirst again: But whosoever drinketh of the water that I shall give him shall never thirst; but the water that I shall give him shall be in him a well of water springing up into everlasting life." [4] It is indeed a strange and moving experience for the new Christian to discover that earth's resources are exhausted. And if one comes across the world's portion and resorts to it, he learns speedily that it is bitter.

If the Marah experience is sent from God expressly to prove us, we may be sure of His blessing and victory if we trust Him. On the other hand, if we backslide, as did Naomi and the prodigal son, we suffer a bitterness that will take its toll. When Naomi returned from Moab, she was hardly recognizable among her friends. They said one to another, "Is this Naomi? And she said unto them, Call me not Naomi, call me Mara: for the Almighty hath dealt very bitterly with me. I went out full, and the LORD hath brought me home again empty." [5] Yes, she had to confess, "I went out full," that is, when she left the land of promise and plenty she walked after her own will and not after the will of God. She learned that backsliding brings bitterness and that others notice the change. It was so with the prodigal son. [6]

But this was not the case with the children of Israel. They were following the path of God's choosing when they met their Marah experience. Moses tells us plainly, "There He proved them." [7] God sent many trials to His

---

[3] Jeremiah 2:13
[6] Luke 15:11-24
[4] John 4:13-14
[7] Exodus 15:25
[5] Ruth 1:19-21

people for the express purpose of proving them.[8] About five hundred years afterward, David wrote, "For Thou, O God, hast proved us: Thou hast tried us, as silver is tried." [9] The Apostle James wrote, "My brethren, count it all joy when ye fall into divers temptations [or testings]; Knowing this, that the trying of your faith worketh patience." [10] Now though it is true that the children of Israel met their Marah experience while following the path of God's choosing, it is equally true that they reacted toward the trial wrongly. "The people murmured against Moses." [11] Behind their complaint was fear and lack of faith, the dread of a slow, torturing death for lack of water. This reaction would have been perfectly natural for the natural man but these were God's children and He was with them. Instead of trusting Him they panicked. This was wrong, and we are warned against such a weak and faithless reaction to trials.[12]

God did not deal with them nor reward them according to their sin because of one man of God among them. Moses "cried unto the LORD." [13] Anyone can murmur, but the trusting child of God will turn to his heavenly Father in prayer. In response to the intercession of Moses, "The LORD shewed him a tree, which when he had cast into the waters, the waters were made sweet." [14] At once they were refreshed and strengthened for the journey.

This tree is a beautiful figure of the cross of Christ.[15]

---

[8] Deuteronomy 8:2,16; Judges 2:22; 3:1,4
[9] Psalm 66:10
[10] James 1:2-3   [11] Exodus 15:24
[12] 1 Corinthians 10:10
[13] Exodus 15:25   [14] Exodus 15:25
[15] Acts 5:30; 10:39; 13:29; Galatians 3:13

To all believers it represents Calvary and the cross on which our blessed Lord died to purchase our redemption. Thus the "preaching [word] of the cross" stands for the gospel,[16] "the offence of the cross" for the stumblingblock by which the wicked stumble,[17] "the enemies of the cross" for those who despise Christ and His atonement,[18] and metaphorically it is used of the true Christian's renunciation of the world.[19]

How do we view the Cross? Can we see the Cross, or are we so blinded with our grief or our greed that we cannot behold it? The Christ of the Cross can sweeten all bitterness. On our pilgrim journey through this world, there will be times of testing, and these might prove to be bitter experiences. Bring the Cross into each experience. Let it mean to you what it meant to Him, self-denial, self-sacrifice, self-renunciation. Look to Jesus who endured the Cross, despising the shame.[20] Remember, it was not God who was on trial; it was His people. He was proving them.

God said to them, "If thou wilt diligently hearken to the voice of the LORD thy God, and wilt do that which is right in His sight, and wilt give ear to His commandments, and keep all His statutes, I will put none of these diseases upon thee, which I have brought upon the Egyptians: for I *am* the LORD that healeth thee." [21] Here at Marah God revealed Himself through a new name—"I am the LORD that healeth thee." This is *Jehovah-rapha*. The word *rapha* appears about sixty times in the Hebrew Old Testament, and it means to cure, to heal, to restore.

---

[16] 1 Corinthians 1:18 [17] Galatians 5:11 [18] Philippians 3:18
[19] Galatians 6:12,14 [20] Hebrews 12:2 [21] Exodus 15:26

The use of the word is not limited to the healing of the physical body, but to moral and spiritual healing as well.

It was in an hour of trial when God revealed Himself to Abraham as *Jehovah-jireh,* and now once more, out of Israel's bitter experience in the wilderness, comes this new and consoling name of God. F. B. Meyer has made a point of the fact that we do not find God revealing Himself in a new name at Elim but at Marah. The pleasant experiences of life do not reveal all the new truth and blessing that await us in God. It was after a conflict and during the fear of enemy reprisals that God said to Abram, "I am thy shield, and thy exceeding great reward." [22] It was in the agony of the conflict with Amalek that Israel came to know *Jehovah-nissi.*[23]

Now, this new revelation of *Jehovah-rapha* comes in a time of severe testing. However, the promise is not an unconditional one, rather its fulfillment is dependent upon God's people meeting certain requirements. Whether the malady be physical, mental, or spiritual, God is abundantly able to heal. But the fact of the matter is He does not always heal. Overcrowded hospitals, psychiatric clinics, and asylums bear witness to the prevalence of disease everywhere.

Moses, the man to whom God revealed Himself in this name, was the first to claim the promise associated with it. When Miriam was smitten with leprosy because of her sin, "Moses cried unto the Lord, saying, Heal her now, O God, I beseech Thee." [24] God answered his prayer and Miriam was healed. Later, in one of his orations on the plains of Moab, Moses testified, "Thy raiment waxed

[22] Genesis 15:1   [23] Exodus 17:15   [24] Numbers 12:13

not old upon thee, neither did thy foot swell, these forty years." [25] David testified to the healing power of *Jehovah-rapha*.[26] Hezekiah was healed and had his life extended fifteen years.[27] These are but a few of the many testimonies in the Old Testament to the healing power of *Jehovah-rapha*.

Turning to the New Testament we learn that our Lord Jesus Christ is *Jehovah-rapha* and that "All the promises of God in Him are yea, and in Him Amen, unto the glory of God by us." [28] He is well known as "the Great Physician," and He Himself said, "They that be whole need not a physician, but they that are sick." [29] He began His public ministry by quoting from Isaiah 61:1, saying, "The Spirit of the Lord is upon Me, because He hath anointed Me to preach the gospel to the poor; He hath sent Me to heal the broken-hearted, to preach deliverance to the captives, and recovering of sight to the blind, to set at liberty them that are bruised." [30] He healed the nobleman's son,[31] the impotent man,[32] the leper,[33] the man with the palsy,[34] the man with the withered hand,[35] the woman who touched Him,[36] and many others. "And Jesus went about all Galilee, teaching in their synagogues, and preaching the gospel of the kingdom, and healing all manner of sickness and all manner of disease among the people." [37] There is no denying that before the Cross, when our Lord and His disciples preached the gospel of the kingdom,

---

[25] Deuteronomy 8:4
[27] 2 Kings 20
[30] Luke 4:18
[33] Matthew 8:1-3
[36] Matthew 9:20-22
[26] Psalm 30:2; 103:3; 107:20
[28] 2 Corinthians 1:20
[31] John 4:46-54
[34] Matthew 9:2-8
[37] Matthew 4:23
[29] Matthew 9:12
[32] John 5:1-18
[35] Matthew 12:9-14

physical healing and the raising of the dead were associated with their ministry.[38]

But what about the present age of grace, the Church Age since the Cross? The command to heal the sick and raise the dead is not found in any of the Epistles written after Calvary. While healing was associated with the gospel of the kingdom, it is not so related with the gospel of the grace of God. Healing is mentioned in several places in the Epistles,[39] but where bodily healing is in view it is left as an individual matter. God is still *Jehovah-rapha*, but He does not always heal. He did not heal Timothy,[40] nor Trophimus,[41] nor Paul.[42] He might not heal you nor me. But He is able, if He wills to do so. He is still *Jehovah-rapha*. Each child of God must wait upon his heavenly Father for himself in the time of sickness.

Then, too, I sometimes feel that in our pursuit of divine healing we fail to consider divine sickness. God may send sickness to us so that He might be glorified,[43] and that His grace and power can be manifested through us,[44] or to discpline us,[45] or punish us,[46] or as an instrument of death.[47] Let us not forget that some form of disease will eventually overtake each of us and each must die,[48] the exception being those who are alive when Christ comes at the rapture. Unless Christ comes first, or we are killed in an accident, we may all expect to get sick and die. Included in those future blessings for which we still wait is the redemption of our bodies.[49]

---

[38] Matthew 4:23; 9:35; 10:7-8
[39] 1 Corinthians 12:29-30; Hebrews 12:13; James 5:14-15; 1 Peter 2:24
[40] 1 Timothy 5:23   [41] 2 Timothy 4:20   [42] 2 Corinthians 12:7-9
[43] John 11:4   [44] 2 Corinthians 12:7-9   [45] Hebrews 12:5
[46] 1 Corinthians 11:30-32   [47] Acts 9:36-37
[48] Psalm 90:10; Romans 5:12   [49] Romans 8:23

Is bodily healing a part of God's provision in the Atonement? There are those who believe that it is, basing their opinions on Isaiah 53:5 and 1 Peter 2:24. I do not believe that it is, except in the sense that the entire corruption of man was settled for at the Cross. Look at the words of Peter, "By whose stripes ye were healed." [50] If healing was in the Atonement, much that Peter wrote would be unnecessary. He addresses himself primarily to those who were suffering. Nowhere does he tell his readers to put their faith in Christ, and then their sufferings would be over. On the other hand, he exhorts them to be patient in suffering. Read Matthew 8:16 and 17, and then notice that it is stated as being fulfilled long before Jesus died upon the cross.

Our blessed Lord is *Jehovah-rapha* who is able to heal any and all sicknesses when it pleases Him. But remember, it is not always His will to administer divine healing. If such promises as Mark 16:17 and 18 are unreservedly for us in this age, then why not heal all the sick and raise all the dead?

One final word: physical healing is possible apart from faith in the Lord Jesus Christ, but salvation is not. Let us not lose sight of the fact that *Jehovah-rapha* is the healer of the soul.[51]

[50] 1 Peter 2:24   [51] Psalm 41:4; 147:3; Jeremiah 3:22

JEHOVAH-SHALOM
(The LORD My Peace)

Some of the brightest pictures in the Bible have for their setting a very dark and unsettled background. Such a setting is seen in the Book of Judges. In this book of twenty-one chapters we have a record of about four hundred and fifty years of Israel's history (Acts 13:19-20). This entire record is a repetition of departure and declension from God. His elect people are identified with their enemies instead of being separated from them. God had made it clear to Israel that they were to drive out the inhabitants from the land.[1] But in this Judah failed,[2] Ephraim failed,[3] Manasseh failed,[4] Benjamin failed,[5] Zebulun failed,[6] Asher failed,[7] and Naphtali failed.[8] These repeated failures resulted in unholy alliances in business, social life, religious life, and marriage. This was indeed a dark period in Israel's history. Their disobedience invoked God's wrath and chastisement upon them,[9] until at last God Himself refused to drive out their enemies.[10]

Four words describe a series of cycles in the life of the nation. They are *sin, servitude, supplication,* and *saviour.*

[1] Exodus 23:31; Numbers 33:52-53,55
[2] Joshua 15:63
[3] Joshua 16:9-10; Judges 1:29
[4] Joshua 17:12-13; Judges 1:27
[5] Judges 1:21
[6] Judges 1:30
[7] Judges 1:31
[8] Judges 1:33
[9] Judges 2:2-3
[10] Judges 2:20-23

231

The people commit sins against the Lord; He then permits a Gentile nation to take them into bondage; they cry unto Him; and He sends a deliverer to save them. Take your Bible and observe these cycles. The first cycle: Judges 3:7-11; the second cycle: 3:12-15,30,31; the third cycle: 4:1-5:31; the fourth cycle: 6:1-24; 7:15-25; the fifth cycle: 8:33-10:5; the sixth cycle: 10:6-11:32; the seventh cycle: 13:1; 14:5-6,19; 15:14-20. This entire period was a series of ups and downs for Israel. It was indeed a very dark and unsettled time for the nation. The last words in the book describe the terrible anarchy that prevailed throughout: "In those days there was no king in Israel: every man did that which was right in his own eyes." [11]

It was in the fourth cycle of Israel's spiritual declension that God appeared to one of the judges, Gideon by name, and revealed Himself as *Jehovah-Shalom*.[12] The Midianites were Israel's oppressors. Their number was so great they appeared as a huge horde of grasshoppers. They took away Israel's crops and cattle and impoverished the people. In that time of severe oppression by the Midianites, God chose Gideon to become the deliverer, to save His people from their enemy. "Midian" means strife, and their treatment of God's children betrayed a character fully in accord with their name. They drove the people into the hills and caves for safety, and then they carried off all of their food. When the people cried to the Lord because of the Midianites, when there was no peace, *Jehovah-Shalom* appeared to Gideon and spoke peace. *Jehovah-Shalom* means "The LORD my Peace."

[11] Judges 21:25   [12] Judges 6:24

The Old Testament usage of this word *shalom* is most informative and instructive. In general, in both the Old and New Testaments, the word signifies the end of all strife and conflict, the removal of everything that causes division or destroys harmony. The word "peace" signifies wholeness or completeness, and it is sometimes translated "whole," [13] "well," [14] "perfect." [15] It expresses the deepest desire and greatest need of the human heart, namely, a harmony of relationship with God, a reconciliation based upon a completed transaction.

As in the case of other names of Jehovah already studied in this series, *Jehovah-Shalom* is connected with an altar. The altar speaks of sacrifice, the only ground of peace with God. When Gideon prepared the kid, the unleavened cakes, and the flour, he laid them on the rock at the command of "the angel of the LORD." Then when Gideon exclaimed, "O Lord GOD [Adonai Jehovah] . . . the LORD said unto him, Peace be unto thee; fear not." [16] "Then Gideon built an altar there unto the LORD, and called it *Jehovah-shalom*." [17] There God removed all fear from His servant's heart by speaking peace. What an occasion for peace and rest, when there was nothing facing the people but fear and restlessness!

Israel's fear and restlessness were the result of her sins. Man as a sinner is at enmity with God, and thus separated from God. That enmity and separation must be done away with if there is to be peace with God, for "There is no peace, saith my God, to the wicked." [18] As already noticed, peace means the end of all enmity and

---

[13] Deuteronomy 27:6   [14] Genesis 43:27
[15] I Kings 8:61; I Chronicles 29:19   [16] Judges 6:19-23
[17] Judges 6:24   [18] Isaiah 48:22; 57:21

conflict and the removal of all that destroys harmony, and that was accomplished by Christ at the cross. "For He is our peace, who hath made both one, and hath broken down the middle wall of partition between us; Having abolished in His flesh the enmity, even the law of commandments contained in ordinances; for to make in Himself of twain one new man, so making peace; And that He might reconcile both unto God in one body by the cross, having slain the enmity thereby: And came and preached peace to you which were afar off, and to them that were nigh." [19] "And, having made peace through the blood of His cross, by Him to reconcile all things unto Himself; by Him, I say, whether they be things in earth, or things in heaven." [20] On the cross "God was in Christ, reconciling the world unto Himself." [21] Now all who have been to Calvary and have received Him can say, "Therefore being justified by faith, we have peace with God through our Lord Jesus Christ." [22] The sin that kept us at distance from God has been put away because "now once in the end of the world hath He appeared to put away sin by the sacrifice of Himself." [23] Through faith in Him we have peace with God, and apart from Him there is no hope of peace.

At least six times in the New Testament God is called "the God of peace." [24] Now we know that "*the* angel of Jehovah" who appeared to Gideon was a theophany or a preincarnate appearance of our Lord Jesus Christ. He is the manifestation of all that Jehovah is, thus "He is our

[19] Ephesians 2:14-17　　[20] Colossians 1:20　　[21] 2 Corinthians 5:19
[22] Romans 5:1　　[23] Hebrews 9:26
[24] Romans 15:33; 16:20; 2 Corinthians 13:11; Philippians 4:9; 1 Thessalonians 5:23; Hebrews 13:20

peace." [25] Christ Himself is the source and measure of our peace. He is "the Prince of Peace," [26] "to guide our feet into the way of peace." [27] He said, "Peace I leave with you, My peace I give unto you," [28] and "These things I have spoken unto you, that in Me ye might have peace." [29] When our hearts are occupied with Christ and we delight in Him, how truly He is to us *Jehovah-Shalom*.

Peace with God is a wonderful experience. It is a settled thing with each one who has received Christ as his personal Saviour. But there are many of God's children who do not enjoy the peace of God. Unfortunately the peace with God has not led them into the peace of God. There are many fearful and frustrated Christians worrying themselves into all kinds of emotional and physical sicknesses. Much of this sort of trouble could be avoided if only God's people would learn to know *Jehovah-Shalom*.

There are two conditions to be recognized if we are to know experientially "the peace of God." The Bible says, "Thou wilt keep him in perfect peace, whose mind is stayed on Thee: because he trusteth in Thee." [30] Now, notice that this peace is not the result of sheer self-determination, but it is ministered by *Jehovah-Shalom* Himself. Perfect peace of mind and freedom from anxiety are known and enjoyed only as we learn to commit all our ways to Him. *Perfect* peace is undisturbed peace. The word "mind" here is the imagination, one of the chief causes of anxiety and worry which rob us of peace. Our blessed Lord, *Jehovah-Shalom* demonstrated it as He hung on the cross, "Who, when He was reviled, re-

[25] Ephesians 2:14   [26] Isaiah 9:6   [27] Luke 1:79
[28] John 14:27   [29] John 16:33   [30] Isaiah 26:3

viled not again; when He suffered, He threatened not; but committed Himself to Him that judgeth righteously." [31] How foolish we are when we let our imaginations carry us away. We can think all kinds of thoughts that rob us of God's peace. Paul wrote of those who "became vain in their imaginations, and their foolish heart was darkened." [32] Afterward he wrote, "Be careful for nothing; but in every thing by prayer and supplication with thanksgiving let your requests be made known unto God. And the peace of God, which passeth all understanding, shall keep your hearts and minds through Christ Jesus." [33] When we trust completely in our heavenly Father, His peace guards as with a garrison, and our hearts and minds are secure.

The second condition for peace is obedience. "O that thou hadst hearkened to My commandments! then had thy peace been as a river, and thy righteousness as the waves of the sea." [34] There is no truer delight nor sweeter serenity than doing the will of God, obeying His Word. The listening and obedient ear knows true peace. Can you say, *Jehovah-Shalom,* the Lord is my peace?

[31] I Peter 2:23   [32] Romans 1:21   [33] Philippians 4:6-7
[34] Isaiah 48:18

JEHOVAH-SABAOTH
(The LORD of Hosts)

The name *Jehovah-Sabaoth* is translated "The LORD of hosts," and it appears more frequently in Scripture than any other of the names of God. For example, in the last three books in the Old Testament we find this name not less than 91 times; 14 times in Haggai, 53 times in Zechariah, and 24 times in Malachi.

The word *sabaoth* means "to mass together, to assemble," the underlying thought being that of warfare. As a general would assemble his army together for combat, so God has His armies, or hosts, that He assembles to fight His cause on earth for the protection of His people. Thus the name *Jehovah-Sabaoth* has come to be associated with warfare. It appears in connection with the movements of Jehovah in times of national crises in Israel.

Stevenson says, "It would be a mistake to think that the title *Jehovah-Sabaoth* refers only to the heavenly hosts. For this word 'hosts' is used also concerning Israel. At the very beginnings of their history as a nation, in their deliverance from Egypt we read, 'all the hosts of the LORD went out from the land of Egypt,'[1] and that term is, from then onwards, frequently applied to them. The title *Jehovah-Sabaoth* therefore embraces both the heav-

[1] Exodus 12:41

237

enly and earthly hosts of the LORD; and the thought expressed in it is the joining of the heavenly forces with the earthly people of God—the bringing of heavenly power to the aid of His elect." We are not in disagreement with this teaching, however it seems quite clear that the "hosts" of the Lord are more often than not the angelic hosts. When Jacob was returning to Canaan, "the angels of God met him. And when Jacob saw them, he said, This is God's host." [2] David recognized that the angels were considered to be the hosts of Jehovah.[3] Actually all of this is not too important. It is not the hosts of the *Lord* that will occupy us in this study but rather the *Lord* of hosts.

But before we proceed in our study, look at a further use of the word "hosts." It is used with regard to the heavenly bodies, more particularly the stars. After God finished the work of creation we read, "Thus the heavens and the earth were finished, and all the host of them." [4] Further on in the Pentateuch we read of "the sun, and the moon, and the stars, even all the host of heaven." [5] Let me remind you at this point that our God and Saviour is the *Lord* of hosts, that is, He is absolutely superior to, and sovereign over His creation, whether that creation be in the realm of the stellar heavens, or angels, or men. All things were created by Him[6] and all things are controlled by Him.[7]

The first appearance of this name in Scripture is at a time of national corruption and confusion.[8] Anarchy prevailed in Israel.[9] Despite the defection of the Israelites,

---

[2] Genesis 32:1-2
[3] Psalm 103:20-21
[4] Genesis 2:1
[5] Deuteronomy 4:19
[6] Colossians 1:16
[7] Hebrews 1:3
[8] 1 Samuel 1:3
[9] Judges 21:25

there was at least one godly Levite from Ephraim, Elkanah by name. Year after year he and his wife kept the
feasts of Jehovah, bringing sacrifices to worship.[10] They
both prayed that God would deliver His people. They
asked God to give to them a baby boy that they might
raise him to be the deliverer of the nation.[11] The point
not to be overlooked, however, is the fact that Elkanah
was conscious that if there was to be deliverance for his
people, *Jehovah-Sabaoth* must bring it to pass, the *Lord*
of the invisible and invincible armies. Both Elkanah and
his wife are crying to *Jehovah-Sabaoth*.

In course of time God answered the prayers of Elkanah
and Hannah, and Samuel was born.[12] The boy's parents
kept their promise to the Lord, and so "Samuel grew, and
the LORD was with him." [13] But Israel had not yet surrendered to the *Lord* of hosts. When Israel attacked the
Philistines, the Philistines killed about four thousand men
in Israel's army. This was proof that *Jehovah-Sabaoth*
was not with them, for His hosts can know no defeat.
Still Israel did not turn to Him. Instead, they turned to
the ark of the covenant for help, and said, "Let us fetch
the ark of the covenant of the LORD out of Shiloh unto
us, that, when it cometh among us, it may save us out of
the hand of our enemies." [14] Here was no crying to God,
no confession of sin, but merely a superstitious belief
that there was some power in the ark. They brought the
ark of the Lord into the camp, but the Lord of the ark
was not there, and the result was disastrous. The Philistines attacked Israel this time, and about thirty thousand

[10] I Samuel 1:1-9   [11] I Samuel 1:10-11   [12] I Samuel 1:20
[13] I Samuel 3:19   [14] I Samuel 4:3

Israelites fell in battle and the ark of God was taken.[15]

Among the thirty thousand slain were Hophni and Phinehas, sons of Eli the priest. When the ninety-eight-year-old priest heard the tragic news, he fell off his seat and broke his neck. This now meant that the nation had no priest, no successor to the priesthood, and no ark of God. During the closing days of the war, the wife of Phinehas gave birth to a son. Upon hearing of the tragic defeat and loss of the nation, as well as the loss of her husband, she named the newborn son *Ichabod,* meaning, "The glory of the Lord is departed." How sad that the *Lord* of hosts was available to His people to deliver them, but they would not turn to Him!

Samuel grew old, and the elders of Israel came to him to ask for a king to rule over them like the Gentile nations. God told Samuel to give the people their request,[16] and Saul was chosen as Israel's first king. At the inaugural ceremony Samuel said to Saul, "Thus saith the LORD of hosts, I remember that which Amalek did to Israel, how he laid wait for him in the way, when he came up from Egypt. Now go and smite Amalek, and utterly destroy all that they have, and spare them not; but slay both man and woman, infant and suckling, ox and sheep, camel and ass." [17] God wanted Saul to know that it would not be the resources of the king that would bring victory, but *Jehovah-Sabaoth.* God knew that many of the Israelites would no longer sense their need of Him now that they had a great military leader like Saul. So he reminds Saul that it is *Jehovah-Sabaoth* who says, "Now go and smite Amalek." When Israel defeated Amalek

[15] I Samuel 4:10-11   [16] I Samuel 8:4-7   [17] I Samuel 15:2-3

back in the days of Moses and Joshua, it was Jehovah who won the battle and who said, "The LORD will have war with Amalek from generation to generation." [18] The battle belongs to *Jehovah-Sabaoth,* and He only can lead to victory and bring deliverance. But Saul was slow to learn this, thus we read, "the Spirit of the LORD departed from Saul." [19]

But God was preparing a younger man to replace the proud and self-centered Saul upon the throne of Israel. He was a ruddy stripling named David, a son of Jesse. In spite of his youth he had learned well the lesson that *Jehovah-Sabaoth* is invincible in battle. David appeared on the scene at a time of national crisis when Israel was at war with the Philistines. His father sent him to the army camp to visit his brothers. He promptly responded in obedience, and early the following morning he was on his way. When he arrived, it was just in time to see the men of Israel, including his own brothers, flee in fear from the challenge of a Philistine by the name of Goliath. The Philistine was a big man to be sure, more than nine feet tall, but not too big for *Jehovah-Sabaoth.* David volunteered to fight Goliath even though King Saul sought to dissuade him. When Saul saw that David would not be dissuaded, he consented, but along with his consent he insisted that David wear his royal armor. This David refused to do, saying, "I cannot go with these." [20] Saul's armor was that of a man after the flesh, and David obviously knew something of the truth that "though we walk in the flesh, we do not war after the flesh: (For the weapons of our warfare are not carnal, but mighty

[18] Exodus 17:16   [19] I Samuel 16:14   [20] I Samuel 17:39

through God to the pulling down of strong holds)." [21] "No man that warreth entangleth himself with the affairs of this life; that he may please Him who hath chosen him to be a soldier." [22] John Bunyan rightly described the Christian life as a "holy war." The struggle is a spiritual one, thus we need to know that it is "Not by might, nor by power, but by My spirit, saith the LORD of hosts." [23]

As Goliath approached David he was preceded by his armor-bearer. He cursed David by his gods and then boasted of what he would do.[24] In his reply David merely testified as to what *Jehovah-Sabaoth* would do.[25] Then David summed up his remarks by saying, "And all this assembly shall know that . . . *the battle is the* LORD's." [26] When Moses led Israel out of Egypt he assured the people that "the LORD shall fight for you." [27] After the successful crossing of the Red Sea the people sang, "The LORD is a man of war." [28] The Lord did fight for them, for their deliverance was a divine work of supernatural power. Explain it as you will, there can be no doubt that a miracle was performed that none but God could accomplish. *Jehovah-Sabaoth* is God's fighting name, and when we turn the battle over to Him, we are assured of victory. So it was with David,[29] and so it can be with each of us. Later, at David's coronation we read, "And David went on, and grew great, and the LORD *God of hosts* was with him." [30]

One of David's first achievements, after he was anointed king, was to bring the ark of God from the

---

[21] 2 Corinthians 10:3-4 [22] 2 Timothy 2:4 [23] Zechariah 4:6
[24] 1 Samuel 17:43-44 [25] 1 Samuel 17:45-46 [26] 1 Samuel 17:47
[27] Exodus 14:14 [28] Exodus 15:3 [29] 1 Samuel 17:45
[30] 2 Samuel 5:10

house of Abinadab in Kirjath-Jearim up to Jerusalem. The procession of thirty thousand men got as far as Nachon's threshing floor, where the cart toppled, and Uzzah put forth his hand to steady the ark, and dropped dead. The ark remained in the house of Obededom for three months.[31] At the end of three months the ark was carried on the shoulders of the priests, according to the instructions God gave to Moses,[32] and brought to Jerusalem amidst the shouts and singing of the people. In the midst of this ceremony celebrating victory, David wrote Psalm 24. "Lift up your heads, O ye gates; and be ye lift up, ye everlasting doors; and the King of glory shall come in. Who is this King of glory? The LORD strong and mighty, the LORD mighty in battle. Lift up your heads, O ye gates; even lift them up, ye everlasting doors; and the King of glory shall come in. Who is this King of glory? The LORD of hosts, He is the King of glory. Selah." [33] This is the first occurrence of this name of God in the Psalter and it shows His sovereignty, but the prophetic anticipation will be finally fulfilled when Christ comes again to establish undisputed rule over all the earth. He is our all-conquering Saviour, the Leader over the armies of Jehovah.

The thought expressed in this name is the divine assistance available to God's children in their hour of need. *Jehovah-Sabaoth* is the Guide and Guardian of His people. Elijah need not fear to appear before Ahab as long "As the LORD of hosts liveth." [34] Likewise Elisha had no fear of the three enemy kings so long "As the LORD of

---

[31] 2 Samuel 6:1-11   [32] Exodus 25:14; Numbers 4:15; 7:9
[33] Psalm 24:7-10   [34] 1 Kings 18:15

hosts liveth." [35] One man of God did not fear the entire Syrian army, but he could say to his servant, "Fear not: for they that be with us are more than they that be with them." [36] The man who cleaves to the *Lord* of hosts learns, as did Elisha the man of God, that "One man of you shall chase a thousand: for the Lord your God, He it is that fighteth for you." [37] In one night *Jehovah-Sabaoth* slayed 185,000 Assyrians in defense of His own people.[38]

Let the people of God take courage and be comforted, for the *Lord* of hosts is our Saviour the Lord Jesus Christ. Infinite and illimitable resources are at His disposal, of which we have not the faintest knowledge. Even though the forces of communism are increasing daily with rapidity we need not fear. We may look to *Jehovah-Sabaoth* with unquestioning confidence.

[35] 2 Kings 3:14 [36] 2 Kings 6:16 [37] Joshua 23:10
[38] 2 Kings 19:31-35

JEHOVAH-SHAMMAH
(The LORD Is Present)

This lovely name of our Lord appears in the last verse of the Book of Ezekiel. We read, "And the name of the city from that day shall be, *The* LORD *is there*." [1] These four words, "The LORD is there," read in the Hebrew, *Jehovah-Shammah*. This name simply means, the *Lord* is present.

The meaning of this compound name of Jehovah has proved a great blessing to God's children down through the centuries. By His various names Jehovah had revealed Himself to His people in His wondrous power, protection, and provision. And now, by the name of *Jehovah-Shammah*, God pledges His presence. This is the last of God's names in the order of their appearance in the Old Testament, however, all that this name epitomizes finds expression frequently in other parts of the Bible.

This name must first be examined in its connection with the great prophecy of Ezekiel. Some teachers have attempted to explain this verse as pertaining to Israel's past history, while others have tried to fit it into the days in which we live, but we believe that it is a prophecy which points most surely to the future. Among evangelical Bible students varying opinions are held as to whether or

[1] Ezekiel 48:35

245

not the Temple will be rebuilt in Jerusalem according to Ezekiel's description. It is not our purpose here to attempt a careful exposition and explanation of the prophet's words, but rather to lay a foundation solid enough upon which we can build so as to apply the meaning of the name, *Jehovah-Shammah.*

One day, quite early in the history of the human race, God chose a particular location on this earth as the place of many of His revelations of Himself. It was situated high on the plateau dividing the Dead Sea Valley from the Mediterranean Sea. There on a bare rock Abraham offered up Isaac, and there God revealed Himself in His name, *Jehovah-jireh.*[2] Later, on that very spot, the Jewish Temple was built by Solomon according to the plans given to David his father. Near the site lay a little town called Salem, or *peace.* Abraham met the ruler of that little town. He was Melchisedec, king of Salem, known also as king of righteousness and king of peace.[3]

In May of 1944, Dr. Donald Grey Barnhouse wrote in *Revelation,* "If we seek for the reason why God chose this particular place as the point of His great revelations of Himself, we may be thrown into great speculation. There had to be a land chosen by Him in which Christ should live and die. There had to be a place where a cross could be planted upon which He should die. There had to be a people from whom could come the virgin who should bring forth the divine Son. . . . God led Abraham to the particular land of Palestine and gave it to him and to his seed after him forever, in an eternal covenant which nothing can change. The fact that the Arabs dominate the

[2] Genesis 22:1-14   [3] Hebrews 7:1-2

land at present is no more pertinent to the fulfillment of God's promises than the fact that the Nazis, in the moment in which I write, happen to occupy France. God is able to order history to His own ends, and many of us think that He is doing a mighty good job of it, moving men and nations after the council of His own will, bringing to pass that which has been so long announced.

"In the midst of the land which God chose there was one spot that He chose for the city which was o be the capital of that nation, and one day is to be the capital of the world. . . . So it came to pass, that in the midst of a world that had turned away from God there came to be a city called Salem, Peace, whose name God changed to 'Jehovah's Peace,' or Jeru-salem."

But when Ezekiel was writing his prophecy, the nation was at the lowest ebb of its history. The city of Jerusalem had been destroyed, the people had been taken captive, and the prophet himself wrote while in captivity. Thomas Whitelaw described the scene as "a land without inhabitants, a city without citizens, a temple without priests, a ritual without worshipers." Because the people had desecrated that hallowed place, the glory of Jehovah had departed.[4] Ichabod was written over the entire place.[5]

Because the history of Jerusalem spells the history of man's rebellion against God, as testified by our Lord Himself,[6] that city has been a battleground, and is to this very day. But Ezekiel was given to see the day when Israel's Messiah will dwell among His people, and they shall cry, *Jehovah-Shammah,* the *Lord* is here. The vision

---

[4] Ezekiel 10:18; 11:22-23   [5] 1 Samuel 4:21
[6] Matthew 23:37

is expanded further through the Prophet Zechariah in chapters 12 through 14 of his prophecy. The Lord Himself will be there in that day.[7] "The Lord will dwell in it forever." [8]

There is no peace today in the city of peace because the Prince of Peace is not there. We are living in days when men are saying, "Peace, peace; when there is no peace," [9] the reason being, "There is no peace, saith the Lord, unto the wicked." [10] Statesmen and military leaders continue to talk about "a just and durable peace," but the Bible is clear in its announcement that peace is not possible so long as the Prince of Peace, our Lord Jesus Christ, delays His coming to Jerusalem. The Lord must be there. Peace did not come from the treaty at Versailles because the Lord was not there; peace did not come from the League of Nations established at Geneva because the Lord was not there; peace did not come from the Court of International Justice established at the Hague because the Lord was not there; peace is not forthcoming from the United Nations (which is already a failure) because the Lord is not there. Peace will come to earth, not from any man-made peace program in any part of the world, but from Jerusalem when the Lord appears in that place.

What practical lessons are there for us in a study like this? It is true that the presence of the Lord with His people has always been the source of their hope and courage and strength. This name for God is by no means limited in its application to a city and a people that are in the future. Just as *Jehovah-Shammah* blessed those with

---

[7] Zechariah 14:4   [8] Psalm 68:16   [9] Jeremiah 6:14; 8:11
[10] Isaiah 48:22; 57:21

His presence who followed Him, before Israel became a nation, even so does His presence go before all who follow Him today.[11]

When God told Abraham to leave his country and kin, He promised to be with him. When Abraham passed off the scene and Isaac appeared, God said, "Sojourn in this land, and I will be with thee." [12] When God had finished with Isaac, He said to Jacob, "Return unto the land of thy fathers, and to thy kindred; and I will be with thee." [13] At Bethel Jacob said, "Surely the LORD is in this place; and I knew it not." [14] When God sent Moses to deliver Israel from the Egyptians, He said, "Certainly I will be with thee." [15] After the death of Moses, the Lord assured Joshua, "As I was with Moses, so I will be with thee." [16] The presence of *Jehovah-Shammah* was a living reality to Abraham, Isaac, Jacob, Moses, Joshua, and every other Old Testament saint who dared to believe God and step out on faith at God's command. At the Red Sea, *Jehovah-Shammah,* the Lord was there. At the banks of Jordan, *Jehovah-Shammah,* the Lord was there.

Now it is one of the most profoundly satisfying of all of the experiences of the Christian to know *Jehovah-Shammah,* the presence of the Lord, in all of life's trials. We need not wait for the fulfillment of Ezekiel's prophetic vision before we can realize the promise, *Jehovah-Shammah.* Of course it is true that we cannot see Him now as we shall see Him then, "For now we see through a glass, darkly; but then face to face" [17] "we shall see Him as He is." [18] But even though we cannot see Him

---

[11] Hebrews 13:5   [12] Genesis 26:3   [13] Genesis 31:3
[14] Genesis 28:15-16   [15] Exodus 3:12   [16] Joshua 1:5,9,17
[17] 1 Corinthians 13:12   [18] 1 John 3:2

now with our physical eyes, we know that He is there. He sends us into all the world, to "all nations," but He assures us, "Lo, I am with you alway, even unto the end of the world." [19] He said, "I will never leave thee, nor forsake thee." [20] He was with Daniel in the lions' den, the Hebrews in the fiery furnace, Jonah in the belly of the great fish, Peter and Paul in prison, John on Patmos, and with every other saint who dared to follow Him by faith.[21]

Even though His presence might not always be realized, He is always there. Every one who is truly a child of God is a temple wherein *Jehovah-Shammah* dwells.[22] Of every saved person it can be said, *Jehovah-Shammah,* the Lord is there. He is present, not merely metaphorically or symbolically, but really, not materially but spiritually. Nor is He merely with us temporarily but permanently. No matter where you are, or what you do, He is always with you if you are a regenerated soul. Possibly your trouble has been that you did not recognize Him, but He has been there nevertheless. The consciousness of *Jehovah-Shammah* will keep us from going where we should not go, and from doing what we should not do. David testified that even if he wanted to escape the presence of *Jehovah-Shammah,* he could not.[23] The present application of this name is both a comfort and a challenge.

[19] Matthew 28:19-20   [20] Hebrews 13:5   [21] Psalm 46:1-5
[22] 1 Corinthians 3:16; 6:19-20; Ephesians 2:21-22
[23] Psalm 139:7-12

THE
SECOND
PERSON

THOU SON OF GOD

O Jesus Christ, Thou Son of God and Son of Man,
Thy love no angel understands, nor mortal can!

Thy strength of soul, Thy radiant purity,
Thine understanding heart of sympathy,
The vigor of Thy mind, Thy poetry,
Thy heavenly wisdom, Thy simplicity,
Such sweetness and such power in harmony!

Thy perfect oneness with Thy God above;
The agony endured to show Thy love!
Thou who didst rise triumphantly to prove
Thou art the Living God, before whom death
And hell itself must shake and move!

Thou Son of God—
Grant me Thy face to see,
Thy voice to hear, Thy glory share;
Never apart from Thee,
Ever Thine own to be,
Throughout eternity.

—BETTY STAM

HIS SONSHIP

"Unto us a son is given." [1]

The unvarnished fact was that even the doctors did not know whose son he was. I shall never forget the incident. The court room was jammed full of interested spectators, sympathizers, and curiosity seekers. At the front of the large, square room sat the lawyers, half facing a stern and serious jury. All eyes were fixed upon a pretty, young girl of twenty-two. She held in her arms a chubby, curly-haired baby boy just four months old. As she sat in the witness stand to testify, she said: "In behalf of my child." The judge was kind and sympathetic. He knew that someone was the father of the child. Turning to the sobbing and much-ashamed young mother, he assured her: "Your child shall have both a name and sufficient support, and it is the business of this court and jury to bring this about. However, an important question must be satisfactorily settled in our minds—'Whose son is he?' "

I do not know whether or not the brilliant judge ever had read the Bible. I only know that the quest of judge and jury was used of God to turn my thinking toward that blessed Book. I too started out that day upon a quest, for I remember how our Lord had said to the Pharisees: "What think ye of Christ? *whose son is He?*" [2] Always it had been my belief, from childhood, that Jesus was the Son of God. I believe it still. But the judge's question sent me to God's Word to grasp the facts, organize them, and then see if I could arrive at a logical con-

[1] Isaiah 9:6   [2] Matthew 22:42

clusion. Since I had always insisted in my mind that a skeptic had no right to doubt or deny spiritual realities until he followed through with his theory of skepticism to its logical end, I now was challenged with the fact that I had no right to declare my faith in Christ until I went through to its logical end and saw where it brought me. This I have done, not fully of course, for we shall never know Him fully until we see Him and are like Him. But I have studied and searched in order to understand more about the majestic theme: "The Sonship of Jesus."

I have concluded that many things in this topsy-turvy world do not make sense. Man has taken it upon himself to run the universe without God, and the result has been this present, whimsical, unorganized, jumbled, and senseless environment in which we find ourselves. But my mind is at rest and my soul is satisfied in regard to the claims of Christ. I am now ready to declare more emphatically than ever that Jesus is all that the Scriptures represent Him to be, the Second Person of the Holy Trinity, God Incarnate, who is to be worshiped and obeyed by all men.

Isaiah said: "Unto us a son is given." But whose Son is He? This statement of the prophet introduces us at once to one of the most exalted themes applied to Jesus, namely, His Sonship. Upon this great doctrine all the interrelated doctrines of Biblical Christianity stand or fall. If for any reason we have an unsound, distorted view of the sonship of Jesus, we stand in danger of being banished from the presence of God.

Jesus is "The Son of God." Here is a divine title that reveals the uniqueness of His Person, particularly since it has to do with Christ's deity. Immediately we see that there must be some marked distinction between Christ as the Son of God and ourselves as sons of God. By the self-designation of our Lord as "The Son of God," He meant that God was His Father in the sense in which God is the Father of none other. Let us make no mistake about this. Nowhere in the realm of science, philosophy, or theology can we discover or soundly reason a natural relationship between God and men such as that which exists between God and Christ.

Jesus Himself taught His unique Sonship when referring to God as "Father." He never said "our Father" when speaking to others except once. The one occasion where He used this term is in the prayer which He taught His disciples. Their request was: "Lord, teach *us* to pray," [3] and Jesus replied: "After this manner therefore pray *ye: Our Father*." [4] Of course this is not "The Lord's Prayer," as it is called by many; but it is a prayer pattern given expressly for the disciples. In it they were taught to pray for forgiveness, something which our Lord never needed. For this reason the prayer can find no application to His sinless life. When He spoke to other men of their relationship to God, He did say: "If ye forgive men their trespassess, *your* heavenly Father will also forgive you: But if ye forgive not men their trespasses, neither will *your* Father forgive your trespasses." [5]

Speaking of little children, Christ said: "In heaven their angels do always behold the face of *My Father*." [6] To encourage believing prayer among His followers, He promised: "If two of you shall agree on earth as touching any thing that they shall ask, it shall be done for them of *My Father* which is in heaven." [7] In answer to Peter's inquiry on forgiveness, Jesus said to forgive a sinning brother "until seventy times seven"; and then He added: "So likewise shall *My heavenly Father* do also unto you." [8] Here Christ is holding conversation with the most intimate of friends and followers. Yet He does not include them in His unique relationship as the "Son of God."

This divine title was used by others whenever they acknowledged the dignity of Christ's Person or His essential deity.

[3] Luke 11:1   [4] Matthew 6:9   [5] Matthew 6:14,15
[6] Matthew 18:10   [7] Matthew 18:19   [8] Matthew 18:35

When the devil tempted our Lord, he made his attack against the divine side of His nature saying: "If Thou be the Son of God, command that these stones be made bread," and "If Thou be the Son of God, cast Thyself down." [9] The demons, having full knowledge of our Lord, cried: "What have we to do with Thee, Jesus, Thou Son of God?" [10] Christ's first meeting with Nathanael provoked a demonstration of divine omniscience, and brought from Nathanael the confession: "Rabbi, Thou art the Son of God; Thou art the King of Israel." [11] A knowledge and a confession of the great truth that Jesus is *the* Son of God is one of the prerequisites to any man's becoming a son of God. The Ethiopian eunuch confessed: "I believe that Jesus Christ is *the Son of God.*" [12]

Dr. Loraine Boettner has said: "In theological language the terms 'Father' and 'Son' carry with them not our occidental ideas of, on the one hand, source of being and superiority, and on the other, subordination and dependence, but rather the Semitic and oriental ideas of likeness or sameness of nature and equality of being. It is, of course, the Semitic consciousness that underlies the phraseology of Scripture, and wherever the Scriptures call Christ the 'Son of God' they assert His true and proper deity. The title signifies a unique relationship that cannot be predicated of nor shared with any creature. As any merely human son is like his father in his essential nature, that is, possessed of humanity, so Christ, the Son of God, was like His Father in His essential nature, that is, possessed of deity. The Father and the Son, together with the Holy Spirit, are coeternal and coequal in power and glory, and partake of the same nature or substance."

Every claim of Jesus Christ, including the confessions of other men, that He was the Son of God is a remarkable expression that shows the eternal relationship between the Father and the

[9] Matthew 4:3,6 [10] Matthew 8:29 [11] John 1:49
[12] Acts 8:37

Son. His title of Son of God is not based upon His Virgin Birth. He did not become the Son of God by virtue of His birth in the manger of Bethlehem, but He was Son of God by inherent right in eternity past. When Isaiah said: "Unto us a son is given," he was not referring merely to the Nativity, for the birth at Bethlehem was a fulfillment of the prophet's preceding statement, "Unto us a child is born." The Son was given before the foundation of the world, and it was He of whom the disciples bore witness when they said: "We believe that Thou camest forth from God." [13] There is no support in favor of the doctrine that the divine relationship between the Father and the Son had its beginning at the Incarnation.

In John 3:16 we read: "For God so loved the world, that He gave His only begotten Son, that whosoever believeth in Him should not perish, but have everlasting life." Here the term "only begotten" does not have reference to the human generation of Christ, but it does speak of that unique relationship in which the Son stands distinct in personality as the Son, yet coequal and eternal with the Father. Elsewhere the Father testified to the eternality of the Son when He said "unto the Son . . . Thy throne, O God, is for ever and ever." [14] It is through the eternal Son that God hath spoken unto us in these last days.[15] Not through One who became His Son has He spoken to the world, but through "One whose relationship to Him as Son stands in antecedent existence both to creation and to His Incarnation." [16] There was never a time when this relationship between the Father and the Son had a beginning. The title of this chapter might well be "The *Eternal* Sonship of Christ."

Jesus is the Son of Mary also. The crowds in the synagogues marveled and were astonished at the wisdom and the mighty

[13] John 16:30   [14] Hebrews 1:8   [15] Hebrews 1:2
[16] W. E. Vine

works displayed by "the carpenter, the son of Mary." [17] And were they not justified in their inquiry, for was He not the son of Mary? The writer believes with all his heart that our Lord is just as much the son of Mary in His humanity as He is the eternal Son of God in His deity. The body of Jesus was not merely an "appearance," as some would have us believe; but it was just as real as the body of any other person. He was very God of very God and very man of very man, a combination of the divine and the human, both of which were needed in order to redeem us. Christ needed to be God in order to give efficacy to His death; and He needed to be man, partaking of flesh and blood, made like unto His brethren, in order to offer His body for a sacrifice on the accursed tree.

The use of the word "conceive" (*sullambano*) when used in reference to Elisabeth is the same as that which is applied to Mary. Luke tells us it was after the announcement of the angel to Zacharias that his wife Elisabeth was to bear a son, that "Elisabeth *conceived*." [18] Then the angel visited Mary and said: "Thou shalt *conceive* in thy womb, and bring forth a son, and shalt call His name JESUS." [19] In other words, writes Dr. Thiessen: "Mary's conception was as true a conception as was Elisabeth's." However, there is one observable difference. When Elisabeth conceived, she had Zacharias as a husband; but when Mary conceived, she had no husband, for the angel assured Joseph: "Fear not to take unto thee Mary thy wife: for that which is conceived in her is of the Holy Ghost." [20] When Jesus Christ was born, He took from Mary His human nature, not Mary's fallen human nature, but human nature apart from sin. If there is any moral mystery in a sinful woman giving birth to a sinless child, we have a satisfactory solution to it in the way that God intervened. God had said through His servant: "The power of the Highest shall overshadow thee." [21]

[17] Mark 6:3   [18] Luke 1:24   [19] Luke 1:31
[20] Matthew 1:20   [21] Luke 1:35

"Overshadow" means to *encase, envelope, imprison.* So Mary was *shut in* (or *hedged about*) by the power of the Highest so that the child was not influenced by Mary's sinful nature. "Therefore also *that holy thing* which shall be born of thee shall be called the Son of God."

Jesus was the son of Mary but not the son of Joseph. His humanity is confined to the virgin mother. If, conversely, our Lord Jesus Christ were not born of a virgin, then His father is not known, and the only logical conclusion is that He was an illegitimate child. Of all such the law says: "A bastard shall not enter into the congregation of the LORD; even to his tenth generation shall he not enter into the congregation of the LORD." [22] If Jesus were not conceived of the Holy Ghost, then He is cursed with the stigma of illegitimacy, and of necessity He would have had to be kept out of the Temple at Jerusalem and the synagogue at Nazareth. But we know that "He came to Nazareth, where He had been brought up: and, *as His custom was,* He went into the synagogue on the sabbath day, and stood up for to read." [23] Certainly if the Jewish fathers thought for one moment that Christ was an illegitimate child, they never would have permitted Him to read publicly from the prophecy of Isaiah. The conception of Jesus Christ was nothing short of a divine miracle, for He had no earthly father.

In a brief article on "The Virgin Birth of Christ," Captain Henry W. Uffelin says: "This was further proved in the demonstration by the rabble crowd who demanded His death outside the judgment hall when they were asked what was to be done with Jesus, and they cried, 'Crucify Him.' He was put to death because in the archives in the Temple at Jerusalem, there was the record of His birth; proof, unmistakably, that He was the rightful heir and legal claimant to the throne of David. On Joseph's side He had no legal right to the throne, because Joseph's line was cut off due to King Jehoiakim's sin in

[22] Deuteronomy 23:2   [23] Luke 4:16

cutting up, destroying, and burning God's Word in a fire on the hearth.[24] He did have the right to the throne, however, on His mother's side, since she was a princess in the house of Nathan. He, therefore, was Israel's rightful King. The record stood! Here is the King, the record cannot be altered or destroyed. Therefore, they crucified the King. This was a direct proof of the virgin birth of our Lord, and places the question beyond debate."

⌘

Christ is called the Son of David. Matthew commences his record of the Gospel by giving us the title of the genealogy of Jesus Christ—"The book of the generation of Jesus Christ, the son of David, the son of Abraham." [25] Here is a relationship between Christ and David that is distinctly stated to be one of sonship. This means that He has a royal connection with Hebrew people, and that He is the true heir to the throne of David. There can be no shadows cast upon this fact. The Virgin Mary was a descendant of David through the house of Nathan, and the Messiah of Israel was to be born of a virgin, one who must be a descendant of David. But lest someone should challenge our Lord's right to the throne on the ground that the virgin had to be the wife of a man who had an unchallenged right to the throne, Matthew shows that Joseph is a descendant of David, and therefore Jesus has a legal right to occupy that throne.

When David was king over Israel, the Lord sent Nathan the prophet to communicate to David the divine covenant: "Thus saith the Lord of hosts, I took thee from the sheepcote, from following the sheep, to be ruler over My people, over Israel: . . . And thine house and thy kingdom shall be established for ever before thee: thy throne shall be established for ever." [26]

[24] Jeremiah 36   [25] Matthew 1:1   [26] 2 Samuel 7:8,16

We know that after the death of David, Solomon ascended the throne and reigned over Israel. It was a reign of peace and prosperity, the Temple being built during that time. The wisdom of Solomon spread far and wide so that it looked for awhile as though his kingdom might be the everlasting kingdom about which God had spoken to David. But the story of Solomon is one of decline and final disaster. The very truths for which the Temple stood were contradicted by Solomon in his folly. Soon after his death, the kingdom of Solomon reaped the bitter fruit that he had sown, and David's kingdom, which was to be an everlasting kingdom according to God, was a total failure in David's son after the flesh.

More than one hundred years after Solomon's death, there arose a mighty prophet in Israel. He was Isaiah, the son of Amoz. Guided by the Holy Spirit, Isaiah prophesied of an everlasting kingdom, the same kingdom which the Lord had promised David: "For unto us a child is born, unto us a son is given: and the government shall be upon His shoulder: and His name shall be called Wonderful, Counsellor, The mighty God, The everlasting Father, The Prince of Peace. Of the increase of His government and peace there shall be no end, upon the throne of David, and upon His kingdom, to order it, and to establish it with judgment and with justice from henceforth even for ever. The zeal of the Lord of hosts will perform this." [27] Under no condition could this have been Solomon's kingdom, for Solomon had died and his body was in the grave when Isaiah spoke these words. Furthermore, Solomon's kingdom had disintegrated. The prophet was looking down the corridors of time to the day when the Son of David, "a greater than Solomon," [28] even our Lord Jesus Christ, would occupy the throne of His father David. Of Solomon we read: "The king made a great throne of ivory, and overlaid it with pure

[27] Isaiah 9:6,7   [28] Matthew 12:42

gold," [29] but it toppled. Of Jesus we read: "Thy throne, O God, is for ever and ever." [30]

Christ, the son of David came, and offered the kingdom to His people, but with unbelieving hearts they rejected it. Those who believed on Him were few in number. We call His public offer at Jerusalem "the triumphal entry," but there was no triumph in that march to the Holy City. Among the multitudes that went before and followed Jesus that day, some shouted: "Hosanna to the *son of David*." [31] But there was no triumph in that entry, only a pathetic entry that ended in crucifixion. The Son of David was here, but He was rejected of men. But one day David's Son will come again. Then the rejected King, the King of kings and Lord of lords will occupy the throne and His enemies shall be made His footstool. In that day shall be fulfilled the promise of the angel Gabriel to Mary: "The Lord God shall give unto Him the throne of His father David." [32]

Christ is called the Son of Abraham. The Abrahamic sonship differs from the Davidic sonship in that, while the Davidic sonship is restricted to David's house and David's people, the Abrahamic sonship extends to "all the families of the earth." [33] When God made His covenant with Abram, He said: "Get thee out of thy country, and from thy kindred, and from thy father's house, unto a land that I will shew thee: And I will make of thee a great nation, and I will bless thee, and make thy name great; and thou shalt be a blessing: And I will bless them that bless thee, and curse him that curseth thee: and in thee shall all families of the earth be blessed." [34] Let us give our attention to the last clause of this promise, *"in thee shall all families of the earth be blessed."* We might ask ourselves

---

[29] 2 Chronicles 9:17   [30] Hebrews 1:8   [31] Matthew 21:9
[32] Luke 1:32   [33] Genesis 12:3   [34] Genesis 12:1-3

the question: "When have all families of the earth been blessed in Abraham?" Surely Abraham did not see the fulfillment of this promise in his day, nor in Isaac's day. In fact neither the patriarchs nor the prophets witnessed a universal blessing in Abraham.

How, then, are all famiiles of the earth to be blessed in Abraham? This is the unfulfilled aspect of the Abrahamic covenant. Some questions remain. Is the present program of God in calling out from among Jews and Gentiles a people for His Name the complete fulfillment of the covenant? Was the promise to Abraham conditional or unconditional? The latter question can be answered briefly. A careful reading of those passages which deal with the Abrahamic covenant will reveal that the promises were unconditional. The covenant is called "everlasting," [35] God ratified it by an oath,[36] and it was given the rite of circumcision as an outward and visible symbol. It is one of the gracious, unconditional promises of God. As regards the first question, we must answer negatively that God's present program in calling out the Church from among Jew and Gentile is not the fulfillment of the Abrahamic covenant. The gospel is being carried to the uttermost part of the earth, but we are not witnessing the universal acceptance of Jesus Christ. Through His death our Lord Jesus Christ reached out in grace to all families of the earth. But every family of the earth has not been blessed through Him.

Christ is the promised Seed, the ground and means of spiritual blessing to the world,[37] but the fulfillment of the promise awaits His coming again. The families of the earth have not acknowledged the sacrificial death of Abraham's Son as an atonement for their sins, but when He comes back to earth, it will be as the Blesser of every family in the earth. All who oppose Him He will smite, and as David's Son He will rule

[35] Genesis 17:7,19   [36] Genesis 15:7-21   [37] Galatians 3:16

with a rod of iron. Then, after His enemies have been destroyed, all will be blessed by Abraham's Seed, the Son of God.

❦

Another title ascribed to Christ, one which He used frequently when speaking of Himself, was the Son of man. Whatever else our Lord meant when He used this title, certainly He was thinking of His manhood, and certainly He sought to draw attention to the fact that He possessed real humanity. But we are not to suppose that the designation of the title, Son of man, is confined to His human nature. There is more than the human connotation here. Furthermore, it was not at His birth as the virgin's son that He was made the Son of man.

It appears quite clear from the teaching of certain Scriptures that Christ possessed an essential glory as the Son of man which is different from the humanity He possessed at His birth. Jesus Himself taught this when speaking to Nicodemus. He was referring to Himself when He spoke of Him "That came down from heaven, even the Son of man," [38] and later when He asked: "What and if ye shall see the Son of man ascend up where He was before?" [39] The martyr Stephen's vision of earthly things grew dim in his dying moments; but as he looked stedfastly toward heaven he saw the heavens opened, "and the Son of man standing on the right hand of God." [40] Who was this Son of man? He was the same heavenly Character whom Daniel saw in the night vision and wrote: "Behold, one like the Son of man came with the clouds of heaven, and came to the Ancient of days, and they brought Him near before Him. And there was given Him dominion, and glory, and a kingdom, that all people, nations, and languages, should serve Him." [41] The Son of man was in heaven before His human birth, for it was He who descended out of heaven, and ascended to heaven

[38] John 3:13   [39] John 6:62   [40] Acts 7:56
[41] Daniel 7:13,14

after His Resurrection from the grave. As Sir Robert Anderson has said: "It was not His human birth that constituted Him the Son of man. That birth, indeed, was the fulfillment of the promise which the name implied; but the Son of man, He declared explicitly, descended out of heaven." The virgin birth was merely a stage in the fulfillment of Christ's mission as the Son of man.

A minister in the Christian Reformed Church writes: "The name 'Son of man' has its origin in the heavenlies. It harks back to that supersensitive region where the council of redemption met. The name finds its origin in that great conference and in the subject about which it met. Redemption strategy was determined upon. And since the proposed program of salvation for mortal men required incarnation of deity it had to be determined upon which of the three persons this task logically devolved. And for it the Son was indicated. Not the Father, nor the Spirit, but the Son was to be made after the fashion of men. He was to become very man, become such by assuming human nature, by becoming 'Son of man' in a word. And that appellation became the exclusive property of the Son henceforth. This gives us the necessary background to any fair evaluation of the name 'Son of Man.' "

Now we wait for this same Jesus to come again—Jesus, Son of God, Son of Mary, Son of Abraham, Son of David, and the Son of man. "For the Son of man shall come in the glory of His Father with His angels; and then He shall reward every man according to his works. Verily I say unto you, There be some standing here, which shall not taste of death, till they see the Son of man coming in His kingdom." [42]

[42] Matthew 16:27,28

JUST FOR THEE

Not for peace and not for power,
 Not for joy and not for light,
Not for truth and not for knowledge,
 Not for courage in the fight,
Not for strength to do Thee service—
 Not for these my prayer shall be;
Not for any gifts or graces,
 But for Thee, Lord, just for Thee.

Make me lonely for Thy presence
 Every earthly friend above,
Make me thirst for Thine indwelling,
 Make me hungry for Thy love,
Till in full and free surrender
 I shall yield my life to Thee;
Only then, in full perfection
 Canst Thou give Thyself to me.

All the beauty that I seek for,
 Every treasure I would own,
Thou art these in rich completeness,
 They are found in Thee alone;
All the loveliness I long for,
 All the best that I would be,
I can never find them elsewhere
 Than in Thee, Lord, just in Thee.

Empty me of all my glory,
 All my boasting, all my pride;
Let my righteousness, my wisdom,
 On Thy cross be crucified;
Fill me then with all Thy fulness,
 All Thy will work Thou for me;
In Thyself in nothing lacking,
 Make me, Lord, complete in Thee.

—Annie Johnson Flint

HIS SUBMISSION

"He humbled Himself." [1]

Complete submission to the Father's will is the lodestone of Christ's attractiveness. He is the perfect example of that which He consistently taught. His spotless character was adorned with the ornament of a meek and quiet spirit as He taught by the Word and by life the need for humbling ourselves under the mighty hand of God and submitting to His will.

Pride is man's greatest sin and the cause of his downfall. "An high look, and a proud heart . . . is sin," [2] and is hated by God. He says: "Pride, and arrogancy, and the evil way, and the froward mouth, do I hate." [3] The Bible speaks out against the proud spirit—"Talk no more so exceeding proudly; let not arrogancy come out of your mouth." [4] "For I say . . . to every man that is among you, not to think of himself more highly than he ought to think." [5] "Be not wise in your own conceits." [6] Paul says that in the last days "men shall be lovers of their own selves . . . proud." [7]

Our Lord said: "Blessed are the meek: for they shall inherit the earth." [8] These words of Christ are, in part, a quotation from Psalm 37:11, where David said: "The meek shall inherit the earth." The inheritance of the meek can never be realized until the proud evildoers shall be cut off and the wicked

[1] Philippians 2:8
[2] Proverbs 21:4
[3] Proverbs 8:13
[4] 1 Samuel 2:3
[5] Romans 12:3
[6] Romans 12:16
[7] 2 Timothy 3:1,2
[8] Matthew 5:5

267

ultimately destroyed from the earth. Alexander Maclaren has said: "He who knows himself and has learned the depth of his own evil will not be swift to blaze up at slights or wrongs. In the future the kingdom of heaven will be a kingdom in the earth, and the meek saints shall reign with the King who is meek and lowly in heart." In our age it is quite contrary to what it will be in the kingdom age. Then "The meek shall increase their joy." [9] Now political power and big business are in the hands of proud aggressors. But he who would be born again to share in the kingdom of God must humble himself, for "God resisteth the proud, but giveth grace unto the humble." [10]

Incongruous is the world's sense of values. It holds in esteem that which is earthly, paltry, and transitory; but it despises that which is spiritually and concurrently precious. Consequently, we value all too little the awful cost that God paid and the travail His soul endured to give a Saviour for the world. Paul said: "Who, being in the form of God . . . equal with God . . . made Himself of no reputation, and took upon Him the form of a servant, and was made in the likeness of men." [11] The first overt act of meekness lay in His being born of a woman. For God the Son, who possesses the very nature and attributes of the Father, to condescend to take into union with Himself the nature of man is an act of immeasurable submission. The world never looked upon a greater demonstration of humility than that which it saw when the eternal Son of God was born a helpless infant, entirely dependent on His mother. He waived His right to assert Himself in an expression of His own power and godhead. The "form of a servant" which Christ took upon Himself was that of bondslave. This same Jesus before incarnation was God, for we have in verse six in the words "form of God" and "equal with God," an expression of

[9] Isaiah 29:19   [10] James 4:6   [11] Philippians 2:6,7

His essential deity. The birth of Jesus was voluntary and exemplifies His self-abnegation for the benefit of mankind.

But if the submission of Jesus is apparent in His being born of woman, it is also evident in the manner of His birth. Before the war American newspapers carried a description of a five-thousand-dollar crib made for a baby born into one of Europe's royal families. Yet when Jesus, the sinless and spotless Son of God, was born of a virgin by a divine miracle, His mother had not so much as a cot or a cradle in which to lay Him. Because there was no room for Him in the inn, He was born in a stable among beasts of burden. Our wonderful Lord became a homeless Stranger and made Himself of no reputation, divesting Himself of His eternal glory and becoming poorer than the poorest. During the first year of the war the King of England laid aside his royal garments, donned the clothing of a workman, and stooped to take his place in a defense factory. But how much greater was the submission of the King of kings—

> "A homeless Stranger amongst us came
> To this land of death and mourning;
> He walked in a path of sorrow and shame,
> Through insult, and hate, and scorning."

In eternity past it was God the Father who had appointed Christ heir of all things. Jesus was the One by whom the worlds were brought into being and He is the One who upholds all things by the Word of His power. Yet we read that He went with Joseph and Mary to Nazareth, "and was subject unto them." [12] Where could one find such submission to the limitations of human life? Like any ordinary child He grew up in

[12] Luke 2:51

the home, labored at the carpenter's bench, and subjected Himself to the struggles and limitations of the average family of that day. Throughout the days of His public ministry He was content to do the will of the Father, caring nothing for earthly possessions. It was to a certain scribe that our Lord said: "The foxes have holes, and the birds of the air have nests; but the Son of man hath not where to lay His head." [13] Boasting was excluded in such a confession; He laid bare His heart. According to Genesis, poverty was to be a part of the curse for man's sin. Here Christ states the fact of the curse of homelessness; for, as Dr. G. Campbell Morgan has said: "The Son of man can only be homed in the very bosom of God."

Mere platitudes do not win the victor's crown. Christ proved Himself to be the submissive Servant on the night in which He was betrayed, with the cruel hours ahead as clear to Him as if they had already gone laboriously by. John says: "He riseth from supper, and laid aside His garments; and took a towel, and *girded* Himself. After that He poureth water into a bason, and began to wash the disciples' feet, and to wipe them with the towel wherewith He was *girded*." [14] Here is the truth in action of Christ's condescension to take His place as a Servant. Could it be that our Lord had lost the consciousness of His deity when He stooped to such a lowly task? We remember that He said: "The Son of man came not to be ministered unto, but to minister, and to give His life a ransom for many." [15] The *girt* towel in the East was a sign of slavery. Peter knew this, and against such an act on the part of our Lord, he was vehement. Only after the death and Resurrection of Christ could he write: "Yea, all of you *gird* yourselves with humility, to serve one another. . . ." [16] Christ's delight to do the work of a slave in serving His disciples is worked out in us when we are willing to serve one another.

[13] Matthew 8:20   [14] John 13:4,5   [15] Matthew 20:28
[16] 1 Peter 5:5 R.V.

All through His earthly life and ministry He relinquished His own self-will as a man in preference to the will of the Father. He could say: "I seek not Mine own will, but the will of the Father which hath sent Me." [17] His life proved the sincerity of His claims. Not even death could tear Him away from the Father's will. When draining the cup to the dregs, agonizing in bloody sweat for our sins, He cried: "O My Father, if it be possible, let this cup pass from Me: *nevertheless not as I will, but as Thou wilt.*" [18]

We stand amazed at such holy meekness displayed by the Lord of Glory in His earthly habitation, but the profoundest utterance of godly humility is expressed in the shameful death of the Cross. As a lamb that is led to the slaughter, so He silently bore all manner of indignities and insolence. He was the One in whom the Father was well-pleased. He it was who could totally say, "Lo, I come to do Thy will, O God." In this greatest drama of human history there were the hands of men that smote Him and drove the nails through His flesh, but we must remember that a righteous and holy God stood behind the scenes. Our Lord's enemies were but "the instruments of God's justice," for "The Lord hath laid on Him the iniquity of us all." [19] When He offered Himself to Israel just before the crucifixion, He said: "Behold, thy King cometh unto thee, *meek.*" [20] A striking combination presents an unforgettable portrait of the Saviour—His *kingliness* and His *meekness*. What a sight! A King on a borrowed beast! A King robed in homespun! "He was rich, yet for your sakes He became poor, that ye through His poverty might be rich." [21]

Is this why men draw back from the Saviour? Do His words, "I am meek and lowly in heart," [22] make no appeal to them? The prophecy concerning His unpretentious beginning, "For He shall grow up before Him as a tender plant, and as a root out

[17] John 5:30
[20] Matthew 21:5
[18] Matthew 26:39
[21] 2 Corinthians 8:9
[19] Isaiah 53:6
[22] Matthew 11:29

of a dry ground," [23] was fulfilled. He did not enter nor leave this world with the pomp and splendor of an earthly king. Is it because of this that men would not have Him? Imperial Rome mocked and scorned His claims. Saturated with luxury, they could not reconcile meekness with sovereignty. But the lowly, rejected Jesus of Judah's cradle and Jerusalem's cross is the eternal King of Glory to be loved and adored by all who will accept Him.

Humility was not confined to the daily living of our Lord. He taught it as a necessary virtue with which all of His followers were to adorn themselves. On one occasion Jesus gave His disciples a mighty lesson on this subject. Calling a little child and setting him in the midst of them, He said: "Verily I say unto you, Except ye be converted, and become as little children, ye shall not enter into the kingdom of heaven. Whosoever therefore shall humble himself as this little child, the same is greatest in the kingdom of heaven." [24] A child is characterized by its freedom from self-sufficiency which results in a spirit of teachableness. Children show eagerness for knowledge by constantly investigating and questioning. Such an attitude must possess anyone who would become a child of God.

Christ condemns the spirit in a man that boasts he knows everything and needs to learn nothing. Such arrogance has kept many out of heaven; for in order to be saved, one must humbly see his own lost and helpless state, and ask: "What must I do to be saved?" God strongly protests the pride of man and bids us turn to His Son for deliverance from this damning evil. In the person of Jesus Christ He teaches us how to be humble. "Into the acid of man's pride He poured the alkali of His own condescending humility. And as a soft answer turneth away wrath, the humility of God turneth away the pride of man."

[23] Isaiah 53:2   [24] Matthew 18:3,4

Turn to the Cross, and behold the meek and lowly Saviour of the world silently and submissively giving Himself in death for you. "Think about it," says Samuel Shoemaker, "and if before that Cross you can find room in your heart for one vestige of human pride, keep it—for I can't."

Our Lord gave to His disciples a lesson on the submissive spirit on the first day of the week of His Passion. They had been filled with the spirit of pride and ambition. Two of them came with their mother to request of Jesus a prominent place in His kingdom. Without hesitation Jesus answered: "Ye know not what ye ask . . . whosoever will be great among you, let him be your minister; And whosoever will be chief among you, let him be your servant." [25] Our Lord was teaching here that wanting to be served and a willingness to serve denoted two different hearts. The first heart wants to be served for its own benefit; the second is ready to make itself useful for the benefit of others. If the person who wants to be first seeks to impress others with his humility, we may be certain that it is mere deceit. Of all false humility Dr. Jefferson says: "There is no vainer form of vanity than just that vanity which apes humility." The submissiveness that Christ calls for on the part of those who would follow Him is a genuine meekness that is born of a sense of one's insufficiency on the one hand, and a sense of the all-sufficiency of Christ on the other.

It was the lowliness of Christ's heart that led Him to receive the worst of sinners, even you and me. And how did He do it? *"He humbled Himself,* and became obedient unto death, even the death of the cross. Wherefore God also hath highly exalted Him, and given Him a name which is above every name: That at the name of Jesus every knee should bow, of things in heaven, and things in earth, and things under the earth; And that every tongue should confess that Jesus Christ is Lord, to the glory of God the Father." [26]

[25] Matthew 20:20-28   [26] Philippians 2:8-11

THE SINLESS SAVIOUR

Before the throne of God above
  I have a strong, a perfect plea,
A great High Priest whose Name is Love,
  Who ever lives and pleads for me.

My name is written on His hands,
  My name is written on His heart,
I know that while in heaven He stands,
  No power can bid me thence depart.

When Satan tempts me to despair
  And tells me of my guilt within,
Upward I look and see Him there,
  Who made an end of all my sin.

Because the sinless Saviour died,
  My sinful soul is counted free,
For God, the Just, is satisfied
  To look on Him and pardon me.

Behold Him there, the risen Lamb,
  My perfect, spotless Righteousness,
The great unchangeable "I AM,"
  The King of Glory and of Grace.

One with Himself I cannot die,
  My soul is ransomed by His blood,
My life is hid with Christ on high,
  With Christ, my Saviour and my God.

                    —C. L. Smith

HIS SINLESSNESS

"And ye know that He was manifested to take away our sins; and in Him is no sin."[1]

To one name alone in all of human history can we attach the sublime word "sinless." Write it beside the name of the most imposing and magnificent on earth and you will revolt against it with your whole being. Then write it before the name of Jesus Christ, the Man of Nazareth, and behold the beauty and truth of its unique application!

On that first Christmas day when Mary's Babe was born in Bethlehem, divinity was clothed upon with the garb of humanity. Veiled in human flesh, the Infinite and the finite came into inseparable union in the Person of Christ Jesus, the God-Man. Therefore Jesus is divine because He is God. Throughout the New Testament we find it repeatedly stated that Christ possessed the attributes of deity and these divine attributes ascribed to Him are applicable to God alone.

Christ is *eternal:*

"In the beginning was the Word."[2]
"Before Abraham was, I am."[3]
"And now, O Father, glorify Thou Me with Thine own self with the glory, which I had with Thee before the world was."[4]

[1] 1 John 3:5   [2] John 1:1   [3] John 8:58
[4] John 17:5

"Thou lovedst Me before the foundation of the world." [5]
"He is before all things." [6]
"Whose goings forth have been from of old, from everlasting." [7]

Christ is *immutable:*

"The heavens are the works of Thy hands: They shall perish; but Thou remainest . . . they shall be changed: but Thou art the same." [8]
"Jesus Christ the same yesterday, and today, and for ever." [9]

Christ is *omnipotent:*

"All power is given unto Me in heaven and in earth." [10]
"Upholding all things by the word of His power." [11]
"All things were made by Him; and without Him was not any thing made that was made . . . He was in the world, and the world was made by Him, and the world knew Him not." [12]

Christ is *omniscient:*

"And Jesus knowing their thoughts." [13]
"He knew all men, And needed not that any should testify of man: for He knew what was in man." [14]
"For Jesus knew from the beginning who they were that believed not, and who should betray Him." [15]
"In whom are hid all the treasures of wisdom and knowledge." [16]

[5] John 17:24
[6] Hebrews 1:10-12
[11] Hebrews 1:3
[14] John 2:24,25

[6] Colossians 1:17
[9] Hebrews 13:8
[12] John 1:3,10
[15] John 6:64

[7] Micah 5:2
[10] Matthew 28:18
[13] Matthew 9:4
[16] Colossians 2:3

Christ is *omnipresent:*

"For where two or three are gathered together in My name, there am I in the midst of them." [17]

"Lo, I am with you alway, even unto the end of the world." [18]

Christ *forgives sins:*

"For this is My Blood of the new testament, which is shed for many for the remission of sins." [19]

"When Jesus saw their faith, He said unto the sick of the palsy, Son, thy sins be forgiven thee. . . . That ye may know that the Son of man hath power on earth to forgive sins, (He saith to the sick of the palsy,) I say unto thee, Arise, and take up thy bed, and go thy way into thine house." [20]

"Repentance and remission of sins should be preached in His name among all nations." [21]

"Behold the Lamb of God, which taketh away the sin of the world." [22]

Inasmuch as we are not attempting to prove the deity of Christ in this chapter, we shall confine our evidences of His deity to the above verses. These are sufficient to show that "the Word" actually became flesh and tabernacled visibly among men, and that Jesus Christ, that man, was God. He possessed the divine nature, and that substantiates the fact of His divinity. This is one of the first principles and pillars of our Christian faith. Christ was Emmanuel—"God with us," God "manifest in the flesh." If the early Church had not been built upon the foundation of the deity of Jesus Christ, she never could have withstood the vicious onslaughts of her enemies.

[17] Matthew 18:20 [18] Matthew 28:20 [19] Matthew 26:28
[20] Mark 2:5,10,11 [21] Luke 24:47 [22] John 1:29

While dealing with the question of the sinlessness of Jesus, it is essential that we understand His human nature. If it were true that the Son of God appeared merely as a ghost and not as a man, then the argument for His sinlessness is useless. But when we read that "the Word was made flesh," we are to understand that God, in the person of His Son, became a real human being, as truly a man as was any man. Those who fail to see the reality of the manhood of Christ are as much in error as those who refuse to accept His deity. F. W. Robertson has said: "There are men so overrefined and fastidious, that they cannot endure the thought of anything spiritual being connected with materialism. They could not believe in anything pure that was also fleshly, for flesh and sinfulness are to them synonymous terms. They cannot believe in the divine humanity, for humanity is to them the very opposite of that which is divine: and accordingly, while admitting the divinity of Jesus, they denied the reality of His materialism. . . . These ultraspiritualists, though they would not believe that the divine Essence could be mingled with human nature without degradation, yet they had no intention of elevating human nature by their own conduct. . . . The most spiritual of all men (the apostles) insisted most earnestly on the materialism of the human nature of our Lord."

In the following Scripture verses we see that, while Christ was divı.ᴢ in the highest sense, He was also perfect humanity, living as a man among men, and being just as much a man in the human relationship as He is equal with God in the divine relationship.

The human parentage of Jesus:

> "And she brought forth her firstborn son." [23]
> "Now when Jesus was born in Bethlehem." [24]

[23] Luke 2:7   [24] Matthew 2:1

"Jesus Christ our Lord, which was made of the seed of David according to the flesh." [25]

"God sent forth His Son, made of a woman." [26]

The human development of Jesus:

"And the child grew, and waxed strong in spirit, filled with wisdom." [27]

"And Jesus increased in wisdom and stature." [28]

The human hunger and thirst of Jesus:

"And when He had fasted forty days and forty nights, He was afterward an hungred." [29]

"Now in the morning as He returned into the city, He hungered." [30]

"There cometh a woman of Samaria to draw water: Jesus saith unto her, Give Me to drink." [31]

On the cross, He cried: "I thirst." [32]

The human suffering of Jesus:

"Thus it is written, and thus it behoved Christ to suffer." [33]

"Though He were a Son, yet learned He obedience by the things which He suffered." [34]

The human death of Jesus:

"The Jews answered him, We have a law, and by our law He ought to die." [35]

"When he had scourged Jesus, he delivered Him to be crucified." [36]

[25] Romans 1:3
[28] Luke 2:52
[31] John 4:7
[34] Hebrews 5:8

[26] Galatians 4:4
[29] Matthew 4:2
[32] John 19:28
[35] John 19:7

[27] Luke 2:40
[30] Matthew 21:18
[33] Luke 24:46
[36] Matthew 27:26

"Jesus, when He had cried again with a loud voice, yielded up the ghost." [37]

"Christ died for our sins according to the scriptures." [38]

Dr. Francis L. Patton said: "Our Lord's life was as completely human as it was completely divine. He suffered; He rejoiced in spirit; He loved; He wept; He formed friendships; He used the language of indignation; He was tempted; He was made under the law; His soul was exceeding sorrowful even unto death. If Christ had no human soul, these references would have no meaning."

It is of the greatest importance that Jesus Christ be fully human, for if His conflicts with sin and Satan were but a deceptive phantasmagoria, then we have nothing to prove. We dare not substitute a phantasm for the incarnate Son of God who was bone of our bone and flesh of our flesh.

Jesus Christ was the only sinless man that ever lived on this earth. You may ask: "How do you know that He was sinless? The Scriptures give an account only of what He said and did. How do you know that in His mind and heart was no guile? Is it not more of a conjecture than a proved fact that for thirty-three years He lived a sinless life when we know of the words and deeds of only about three years of His life?"

David Strauss leads us to a satisfactory answer to these questions when he said that Jesus Christ possessed "a conscience unclouded by the memory of any sins." Spiritually-minded men like Isaiah confessed: "Woe is me! for I am undone; because I am a man of unclean lips";[39] David cried: "I acknowledge my transgressions: and my sin is ever before me";[40] the mighty Apostle Paul said: "Christ Jesus came into the world to save

---

[37] Matthew 27:50 　　[38] 1 Corinthians 15:3 　　[39] Isaiah 6:5
[40] Psalm 51:3

sinners; of whom I am chief." [41] The saintliest among the redeemed of the Lord retain the memory of past sins and live in regret and remorse. "If we say that we have no sin, we deceive ourselves, and the truth is not in us." [42] Like Job, we must admit: "Behold, I am vile." [43] Do not think for one moment that the higher a man rises in spiritual progress the more reluctant he is to acknowledge his shortcomings. Contrariwise, the saint with the deepest spiritual insight, with the largest life, and with the most intimate fellowship with God is the man who falls humbly with his face in the dust. Now all testimony credits Jesus with being a good man, yet He never showed signs of repentance, evidences of regret. Nor did He ever give expression to contrition or remorse.

When Jesus taught His disciples to pray, they were to pray after this manner: "Forgive us our debts." [44] He was telling them they had sins which needed to be forgiven. In fact, while Christ was nailed to His Cross, He prayed: "Father, forgive them," [45] but never once was He known to pray: "Father forgive *Me.*" The recorded prayers of our Lord do not reflect the slightest shadow on His moral character. As we study carefully His biography there cannot be found one single stain. Peter Bayne, in "The Testimony of Christ to Christianity," has said: "No vice that has a name can be thought of in connection with Jesus Christ. Ingenious malignity looks in vain for the faintest trace of self-seeking in His motives; sensuality shrinks abashed from His celestial purity; falsehood can leave no stain on Him who is incarnate truth; injustice is forgotten beside His errorless equity; the very possibility of avarice is swallowed up in His benignity and love; the very idea of ambition is lost in His divine wisdom and divine self-abnegation."

Philip Schaff has pointed out the fact that if Jesus Christ committed one sin, then, in view of His own personal testimony

---

[41] 1 Timothy 1:15   [42] 1 John 1:8   [43] Job 40:4
[44] Matthew 6:12   [45] Luke 23:34

we are left only "the choice between absolute purity and absolute hypocrisy: such hypocrisy as would be the greatest moral monstrosity on record." If Jesus Christ ever had committed a single sin, then He was conscious of His sin as all sinners are, and therefore He can be charged with fraud and trickery. But the sinlessness of Jesus is agreed to by His enemies as well as His own followers, and it is attested to by the absence of any record of misdoing on His part. If the testimony of heathen and holy men alike to the sinlessness of Christ is false, then Jesus proved to be a master-deceiver, and "such an example of successful hypocrisy would be itself the greatest miracle ever heard of in the world." But did He commit any act of sin? Was His conscience free from all guilt and stain? In answering these questions, we admit that, so far as the whole human race is concerned, "There is none righteous, no, not one. . . . For all have sinned, and come short of the glory of God." [46] But all available records prove conclusively that *Jesus Christ, the sinless Son of God, is the one solitary exception to the universal law of sin.*

❧

When the angel Gabriel announced to Mary that she would become the mother of Jesus, he said: "That holy thing which shall be born of thee shall be called the Son of God." [47]

The Apostle Peter, who shared close fellowship with Christ, describes Him as the One "who did no sin, neither was guile found in His mouth," [48] and affirms that man is redeemed "with the precious blood of Christ, as of a Lamb without blemish and without spot." [49]

The writer of the Epistle to the Hebrews says that Christ "was in all points tempted like as we are, yet without sin," [50] that He was "holy, harmless, undefiled, separate from sin-

[46] Romans 3:10,23
[49] 1 Peter 1:19
[47] Luke 1:35
[50] Hebrews 4:15
[48] 1 Peter 2:22

ners," [51] and that Christ, "through the eternal Spirit offered Himself without spot to God." [52]

The Apostle John firmly asserts that "in Him is no sin." [53]

There were enemies and disinterested persons who testified to the sinlessness of Jesus. The traitor Judas, stricken with remorse, admitted: "I have sinned in that I have betrayed the innocent blood." [54] The wife of Pontius Pilate said: "Have thou nothing to do with that just man." [55] Even Pilate himself, when washing his hands before the multitude, weakly announced: "I am innocent of the blood of this just person." [56] Finally, one of the thieves who was crucified with our Lord said: "We receive the due reward of our deeds: but this man hath done nothing amiss." [57]

In establishing His sinlessness, Jesus testifies of Himself, saying: "I do always those things that please Him [the Father]." [58] "Which of you convinceth [or convicteth] Me of sin?" [59] "The prince of this world cometh, and hath nothing in Me." [60] "I have kept My Father's commandments, and abide in His love." [61]

Dare we question the sinlessness of Jesus? Not one of us can study the life of the Holy One without being convinced that here is a Person who was infinitely more than any man ever dared to claim for himself. To know the Son of God as He lived on earth is to acknowledge that here was a man who truly was different from all others.

Not only did Jesus tower above all men in holiness, but He forgave sins. The purpose of Christ's coming into the world was to forgive sins and save sinners. Always He showed a deep concern and a heart interest in the salvation of others, but at no time did He show the least concern for His own salvation. He needed no salvation, no cleansing, no deliverance. For two

[51] Hebrews 7:26
[54] Matthew 27:4
[57] Luke 23:41
[60] John 14:30

[52] Hebrews 9:14
[55] Matthew 27:19
[58] John 8:29
[61] John 15:10

[53] 1 John 3:5
[56] Matthew 27:24
[59] John 8:46

thousand years the worst of sinners have received from Him divine assurance of forgiveness. Paul defends the sinlessness and the saviourhood of Jesus when he says that God "hath made Him to be sin for us, *who knew no sin;* that we might be made the righteousness of God in Him." [62] If it were untrue that Jesus Christ "knew no sin," He would have been unfit to become our Sin-Bearer. Jesus Christ was a sin-offering, but He was never a sinner. The exhaustive research of twenty centuries could not find one blemish in His character, but millions have experienced His power and willingness to forgive them their sins. "Thou shalt call His name Jesus: for He shall save His people from their sins." [63] Here it is announced before His birth that Jesus would be the Saviour. He was the perfect Sacrifice, without blemish and without spot. "Behold the Lamb of God, which taketh away the sin of the world." [64]

Perhaps the most forceful argument for the sinlessness of Jesus is His own Resurrection from the dead. We know that death is the result of sin—"By one man sin entered into the world, and death by sin," [65] "And sin, when it is finished, bringeth forth death." [66] Since sin causes the death of all men, Jesus Christ would have remained in the grave had He ever been guilty of sin.

All that the human heart needs or could ask for is found in the Person of God's Son, the Lord Jesus Christ. The whole divine plan of salvation for man is bound up in His absolute sinlessness. So it is Christ, the spotless One, who suffered on the Cross for our sins, and whosoever shall call upon His name "shall be saved." [67]

[62] 2 Corinthians 5:21
[65] Romans 5:12
[63] Matthew 1:21
[66] James 1:15
[64] John 1:29
[67] Romans 10:13

THE LORD OUR SHEPHERD

Through all the vanished years,
Lord Jesus, I have known Thy Shepherd-care.
Should things uncertain fill my heart with fears?
And should the future cause me to despair?
Ah no, the memories of pastures green
And sparkling streams breathe courage to my heart.
Shekinah still beams on in glorious sheen.
I shall not want, for Thou my Shepherd art.

And should my path lead through the wilderness,
Through desert regions, where no bread I see,
Should sore temptations fill me with distress,
Still, my Redeemer, I will trust in Thee!
Thou still hast ways and means Thy flock to feed,
Though all the world no pasture should impart.
Thou still canst well supply my every need.
I shall not want, for Thou my Shepherd art!

Thou, too, hast wept. Thou, too, hast suffered loss,
Hast hungered, borne temptation's subtle blow.
Thy holy Hands were nailed to Calv'ry's Cross;
Earth's every pain and grief Thou well didst know;
Thus Thou art able well to comfort me,
Should I be wounded by the arrow's dart.
Let come affliction and adversity,
I shall not want, for Thou my Shepherd art!

Redeeming love caused Thee to die for me.
Thy precious blood washed all my sins away;
Thy Father's arms embrace me tenderly;
Thy Spirit bids me fear not, come what may.
Thy death has won eternal life for me,
My journey Heavenward Thou well canst chart.
O Saviour mine, till Eden's gates I see,
I shall not want, for Thou my Shepherd art!

—ANNA HOPPE

HIS SHEPHERDING

"I am the good shepherd: the *good shepherd* giveth His life for the sheep." [1]

"Now the God of peace, that brought again from the dead our Lord Jesus, that *great shepherd* of the sheep . . ." [2]

"And when the *chief Shepherd* shall appear, ye shall receive a crown of glory that fadeth not away." [3]

Modern educators advocate the method of leading from the known to the unknown. The Master Teacher used this method continually. Metaphorically, He called Himself a Door; once, a Light; once, a Vine; and often, a Shepherd. To a nation procreated in pastoral lore, the duty incumbent upon a shepherd was no unknown thing. A cold unimaginative intellect cannot feel the tenderness that the name *Shepherd* connotes. Only a spiritual man whose spirit and soul are aflame with divine fire can analyze and interpret the language of our Lord, and surely the Word of God leaves no doubt in a believer's mind as to the ministry of Christ our Shepherd.

A most familiar sight in the Holy Land is that of the shepherd with his flock. Such tender relationship is rare between man and animal. The shepherd's life is one of whole and complete surrender to the guarding of the sheep in his care. Out on the hillside and in green pastures he devotes every minute of the day and night providing for them and, if need be, protecting them. Wild beasts, tribal animosities, and thieves ever threaten the peace of his quiet pastures, demanding a strict vigilance.

[1] John 10:11   [2] Hebrews 13:20   [3] 1 Peter 5:4

286

It is not uncommon in moments of extreme danger that the shepherd makes the supreme sacrifice to win safety for his sheep. Though we cannot balance the scale of values, the fact remains. On the one side is the life of a man; on the other, the life of a sheep. One would surely say the former far outweighs the latter, whatever the basis of value. To a people impregnated with such pastoral lore and life, Jesus said, "I am the good shepherd; the good shepherd giveth His life for the sheep." [4]

This heavenly revelation of Christ as the Good Shepherd reveals the scope of His purpose in coming to earth. The world needed in Christ's day, and still needs today, the Good Shepherd. Satan, going about like a roaring lion, has been tracking down the sheep, seeking whom he may devour. He commenced molesting the sheep in the Garden of Eden: Adam and Eve scarcely had entered into the joy of the first paradise when Satan appeared. Approaching his victims subtly like a wild beast in sheep's clothing, he led our first parents astray. Ever since that fatal hour the human race has been led on the downward course away from God.

The prophet says: "All we like sheep have gone astray. . . ." [5] Speaking through the prophet Ezekiel, God said: "My sheep wandered through all the mountains, and upon every high hill: yea, My flock was scattered upon all the face of the earth, and none did search or seek after them." [6] These words of the prophet show that we are exceedingly mundane. The Apostle Peter reminds believers: "Ye were as sheep going astray." [7] Sheep are weak and vacillating. It is the custom in some stockyards to employ a goat. Whenever a shipment of sheep arrives, the goat is placed at the foot of the runway to lead the sheep to their death. Usually, without hesitancy, the

[4] John 10:11   [5] Isaiah 53:6   [6] Ezekiel 34:6
[7] 1 Peter 2:25

whole flock of sheep will accept the goat's leadership and walk directly to the slaughter. The gullibility of man and the false leadership of satanic systems have sent millions to Christless graves and to eternity in hell. Dictators, atheists, and infidels in the classroom, and false prophets in the pulpit have misled multitudes. Dr. Walter Maier has said: "Every century of history is marked by deep sorrows which have come from blind obedience to false leaders." Indeed man needs someone to guide him aright.

Sheep have a very poor sense of direction and oftentimes wander aimlessly, hurling themselves blindly over a cliff to their death. It is not uncommon for a sheep to stray from the flock and lose its way. Men are constantly losing their way. Like lost sheep, they have no sense of direction. "They wandered in the wilderness in a solitary way; they found no city to dwell in. Hungry and thirsty, their soul fainted in them." We are not tirading when we declare that America has lost its sense of moral direction. The fact is sad, but it is true nevertheless. Our courts are kept busy and our penitentiaries are kept full trying to track down (or keep up with) the criminals who are guilty of sex crimes, murder, robbery, drunkenness, and gambling. This debased and degenerate age needs to lift its head to hear the Good Shepherd say: "I am the way, the truth, and the life: no man cometh unto the Father, but by Me." [8]

Who of us will not agree that we have lost nationally our sense of spiritual direction? There was a day when Sunday was a holy day for the American people. Great crowds, consisting of whole families, went regularly to church. But we are straying fast. The theater, the sports arena, and countless other pleasure resorts are crowded, while many of our churches are suffering from the poorest attendance in recent years. Problems that related to the nation, the family, and individuals used to bring people to their knees in prayer and to the Bible for guidance.

[8] John 14:6

Today these things send people to spiritist mediums, fortune-tellers, and teacup readers. Throngs are traveling the broad road that leads to destruction, and like wandering sheep with no sense of direction, they go farther from God and nearer to the pit of déstruction. While the preaching of the gospel of Christ is enjoying its heyday, and the radio, foreign missions, large evangelistic campaigns, books, and great youth movements are sweeping the world, multitudes continually and contemptuously turn their back upon the Saviour's outstretched arms and gracious invitation to be saved.

All this shows us that we need the Good Shepherd. God never could have accepted our sin-scarred lives as they were, but, praise His Name, "the Good Shepherd giveth His life for the sheep." Here in this single sentence is stated with crystal clarity the doctrine of the sacrificial and substitutionary death of Christ for sinners. The death of the Good Shepherd was not the death of a martyr. Calvary's Cross revealed the death of deity. When writing to believers, the Apostle Peter declared: "For ye were as sheep going astray; but are now returned unto the Shepherd and Bishop of your souls." [9] Who is this Shepherd? In centuries past Jehovah was known to the Israelites in His shepherd character. All Israel was familiar with the immortal words of David where he said: "The *Lord* is my shepherd." [10] When Peter wrote of Christ as the Shepherd and Bishop of our souls, it was in connection with the death of Him, "Who His own self bare our sins in His own body on the tree," [11] Peter was reaffirming the deity of Christ. Jehovah was the Shepherd, for "Thus saith the Lord God; Behold, I, even I, will both search My sheep, and seek them out," [12] and that Shepherd was Christ.

In Him there would be no want. Those who are following Christ are following the Good Shepherd, and can say: "I shall

[9] 1 Peter 2:25   [10] Psalm 23:1   [11] 1 Peter 2:24
[12] Ezekiel 34:11

not want for *rest*," for "He maketh me to lie down in green pastures." [13] I shall not want for *refreshing*, for "He leadeth me beside the still waters." I shall not want for *security*, for "He restoreth my soul." I shall not want for *guidance*, for "He leadeth me in the paths of righteousness for His name's sake." I shall not want for *peace*, for "I will fear no evil." I shall not want for *companionship*, for "Thou art with me." I shall not want for *comfort*, for "Thy rod and Thy staff they comfort me." I shall not want for *sustenance*, for "Thou preparest a table before me in the presence of mine enemies." I shall not want for *power*, for "Thou anointest my head with oil." I shall not want for *anything*, for "my cup runneth over." I shall not want for *mercy*, for "surely goodness and mercy shall follow me all the days of my life." Nor shall I want in the future life, for "I will dwell in the house of the Lord for ever." [14]

Are you following the Good Shepherd who offered Himself as a sacrifice for you? We all deserve the wrath and judgment of the Almighty, but in this the day of grace we can be saved by His death. He braved the perils of His enemies and went to the grave to redeem the sheep that had strayed. Under the dispensation of law the lambs were put to death for the Shepherd, but under the present covenant of grace the Shepherd was put to death for the lambs. This He did willingly, for He said: "I lay down My life for the sheep . . . I lay it down of Myself." [15] Can you say, "The Lord Jesus is *my* Shepherd"?

> "This Shepherd so kind, had me in His mind,
> When He laid down His life for His sheep."

Dr. Walter Maier tells how three American travelers went to the top of Mount Calvary some years ago, cut a small piece of wood there, and had it made into a walking stick. Upon returning to America they presented their trophy to Governor

[13] Psalm 23:2   [14] Psalm 23:2-6   [15] John 10:15,18

George Briggs of Massachusetts and said: "We wanted you to know that, when we stood there at Calvary, we thought of you." The governor thanked them for the gift, but added: "I am still more thankful, gentlemen, that there was another One who thought of me there."

Have you ever given consideration to the wonderful truth that the Good Shepherd gave His life for *you?* There at Calvary He offered Himself in death to lead the straying sheep into the fold. Though the ninety and nine safely lay in the shelter of the fold, the tender Shepherd's care sent Him out into the dangerous mountains to rescue the one that was sick and helpless and ready to die. That one was you. Say with the Apostle Paul: "The Son of God, who loved *me,* and gave Himself for me." [16]

"Now the God of peace, that brought again from the dead our Lord Jesus, that *great shepherd* of the sheep, through the blood of the everlasting covenant, Make you perfect in every good work to do His will, working in you that which is wellpleasing in His sight, through Jesus Christ; to whom be glory for ever and ever. Amen." [17]

It is not enough that the Good Shepherd died, though it is good that He died. Our eternal redemption cannot rest solely upon the power of Christ's death. The sheep need to be saved, but they need to be kept as well. A dead shepherd would be incapable of guiding, caring for, nursing, or delivering the sheep. When the Good Shepherd laid down His life for the sheep, that was merely the beginning of the mighty rescue. If His body is yet in the grave, the believer's future is gloomy. But He conquered death and the grave, thereby revealing His power to care for His own. This is *the* gospel: "Christ died for our sins according to the scriptures; and that He was buried,

[16] Galatians 2:20   [17] Hebrews 13:20,21

and that He rose again the third day according to the scriptures." [18]

The Resurrection of the Shepherd promises the same for the sheep. "If Christ be not risen," says Paul, "then is our preaching vain, and your faith is also vain . . . ye are yet in your sins . . . they also which are fallen asleep in Christ are perished . . . we are of all men most miserable." [19]

Anton Mauve became famous as a painter of sheep. Two of his most popular paintings are "Sheep in Spring" and "Sheep in Autumn." Doubtless Mauve meant the two to be interpreted together. "Sheep in Spring" pictures the flock going out to pasture. "Sheep in Autumn" depicts them returning home, for it is eventide and the shadows are lengthening. Are we not reminded of the long journey of the Great Shepherd's sheep? It is the journey of life and the return to the heavenly home. It is not incredible that the Great Shepherd should raise His sheep from the grave. He has promised that the grave shall be conquered, death shall be destroyed, and that the sheep shall be raised to live forever in the eternal fold. Hear Him say: "Because I live, ye shall live also." [20]

This world is a howling, menacing wilderness in opposition to all who follow the Great Shepherd. And every opposing force makes it increasingly difficult for the sheep to follow Him. Following Jesus cannot be done in our own strength. But exalted at the Father's right hand, the Great Shepherd leads His flock: "Wherefore He is able also to save them to the uttermost that come unto God by Him, seeing He ever liveth to make intercession for them." [21]

"And when the Chief Shepherd shall appear, ye shall receive a crown of glory that fadeth not away." [22]

[18] 1 Corinthians 15:3,4   [19] 1 Corinthians 15:14, 17-19   [20] John 14:19
[21] Hebrews 7:25   [22] 1 Peter 5:4

We recall that the Good Shepherd had said: "I give unto them [My sheep] eternal life; and they shall never perish, neither shall any man pluck them out of My hand." [23] As the *Good Shepherd,* He gave His life to save the sheep; as the *Great Shepherd,* He rose again to sustain the sheep; as the *Chief Shepherd,* He will come again to lead the sheep home to their rewards and to share with Him in righteous rule when He sits upon the throne of David. Briefly, the shepherd character of our Lord is threefold: He died to save; He lives to keep; He is coming to reward.

Peter says: "The chief Shepherd *shall* appear." Paul wrote: "The Lord Himself shall descend from heaven with a shout." And not one of His sheep will fail to hear that shout, for the Shepherd Himself said: "The sheep follow Him: for they know His voice," [24] and then, as though to make the application more personal and sure, He added: "My sheep hear My voice, and I know them, and they follow Me." [25] There are many false christs in the world who are leading many astray simply because those sheep cannot discern the sound of the voice. But the flock of the Chief Shepherd will not follow the stranger, "but will flee from him: for they know not the voice of strangers." [26]

One day near Jerusalem a shepherd awoke to find some Turkish soldiers driving away some of his sheep. He was alone and had no way of regaining his sheep, but suddenly an idea flashed through his mind. He waited till the soldiers were passing through a gulley and up a steep hill. Then he put his hands to his mouth and shouted in the same manner that he did each morning when he led his sheep out to pasture. Suddenly the sheep turned and rushed down the hillside and up the other before the soldiers were able to stop them. Then the shepherd quickly led them to a hiding place.

The Lord Jesus is our Shepherd. Of course He neither slum-

[23] John 10:28   [24] John 10:4   [25] John 10:27
[26] John 10:5

bers nor sleeps, but one day He will call us from the dangers and enemies of this world, and we shall see the Chief Shepherd who died and rose again and has come for His own even as He had promised. And then—

> "All that the Father gave
>   His glory shall behold,
> Not one whom Jesus came to save
>   Is missing from His fold."

OPEN MY EYES

Open my eyes, that I may see
This one and that one needing Thee,
Hearts that are dumb, unsatisfied,
Lives that are dead, for whom Christ died.

Open my eyes in sympathy,
Clear into man's deep soul to see;
Wise with Thy wisdom to discern,
And with Thy heart of love to yearn.

Open my eyes in faith, I pray;
Give me the strength to speak today,
Someone to bring, dear Lord, to Thee:
Use me, O Lord, use even me.

—Elizabeth A. Scott

HIS SOUL-WINNING

"For the Son of man is come to seek and to save that which was lost." [1]

The primary purpose of Christ's coming into the world was to win the lost to personal faith in Himself as the Son of God and the Saviour of men. At no time did He allow other tasks, no matter how important they appeared to be, to relegate His primary purpose to the background. At times He engaged Himself in deeds of social service, or, as in many instances, He spent time in training His disciples for service; but every task to which our Lord gave Himself had as its ultimate goal the salvation of the lost. This was the will of the Father, and to that end Jesus consecrated all His efforts, even to the sacrificing of His very life on the Cross.

For Christ to carry out His mission He had to have a message. Whether His audience was an individual or a congregation of thousands, it was necessary that He have something to say; for "faith cometh by hearing." [2] We know that He did have something to say; for whenever He spoke, His message aroused interest. Sometimes men were stirred to bitter resentment, while on other occasions He won the eager and enthusiastic approval of His hearers. But whether the crowds were against Him or in favor of Him, every opportunity was seized upon to declare the same message.

❧

[1] Luke 19:10   [2] Romans 10:17

296

What was Christ's message? We are told that "Jesus came into Galilee, preaching the *gospel* of the kingdom of God, And saying . . . repent ye, and believe the *gospel.*" [3] The gospel is the evangel, God's message of salvation. It is the one and only true message of good tidings that assures man of a hope beyond the grave. When seeking the lost, Jesus never dealt with generalities but with personalities. This contributed to His success as a soul-winner.

Sin was never winked at or varnished over. Jesus observed the bewildered morass of sinful human nature, and with boldness He condemned every form and appearance of evil. He did not alter His message to conform to the different classes. He won to himself human derelicts, demon-possessed men, theological professors, royalty, and the rich. He succeeded because He broke through all race and class barriers and put the whole of humanity on one common level.

Christ's view of the human race was not that adopted by the modernist who recently made the statement that "all are brothers, and therefore all must be the sons of God. Sin is without penalty, consequently there is no need of hell." The modernist calls Christ his "perfect example," but he has not so learned Christ. Tenderness was not a missing note in our Lord's soul-winning efforts, yet He dared to expose sin and to speak out the Father's hatred against it as well as to preach a literal hell, a place of punishment for all who would not repent. Christ believed with the psalmist who, under divine inspiration, wrote: "They are all gone aside, they are all together become filthy: there is none that doeth good, no, not one." [4] Jesus Christ, who knew what was in man, *"came not to call the righteous, but sinners to repentance."* [5]

Is it not true that Christ's Church is weakest in her greatest responsibility because of a strange reticence to speak of sin?

[3] Mark 1:14,15   [4] Psalm 14:3   [5] Luke 5:32

Soul-winning efforts are waning because some church leaders have adopted unbiblical, false views concerning sin.

The story is told of an Indian evangelist who was interrupted in his sermon by a flippant youth, who said: "You talk to us about the burden of sin. I feel none. How heavy is it—ten, fifty, or eighty pounds? What is its weight?"

The evangelist replied: "If you laid ten, fifty, eighty, or one hundred pounds on a corpse, would it be conscious of the load?"

"Certainly not," said the youth. "A corpse is dead."

"Exactly so," answered the evangelist. "That is why you are unconscious of the load of sin; you are *'dead in trespasses and in sins.'*" Paul says: "And you hath He quickened, who were dead in trespasses and sins." [6]

Jesus awakened His hearers to a consciousness of sin, for just as long as men are not aware of this condition they will have no desire to be saved from it. No patient will submit to a remedy until he knows he is sick. The thinnest kind of preaching is the moralistic preaching that does not grapple with the fact of sin. "If we say we have no sin, we deceive ourselves, and the truth is not in us." [7] To do an effective piece of work in winning the lost to Christ we must point out the fact of sin; for, as Dr. J. S. Whale states in *Christian Doctrine,* "Public Enemy Number One is neither ignorance nor stupidity nor defective social environment but *sin.*" We have no gospel to preach when we remove the fact of sin and the hatred and wrath of God against sin. Dr. Robert G. Lee remarks: "God looks on sin and sinning as you would look on a dagger that pierced your mother's heart as it was thrust therein by the hand of a murderer—with righteous revulsion. God looks on sin as you would look on a rattlesnake if you found it coiled in your baby's bed—with holy hate. God looks on sin as you would look on the vulture that would pick out the eyes of your darling child and leave it blind the rest of its days. God looks on sin as you

[6] Ephesians 2:1   [7] 1 John 1:8

would look on a buzzard in your dining room. God looks on sin as you would look on the finger prints of the lust demon on the lily-white throat of your fair daughter. God looks on sin as you would look on the footprint of your home's despoiler. God hates sin. The Bethlehem manger says so. The thorns on His brow and the nails in His hands and the spear in His side and the blood on His cheek and chin and knee, blood in drops, blood in rills, blood in pools at the foot of the Cross—all these say so! The Cross says so. The empty tomb in the garden says so." Jesus knew the Father hated sin. He hated sin also. That is why He did not hesitate to speak out against it. And until we accept God's view of sin, even as Paul did when he saw it as something "exceeding sinful," we cannot engage ourselves in a fruitful and an effective effort of winning the lost to Christ. If we are to imitate the example of Christ in soul-winning, then we must understand something of the immense burden of sin that weighs heavily upon the world.

The gospel that Jesus preached and taught not only revealed sin, but it offered the only remedy. The soul that is sick cannot be cured with a mere diagnosis; it longs for deliverance. Jesus laid bare the sins of pride, hypocrisy, idol worship, and false religion; but He offered the remedy also. He never was bewildered or uncertain about the sinner's need. When dealing with matters of the soul our Lord spoke authoritatively. His hearers had no cause to question the solution He offered for the ills of man because "He taught them as one having authority." [8]

Nicodemus came to Jesus and heard the Saviour say: "Ye *must* be born again." [9] This leader of Israel could not mistake his personal need, for Jesus appealed directly to Jewish Scriptures, and used almost the same language as the Prophet Ezekiel where he said: "Then will I sprinkle clean water upon

[8] Matthew 7:29. Mark 1:22   [9] John 3:7

you, and ye shall be clean: from all your filthiness, and from all your idols, will I cleanse you. A new heart also will I give you, and a new spirit will I put within you: and I will take away the stony heart out of your flesh, and I will give you an heart of flesh. And I will put my spirit within you." [10] Such was our Lord's method of dealing with the lost. Can we hope to improve upon this matter? We err if we try. Bible preaching and Bible teaching in soul-winning are most profitable. The Apostle Paul sought no other methods in his labors for Christ. "And Paul, as his manner was, went in unto them, and three sabbath days reasoned with them *out of the scriptures*." [11] Charles H. Spurgeon was successful as a soul-winner, and yet he could earnestly say: "If I have gone beyond what that Book has taught, may God blot out everything that I have said! I beseech you, never believe me if I go an atom beyond what is plainly taught there. I am content to live and die as the mere repeater of scriptural teaching." It was Scripture that stirred the Ethiopian eunuch to conviction, and when Philip the evangelist witnessed to him, he "began at the same scripture, and preached unto him Jesus." [12] And Philip got his man through to Christ.

The two travelers on the road to Emmaus were weary and discouraged and without hope. Then Jesus came, "And beginning at Moses and all the prophets, He expounded unto them in *all the scriptures* the things concerning Himself." [13] Then we read that "their eyes were opened, and they knew Him." Little wonder! They had heard that which God has promised to bless. He has said: "So shall My Word be that goeth forth out of My mouth: it shall not return unto Me void, but it shall accomplish that which I please, and it shall prosper in the thing whereto I sent it." [14] When witnessing to the chief priests and elders in the Temple, Jesus asked: "Did ye never read in the

[10] Ezekiel 36:25-27a   [11] Acts 17:2   [12] Acts 8:35
[13] Luke 24:27   [14] Isaiah 55:11

scriptures . . . ?" [15] To the Sadducees who doubted the Resurrection, He said: "Ye do err, not knowing the *scriptures*." [16] He challenged the Jews to "Search the *scriptures*." [17] If some of the disciples were confused at the empty sepulcher of Christ, it was because "they knew not the *scripture,* that He must rise again from the dead." [18] Let us, like Apollos of Alexandria, become "mighty in the scriptures." [19] Then we too can be certain of fruit in our soul-winning endeavors even as this man was who "mightily convinced the Jews, and that publickly, shewing by the scriptures that Jesus was Christ." [20]

Included in Jesus' continuous soul-winning campaign was His work with individuals. He did not seek the crowds. He was content to labor in tenderness and compassion with one sinner. *Individual Work for Individuals,* the title of a book, expresses the personal evangelism of Jesus. Think of the converts from many walks of life who discovered the Saviour because of His personal work among men—Peter and Andrew, Levi the son of Alphaeus, Philip, Nicodemus, the woman at the well, Zacchaeus, the maniac of Gadara, the Roman centurion, the thief on the cross, and others. The value and importance of soul-winning cannot be estimated by numbers. To win one may mean that you have won many. Andrew brought Simon—only one—but that one was many; for Simon, under God, brought three thousand in one day. Ezra Kimball, a Sunday school teacher, won D. L. Moody to Christ—only one—but that one was many; for Moody moved two continents toward God. Again it was Robert Lee who said: "Just as one digit is valuable in the multiplication table, and one letter in the alphabet—far more valuable is the conviction of the value of just one soul in God's sight." Personal soul-winning is the responsibility of

[15] Matthew 21:42
[18] John 20:9
[16] Matthew 22:29
[19] Acts 18:24
[17] John 5:39
[20] Acts 18:28

every Christian. It must become the normal life of each parish if we expect God to bless our churches, our families, and our nation. It is just as much the duty incumbent upon the laity as the responsibility assigned to the clergy.

～

As we journey with Christ after the lost we observe how important He considered prayer in His own life. Not only did He talk to men about God, but He communed with His Father about men. Sometimes we find it easier to do the former. Fruitless efforts are caused oftentimes by prayerlessness. Jesus predicted the downfall of Simon Peter, but added: "I have prayed for thee, that thy faith fail not. [21] When He chose disciples for this mighty work, Luke says, "He went out into a mountain to pray, and continued all night in prayer to God." [22] When Saul of Tarsus met Jesus, he later became the greatest evangelist and soul-winner the Christian Church has had in all of her history, and that because he adopted the Saviour's methods. Hear him say: "Without ceasing I make mention of you always in my prayers." [23] To the Ephesians he wrote: "Making mention of you in my prayers." [24] The saints at Philippi could rejoice that in "every prayer" Paul made request for them, and at Colosse they doubtless reread his comforting words —"praying always for you." [25] We exercise a deep concern for the lost when we speak to men about our Saviour, but the intensity of that compassion increases when we weep on bended knees before God in their behalf.

Soon after Gypsy Smith's conversion he became burdened for the salvation of his uncle. Knowing that among gypsies it was considered improper for children to address their elders on the matters of duty and personal responsibility, the boy prayed that somehow God would open the way.

[21] Luke 22:32
[24] Ephesians 1:16
[22] Luke 6:12
[25] Colossians 1:3
[23] Romans 1:9

One day his uncle noticed a hole in the knee of his trousers, and said: "Rodney, how is it that you have worn the knees of your pants so much faster than the rest of them?"

"Uncle," replied the boy, "I have worn them out praying for you, that God would make you a Christian."

There was a silence for a few moments, and then, putting his arm around the boy and drawing him close to his breast, the uncle acknowledged his need of Christ. Together they knelt and the gypsy boy's prayer was answered.

This business of soul-winning is yours and mine. It is the charge committed to the church and each of its members. Dr. Walter Maier asked in one of the Lutheran Hour Broadcasts: "What is a church profited if it has millions of dollars in real estate and investments, while men and women are dying every second of the day without knowing the Lord? What advantage has a religious group if its legacies and investments tower into the tens of millions, yet it does not use these funds for calling sinners to repentance?" Will there be souls in heaven because you witnessed, prayed, or gave gifts for the cause of Christ and the salvation of the lost? Will we busy ourselves in the spreading of the gospel, or will we leave it for others? Will we adopt the message of our Lord and go after the lost? If you, reader, are encouraged to win one soul to Christ, it will help solve the problems in your church, and you will receive great blessing.

> Lord, lay some soul upon my heart,
> And love that soul through me;
> And may I bravely do my part
> To win that soul for Thee.

> Lord, lead me to some soul in sin,
> And grant that I may be
> Endued with power and love to win
> That soul, dear Lord, for Thee.

A PARTING HYMN WE SING

A parting hymn we sing,
Around Thy table, Lord;
Again our grateful tribute bring,
Our solemn vows record.

Here have we seen Thy face,
And felt Thy presence here,
So may the savor of Thy grace
In word and life appear.

The purchase of Thy blood—
By sin no longer led—
The path our dear Redeemer trod
May we rejoicing tread.

In self-forgetting love
Be our communion shown,
Until we join the Church above
And know as we are known.

—A. R. WOLFE

HIS SONG

"And when they had sung an hymn, they went out into the mount of Olives." [1]

"I will sing with the spirit, and I will sing with the understanding also." [2] This is the interpretation of the heavenly chorister in the heavenly choir of regenerate hearts. No Satan-owned individual can match the tone of this ethereal choir. The jazz and jive of hell are but frightful dissonance in this blessed rendition of the song of the redeemed.

In Satan's delusory way he offers his fraudulent ballads and canticles, a beggarly makeshift for a melody which emanates from a heart filled with the grace of God. A degenerate life, knowing no difference, apparently enjoys the thrill of the sensual for a few hours; but when it is over, the soul is emptier and the groanings deeper than when the pleasure began. Satan's music is a sedative, the wearing off of which makes the pain more acute. God has declared: "I will turn . . . your songs into lamentation . . . and I will make . . . the end thereof as a bitter day." [3]

Earth's groanings complain of the wounds sinners have inflicted upon themselves in their departure from God. "Wherefore . . . through all her land the wounded shall groan." [4] When David sinned he expressed deep distress and agony of spirit. Then he cried: "I am weary with my groaning." [5] All of the trials, sorrows, and brokenness of heart are brought on

[1] Matthew 26:30   [2] 1 Corinthians 14:15   [3] Amos 8:10
[4] Jeremiah 51:52   [5] Psalm 6:6

306

by disobedience to God. Job said that because of their sins "men groan from out of the city, and the soul of the wounded crieth out." [6]

When Jesus was here upon earth the hearts of men were wicked. Malefic practices branded the age as sinister. Dr. G. Campbell Morgan gives us a graphic picture of conditions in Christ's day—"The king is there, degenerate. The Temple is there, desecrated. The priesthood is there, degraded. The people are there, debased." Our Lord had come to save men from their sins and bring them into right relation with God. But instead of receiving Him as their Messiah and Saviour, they spurned Him. Consequently, the world of Christ's day groaned under the staggering weight of sin. There was no song.

Though the Bible sounds the dolorous note of the lost condition of man and his unhappy end if he does not repent, yet it is the world's greatest song book. Besides this, it has furnished Handel, Stainer, Mendelssohn, and others with inspiration to compose some of the world's finest music. But few can sing the songs of Zion at any time. Contrariwise, a child of God can make melody in his heart under any circumstance. Our Lord sang a hymn in the face of death, and so the ministry of song and music won the approbation of God Himself.

Some religious groups ban all types of music from their meetings. Certainly this is not in accord with the Holy Scriptures. When God miraculously delivered the children of Israel out of Egypt, "Then sang Moses and the children of Israel this song unto the Lord . . . The Lord is my strength and song." [7] When the stars in their courses fought against Sisera, Deborah and Barak sang: "I . . . will sing unto the Lord; I will sing praise to the Lord God of Israel." [8] David, the sweet singer of Israel, said: "Sing unto the Lord, O ye saints of His, and give thanks at the remembrance of His holiness." [9] "Praise the

[6] Job 24:12   [7] Exodus 15:1,2   [8] Judges 5:3
[9] Psalm 30:4

LORD with harp: sing unto Him with the psaltery and an instrument of ten strings. Sing unto Him a new song; play skilfully with a loud noise." [10] Isaiah said: "Sing unto the LORD; for He hath done excellent things." [11] Jeremiah cried: "Sing unto the LORD, praise ye the LORD." [12] We would need pages to quote the passages that call upon the redeemed of God to sing praise unto Him. The large place in the Bible that is given to music and song shows that there is power in this type of ministry. Dr. P. W. Philpot has often told how he was saved on a street corner in Canada through the singing of a gospel hymn. Many hardened hearts that have steeled themselves against the preaching of God's Word have responded to the tender appeal of a song.

❧

Look with me at the song that Jesus sang:

"And when they had sung an hymn, they went out into the mount of Olives." [13]

The hour in which our Lord and His disciples sang was a trying one indeed. The shadow of the Cross of Calvary hovered over them. The crucifixion was only a few hours away. Soon He would be nailed to His cross in suffering agony and His followers would be persecuted by the rulers. And yet we are told that they sang "an hymn." We may be sure that Jesus sang, for He Himself said: "In the midst of the church will I sing praise unto Thee." [14]

Jesus sang because it was fitting for Him to sing on that occasion. It was at the season of the Passover when every Jew sang the hallel. The hallel was a small hymn book consisting of Psalms 113 to 118. This special hymnal appears at

---

[10] Psalm 33:2,3   [11] Isaiah 12:5   [12] Jeremiah 20:13
[13] Matthew 26:30   [14] Hebrews 2:12

the exact mathematical center of the Bible. Though we have never been able to discover the music that was used for the singing of the psalms, it was the interpretation of the words that mattered most. He sang with the Spirit and with a full understanding of the suffering and the ultimate joy of the Cross to follow.

The six hymns were not sung at the same time but at different times during the Passover. The one hundred eighteenth Psalm was reserved for the close of the feast, and since we are told clearly that they sang "*an* hymn" before their departure, we may conclude that it was the last of the six.

It was a psalm of praise for the *mercy* of God.

"O give thanks unto the LORD; for He is good: because His mercy endureth for ever. Let Israel now say, that His mercy endureth for ever. Let the house of Aaron now say, that His mercy endureth for ever. Let them now that fear the LORD say, that His mercy endureth for ever. I called upon the LORD in distress: the LORD answered me, and set me in a large place." [15]

Mercy implies compassion so great as to enable one to forbear even when justice demands punishment, and to give help or comfort to the most undeserving. The average man on the street feels that the world owes him a living and that God is cruel if he suffers a mishap or ill health. Yet we live and move and have our being by an act of the kindness of God. Our sin-scarred world deserves the judgment that came upon Sodom and Gomorrah, but God in mercy permits man to carry on, offering him every opportunity to repent and be saved. "It is of the LORD's *mercies* that we are not consumed, because His compassions fail not." [16] Mercy is a benevolence of God that

[15] Psalm 118:1-5   [16] Lamentations 3:22

He has never withheld from man. "O give thanks unto the LORD; for He is good: for His mercy endureth for ever."

Mercy is the sinner's only plea. On no other ground can he be forgiven. When Jesus passed by, the two blind men cried: "Thou Son of David, have mercy on us." [17] The Syrophenician woman cried: "Have mercy on me, O Lord, thou son of David; my daughter is grievously vexed with a devil." [18] When our Lord came down from the Mount of Transfiguration, "there came to Him a certain man, kneeling down to Him, and saying, Lord, have mercy on my son: for he is lunatick." [19] Every one of us deserves to be doomed to eternal punishment and dragged into hell; but, thank God, the door of mercy is open wide. "Not by works of righteousness which we have done, but according to His *mercy* He saved us, by the washing of regeneration, and renewing of the Holy Ghost." [20] Our Lord was singing a song of praise for the mercy of God in behalf of those who had rejected Him.

> "There's a wideness in God's mercy,
> Like the wideness of the sea.
> There's a kindness in His justice
> Which is more than liberty.
>
> "There is welcome for the sinner,
> And more graces for the good.
> There is mercy with the Saviour,
> There is healing in His blood."

"O give thanks unto the LORD; for He is good: for His mercy endureth for ever."

It was a psalm of praise for the *might* of God.

The LORD is on my side; I will not fear: what can man do unto me? The LORD taketh my part with them that help me:

[17] Matthew 9:27 [18] Matthew 15:22 [19] Matthew 17:14,15
[20] Titus 3:5

therefore shall I see my desire upon them that hate me. It is better to trust in the LORD than to put confidence in man. It is better to trust in the LORD than to put confidence in princes. All nations compassed me about: but in the name of the LORD will I destroy them. They compassed me about; yea, they compassed me about: but in the name of the LORD I will destroy them. They compassed me about like bees; they are quenched as the fire of thorns: for in the name of the LORD I will destroy them. Thou hast thrust sore at me that I might fall: but the LORD helped me. The LORD is my strength and song, and is become my salvation. The voice of rejoicing and salvation is in the tabernacles of the righteous: the right hand of the LORD doeth valiantly. The right hand of the LORD is exalted: The right hand of the LORD doeth valiantly.[21]

Almost eight hundred years before Christ was born, it was prophesied of Him: "For unto us a child is born, unto us a son is given: and the government shall be upon His shoulder: and His name shall be called Wonderful, Counsellor, *The mighty God*, The everlasting Father, The Prince of Peace." [22] His name is "The mighty God." The total depravity of man cries for a mighty Deliverer. The breakdown of home life, widespread social immorality, and the vast underworld of crime all prove that One is needed who is mighty to save. The prophet quotes our Lord's own words: "I the LORD am thy Saviour and thy Redeemer, *the mighty One* of Jacob." [23] "There is no Saviour beside Me." [24] The unsaved yet in their sins will continue to groan until they are delivered by the mighty arm of God.

We, who have believed and are saved, know that He has power not only to save us but also to change our wailings to singing. We can testify that He does compass us about with "songs of deliverance," [25] and "He hath put a new song in my

[21] Psalm 118:6-16
[24] Hosea 13:4
[22] Isaiah 9:6
[25] Psalm 32:7
[23] Isaiah 49:26

mouth, even praise unto our God." [26] The Psalmist said: "I call to remembrance my song in the night." [27] Now that he had found the merciful and mighty Saviour, there was no need to have to wait till the morning for his song. Though the night was dark all around him and left behind it a trail of terror, the presence of the Saviour caused him to burst forth into a hymn of praise. Jesus gives no song to skeptics and doubters but only to the soul that trusts Him. Faithless lives are songless lives. Jesus could sing in His darkest hour because He believed that the purposes of God would ultimately triumph. When the mighty Hebrew apostle and his companion were thrust into prison at midnight, the darkest hour, "Paul and Silas prayed, and sang praises unto God." [28] The trusting child of God can sing:

> "There is never a day so dreary,
> But God can make it bright;
> And unto the soul that trusts Him
> He giveth songs in the night."

Great times of singing are predicted for the future. Israel has no song today, but the Bible forecasts the day when God shall deliver her by His divine might. "Sing, O barren [Israel], thou that didst not bear; break forth into singing, and cry aloud." [29] Israel has bright prospects for the future. "I have redeemed thee. Sing, O ye heavens; for the LORD hath done it: shout, ye lower parts of the earth: break forth into singing, ye mountains, O forest, and every tree therein: for the LORD hath redeemed Jacob, and glorified Himself in Israel." [30] There is no song for Jew or Gentile without the Saviour. But after we have come to know Him we can sing even as we pass through the valley of the shadow of death. When twenty African tribesmen killed Bishop Hannington, he died singing:

[26] Psalm 40:3   [27] Psalm 77:6   [28] Acts 16:25
[29] Isaiah 54:1   [30] Isaiah 44:22,23

> "Safe in the arms of Jesus,
> Safe on His gentle breast,
> There by His love o'ershaded
> Sweetly my soul shall rest."

Because Jesus sang we too have a song. Perhaps there are some with little capacity to sing here on earth, but in heaven all the redeemed shall sing together in blessed harmony around the throne of God. We shall sing in unison the song of redemption through the Blood of Christ. Until our Saviour comes to gather us unto that heavenly choir, let us seek to please Him by our lives. In that day, "He will joy over thee with singing." [31]

> "Come let us sing the matchless worth,
> And sweetly sound the glories forth
>   Which in the Saviour shine.
> To God and Christ our praises bring:
> The song with which high Heaven will ring,
>   'Praises for grace divine.'

> "How rich the character He bears,
> And all the forms of love He wears,
>   Exalted on the throne;
> In songs of sweet untiring praise,
> We e'er would sing His perfect ways,
>   And make His glories known.

> "And soon the happy day shall come,
> When we shall reach our destined home,
>   And see Him face to face;
> Then with our Saviour, Lord, and Friend,
> The one unbroken day we'll spend
>   In singing still His grace."

[31] Zephaniah 3:17

HE WENT A LITTLE FARTHER

He went a little farther,
  All alone,
  Into the darkest night this world has known;
The ancient olive trees a vigil kept,
Disciples slept.

He went a little farther,
  To a tree
  That stretched its cruel arms o'er Calvary;
No other could have suffered in the stead
Of Him who bled.

He went a little farther;
  Fear and gloom
  Encompassed those who laid Him in the tomb;
Forgotten was His promise unto men
To rise again.

He went a little farther;
  Christ arose
  Triumphant over sin and death, our foes,
And now in heaven lives to intercede
For human need.

He went a little farther—
  Wondrous thought;
  For you, for me, He has salvation bought;
We choose to live or die eternally.
Which shall it be?

—MARJORIE B. ROBINSON

HIS SOLITUDE

"And Jesus was left alone." [1]

Alone. There is a physical aloneness caused by separation of one from one's fellows, a time when one is seen, touched, or heard by no others. But there is an aloneness of the soul when the soul is surrounded by a stratosphere of seclusion which no human being is able to penetrate. Voices within clamor for companionship, but no one can answer them. Human kindness and warmest friendships cannot touch. Earth becomes a wilderness. We are alone.

Someone has said: "In the plainest sense of the word we are lonely, and cannot be otherwise. Those who know and love us best know not half the reasons why we sigh or smile. Men and women may live together in what seems the closest intimacy for years, and yet keep within their hearts reserved and barriered chambers to which neither has the key. . . . Our life may be spent among crowds, and yet the vast silence which encloses the heart may never once be broken."

There is an abysmal aloneness that waits to engulf the lost sinner as he stands before God's throne of justice to receive the eternal decree. He will be alone before God; no one will plead his cause. The night of loneliness will encompass him. There will be none to help.

There is a loneliness from which God in His mercy has delivered every blood-washed saint. Reflect for a moment upon the

[1] John 8:9

loneliness from which Christ your Saviour has delivered you.
Having meditated even briefly, can you do ought but run to
the altar of your heart and offer the sacrifice of praise to the
all-wonderful One who has promised, "Lo, I am with you alway?"

Words cannot portray nor imagination conceive the awful
cost to God to give the assurance of His abiding presence.
Christ suffered, bled, and died—alone.

Loneliness was not a new experience for Jesus as He set His
face toward the Cross. Nor did it have its inception in the
shadow of Calvary. His life was lived in extreme loneliness.
Though His birth was announced by the prophets centuries
before, the fact remains that Mary laid her Saviour, the King
of Glory in a lowly manger. Though thousands lived in anticipation of the coming of the Messiah, He came all the way
from the heavenly mansions to an earthly stable, unnoticed.
Though an angelic choir sang as they heralded His birth, yet
only a few humble shepherds sought Him to worship Him.
The world should have bowed at His infant feet. Instead,
political authorities sought the young Child's life. For Him
"there was no room." [2] No room in the inn; no room in the
minds of potentates; no room in the hearts of His own.

Then there was the loneliness of His early boyhood days.
We dare not intrude with any fanciful imaginations of our own
into the hallowed silence of those intervening years from the
return from Egypt to the temple experience at twelve years of
age. However, from our reading of the New Testament we may
conclude that Jesus had brothers who, "in their unbelieving
state, must have been somewhat harsh and unsympathetic men.

[2] Luke 2:7

At all events they never believed on Him during His lifetime, and it is not likely that they were close companions to Him in Nazareth. *He was probably much alone.*" [3] Our Lord doubtless looked back to those earlier years when He Himself testified: "A prophet hath no honour in his own country." [4]

Think of the solitude of His experience at the age of twelve. When His parents took Him to Jerusalem at the time of the Passover, He entered into spiritual intercourse with the great rabbis in the Temple, both hearing them and asking them questions. A pang of loneliness stabbed His heart as His mother said: "Son, why hast Thou thus dealt with us? behold, Thy father and I have sought Thee sorrowing." [5] At once He saw that they did not understand His divine mission. He was alone in the purpose for which He came, and from His lonely heart, He asked: "Wist ye not that I must be about My Father's business?" [6]

As He ministered among men He was often alone. We see the solitariness of the Saviour when the scribes and Pharisees brought to Him a woman taken in adultery. "They say unto Him, Master, this woman was taken in adultery, in the very act." Then Jesus, after writing on the ground, said: "He that is without sin among you, let him first cast a stone at her. . . . And they which heard it, being convicted by their own conscience, went out one by one, beginning at the eldest, even unto the last: and *Jesus was left alone.*" [7]

Here we have one of the reasons why Jesus was so often *alone*. He demanded from all men purity of life. He never played favorites nor compromised with sin. His searching and scorching words so convicted men of their unrighteousness that they were driven from His holy presence one by one until He

[3] James Stalker   [4] John 4:44; Matthew 13:53-57
[5] Luke 2:48   [6] Luke 2:49   [7] John 8:3-9

was left alone. Christ "was the true Light, which lighteth every man that cometh into the world," [8] and whenever man approached Him, his deeds were made known. Since contact with Jesus exposes sin, man refused to come to the Light "lest his deeds should be reproved." [9] Little wonder that the scribes and Pharisees fled from His presence one by one until Jesus was left alone. Though many have believed in Him, our Lord is lonely still, for this pleasure-mad generation of ours cannot stand to be in His presence. He suffers in solitude today because of the rebellion of sinners who spurn His love. But Christ shall not be lonely long, for when He comes to gather His own to Himself, "He shall see of the travail of His soul, and shall be satisfied." [10]

It was not an infrequent experience for our Lord to be alone when He prayed. Luke says: "And it came to pass, as He was alone praying." [11] It has been said that the loneliness of Christ was caused by the divine elevation of His character. His soul longed for solitude in prayer. There must have been times when the Sinless One sought retirement to commune with the Father. Even we frail creatures of the dust have experienced those moments when we wanted to be shut away, alone with God. Perhaps they are not as frequent as they should be. Yet our Lord engaged in secret prayer often—"He withdrew Himself into the wilderness, and prayed." [12]

> "And it came to pass in those days, that He went out into a mountain to pray, and continued all night in prayer to God." [13]

> "And He was withdrawn from them about a stone's cast, and kneeled down, and prayed." [14]

[8] John 1:9
[9] John 3:19,20
[10] Isaiah 53:11
[11] Luke 9:18
[12] Luke 5:16
[13] Luke 6:12
[14] Luke 22:41

It is interesting to note that even when our Lord prayed in the presence of others there was a solitude of soul He could not escape. In a most arresting statement, Luke says: "As He was alone praying, His disciples were with Him." [15] At first glance these facts appear incompatible—"He was alone . . . His disciples were with Him." But the word intervening between these two statements makes all the difference. It is the word *"praying."* Here we are given deep insight into the prayer life of our Lord. He did not pray as other men prayed. Every sinner must approach God through a Mediator, pleading divine mercy because of a sin-stained life. But Jesus needed no mediator. Having no sin of His own He never had cause to plead mercy and pardon. He prayed on a higher plane than any other man. While the disciples were with Him when He prayed, He was praying alone, in a sphere known only to Himself. In a sense it is true that every time Christ prayed, it was alone.

⌇

Here is another reason for the loneliness of Jesus. He was misunderstood. It was enhanced as His efforts to make them understand increased. Loneliness must have stabbed Him when His own people refused Him. Think of it! "He came unto His own, and His own received Him not." [16] He was their King, and He offered Himself as such; but in their deliberate refusal and rejection of Him they drove the arrow of solitude into His heart afresh. For three years Christ labored among them day and night only to see them spurn His love and turn from His teachings. As Jesus foresaw the terrible doom of Jerusalem and her severance from Him, the loneliness was more than His heart could bear. Hear Christ's lamentation: "Jerusalem, Jerusalem . . . how often would I have gathered thy children together, as a hen doth gather her brood under her wings, and ye would not!" [17]

Surely your heart is crying out its love to Him anew, but as we look reverently upon that memorable scene in the garden of Gethsemane we see even a deeper loneliness than the Saviour has shown heretofore. The keenest sorrow is often a solitary one, the sharpest agony known to the suffering soul alone. The agony of our Lord's passion was no exception. It was not alleviated because others were near to share the blow and to offer Him their caresses of consolation, for He was alone. Where were all who had professed to be His followers? Had there not been a great host of disciples who had sought Him so unceasingly that He had to resort to the mountain to be alone? But there came a day when He tried to teach them spiritual things concerning bread that comes out of heaven, and "From that time many of His disciples went back, and walked no more with Him." [18] Had there not been twelve of His apostles, who had traveled, eaten, talked, and lived with Him for three full years of ministry? No, for Judas was at that moment plotting with the conspirators against Him. Were there not at least eleven? No, for He had said to them as they approached the gate, "Sit ye here, while I go and pray yonder." Were there not three who shared the most intimate experiences of the body and the soul of Jesus, even Peter, James, and John? We do not read far into the Scriptures until we have discovered that even these three were now sleeping. The garden was indeed a hallowed place of solitary suffering. The battle that Jesus fought in this dark hour He must of necessity fight alone. This was the prediction of the ancient prophet—"I have trodden the winepress alone." [19]

❧

[17] Luke 13:34   [18] John 6:66   [19] Isaiah 63:3

If your soul can look upon one more scene, behold the loneliness of the Cross. His trial and condemnation are now past. Having been led to Calvary's hill and nailed to the cross, He hangs suspended between heaven and earth. From those tender lips so full of grace and truth came an utterance that expressed the immeasurable depth of His loneliness. "My God, My God, why hast Thou forsaken Me?" [20]

The scene is closed; we dare not trespass our gaze any deeper into such sanctitude. Suffice it to say that on the Cross Jesus was bearing the load of the world's sin. He was encircled by the sins of every man of all ages. And seeing that the Father was of purer eyes than to behold sin, He hid His face from the horrible scene. *Forsaken!* What a tragic word! *Deserted. Alone.* When Jesus walked among men He could testify: "I am not alone, because the Father is with Me." [21] But here, in the darkest hour of the world's history, He was left to die, abandoned by God.

> "Yea, once Immanuel's orphaned cry
>   His universe hath shaken,
>   It went up from His holy lips,
>   My God, I am forsaken."

Author's pen or painter's brush will never be able to portray the Saviour's solitude when "the Lord hath laid on Him the iniquity of us all." [22] The awful cost He paid to give us the consolation of His eternal companionship!

> "Alone, Alone,
>   He bore it all alone,
>   He gave Himself to save His own,
>   He suffered, bled, and died,
>   Alone, Alone."

[20] Matthew 27:46   [21] John 16:32   [22] Isaiah 53:6

THE SILENCE OF GOD

Jehovah saith no more; the voice of God hath ceased.
No more by vision or by dream, by prophet or by priest,
By ephod or by teraphim, by angel or by star,
By altar or by sacrifice, He speaketh from afar.

No more—He saith no more; the silent heavens wait;
The silent angels keep their watch beside the open gate;
The silent Christ bends low with tender, pitying face,
To see if one more soul on earth will seek God's offered grace.

Jehovah saith no more. Why should he speak again
When His last word is echoing yet within the ears of men?
But they refuse to hear, and through the flying days
They eat and drink and buy and sell, and go their careless ways.

Jehovah saith no more. His last great Word is said
Till from the earth and sea His voice shall call the dead;
Till like the thunder's peal His judgment word is hurled
To shake with awful wrath the unbelieving world.

But now His voice is still. O ye whose hearts have heard,
Ye are the voice of God to speak His gracious word.
Repeat it to the sons of men, though they the call ignore,
For, save as ye shall speak His word, Jehovah saith no more.

—ANNIE JOHNSON FLINT

HIS SILENCE

"He was oppressed, and He was afflicted, yet He opened not His mouth." [1]

More than seven hundred years before Christ was born, the prophet Isaiah predicted the silence of Jehovah's suffering Servant. In the fulness of time Jesus was born, and at the close of thirty-three years on earth He was put to death on the cross. Despised and rejected, stricken, smitten of God and afflicted, bruised and oppressed, Christ maintained a sublime and majestic silence through all His suffering. Not long after our Lord's ascension the Ethiopian eunuch was reading the sacred scroll that contained Isaiah's message, and his eyes rested upon the words, "He was led as a sheep to the slaughter; and like a lamb dumb before his shearer, *so opened He not His mouth.*" [2] Being somewhat perplexed by the statement, the eunuch asked of Philip: "Of whom speaketh the prophet this? . . . Then Philip opened his mouth, and began at the same scripture, and preached unto him Jesus." [3]

The ancient preacher spoke well when he said: "A time to keep silence, and a time to speak." [4] This is a lesson we all might learn, for "to speak or not to speak" is a dilemma we face often. Even to His dying moments, our Lord was a master in every situation in which He found Himself. Some men seize upon their last moments to make a great declaration, discharge a responsibility, build up a defense, or ease their conscience.

[1] Isaiah 53:7 [2] Acts 8:32 [3] Acts 8:34,35
[4] Ecclesiastes 3:7

But with Jesus every situation was carefully analyzed; and even before the chief priests, there were occasions when He stood in stony silence. When the judgment hall was thronged with eager listeners and Christ had opportunity to array His divine wisdom, to the amazement of the crowds, He remained speechless.

This issue is not an easy one to settle. So frequently we say the wrong thing and then regret that we have spoken at all. On the other hand some of us have repented more than once because of a cowardly silence when we should have spoken out boldly. Peter doubtless stands out here as an example of human failure. Either he said the wrong thing at the wrong time or else he stood in shameful silence denying the Lord who loved him. But the more Peter studied His Saviour the more he learned about the subject of speech and silence. Now may the Holy Spirit be pleased to speak to our hearts as we look at the silence of Jesus.

Jesus was silent on the interrogation of Annas. After Christ's betrayal and arrest the officers "led Him away to Annas first." [5] Annas, in Scripture, is called "the high Priest," [6] and it was before him that our Lord underwent the first judicial examination. He questioned Christ concerning "His *disciples,* and of His *doctrine.*" [7] The high priest was eager to know who Christ's disciples were and just how far they had been influenced by His teaching. Then looking for something that he might use with which to press charges against Jesus, Annas questioned Him about His doctrine; that is, what our Lord taught, the principal points of His creed. This was not the inquiry of an honest man. Annas was hoping by reason or argument to deduce from our Lord's statements some word upon which he could condemn Christ to death. The bold reply of Jesus is noteworthy.

[5] John 18:13   [6] Acts 4:6; 23:2   [7] John 18:19

"Why asketh thou Me? ask them which heard Me." [8]

Why was Jesus silent concerning His disciples and His doctrine? Certainly there was nothing to hide. For three years He had taught openly and gained not a few followers. Whenever His disciples were wrongly accused Christ defended them. When the Pharisees condemned them for plucking corn on the Sabbath Jesus stood in their defense.[9] And at no time was He ashamed of His doctrine. It is repeated often in the Gospels that "they were astonished at His doctrine." [10] When He taught in the Temple Jesus told the Jews: "My doctrine is not Mine, but His that sent Me. If any man will do His will, he shall know of the doctrine, whether it be of God, or whether I speak of Myself." [11]

Why then was Jesus silent about the questions that Annas had asked? To know the heart of Annas is to know the answer to the silence of Jesus. Annas was the shrewd, sinister, and highly successful politician of Christ's day. His was a selfish interest. He never had the people at heart. His scheming and ruthless tactics had labeled him as a political rogue more than a priest of God. His crooked hands already had seized more than he could hold. When age sapped Annas of his vitality, one by one he made his five sons high priests. And when each had served his term Annas chose his son-in-law, Caiaphas. He bullied and bribed his way into the office of political rule. His real power and hatred for Christ were shown when our Lord's enemies hurried Him to Annas first. Annas had no honor. His system of dishonesty was diametrically opposed to the teaching of Christ. The insincerity and deceit in the heart of Annas were all known to our Lord. God "looketh on the heart." [12]

It was not a case of soul-hunger or spiritual anxiety with Annas. His only purpose was to entice and entrap Jesus so that

[8] John 18:21 [9] Luke 6:1-5
[10] Matthew 7:28; 22:33; Mark 1:22; 11:18; Luke 4:32
[11] John 7:16,17 [12] 1 Samuel 16:7

he might hasten His death. Thus Jesus became the stern, silent Listener, having perceived the wickedness in the heart of Annas. Do not think the Saviour cruel for His refusal to explain the doctrine of God. He is only too glad and gracious to answer a sincere inquirer. Jesus explained the new birth to Nicodemus, taught the woman at the well how to worship God, and explained to Thomas the way to heaven. Having full knowledge of the disingenuous spirit of Annas, Christ refused to be caught in his trap. He would not answer.

There is a silent heaven to all who have the spirit of Annas. God despises insincerity. When Joshua gave his last charge to Israel before his death, he said: "Fear the LORD, and serve Him in sincerity and in truth." [13] To be sincere means to be "unmixed, pure, unsullied." The sincere Christian is no hypocrite. Contrariwise, there is a corruptness in him who feigns piety but who is doubleminded. And though the insincere man attends church regularly, gives generously, and says prayers frequently, he gets no response from God. To him the Lord remains sternly reticent. Sincerity was the burden of the Apostle Paul's heart when he wrote to believers at Philippi: "And this I pray . . . that ye may be *sincere* and without offence till the day of Christ." [14]

Jesus was silent before Caiaphas. After Christ had refused to answer Annas regarding His disciples and His doctrine, "Annas had sent Him bound unto Caiaphas the high priest." [15] "Now Caiaphas was he, which gave counsel to the Jews, that it was expedient that one man should die for the people." [16]

After the witnesses had testified against Jesus in Caiaphas' court, the high priest asked Him: "Answerest Thou nothing? what is it which these witness against Thee? *But Jesus held His peace*." [17] Mark tells us that "He held His peace, and

[13] Joshua 24:14   [14] Philippians 1:9,10   [15] John 18:24
[16] John 18:14   [17] Matthew 26:62,63

answered nothing." [18] We find little difficulty in understanding the silence of Jesus before Caiaphas.

We notice first that Caiaphas had brought "false witnesses" to appear against Christ.[19] There was no honest effort to find out if Jesus was guilty; they merely assumed that He was. Having built up their case against Christ, the leaders of the Sanhedrin proceeded to hire false witnesses. And false they were! Pointing to our Lord, they testified: "This fellow said, I am able to destroy the temple of God, and to build it in three days." [20] Now no such statement had ever been made by Christ. He had said: "Destroy this temple, and in three days I will raise it up";[21] but He had been speaking of His own body and not the temple building.

Jesus saw through their plans. He was being incriminated. The Sanhedrin knew the witnesses were false; the witnesses themselves knew they were lying; and Christ knew full well the purpose of the lie. They convened with the determination to put Him to death. It was useless for our Lord to answer their charges. Whenever a man bears false witness against God and His Son, that man has sealed his own doom. No amount of ritual or ceremony on the part of the religious rulers in the temple could have appeased the wrath of God. He remained silent and refused to respond to their false worship. Little wonder that there are so many God-forsaken churches in our land! When modernists bear false witness, denying our Lord's virgin birth, vicarious atonement, and resurrection, they call upon Him in vain. He refuses to answer those who speak falsely of Himself.

Jesus was silent before Caiaphas, not because of the false witnesses merely, but because of the character and conduct of Caiaphas. Do not forget that Caiaphas ruled that unscrupulous crowd of money-changers that Christ had driven out of the

[18] Mark 14:61 [19] Matthew 26:59; Mark 14:57
[20] Matthew 26:61 [21] John 2:19

Temple. From that moment he determined that Jesus would be forever removed from his path, for the action our Lord took against the temple racketeers cut the fabulous income of the hierarchy. Caiaphas had prejudged Jesus when he slyly committed himself that Christ must die: "And one of them, named Caiaphas, being the high priest that same year, said unto them . . . it is expedient for us, that one man should die for the people." [22] Dr. Black says: "Prejudging is not judging. It argues a closed mind and a shut heart. That is fatal. Caiaphas, for instance, already knew what he was going to do with Jesus. When Christ looked at him, He was looking at a shut gate, locked and barred." The session before Caiaphas was a mock trial. In the mind of the high priest, Jesus was judged already.

Today men are condemning Christ before hearing Him. They deny His saving power before they taste and see that the Lord is good. They condemn the Bible, yet they have not studied it for themselves. They find all manner of fault with the church, yet they have not joined nor supported it. Because of preconceived ideas, misconceptions, and false teachings, Jesus is prejudged by men before they meet Him face to face. Any who condemn Him before He is heard, He will not answer. The Judged becomes the Judge, and in silence He condemns all who will not reason.

Jesus was silent before Pontius Pilate. When Caiaphas saw that his cunningness failed before the wisdom of the Son of God, he allowed some to spit in His face, and buffet Him; "and others smote Him with the palms of their hands," [23] and then they delivered Christ to Pilate. Already the testimony of the false witnesses had been passed on to Pilate, but one would feel that He could expect a fair hearing in a Roman court. In

[22] John 11:49,50   [23] Matthew 26:67

some respects we must agree that Pilate conducted himself well as a Roman governor. But as his conversation with Christ progressed he allowed his weaknesses and his true self to come more and more to the front. "Pilate said unto Him, Hearest Thou not how many things they witness against Thee?" "And He answered him to never a word; insomuch that the governor marvelled greatly." [24]

Now why did our Lord refuse to answer Pilate?

We do not think it by accident that Pontius Pilate is the only man whose name is mentioned in the "Apostle's Creed." Millions of people all over the world have declared in many different languages that they believed Jesus Christ, God's only Son, our Lord, "Suffered under Pontius Pilate."

Of Pilate it is written: "When he had scourged Jesus, he delivered Him to be crucified." [25] At the hands of this crooked politician the Saviour was subjected to the agony of indescribable torture. Blow after blow was rained on His defenseless body. They smote His face with the palms of their hands and pummeled Him with clenched fists. The scourging of Christ was worse than any modern method of punishment. The Son of God was stripped and tied and then whipped with rawhide, the thongs being tipped with sharp lead. Then the cruel and heartless hierarchy stood by while the Saviour's back was cut open by inhuman brutality. Such was the suffering of Christ at the hands of Pilate. But through it all our Lord was silent.

But why was Jesus silent in the presence of Pilate before He was scourged? First, I believe that Pilate was a coward, and because he lacked the courage of his convictions there was nothing that Jesus had to say to a man that was a weakling. The Jews said to Pilate: "We have a law, and by our law He ought to die, because He made Himself the Son of God."

"When Pilate therefore heard that saying, *he was the more afraid.*" [26]

[24] Matthew 27:14   [25] Matthew 27:26   [26] John 19:7,8

Pilate knew full well that Christ had done nothing worthy
of death, but instead of releasing his prisoner he condemned
Christ to death for fear of the people. He thought more of his
life and his job than he did of the eternal destiny of his own
soul. Having agreed to release Barabbas, the people's choice, the
cowardly Pilate sought to shift his responsibility of Christ on
someone else when he asked: "What shall I do then with Jesus
which is called Christ?" [27] This was a question that Pilate had
to answer for himself, but having played the role of a coward,
he sought to put the issue to the crowd. It was Pilate's personal
question. He had Christ on his hands and had to decide for Him
or against Him; but instead, he decided on a middle course
and sought a compromise measure.

> "But Jesus yet answered nothing; so that Pilate mar-
> velled." [28]

Pilate is at once terrified and frantic. No, Jesus is not impatient and angry with Pilate. He simply knows that it is vain
to answer a coward. When our only response to the Truth is
fear and cowardice, then the Truth becomes silent to us. If
when the true Light is put before our eyes we shrink back as a
pusillanimous man, then for us that Light refuses to shine.
It was so in the case of Peter. The fisherman-disciple had lost
all courage when he denied his Lord in the presence of the maid,
but Jesus said never a word to Peter. Instead, we are told: "The
Lord turned, and looked upon Peter." [29] That was all—He
looked! The silence of Jesus condemned the cowardly Peter so
that he "went out, and wept bitterly." Christ has no answer to
those who know the truth but lack the courage of their convictions.

"What shall I do then with Jesus which is called Christ?" On
this question we cannot remain neutral. It is for you and me to

[27] Matthew 27:22   [28] Mark 15:5   [29] Luke 22:61

decide as well as it was for Pilate. If for fear of losing our prestige, popularity, or position we leave the answer to the mob while we draw fearfully and cowardly back, then Christ will have nothing to answer us. "When Pilate heard of Galilee, he asked whether the man were a Galilaean. And as soon as he knew that He belonged unto Herod's jurisdiction, he sent Him to Herod, who himself also was at Jerusalem at that time. And when Herod saw Jesus, he was exceeding glad: for he was desirous to see Him of a long season, because he had heard many things of Him; and he hoped to have seen some miracle done by Him. Then he questioned with Him in many words; but He answered him nothing." [30]

Finally, as we have it here, Christ was silent before Herod—"He answered him nothing." Luke tells us that when Herod saw Jesus "he was exceeding glad." As far as we have any record this is the first time that Jesus and Herod met face to face. Why was Herod glad? He hoped to see Jesus perform some miracle. He had heard of our Lord's wonder-working power, and as Dr. Morgan says: "He expected some thrill for his degenerate, burnt-out life." Herod was a man of vile passions who became debauched by his lecherous villainy. He was enslaved by sin; but more than that, Herod was in love with his sin.

The corrupt and evil heart of Herod is obvious as we take one quick glance at his life. Herod Antipas was his name, and he became ruler of the province which contained Galilee. He was king during the lifetime of Jesus. When we first see him in the New Testament record, his hands are stained with the blood of one of God's choice servants. Of John the Baptist, our Lord said: "Among them that are born of women there hath not risen a greater than John the Baptist." [31] Matthew tells us

[30] Luke 23:6-9   [31] Matthew 11:11

also that Herod sent "and beheaded John in the prison." [82] This action of Herod only increased the intensity of his wickedness, for he was living unlawfully at that time with Herodias, his brother Philip's wife.

We know our Lord's estimate of Herod. When Jesus and His disciples entered Herod's territory preaching and teaching before the people, "The same day there came certain of the Pharisees, saying unto Him, Get Thee out, and depart hence: for Herod will kill Thee."

"And He said unto them, Go ye, and tell that fox." [83]

In his volume, *The Day of the Cross*, Dr. W. W. Clow says: "The story of Herod in the Gospel page is the history of the soul of a worldling." Here is a true estimate of the man. The worldly forces of evil became Herod's playground. He was absorbed in his sins and was satisfied to remain absorbed. Christ has nothing in common with a worldling who is in love with his sins, so He remains silent in the presence of Herod. Says Dr. Bruner: "Here we have, not Jesus on trial before Herod, but 'the spirit of this world' incarnate in Herod the worldling, on trial before that One who shall abide when the world and the lust thereof are passed away." Jesus has nothing to answer a pleasure-loving and sensual people who refuse to repent and turn from their evil ways.

This is the day of grace. "God . . . Hath in these last days spoken unto us by His Son." [84] The door of mercy is still open to all, even to those who are possessed of the spirit of Annas, Caiaphas, Pilate, or Herod. Men who are gripped by insincerity, falseness, cowardice, stubbornness, and vice may still be delivered from any and all kinds of sin. God, in His Word, still pleads for men to come in confession of their sins and be saved.

[82] Matthew 14:10   [83] Luke 13:31,32   [84] Hebrews 1:1,2

If you heed His invitation now, He will forgive you and cleanse you from all unrighteousness, but if you reject His loving offer of pardon you must pay at the day of judgment. In that day God will have become your Silent Judge.

CONSECRATION

Take my life and let it be
Consecrated, Lord, to Thee.
Take my moments and my days,
Let them flow in ceaseless praise.

Take my hands and let them move
At the impulse of Thy love.
Take my feet and let them be
Swift and beautiful for Thee.

Take my voice and let me sing
Always, only, for my King.
Take my lips and let them be
Filled with messages for Thee.

Take my silver and my gold,
Not a mite would I withhold.
Take my intellect and use
Every power as Thou shalt choose.

Take my will and make it Thine,
It shall be no longer mine.
Take my heart—it is Thine own,
It shall be Thy royal throne.

Take my love: my Lord, I pour
At Thy feet its treasure-store.
Take myself, and I will be
Ever, only, all for Thee.

—FRANCES RIDLEY HAVERGAL

HIS SANCTIFICATION

"And for their sakes I sanctify Myself, that they also might be sanctified through the truth." [1]

"I sanctify Myself." Is it not a very strange combination of words coming from the lips of our Lord? This statement was uttered by Christ in His great prayer as His earthly ministry drew to a close. It is recorded by Saint John only, and it consti-tutes the whole of the seventeenth chapter of the Gospel record that bears his name. Dr. G. Campbell Morgan has said: "When we come to this chapter we are at the center of all the sanctities. . . . Through this prayer we are permitted to come into the sanctity of the thinking of Jesus in the presence of His Father, immediately before His Cross." When our Lord prayed, He prayed on a level above that of any other person. Whenever we pray, it is through a divine Mediator only, but Christ was the Perfect Man, and therefore needed no mediator.

We approach this seventeenth chapter of John humbly and reverently, for we have before us the sanctum sanctorum of the Gospel. Personally, I do not see the faintest ray of hope that we shall ever comprehend here the full meaning of this great prayer of our Lord. Here the soul of Christ is poured forth before our very eyes, but the finite mind will never fathom the source. Among others, three Puritan preachers have attempted an ex-position of this chapter, and though their sermons comprise 1700 large pages, neither Newton, Manton, nor Burgess makes

[1] John 17:19

any claim to have given a complete or exhaustive treatment of its contents. In this brief meditation we shall consider a part of verse nineteen only, *"And for their sakes I sanctify Myself."*

❧

Some may question Christ's need for sanctification. It is true that in one sense our Lord needed no sanctification, for He "is holy, harmless, undefiled, separate from sinners, and made higher than the heavens." [2] This makes Christ's statement a difficult one to understand. It is quite clear, however, that the word *sanctify* does not carry with it the popular conception of making holy. As F. W. Robertson has said: "He could not by an inward effort or struggle *make* Himself holy, for He was that already."

A true interpretation of our Lord's statement rests upon a proper understanding of the word *sanctify*. We know that when Jesus used it in reference to Himself, He did not mean holy or righteous.

God had said to Jeremiah: "Before thou camest forth out of the womb I sanctified thee, and I ordained thee a prophet unto the nations." [3]

Here the word means *set apart,* for in His divine omniscience God saw Jeremiah set apart for the work of a prophet. This is rightly termed positional sanctification, for it has to do with Jeremiah's position and his relationship to the prophetic office. God had set him apart positionally. In exactly the same way all believers are set apart by God. We are positionally sanctified and are, therefore, saints before God. Writing to the church at Corinth, Paul addresses his Epistle, "Unto the church of God which is at Corinth, to them that are *sanctified* in Christ Jesus, called to be saints." [4] The sanctified are not sinlessly perfect, but are those set apart to God in Christ Jesus. The very moment a man puts his trust in the Lord Jesus for salvation from sin, that

[2] Hebrews 7:26 [3] Jeremiah 1:5 [4] 1 Corinthians 1:2

instant he becomes a saint and is positionally sanctified. "By the which will we are sanctified through the offering of the body of Jesus Christ once for all." [5] All believers are imperfect in this life. Nevertheless they are positionally set apart and are therefore saints. The Corinthian Christians had fallen into error and sin. Still Paul said: "But ye are washed, but ye are sanctified." [6]

Though Jeremiah was set apart (or sanctified) by God for the prophetic office, he had yet to sanctify (or devote) himself to the work that was assigned to him by God. At first Jeremiah offered excuses why he should not be God's prophet, and when the Lord assured him of His holy presence, Jeremiah agreed in his heart to obey God. He sanctified himself *practically* to a task that God had sanctified him to *positionally*. He devoted Himself to the work that God had appointed him to do. The same was true of Isaiah who said: "Here am I; send me." [7] The Apostle Paul testifies: "But when it pleased God, who separated me from my mother's womb, and called me by His grace, To reveal His Son in me, that I might preach Him among the heathen; immediately I conferred not with flesh and blood." [8] Here is Paul's positional sanctification, called and separated to the work of the gospel before he was born. But before Saul of Tarsus became the mighty apostle to the Gentiles he had to sanctify (or devote) himself willingly to that work. And he did that very thing when he cried: "Lord, what wilt Thou have me to do?" [9]

"Moses had said, Consecrate yourselves to day to the Lord." [10] Dr. E. Y. Mullins has said: "In Paul's writings there is frequent exhortation to consecration or sanctification in the sense of devotement to God." It is in this sense of "devotement," or the state of being devoted to God, that we shall use the term sanctification. Moses was saying in effect, "Devote yourselves unto the Lord. Become the devotees of God."

5 Hebrews 10:10   6 1 Corinthians 6:11   7 Isaiah 6:8
8 Galatians 1:15,16   9 Acts 9:6   10 Exodus 32:29

This is exactly what our Lord meant when He said: "I sanctify Myself." God the Father already had sanctified the Son for the work of redemption, for we read of Jesus, "Whom the Father hath *sanctified*, and sent into the world." [11] Jesus Christ was set apart for the purpose of redeeming lost humanity, for, says the Apostle John: "The Father sent the Son to be the Saviour of the world." [12] After He had come it was left with the Son to devote Himself to His unfinished task, so He set Himself apart to complete redemption's plan.

❧

Jesus Christ was devoted to the truth. On one occasion He said: "I am . . . the truth." [13] The written Word is truth, but He, the living Word, is *the* Truth. John says that He is "full of grace and truth." [14] While the law was given by Moses, "grace and *truth* came by Jesus Christ." [15]

Our Lord was devoted to the truth in His preaching. His first recorded message in the synagogue showed His devotion to the truth. As He took His place behind the sacred desk, "there was delivered unto Him the book of the prophet Esaias" [or Isaiah].[16] From one of the greatest of the Old Testament prophets our Lord read and expounded. On one occasion the devil made up Christ's audience. Three times the tempter sought to lead Him astray, but Jesus proved His devotedness to the Word. Not even the powers of hell could shake Him from the truth. Hear Him answer:

"Man shall not live by bread alone, but by every word that proceedeth out of the mouth of God." [17]

"Jesus said unto him, It is written." [18]

"Get thee hence, Satan: for it is written." [19]

[11] John 10:36
[14] John 1:14
[17] Matthew 4:4
[12] 1 John 4:14
[15] John 1:17
[18] Matthew 4:7
[13] John 14:6
[16] Luke 4:17
[19] Matthew 4:10

In His refusal to compromise with evil our Lord proved that devotedness to the truth would bring the victory. The chief weapon that Christ used in resisting Satan was the Word. Paul said: "Take . . . the sword of the Spirit, which is the word of God." [20] The great apostle knew that we could not fight the good fight of faith unless we were fully equipped with the God-provided implement of war. We need a sharp, offensive weapon that will deal the death blow to the ministers of Satan who teach the doctrines of demons. There are some modern preachers of our own day who deny that the Bible is the inspired Word of God. Others hold that the Bible merely contains the Word of God and that only parts of it can be accepted. These twentieth century Pharisees are strangers to the Sword of the Spirit.

In sanctifying Himself to the truth, Jesus always was prepared to face the enemies of God's Word. Repeatedly He wielded the Sword of Truth in answering the scribes and Pharisees. Though they were offended by His doctrine, He never departed from what He knew was right. When they accused the disciples of transgressing the tradition of the elders, Jesus answered them, "For God commanded, saying . . . well did Isaiah prophesy of you." [21] Jesus was hated because of His words, but He refused to be silenced. He knew that the Word was a terror to evildoers. Still He fearlessly proclaimed it.

Let us not forget "the Word of God is quick, and powerful, and sharper than any two edged sword, piercing even to the dividing asunder of soul and spirit, and of the joints and marrow, and is a discerner of the thoughts and intents of the heart." [22] There is need for the Word of God to be spoken in the power of the Spirit even though men do not want it. We have the promise of God, "It shall not return unto Me void, but it shall accomplish that which I please, and it shall prosper

[20] Ephesians 6:17   [21] Matthew 15:4,7,12   [22] Hebrews 4:12

in the thing whereto I sent it." [23] "Preach the Word," says Paul, "be instant in season, out of season." [24] Are we devoted to God's Word? Are we regular in our private reading and study of the Bible for personal experience?

Our Lord proved His devotion to the truth by practicing it. Some men can preach a practical sermon but they seem to have great difficulty in practicing what they preach. With Christ it was a case of preaching what He practiced. We have stated already that not one of us will arrive at the state of sinless perfection in this life. However, we are not dabbling in the realm of conjecture when we say that Jesus was absolutely sinless. He could speak out boldly against the sins of lying, stealing, covetousness, adultery, envy, backbiting, or hatred without fear of repercussion. He did no sin, in Him was no sin, and He was separate from sinners. During His entire lifetime upon earth Christ devoted Himself to the preaching and practicing of the truth.

The Bible speaks often of devotion to the truth. The Apostle Paul wrote: "Holding forth the word of life," [25] "Hold fast the form of sound words," [26] "Holding fast the faithful word." [27] Here he is pleading for loyalty and devotion to the truth of God, for when we are holding to the truth we may expect the truth to hold us. Earlier in His prayer our Lord besought the Father in behalf of His disciples and prayed: "Sanctify them through Thy truth: Thy Word is truth." [28] As we are enlightened by the Word we must live by the Word. When we do not rebel and steel ourselves against the truth, it will purify our lives.

Not only was our Lord devoted to the *truth*, but He sanctified Himself to a *task* as well. His coming into the world was no

[23] Isaiah 55:11
[24] 2 Timothy 4:2
[25] Philippians 2:16
[26] 2 Timothy 1:13
[27] Titus 1:9
[28] John 17:17

fortuitous event. Jesus Himself said: "For the Son of Man is come to seek and to save that which was lost." [29] Seeking and saving lost souls was His work. And in all of His life and service He could not be veered from His course. Larger opportunities and higher salaries sometimes cajole us into new fields of endeavor; but His life work was never a contingency with Jesus. Just before His birth an angel of the Lord appeared to Joseph, and said: "Thou shalt call His name JESUS [meaning Saviour]: for He shall save His people from their sins." [30] To that task of saving men Christ devoted Himself without mental reservation. He prayed: "And for their sakes I sanctify Myself." He set Himself apart to live and to die for others. That was His mission, and not once did He permit any person or power to change His course.

By a solemn act Jesus Christ dedicated Himself to deliver sinful humanity from the penalty and the power of sin. By His death and Resurrection He sanctifies positionally all that believe in Him. Now He asks that we set ourselves apart to the task of taking His gospel to the uttermost part of the earth. He said: "Ye have not chosen Me, but I have chosen you, and ordained you, that ye should go and bring forth fruit, and that your fruit should remain." [31] He has ordained us (or set us apart) to be witnesses of His gospel. Will we devote ourselves to this glorious work or will we allow cares, pleasures, and pastimes to occupy our time? Jesus could say: "I have glorified Thee on the earth: I have finished the work which Thou gavest Me to do." [32] When He prayed thus He was certain of His Cross, so that when He hung dying on it, His last cry was "It is finished." Let us, like our Lord, find the perfect plan of God for our lives, and then in love and loyalty to Him, say, "I sanctify myself." Even now He stands at your heart's door; and as He seeks to possess you, He asks: "Who then is willing to consecrate his service this day unto the Lord?" [33]

[29] Luke 19:10 [30] Matthew 1:21 [31] John 15:16
[32] John 17:4 [33] 1 Chronicles 29:5

"THOU REMAINEST"

"Thou remainest," blest Redeemer,
Lord of peace and Lord of strife;
Jesus, Saviour, Lord forever,
"Thou remainest," Christ my life.

Satisfying ev'ry longing
Of my sinful soul for grace;
From my weakness never turning,
"Thou remainest," Christ my peace.

One by one my loved may leave me,
Voices sweet no more be heard;
But of God naught can bereave me,
"Thou remainest," Christ my Lord.

When from earth Thou, Lord, shalt call me,
Calm I'll lay my burden down;
For I know, whate'er befall me,
"Thou remainest," Christ my crown.

—D. W. WHITTLE (EL NATHAN)

HIS STEADFASTNESS

"He steadfastly set His face to go to Jerusalem." [1]

Ours is a flabby age. Should we find one person who tenaciously holds on to some principle, purpose, or pursuit of life, we have found the exception rather than the commonplace. The lost are groping to find a purpose for life, and having found it, they are bewildered to realize they have no power to effect it. The removal of the callous on the surface lays bare a flabbiness and fickleness that becomes the more abhorrent to us as we gaze upon the steadfastness of Christ.

One of the most wonderful characterizations of our Lord is that of the "set face," the determination to fulfill the eternal resolve and purpose of His soul. The gifted artists of the centuries have combined to give us many wonderful portraits of the Saviour, but none has used the steadfast face of Jesus as material for his masterpiece. And yet Christ's steadfastness is one of the distinguished characteristics of His whole life. Knowing the eternal will of the Father, our Lord came to fulfill it fully, and not even the devil could bend or break His will. He expressed a singleness of purpose in the words, "Lo, I come to do Thy will, O God."

It was the plan of God the Father to send the Son to be the Saviour of the world. In eternity past the method of man's redemption was agreed upon by all three Persons of the Godhead. Calvary was no mere afterthought. Jesus was the Lamb

[1] Luke 9:51

slain before the foundation of the world. It was the perfect will of God for Him to complete the divine mission in giving Himself in sacrificial death for sinners. His task was not an easy one. Every day of His life Jesus lived in anticipation and expectation of the shameful death by crucifixion.

"He steadfastly set His face to go to Jerusalem." [2]

In the face of satanic effort to thwart the carrying out of His mission, we see Him proceeding to the accomplishment of that work of redemption. Obviously Christ had a clear conception of His mission when He was but a boy of twelve. The temple scene at Jerusalem, when He sat down with the rabbis to discuss the fine points of the law, gives evidence of Christ's firmness and determination to continue in the things of His Father. When Mary and Joseph found Him in the Temple, His mother said: "Son, why hast Thou thus dealt with us? behold Thy father and I have sought Thee sorrowing." Then we have the first recorded words from the lips of the boy Jesus. He answered: "How is it that ye sought Me? wist ye not that I *must* be about My Father's business?" [3] Though His earthly parents did not understand Him, Jesus told them that the theme of His life was to be about the things of His Father. It was a divine imperative—"I *must* be about My Father's business."

"*I must.*" In these words our Lord expressed steadfastness. There is glory in going on, but the final crown is never won until the Cross. So that His life would be one of enduring discipline, Jesus made His decision early. He made steadfastness the keynote of His early life, and throughout His whole earthly ministry the peremptory word *"must"* constrained Him to finish the work that the Father had given Him to do.

[2] Luke 9:51   [3] Luke 2:49

In His steadfastness Jesus carried His message of divine love and life to all men. We feel called and confined to a certain function or province. We settle down to one country or community. In Capernaum the people sought Him that He should not depart from them. But He replied: *"I must preach the kingdom of God to other cities also: for therefore am I sent."* [4] "He came unto His own, and His own received Him not." Then as He spoke of His great redemption, He said:

"I lay down My life for the sheep."
"And other sheep I have, which are not of this fold: them also I *must* bring." [5]

The world was His field. When His sheep of the Jewish fold rejected Him, He turned to the other sheep, the Gentiles, for, said He: "Them also *I must bring*." In order to fulfill the divine program and the prophetic Word, Christ provided salvation for all men. Just prior to His death He reminded the disciples that, "The gospel must first be published among all nations." [6]

God's *must* in our Saviour's life was a tremendous driving force toward expeditiousness. Jesus knew His life on earth would be short-lived, and therefore there was no time to be wasted. When He saw the need of the blind man He would not be delayed by discussing with His disciples the cause of the man's blindness. He interrupted their interrogations by stating: "I must work the works of Him that sent Me, while it is day: the night cometh, when no man can work." [7]

While Jesus was here on earth it was "day." When man rejected and crucified Him, and He left this earth, it became "night." As He saw the shadow of His Cross He hurried to complete the task that was His. It was the Spirit of Christ that lay hold of the mighty Apostle Paul when he said: "The night

[4] Luke 4:43   [5] John 10:15,16   [6] Mark 13:10
[7] John 9:4

is far spent, the day is at hand: let us therefore cast off the works of darkness, and let us put on the armour of light." [8] Elsewhere Paul pleads for "redeeming the time." [9] O Christian, this is our daylight; it will soon be gone. Opportunities we lose now can never be retrieved. The resoluteness of our Lord Jesus Christ should drive us to expeditiousness. "Whatsoever thy hand findeth to do, do it with thy might; for there is no work, nor device, nor knowledge, nor wisdom, in the grave, whither thou goest." [10]

There is yet a further note in the *must* of God as it affected the life of Christ. As yet He had not reached Jerusalem toward which "He stedfastly set His face." Why did Jerusalem constrain Him? To Christ all Jerusalem, its civic and religious system, was rancorous. Clemency was never shown. All assailed His every act. But Jerusalem needed Him, so He must go. He foretold her destruction when He said: "And when ye shall see Jerusalem compassed with armies, then know that the desolation thereof is nigh." [11] Though our Lord knew of that city's deliberate rejection of Him and of her doom, His love for her never waned. Still He lamented over the city and cried: "O Jerusalem, Jerusalem, which killest the prophets, and stonest them that are sent unto thee; how often would I have gathered thy children together, as a hen doth gather her brood under her wings, and ye would not!" [12]

But Christ did not labor and love in vain. Even though Jerusalem has been the object of much scorn and suffering, it is only "in part," [13] "until the times of the Gentiles be fulfilled." [14] The mighty rehabilitation when her "desert shall rejoice, and blossom as the rose" [15] has already sprouted. It is even as

[8] Romans 13:12
[9] Ephesians 5:16
[10] Ecclesiastes 9:10
[11] Luke 21:20
[12] Luke 13:34
[13] Romans 11:25
[14] Luke 21:24
[15] Isaiah 35:1

the apostle testifies in the Patmos vision—"And there came unto me one of the seven angels . . . And he carried me away in the spirit to a great and high mountain, and shewed me that great city, the holy Jerusalem, descending out of heaven from God." [16]

Jerusalem was not only the object of the Saviour's love; it was the place of His sufferings. "From that time forth began Jesus to shew unto His disciples, how that He must go unto Jerusalem, and suffer many things of the elders and chief priests and scribes, and be killed, and be raised again the third day." [17]

Our Lord's choice to suffer at Jerusalem has shaken the whole world, which has not ceased to marvel at Christ's tenacity of purpose in yielding to the shameful death by crucifixion. His disciples could not sound such resoluteness to the torture that awaited Him. Rebuking Him, they said: "Be it far from Thee, Lord: this shall not be unto Thee." [18] But He had pledged Himself years before He had come into this world. The prophet Isaiah, quoting the Holy One of God, said: "For the Lord God will help me; therefore shall I not be confounded: *therefore have I set My face like a flint,* and I know that I shall not be ashamed." [19]

The Son of Man must suffer many things. He chose the Cross in ages past, and He could not deny Himself. The prophets portrayed Him as the suffering Servant of Jehovah. With a calm confidence that His death would deliver mankind from the penalty and the power of sin, He resolutely fixed His eye upon the place where He knew suffering would be His. The human thing to do would be to go anywhere else but to Jerusalem, for this was the city of danger and peril. However, the *must* of Christ's sufferings was "the divine and eternal counsels of God operating in Him and through Him, and driving Him along that pathway." [20]

[16] Revelation 21:9,10   [17] Matthew 16:21   [18] Matthew 16:22
[19] Isaiah 50:7   [20] Dr. G. Campbell Morgan

After Pentecost Peter had a new concept of the *must* of Christ's sufferings. When he preached his first sermon in the power of Pentecost, he declared: "Him, being delivered by *the determinate counsel* and foreknowledge of God, ye have taken, and by wicked hands have crucified and slain." [21]

The mighty apostle would not allow those responsible for Christ's death to think for a moment that Jesus died a helpless victim or went to a martyr's death. He would have them know that the Saviour's death was "by the determinate counsel and foreknowledge of God." That means that it was according to God's settled purpose. The Leader of this small band of disciples deliberately walked into what He knew would mean certain death for Himself. Though they were dismayed and filled with fear when He first told them, He insisted: "Behold, we go up to Jerusalem; and the Son of man shall be betrayed unto the chief priests and unto the scribes, and they shall condemn Him to death." [22] But now they knew that "the Son of man came not to be ministered unto, but to minister, and to give His life a ransom for many." [23] Jesus chose the Cross and went to Jerusalem to His death absolutely of His own free will. It was His settled purpose before sin entered into the world. Therefore when He came, the Cross was a solemn necessity which drove Him toward Jerusalem until His death was accomplished. The death of Jesus Christ was a deliberate laying down of His life, a voluntary substitution that He might deliver sinners from eternal condemnation. If atonement were to be made, it was absolutely necessary that Christ, the sinless One, should shed His blood for remission of sin.

❦

Yet one deeper note is sounded in the *must* of the Saviour. If Christ struggled with varied forces that sought to keep Him

[21] Acts 2:23   [22] Matthew 20:18   [23] Matthew 20:28

from going to the Cross, His greatest battle was to remain on that Cross after His enemies had nailed Him to it. At no time in our Lord's life was His steadfastness so much in evidence as when the crowds challenged His deity as He hung upon His Cross. "And they that passed by reviled Him, wagging their heads, And saying, Thou that destroyest the temple, and buildest it in three days, save Thyself. If Thou be the Son of God, come down from the cross. Likewise also the chief priests mocking Him, with the scribes and elders, said, He saved others; Himself He cannot save. If He be the King of Israel, let Him now come down from the cross, and we will believe Him." [24]

These final taunts of the priests hurled against the bleeding, dying Son of God challenged His claims to deity. They cried: "If Thou be the Son of God, come down from the cross." Their cry is filled with doubt—"If." But there is no "perhaps" or "probably" attached to this issue. He was and is the Son of God. The Father had testified: "This is My beloved Son." And yet the rabble-rousing mob cast their denunciations in His teeth. But, mark you, the same power that stilled the storm, raised the dead, and which hardly twelve hours before had cast an armed guard prostrate to the ground, could have silenced and paralyzed all who stood about Him. Furthermore, legions of angels stood at attention ready to answer His call. One word from His parched lips and His enemies would have been annihilated. Yes, Jesus could have accepted their challenge and, without difficulty, come down from the cross. But, thank God, He steadfastly stayed on it, for without the crucified Christ there could have been no Christianity. Any one of us would have fallen into the enemy's trap, but our Lord remained resolute.

Then His tormentors derided Him: "He saved others; Himself He cannot save." How true! *He saved others.* That was the

[24] Matthew 27:39-42

purpose of His coming, "For the Son of man is come to seek and to save that which was lost." [25] But what a sad misconception they had when they sneered: "Himself He *cannot* save." Our Lord did have the power to come down from the cross but He *would* not. They should have said: "Himself He will not save." Had Christ answered their devilish taunts the whole human race would have been plunged into darkness and condemnation and lost forever. A crossless Christ would have meant eternal tragedy. The Saviour might have chosen some quick and sudden method to die. But no! He persisted in crucifixion, the long, painful, excruciating death. With each moment that He hung on the Cross the fever increased its raging and the burning wounds increased their pain. Yet He refused to come down until He had completed the wonderful plan of redemption. Having loved His own He loved them unto the end. Bless the Lord! Christ steadfastly remained on the Cross.

❧

This brief glimpse of the Saviour's determination shamefully reveals our own instability and our lack of resolution. We need to settle the vital issues of life with a fixed purpose and with promptitude. We are short on the spirit to face danger and suffering. Yet this sin-scarred age in which we live cries for immediate action on the part of Christ's followers. The Apostle Paul saw the peril in his day, so writing to Timothy, he stripped his sympathy of all false sentiment when he said: "My son, be strong in the grace that is in Christ Jesus. Thou therefore endure hardness, as a good soldier of Jesus Christ." [26]

Paul did not pen these words from an elaborate suite in a hotel. The quivering hand that held the quill was manacled with a felon's chain. The preacher was shivering in a damp

* Luke 19:10   [26] 2 Timothy 2:1,3

dungeon without his cloak which he had left at Troas. He was expecting with the dawn of each new day that some stern-faced executioner would unlock his cell door and lead him to his death. Yet there was no sign of wavering in his spirit, no plea for help or release, no expression of regret that he hazarded his life in the great crusade for Christ, not even perturbation. The stones of Lystra or the stripes of Philippi could never strip him of his courage. He was "the prisoner of Jesus Christ," and "it makes a world of difference if you take Jesus into jail with you. Jesus can turn a prison into a paradise, a prisoner's bench into a pulpit, a felon's bonds into a silent exposition of His gospel." [27] Here is a challenge to those of us who are so easily browbeaten and so frequently daunted and discouraged.

Paul was following in the steps of his Master. Why do we not follow? The *must* of the Saviour's sufferings must be produced in all who will be His disciples. The Apostle Peter said: "Ye are partakers of Christ's sufferings." Therefore we ought not to think it strange concerning the fiery trial which is to try us, as though some strange thing happened to us,[28] for, in due time, when our Lord is revealed in His glory, our rejoicing will be yet greater.

Let us, with fixed determination, "forgetting those things which are behind, and reaching forth unto those things which are before . . . press toward the mark for the prize of the high calling of God in Christ Jesus." [29] "Nothing wavering. For he that wavereth is like a wave of the sea driven with the wind and tossed." [30] It is not enough to commence with Christ; we must continue firm unto the end. "For we are made partakers of Christ, if we hold the beginning of our confidence steadfast unto the end." [31]

[27] R. Moffat Gautrey   [28] 1 Peter 4:12,13   [29] Philippians 3:13,14
[30] James 1:6   [31] Hebrews 3:14

"Filled with the Spirit, fitted for service,
All that I am to Jesus I give.
Filled with the Spirit, doing His bidding,
Only for Jesus now would I live."

MATCHLESS HANDS

His hands were laid in blessing on the head
Of each small, trusting child who came to Him;
And by their touch He gave life to the dead,
Health to the sick, and light to eyes grown dim.
The lame were strengthened, lepers were made clean,
The hungry fed, the thirsty satisfied;
The demon-ridden, freed from bonds unseen,
Praised the blest hands whose power men have denied.

And in those gentle palms, the cruel nails
Made the eternal scars that still proclaim
The love of God that changes not, nor fails
One need of those who call upon His name.
Death could not bind His hands, nor could the grave
Render them powerless, for beneath their tips
Hell's ramparts crumbled, and a joyous wave
Of souls surged up, His praises on their lips.

Those matchless hands, outstretched, are pleading now,
"O weary, sinsick soul, come unto me."
I can resist them not, Lord; so I bow
Low at Thy feet for all the world to see.
Take Thou this useless lump of human clay,
Distorted in the making—shaped so ill—
Break its spirit in Thy hands; then I pray,
Refashion it according to Thy will.

—Eunice L. Newman

HIS SCARS

"His visage was so marred more than any man, and His form more than the sons of men." [1]

> Five bleeding wounds He bears,
> Received on Calvary;
> They pour effectual prayers,
> They strongly pray for me:
> "Forgive him. Oh! forgive," they cry,
> "Nor let that ransomed sinner die."
>
> —Charles Wesley

Do the Scriptures remain almost silent on the beauty and grace of the Lord Jesus as He lived His earthly life because no words could adequately describe His loveliness? Yet we have this said of Him: "Thou art fair . . . yea, pleasant." Truly He was the "rose of Sharon" and the "lily of the valleys" as He walked this earth. "His head is as the most fine gold . . . His eyes are as the eyes of doves by the rivers of waters . . . His cheeks are . . . as sweet flowers: His lips like lilies, dropping sweet smelling myrrh. . . . Yea, he is altogether lovely." [2]

Though the Scriptures permit us to behold His beauty through the eye of faith, yet it is the sight of the bleeding Christ that has brought more men into right relation with God than any other. He was bruised for our iniquities. "His visage was so marred more than any man, and His form more than

[1] Isaiah 52:14   [2] Song of Solomon 5:10-16

the sons of men," [3] for our justification. One cannot gaze long at such exemplification of divine justice, limitless love, and grace without being transformed. Behold the scars!

∾

There were the scars of the scourging. Scourging was one of the severest methods of punishment in Christ's day. In the Latin we have *excoriare; ex* which means "off," and *corium*, meaning "skin." This word was used to convey the thought of stripping off the skin. In a vivid portrayal the Prophet Isaiah depicts the scourging of Jehovah's suffering Servant.

> "I gave My back to the smiters, and My cheeks to them that plucked off the hair: I hid not My face from shame and spitting." [4]

> "But He was wounded for our transgressions, He was bruised for our iniquities: the chastisement of our peace was upon Him; and with His stripes we are healed." [5]

Such treatment was reserved for criminals of the lowest type. Yet the back of Jesus was lashed and whipped until it was cut and bleeding, and not once did He wince or withdraw from the many stripes. Though He was not the sinner or the criminal, He was paying in full for the world's outrageous sins and crimes against the holiness of God. The Apostle Peter interprets for us the divine purpose in the scars of the scourging: "Who His own self bare our sins in His own body on the tree, that we, being dead to sins, should live unto righteousness: by whose stripes ye were healed." [6] Peter is in perfect harmony with Isaiah in the interpretation of the reason for Christ's sufferings, for more than seven hundred years before Christ was born the prophet said: "He was wounded for our transgressions, He was

[3] Isaiah 52:14   [4] Isaiah 50:6   [5] Isaiah 53:5
[6] 1 Peter 2:24

bruised for our iniquities: the chastisement of our peace was upon Him, and with His stripes we are healed." Our bodies are scarred *by* sin, but the body of our glorified Redeemer was the only body scarred *for* sin. In the Saviour's scourging, God was laying on Him the iniquity of us all.

Be it to the shame of man that he can see the spectacle of Calvary and pass by it unmoved. It is tragic for anyone to become so accustomed to the scourgings and stripes of the Crucified that he can glance upon Him as just another passing attraction to the eye. R. Moffat Gantrey, a minister in the Wesleyan Methodist Church of England, has said that our hearts have grown callous because they are accustomed to His anguish. "We are no longer awed by the unutterable sorrow of the Lamb. If angels have hearts to break, they must have broken their very hearts when they saw what man had done to God's Well-Beloved. If angels have tears to shed, they must have wept tears of blood as they marked the base indignities which man had heaped upon the wondrous Saviour of the world. It was a sight at which heaven shuddered, and from which the angels veiled their faces with their wings, unable to behold the tragic evidences of our tremendous shame."

Those scars that were once the object of the laughter and scorn of man have become the source of light and salvation to all who believe. That same scourged and scarred back of Jesus hides the sin of every blood-washed child of God. "Behold, for peace I had great bitterness: but Thou hast in love to my soul delivered it from the pit of corruption: for Thou hast cast all my sins behind Thy back." [7] Yes, "they led Him away, and delivered Him to Pontius Pilate the governor . . . and when he had scourged Jesus, he delivered Him to be crucified." [8] But let us not forget that in every blow that struck the back of the Saviour, "God was in Christ, reconciling the world unto Himself." [9] What an awe-inspiring, transcending thought! By

[7] Isaiah 38:17   [8] Matthew 27:2,26   [9] 2 Corinthians 5:19 .

those stripes we are healed. In the resurrection day the redeemed shall stand in His presence with perfect, glorified bodies, but as we gaze upon the scars of our Lord's scourging we shall be reminded of the infinite cost of our redemption.

Then there were the scars of the spikes. It is universally known that when our Lord was crucified on the cross, His body was fastened to it by the spikes that were driven through His hands and His feet. He said through the Psalmist: "They pierced My hands and My feet." [10]

Have you ever considered the hands of Jesus? His holy hands did not deserve the scars of the nails that were put there.

His are the mighty hands that hold all of time and eternity. The Psalmist testified: "My times are in Thy hand." [11]

His are the hands of mercy. David prayed: "I am in a great strait: let me fall now into the hand of the Lord; for very great are His mercies." [12] The blood that dripped from His wounded hands tells us that it is "not by works of righteousness which we have done, but according to His mercy He saved us, by the washing of regeneration, and renewing of the Holy Ghost." [13] All who ever hope to be saved from hell must be saved by His mighty hand, for, "Behold, the Lord's hand is not shortened, that it cannot save." [14] Christ can cleanse the vilest and most degraded sinner, for we read concerning a leper that "Jesus put forth His hand, and touched him, saying, I will; be thou clean. And immediately his leprosy was cleansed." [15] In mercy He blesses little children. We read that "He took them up in His arms, put His hands upon them, and blessed them." [16]

His are the hands of deliverance. Did not the prophet say: "The hand of our God was upon us, and He delivered us from the hand of the enemy"? [17] God, by His hand, delivered the Is-

[10] Psalm 22:16
[11] Psalm 31:15
[12] 1 Chronicles 21:13
[13] Titus 3:5
[14] Isaiah 59:1
[15] Matthew 8:3
[16] Mark 10:16
[17] Ezra 8:31

raelites. Faithless Peter stepped off his ship to walk on the water, but fear gripped him and he commenced to sink, "and immediately Jesus stretched forth His hand, and caught him." [18] Even now the world seeks to lure the Christian, and Satan desires to slay him, but "Though he fall, he shall not be utterly cast down: for the LORD upholdeth him with His hand." [19]

His are the hands of assurance and safety. The believer's remarkable deliverance from the penalty of sin is an eternal one. Jesus said: "I give unto them eternal life; and they shall never perish, neither shall any man pluck them out of My hand. My Father, which gave them Me, is greater than all; and no man is able to pluck them out of My Father's hand." [20]

When Christ comes back again, "One shall say unto Him, What are these wounds in Thine hands? Then He shall answer, Those with which I was wounded in the house of My friends." [21] Yes, our risen Lord carries the scars of the spikes in His hands today, and those wounds are the sure evidence of His Saviourhood. Those scars were the proofs whereby He showed Himself alive after His Resurrection. When He appeared to His disciples after the Resurrection, "He shewed unto them His hands." [22] The scars in His hands strengthen our faith in the One whom we have trusted for eternal life, even Jesus Christ, who was dead, but who is alive forevermore.

R. Moffat Gantrey related the following incident in his sermon entitled "The Pierced Hands":

"Not many months ago, in an Oxfordshire village, an old saint lay dying. For over eighty years she had been on pilgrimage to Zion, until her face had grown bright with heaven's approaching glory. An Anglo-Catholic priest, under the entire misapprehension that none of his parishioners could find access to the City unless he unlocked the gate, called to visit her. 'Madam,' he said, 'I have come to grant you absolution.'

[18] Matthew 14:31   [19] Psalm 37:24   [20] John 10:28,29
[21] Zechariah 13:6   [22] John 20:20

"And she, in her simplicity, not knowing what that word meant, inquired, 'What is that?'

" 'I have come to forgive your sins,' was the reply.

" 'May I look into your hand?' she answered. Gazing for a moment into the hand of the priest, she turned and looked him squarely in the face and said, 'Sir! You are an imposter.'

" 'Imposter!' the scandalized cleric protested.

" 'Yes, sir, an imposter! *The Man who forgives my sin has a nail-print in His palm.'* "

We fully believe in the biblical record of what Christ's hands have wrought in creation, for "Of old hast Thou laid the foundation of the earth: and the heavens are the work of Thy hands." [23] But greater still than the work of creation by His hands is the amazing and finished work of redemption. When we see our wonderful Creator-Redeemer God, there will be a scar in each hand; the scar of the spike which the executioner's hammer had driven through those hands of love and power.

There is a strange but striking passage in the prophecy of Isaiah. "Can a woman forget her suckling child, that she should not have compassion on the son of her womb? yea, they may forget, yet will I not forget thee. Behold, I have graven thee upon the palms of My hands." [24] We know of mothers who have neglected and forgotten their own children, but we may be assured that our heavenly Father who has purchased us and made us His own children by the blood of His only begotten Son will never forget His own. And why? Because He has engraved their names in the palm of His hands. His are the hands of eternal remembrance of a right relationship between the sons of men who have trusted in the Lord Jesus Christ. When finally we arrive at home to be with the Lord, the scars in His hands will guarantee us that we shall ever be with the Lord.

∽✷

[23] Psalm 102:25   [24] Isaiah 49:15,16

But there are scars in Jesus' feet also. We remember how He said: "They pierced My hands *and My feet*." [25] Before those wounds were cut into the Saviour's feet, He sought the streets and the lanes for the lost and needy. In His untiring service to the world, His were feet of beauty—"How beautiful upon the mountains are the feet of him that bringeth good tidings, that publisheth peace." [26]

Mary, in her hour of sorrow and bereavement, was comforted at the feet of Jesus—"Then when Mary was come where Jesus was, and saw Him, she fell down at His feet, saying unto Him, Lord, if Thou hadst been here, my brother had not died." [27]

When Jesus came to Bethany, we are told that Mary "sat at Jesus' feet, and heard His word." [28] At the nail-scarred feet of the Saviour multitudes have come since Mary's day, and they are coming still, to learn wisdom from above.

Christ's feet are the only feet worthy of worship. When the two Marys came to the tomb on the morning of the Resurrection, "Jesus met them, saying, All hail. And they came and held Him by the feet, and worshipped Him." [29]

Large numbers were brought to His feet for healing—"And great multitudes came unto Him, having with them those that were lame, blind, dumb, maimed, and many others, and cast them down at Jesus' feet; and He healed them." [30]

As the sovereign Head of the Church which is His Body, all things are under His feet—"And hath put all things under His feet, and gave Him to be the head over all things to the church." [31] How it must have grieved our Lord down through the centuries to gaze upon the ignorant masses bowing themselves before the feet of popes and bishops! But the future is bright with promise and prospect, "For He must reign, till He hath put all enemies under His feet." [32] One day they pierced

[25] Psalm 22:16
[28] Luke 10:39
[31] Ephesians 1:22
[26] Isaiah 52:7
[29] Matthew 28:9
[32] 1 Corinthians 15:25
[27] John 11:32
[30] Matthew 15:30

and scarred His holy feet with spikes, but those scarred feet will one day trample down the enemies of our God and His Christ.

We must hasten to consider the scars of the thorns. Matthew says: "And when they had platted a crown of thorns, they put it upon His head." [33] The human mind with its limitations finds it difficult to conceive of this coronation when the Head that was graced with the glory of God was suddenly seized by wicked hands and crowned with thorns, "the head upon which all the angelic adoration was heaped."

When our Lord left heaven the world viewed the greatest act of humility it had ever known. Christ, the King of glory, had left the ivory palaces to become the hated and despised Carpenter of Nazareth. So poor and lowly did He become that on one occasion He said: "The foxes have holes, and the birds of the air have nests; but the Son of man hath not where to lay His head." [34] It was this humble and homeless head that His enemies smote and pierced with thorns.

Thorns had their beginning in the garden of Eden. Thorns and thistles were a part of the curse pronounced upon the earth when Adam and Eve sinned. God had said: "Cursed is the ground . . . Thorns also and thistles shall it bring forth to thee." [35] Thus our Lord, who knew no sin, was made sin for us when the emblem of sin was pressed upon His brow. Thorns are a part of the curse, but the Christian rejoices as he reads Paul's triumphant declaration of deliverance—"Christ hath redeemed us from the curse of the law, being made a curse for us." [36]

There is a prophetic utterance that says: "All the land shall become briers and thorns." [37] This prophecy has had a re-

[33] Matthew 27:29   [34] Matthew 8:20   [35] Genesis 3:17,18
[36] Galatians 3:13   [37] Isaiah 7:24

markable fulfillment, not only in Palestine, but in all the world. But the future is brightened by words from the same divinely-inspired spokesman as he points ahead to the millennial age when the curse of sin is lifted and the thorns have disappeared. "For ye shall go out with joy, and be led forth with peace: the mountains and the hills shall break forth before you into singing, and all the trees of the field shall clap their hands. Instead of the thorn shall come up the fir tree, and instead of the brier shall come up the myrtle tree." [38]

As we look upon the scars of Jesus caused by the thorns, we are reminded now, and we shall be reminded throughout all of eternity, that our Saviour bore on His blessed brow the curse for our sins. When He comes to reign, there shall be "no more curse." Then shall He be crowned King of kings and Lord of lords.

> "Crown Him with many crowns,
> The Lamb upon the throne;
> Hark! how the heavenly anthem drowns
> All music but its own!
> Awake, my soul, and sing
> Of Him who died for thee;
> And hail Him as thy matchless King
> Thro' all eternity."

But tarry longer! Let us look at one scar more. His side bears a wound, for which knowledge of the occasion and cause we are indebted to the Apostle John. Only the beloved disciple relates this curious incident. "But one of the soldiers with a spear pierced His side, and forthwith came there out blood and water." [39] Thus with a stroke of the soldier's spear a great prophecy was fulfilled—"They shall look upon Me whom they have pierced." [40]

[38] Isaiah 55:12,13   [39] John 19:34   [40] Zechariah 12:10

The piercing of the Saviour's side remains as immortal evidence of both His death and Resurrection. The heart is the very seat of life, and the piercing of the Roman spear supplies proof that Christ's life was extinguished. His heart ceased to beat, and He actually died. If His death were not real, His Resurrection also was not real, and we are yet in our sins. But we know that Jesus died, and consequently His death has become the guarantee that sin has been paid for in full. He said: "This is My blood of the new testament, which is shed for many for the remission of sins." [41] After His Resurrection He appeared to the disciples, and "He shewed unto them His hands and *His side*." [42] To Thomas, Jesus said: "Reach hither thy hand, and *thrust it into My side:* and be not faithless, but believing." [43]

Have you trusted Him fully for salvation from sin? His wounded side tells us that the prophet's mighty prediction has been fulfilled: "There shall be a fountain opened . . . for sin and for uncleanness." [44] Either His scars will break your heart and move you toward the Saviour and everlasting life, or else you will turn away in willful rejection of Him and your soul shall be lost forever.

> "Wounded for me, wounded for me,
> There on the cross
> He was wounded for me;
> Gone my transgressions, and now I am free,
> All because Jesus was wounded for me."

[41] Matthew 26:28   [42] John 20:20   [43] John 20:27
[44] Zechariah 13:1

HE DIED FOR YOU

He died for you, that Man upon the tree
Whose head was hung in shame and agony.
No pow'r of words can e'er describe the grief
It cost that Man your soul to bring relief.
Not thorny crown, nor nails through guiltless hands,
Not pinioned feet did break the awful bands,
But rather death; one of the Trinity,
God's Son, made sin for your eternity;
His blood outpoured from spear-wound in His side
For thorough cleansing when by faith applied;
This was the price, and justice had its due
When once for all, in love, He died for you.

—WILLIAM J. RIEHL, JR.

HIS SUFFERING

"Awake, O north wind; and come, thou south; blow upon my garden, that the spices thereof may flow out." [1]

How tenacious is the snare of things that are seen! How essential it is that God keeps us living in the realm of the unseen! No life is completely furnished without sorrow, for there is a supernatural power in it which has never been fathomed by human reason. When our being lies perfectly still, all struggling ceased, under the hand of God and the quietness of eternity has settled down in our souls, then it is that the Holy Spirit works the mystifying perfecting of our selves.

Not one person in all the world is exempt from sorrow. Philosophers of every age have acknowledged it. Biographers, no matter how shallow the treatise, have recorded it. Experience has confirmed it. From the fact of suffering there is no escape. It sinks its fangs deeply into rich and poor, high and low, saved and lost.

Except for natural causes and war, perhaps the greatest injuries have been inflicted upon men because of their religious convictions. Since the vicious slaying of John the Baptist, the first recorded martyr who died for the testimony of Jesus Christ, there has been no intermission in the attacks on the followers of Christ. History is revealing in its gruesome accounts of human suffering inflicted upon thousands of His disciples. Battered and bleeding bodies of helpless, humble believers have

[1] Song of Solomon 4:16

been dragged through rough streets. Men, women, and children have been made to kneel while the axeman's blade severed their heads from their bodies. Christians have been crucified; some have been torn limb from limb by furiously voracious beasts, while others were dipped into boiling pitch. These are but a few of the many methods of torture used by the enemies of Christ in the years since the Lamb of God was slain on Calvary. We wince as such atrocities are recounted.

There is the torture of the mind and the agony of the soul —that escapeless, gnawing suffering which no other person can truly share. Records of this are uncommon; words do not adequately portray it.

Are you brokenhearted because one with whom you shared your confidences has betrayed you? Jesus said: "Yea, Mine own familiar friend, in whom I trusted, which did eat of My bread, hath lifted up his heel against Me." [2] Are you misunderstood and do your associates not value your taste nor your choices? Jesus could say: "I said unto them, If ye think good, give Me My price; and if not, forbear. So they weighed for My price thirty pieces of silver." [3] Have friends or loved ones forsaken you? All the disciples forsook Jesus and fled. Do others torment you until you sting with shame? Jesus said: "I gave My back to the smiters, and My cheeks to them that plucked off the hair: I hid not My face from shame and spitting." [4] "The assembly of the wicked have inclosed Me: they pierced My hands and My feet." [5] Do the injustices done you inflame you until you think you must retaliate? Jesus was afflicted, "yet He opened not His mouth." [6] Do you believe no one cares? Jesus declared: "I looked for some to take pity, but there was none; and for comforters, but I found none. They gave Me also gall for My meat; and in My thirst they gave Me vinegar to drink." [7] Do you feel that the burden you must carry is too

[2] Psalm 41:9
[5] Psalm 22:16
[3] Zechariah 11:12
[6] Isaiah 53:7
[4] Isaiah 50:6
[7] Psalm 69:20,21

great? Then listen to this magnificent declaration: "The Lord hath laid on Him the iniquity of us all." [8] "Surely He hath borne our griefs, and carried our sorrows." [9]

❧

The sufferings of Christ were *voluntary*. F. W. Farr expresses it thus: "He did not suffer with the impassive and imperturbable resignation of a stoic. He suffered willingly and cheerfully. He was not taken by surprise. He knew from the beginning what would befall Him." The idea of Christ's death being that of a martyr is nowhere to be found in Scripture. He did not fall prey to His sufferings as a helpless victim who could not defend Himself. While ignorant men heaped humiliation, shame, and suffering upon Jesus, He endured it all voluntarily. It would not be otherwise in view of His own oft-repeated statements like the following: "From that time forth began Jesus to shew unto His disciples, how that He must go unto Jerusalem, and *suffer many things.*" [10] "Likewise shall also the Son of man *suffer.*" [11] "With desire I have desired to eat this passover with you *before I suffer.*" [12]

The sufferings of Christ were according to the divine plan that was prearranged before the Incarnation of the Son of God. Jesus taught this truth. He rebuked the two disciples as they journeyed that day to Emmaus. "Then He said unto them, O fools, and slow of heart to believe all that the prophets have spoken. Ought not Christ to have suffered these things?" [13] Millenniums before His birth at Bethlehem He volunteered to suffer. The Old Testament Scriptures "testified beforehand the sufferings of Christ." [14] Paul says: "For I delivered unto you first of all that which I also received, how that Christ died for our sins according to the scriptures." [15] The only Scriptures in Paul's day were those that comprised the Old Testament, and

[8] Isaiah 53:6 [9] Isaiah 53:4 [10] Matthew 16:21
[11] Matthew 17:12 [12] Luke 22:15 [13] Luke 24:25,26
[14] 1 Peter 1:11 [15] 1 Corinthians 15:3

of these our Lord Himself was the Author. Therefore He must have offered Himself in eternity past.

As the Good Shepherd Jesus suffered intentionally and unconstrainedly. He said: "I am the good shepherd: the good shepherd giveth *His life* for the sheep." [16] "Therefore doth My Father love Me, *because I lay down My life,* that I might take it again. No man taketh it from Me, but *I lay it down of Myself.*" [17] No man could take the life of Jesus Christ except He willed it. "I am the Life," He said. Therefore there can be no power or force that can compel Him to lay down His life. As He hung upon the Cross, the Roman soldiers offered Him a sedative to ease His sufferings and make His death less excruciating, but the suffering Saviour spurned the offer, for we read: "When He had tasted thereof, He would not drink." [18] He volunteered to suffer consciously. Therefore we are convinced that He faced the agonies of Calvary knowingly and willingly.

Culross wrote: "When we suffer, how hard we find it to be still! The flames of resentment—how they leap up in our bosom, and flush our cheek with angry red! What impatience there often is, what murmuring, what outcry, what publishing of our sorrow! But the spirit of the Saviour is loftier and grander unutterably. In sublime and magnanimous silence He endures to the uttermost, sustained by His mighty purpose and by the conviction, *Jehovah wills it.*"

The sufferings of Christ were *vicarious.* Vicarious suffering is that which one suffers in the stead of another. When one suffers voluntarily in such a way, one acts nobly. It is not uncommon to hear of a man taking on himself the punishment that someone else has deserved. In a lonely cemetery near

---

[16] John 10:11   [17] John 10:17,18   [18] Matthew 27:34

Palmyra, Missouri, a modest marble tombstone bears this inscription:

> "This monument is dedicated to the memory of Hiram Smith, who was shot at Palmyra, October 18, 1862, as a substitute for William T. Humphrey, my father."

During the Civil War William Humphrey, along with nine other Southern sympathizers from Palmyra, were found guilty of abducting a Northern farmer. For their crime they were to be executed, but for some reason William Humphrey was spared on condition that a substitute die in his place. With only a little time remaining before the execution, twenty-two year old Hiram Smith offered to die and was shot in Humphrey's stead. That was a vicarious sacrifice.

The word *vicarious* describes accurately the *how* of Christ's sufferings. But Christ's vicarious sufferings differ greatly from Hiram Smith's vicarious sufferings. Hiram Smith offered himself at the last minute with but a few moments between death and the man who was sentenced to die. Jesus Christ volunteered to die as your substitute and mine "before the foundation of the world." [19] By His sufferings Jesus took upon Himself the sufferings we deserved to bear, and bore them in His own person that we might be delivered from them. We might have been left to ourselves to bear the judgment of our own iniquity; but instead of man being abandoned to his own fate, God in His infinite wisdom and indescribable love has found a better way. The Son of God agreed to become our Substitute, and thus we read: "He was wounded for *our* transgressions, He was bruised for *our* iniquities . . . the Lord hath laid *on Him* the iniquity of *us all.*" [20] "For Christ also hath once suffered for sins, *the just for the unjust,* that He might bring us to God, being put to death in the flesh, but quickened by the Spirit." [21] By no

[19] 1 Peter 1:20 [20] Isaiah 53:5,6 [21] 1 Peter 3:18

other interpretation of the Holy Scriptures, by no bold denial of the facts in the case, nor by false deception can we escape (and thank God we do not want to escape) the all-glorious and eternal truth that Jesus Christ "gave Himself a ransom for all." [22]

In His sufferings Christ was *victorious*. To what chief end and purpose did the Saviour offer Himself? Since we have discovered the *why* of His sufferings, we have a right to investigate whether or not it resulted in success. Were the eternal plans of God frustrated or fulfilled when Jesus died? Are we merely to present a posthumous award, and continue in sorrow and despair with the idea that His valor was in vain? Or did His sacrifice gain the victory?

Since Christ "gave Himself a ransom for all," it was necessary that the wall of partition between Jew and Gentile should be broken down. The Mosaic code and the Jewish ritual were not to be despised, for they were ordered by Jehovah; but these erected a middle wall of partition between Jew and Gentile. And each of us knows too well the bitterness that has raged between the two down through the centuries, especially the hatred and the heated attacks against the Jew. On the wall in a temple of old, separating the court of the Gentiles from the court of the Israelites, there was found the following inscription: "Let no Gentile, let no man of the nations, go beyond this wall on pain of death." To the Jew of old the Gentiles were poor, wandering outcasts, "aliens from the commonwealth of Israel, and strangers from the covenants of promise, having no hope, and without God in the world." [23] The Gentiles had no claim upon the promised Messiah, for Israel possessed the promises. Jesus Himself said to the woman at Sychar that "salvation is of the Jews." [24] Though the Syrophenician woman fell at

[22] 1 Timothy 2:6   [23] Ephesians 2:12   [24] John 4:22

His feet and cried: "Have mercy on me, O Lord, Thou Son of David," [25] the Scripture says that "He answered her not a word." [26] As a Gentile she had no claim upon Him. But the sufferings of the Saviour have accomplished what no other could do. Blessed be God! The blood of Christ has broken down the dividing wall between Jew and Gentile, which wall was the law. And now in the Cross of Christ the enmity has been slain, and the Gentile and the Jew who have likewise trusted the Saviour are gathered together in one body. Jesus suffered "that He might reconcile both unto God in one body by the Cross, having slain the enmity thereby." [27] This is God's masterwork, accomplished through the sufferings of His Son. This was a glorious victory! This was a mighty reconcilation that was humanly impossible. Apart from the sufferings and death of our Saviour, the "one new man" whom He "hath made both one" would not exist. The Jew and the Gentile as individual sinners are on equal footing. Whether occidental or oriental, Aryan or non-Aryan, all men can and must meet at the Cross of Christ. There God intervened for the hopeless Gentile and the unbelieving Jew alike, and provided a way of salvation for both through a world Saviour. We have yet to find any natural way in which the Jew and the Gentile could find a way of conciliation. But Christ, in His sufferings, cancelled the debt of both and made peace by the blood of His Cross. What a glorious victory!

Among the manifold victories wrought through the sufferings and death of the Saviour is the all-glorious triumph over the evils of this present world. In the death of His Son, God provided man with a remarkable deliverance from the daily practice of sin. Here is something that neither education nor philosophy nor civilization nor reformation could accomplish. Man is universally the slave of sin, sometimes a willing victim and sometimes an unwilling victim; and it is concluded in our day that all moral improvements have failed to rid the heart

[25] Matthew 15:22   [26] Matthew 15:23   [27] Ephesians 2:16

of its tendency to do evil. History shows that many of the ancient philosophies and religions degraded life by their vile teachings and immoral practices. They were powerless to supply the need for victory over sin. We are not despising the noted lawmakers and the many worthwhile attempts at reforms, but we all must agree that every effort has proved conclusively that the methods of men have failed. After six thousand years of human history God still sees "that the wickedness of man [is] great in the earth, and that every imagination of the thoughts of his heart [are] only evil continually." [28]

But delivered out of this morass of humanity there is to be found a body of true believers in the Lord Jesus Christ who are living daily a life of victory over the temptation to do wrong. These constitute the body of Christ and are the saved out of all the nations of the world. Were you to ask the true child of God to reveal the secret of power over sin, he might answer in one word—"Delivered!" Such an one has learned that Christ "gave Himself for our sins, that He might *deliver* us from this present evil world." [29] All sin exacts a penalty and exercises a power over its victims. But Christ, in His sufferings and death, did the work that no other could do. He defeated Satan and destroyed the power of sin. Out of personal experience and by the wisdom of God, the Apostle Paul wrote: "For sin shall not have dominion over you. . . . Being then made free from sin, ye became the servants of righteousness." [30] We know that Satan is the prince and the power of this world, but, praise God, we can believe the Word of God—"Ye are of God, little children, and have overcome them: because greater is He that is in you, than He that is in the world." [31] The suffering Saviour is "the Lamb of God, which taketh away the sin of the world." [32]

> "And thou shalt know blest fellowship with Me,
>   Whose broken heart of love hath healed the world."

[28] Genesis 6:5
[31] 1 John 4:4
[29] Galatians 1:4
[32] John 1:29
[30] Romans 6:14,18

BENEATH THE CROSS OF JESUS

O safe and happy shelter,
  O refuge, tried and sweet,
O trysting-place, where heaven's love
  And heaven's justice meet.
As to the holy patriarch
  That wondrous dream was given,
So seems my Saviour's Cross to me,
  A ladder up to heaven.

There lies beneath its shadow,
  But on the farther side,
The darkness of an awful grave,
  That gapes both deep and wide,
And there between us stands the Cross,
  Two arms outstretched to save,
Like a watchman set to guard the way
  From that eternal grave.

Upon the Cross of Jesus,
  Mine eyes at times can see
The very dying form of One
  Who suffered there for me;
And from my smitten heart, with tears,
  Two wonders I confess,
The wonder of His glorious love,
  And my own worthlessness.

—ELIZABETH CLEPHANE

HIS SAVIOURHOOD

"For unto you is born this day in the city of David a Saviour, which is Christ the Lord." [1]

The world is extravagant with words and lavishes upon many the pleasing titles of potentate, deliverer, philanthropist, savant, and philosopher. To One alone goes the title of Saviour, for a peculiar divineness and holiness attach themselves to this name. Though the world may grant titles profusely, God has said: "I, even I, am the Lord; and beside Me there is no saviour." [2] "I the Lord am thy Saviour and thy Redeemer." [3]

The title *Saviour*, the noun *salvation*, and the verb *to save* are found in every book in the New Testament. The common origin of these words is the Latin *salvare*, meaning to make safe, to secure. The original thought was that of preservation from injury or danger, but in theology it means to deliver from the penalty and power of sin; to preserve from final and everlasting punishment. Saving souls from eternal death is not a human task; it is a divine accomplishment—"Salvation is of the Lord." [4]

It is our purpose in this chapter to discuss the Saviourhood of Jesus Christ and to prove that He is the only complete Saviour of the race. The Apostle John writes: "We have seen and do testify *that the Father sent the Son to be the Saviour of the world*." [5] Regardless of what churches and creeds have to offer

[1] Luke 2:11 [2] Isaiah 43:11 [3] Isaiah 49:26; 60:16
[4] Jonah 2:9 [5] 1 John 4:14

374

this sin-scarred and doomed world, we repeat the immortal declaration of the Apostle Peter: "Neither is there salvation in any other: for there is none other name under heaven given among men, whereby we must be saved." [6] Peter does not leave his listeners in doubt regarding the One of whom he is speaking. He says it is "by the name of Jesus Christ of Nazareth." [7] Salvation is never granted in your name, nor in your parent's name, nor in the name of your church. Jesus insists: "I am the way . . . no man cometh unto the Father, but by Me." [8]

Mankind's lost estate cries for a Saviour. False philosophy teaches that all men are the children of God and that all will eventually arrive at the same destination. They are in favor of all of the religions of the world, for, they say, "It matters not what one believes. Follow the religion of your own choosing, for each is but a different road to the common destination of all men. You choose yours, but let me choose my own." Such logic is the devil's lie. Whether we like the thought or not, the world of humanity is *lost*. This is the picture that the Bible gives us of all human life apart from the salvation that God has prepared and presented to us through Jesus Christ.

"All we like sheep have gone astray." [9]

"Behold, I was shapen in iniquity; and in sin did my mother conceive me." [10]

"The heart is deceitful above all things." [11]

"For there is not a just man upon earth, that doeth good, and sinneth not." [12]

"There is none that doeth good, no, not one." [13]

"For all have sinned and come short of the glory of God." [14]

[6] Acts 4:12
[9] Isaiah 53:6
[12] Ecclesiastes 7:20
[7] Acts 4:10
[10] Psalm 51:5
[13] Romans 3:12
[8] John 14:6
[11] Jeremiah 17:9
[14] Romans 3:23

These and many other Bible passages depict the total depravity of man. In spite of the false religions that deny the existence of sin, the Word of God refers to every unbeliever as "dead in trespasses and sins." [15]

God's call to men everywhere to repent of their sins and seek the Lord, to reason together with Him, to accept His gracious gift of salvation through Jesus Christ implies the fact of man's lost and sinful condition. The Bible contains a universal appeal to men to get right with God through faith in His Son. Certainly the repeated pleadings of the Lord are significant in themselves. From the call of God to Adam to the final invitation in Revelation, the Bible is a personal invitation to sinners. *"Come"* is the plea of the Saviour—

"*Come* now, and let us reason together, saith the LORD: though your sins be as scarlet, they shall be as white as snow; though they be red like crimson, they shall be as wool." [16]

"Ho, every one that thirsteth, *come* ye to the waters." [17]

"*Come* unto Me, all ye that labour and are heavy laden, and I will give you rest." [18]

"And the Spirit and the bride say, *Come*. And let him that heareth say, *Come*. And let him that is athirst *come*. And whosoever will, let him take the water of life freely." [19]

"*Come* ye sinners, poor and needy,
Weak and wounded, sick and sore;
Jesus ready stands to save you,
Full of pity, love and power."

In his volume entitled *One Thing Needful*, J. Harold Gwynne had said: "The world situation today, the sad condition of humanity at the present hour remind us very forcibly and tell us most insistently how lost, bewildered, and depraved the human race is. The horrors of modern warfare cry *lost*. The vast

[15] Ephesians 2:1   [16] Isaiah 1:18   [17] Isaiah 55:1
[18] Matthew 11:28   [19] Revelation 22:17

underworld of crime cries *lost*. The shameful prevalence of social immorality and attending evils is a tragic cry of *lost*. The bewilderment, the secularism, the loss of faith in educational circles cry *lost*. The spiritual lethargy, the soiled garments, the lack of vision, passion and power in the Church cry out *lost*. We know from everyday human experience that we are far from God and that we need His seeking love and saving help."

"For the Son of man is come to seek and to save that which was lost." [20]

The Philippian jailer cried: "What must I do to be saved?" [21] But before he raised the question he had a consciousness that he was *lost*. There comes a time in the life of very man when God speaks in an unmistakable way concerning the welfare of his own soul. The first question that enters the mind of the awakened sinner is "What must I do to be saved?" And be sure, the answer never has varied. The apostles came with the one and only answer: "Believe on the Lord Jesus Christ, and thou shalt be saved." [22] Here is the very heart of the evangel. All of the values of evangelical preaching are bound up in this one statement. The answer to the soul's quest for deliverance from the penalty and power of sin can never be found in altars and images, rituals and ceremonies. The conditions of salvation are not optional. There is but one. God has made it and it dare not be changed. You must trust Jesus Christ as the only Saviour from your sin or you must be eternally lost.

Christ came to be your Saviour. Before He was born the angel of the Lord said: "Thou shalt call His name JESUS: for He shall *save* His people from their sins." [23] *Jesus* is a Greek form of the Hebrew *Joshua*, and means *Saviour*. At the time of His birth the

[20] Luke 19:10   [21] Acts 16:30   [22] Acts 16:31
[23] Matthew 1:21

angel added: "Unto you is born this day in the city of David a *Saviour*, which is Christ the Lord." [24] Christ's was a mission of rescue. "The Son of man came not to be ministered unto, but to minister, and to give His life a ransom for many." [25] This is the gospel, and "it is the power of God unto *salvation*." [26] Not unto reformation, civilization, or education. "Salvation is a word for a lost man, and for none other. Men are involved either in salvation, or in its opposite, perdition." For nineteen hundred years God has been concentrating on man's salvation through the sacrifice of His Son. Dr. Ralph Turnbull has said: "Don't object to this word 'salvation.' It is the only word adequate to describe what God offers to sinning man."

Many of this world's emperors have carried the title "saviour." They were looked upon as the saviours of the people, but none of them could pledge his subjects any hope beyond the grave. Dr. Wuest says: "Now comes Christianity with its imperialistic announcement, 'For unto you is born this day in the city of David a *Saviour*, which is Christ the Lord.' What motive would they have for transferring their allegiance from a world-saviour who gave them the comforts of life and at the same time allowed them to go on in their sins, to the Lord Jesus, especially when allegiance to this new Saviour could very well result in their crucifixion by Rome? And yet for the first three hundred years of history of the church, tens of thousands willingly embraced this new Saviour and went to a horrible death. How explain this? The only answer is that the supernatural power of God was operative in their hearts. The Samaritans said: "We have heard Him ourselves, and know that this is indeed the Christ, the *Saviour* of the world." [27] Wherever Christ is recognized in the heart as Saviour, there is a never-dying allegiance to Him over the ever-failing "saviours" of the world.

❧

[24] Luke 2:11
[27] John 4:42
[25] Matthew 20:28
[26] Romans 1:16

It is eternally written that "He is able to *save* . . . to the uttermost." [28] What a tremendous statement! He has ability that knows no inability. So important is this truth of the ability of Christ, it forms the foundation of the Christian faith and life. He is able—O blessed thought! We need to occupy ourselves with the power of the living Saviour. He is able to save and to continue saving.

But He is able to save *to the uttermost*. The salvation that He offers is comprehensive and complete. The word *uttermost* means "completely." It is found in one other place in Scripture, in the story of the woman who had an infirmity for eighteen years.[29] Luke says she "had a spirit of infirmity eighteen years, and was *bowed together* [or to the uttermost], and could in no wise lift up herself." This poor woman was bound completely, or bound to the uttermost so that she was unable to help herself, so the Saviour of man reached to the uttermost of her helplessness and saved her. Thus Christ fulfills His saving mission by saving those who are unable to save themselves. Here is an accurate picture of lost humanity. Bound by the fetters of sin man cannot loose himself; but Christ, the uttermost Saviour, is able to save to the uttermost depth of our inability. *"For by grace are ye saved through faith; and that not of yourselves: it is the gift of God."* [30]

Then Christ is able to save to the uttermost depth of our ignorance. How ignorant the natural man is of the things of God! "Neither can he know them, because they are spiritually discerned." [31] Nicodemus was an educated and learned Jew, but when Jesus spoke to him about the only way of salvation, "Nicodemus answered and said unto Him, How can these things be?" The seeking Saviour did not leave this Jewish ruler to think the thing through for himself. Christ saw his plight, and reaching down to the depth of his ignorance, the Saviour

---

[28] Hebrews 7:25   [29] Luke 13:10-13   [30] Ephesians 2:8
[31] 1 Corinthians 2:14

uttered what is perhaps the most loved passage in all the Bible—"For God so loved the world, that He gave His only begotten Son, that whosoever believeth in Him should not perish, but have everlasting life." [32] Who among us cannot understand it? Little children have learned it and through it have embraced the Saviour and followed Him all of their lifetime.

One final word! The Saviour's work is not completed. Salvation is threefold—past, present, and future. Christ has saved us from the *penalty* of sin, and so perfect is this work of God that the saved are said to be safe forever—"There is therefore now no condemnation to them which are in Christ Jesus." [33] Then Christ saves His own even now from the reigning *power* of sin—"For I know that this shall turn to my salvation through your prayer, and the supply of the Spirit of Jesus Christ." [34] Now finally, the believer is yet to be saved from the *presence* of sin—"For now is our salvation nearer than when we believed." [35]

The hope of each Christian is the promised return of Jesus Christ, when he shall meet the One who bought him, face to face. Our great God became our great Saviour. Is He your Saviour?

"Looking for that blessed hope, and the glorious appearing of the great God and our *Saviour* Jesus Christ." [36]

[32] John 3:16
[35] Romans 13:11
[33] Romans 8:1
[36] Titus 2:13
[34] Philippians 1:19

FOR SINNERS SLAIN

Dear Substitute for sinners slain,
Oft Thou hadst lack of bread;
Yet Thine the hands that broke the loaves
And multitudes were fed.

When wearied Thou didst seek Thy rest,
But winds obey Thy will;
The storm Thou makest it a calm,
The waves thereof are still.

They pierced Thy hands at Calvary,
Thou blessed Sacrifice;
Yet Thou didst ope to the redeemed
The gates of paradise.

Dear Substitute for sinners slain,
Lord Jesus, mine Thou art:
Thou very God and very Man
Hast reached this sinner's heart.

—LOUISE B. EAVEY

HIS SACRIFICE

"Even Christ our Passover is sacrificed for us." [1]

A sacrifice is an offering of anything to God with the idea of giving thanks, making atonement, or seeking conciliation. Of course this definition is confined strictly to the biblical idea of sacrifice. Who of us has not thought about the sacrifice of the millions of lives and the multiplied billions of dollars which were offered as the price for American liberty? Yet these sacrifices, though a serious loss to us all, do not fit into the same category as the sacrifice of Jesus. The lives offered on the world's battlefields are powerless to atone for the sins of either the one sacrificed or those for whom the sacrifice was made.

The biblical significance of sacrifice is associated with sin. We do not read of a sacrifice until after we read of sin's entrance into the world. When we read in Genesis 3:21: "Unto Adam also and to his wife did the Lord God make coats of skins, and clothed them," we notice that it was after the fall and the subsequent pronouncement of judgment. Adam had provided an apron for himself, but it was an ineffectual covering. God came upon the scene with a garment that was obtained through bloodshedding. Before there could be a covering for sin, there had to be a sacrifice. This is God's first overt revelation of a sacrifice for sin, and it pointed forward to the Cross at Calvary where the Lamb of God would be sacrificed for the sin of the world.

[1] 1 Corinthians 5:7

In the biblical account of sacrifices we see complete deliverance from the penalty and power of sin. In the first eleven verses of Exodus, chapter twelve, we have a full description of the sacrifice that was to be slain for the deliverance of Israel out of the bondage of Pharaoh in Egypt. It is called the "LORD's passover," [2] and we know without any question that it is a type of our Lord Jesus Christ, for the Apostle Paul by the inspiration of the Holy Spirit says: "For even Christ our passover is sacrificed for us." [3] Readers of the New Testament are quick to note the significance of Israel's lamb with "the Lamb of God, which taketh away the sin of the world." [4] There are several striking facts about the paschal lamb that are outstanding and essential, and each teaches some truth concerning Christ our Sacrifice.

The first words that God gave when He instituted the Passover were: "This month shall be unto you the beginning of months: it shall be the first month of the year to you." [5] Israel was then in the seventh month of the civil year which was running its ordinary course when God instituted the change. The Lord had not been having His way in the lives of the people, but now a new commencement must be made and that not without Him—*It shall be the first month of the year to you.* Man had a way of reckoning time but it was apart from redemption. Now God is going to take account of things, but it must begin with a sacrifice for redemption. We see the counterpart of this truth in the sacrifice of Christ on the Cross. The first six months of the Jewish year prior to the Passover were to be blotted out, with God's people making a new start and the past gone forever. Do you not see the application here? Everything in man's life previous to conversion is of little significance. We

[2] Exodus 12:11; Leviticus 23:5   [3] 1 Corinthians 5:7   [4] John 1:29
[5] Exodus 12:2

hear people speak of *life,* but until one is "born again"[6] he has not begun to live.[7] Life begins at second birth. Then we become "new creatures" in Christ.[8] Only as we appropriate the sacrifice of our Lord do we commence to understand life. Jesus said: "He that believeth not the Son shall not see life; but the wrath of God abideth on him."[9] Recently one of the young men in the church where I am serving as pastor said: "Pastor, today is my birthday." When I asked him how old he was, he answered: "Three years old today." It was three years before that I had picked him up with my car on the highway, and he accepted Christ as his personal Saviour. He had two birthdays, and he was emphasizing the one when he actually began to live, when he was born again. The sacrifice of Christ at Calvary, when He hung upon a literal cross of wood and shed His life blood, is man's only hope of salvation from death and hell. Our Lord promises: "He that . . . believeth on Him that sent Me, hath everlasting life, and shall not come into condemnation; but is passed from death unto life."[10] Have *you* begun life with Him? How many birthdays do you have? His sacrifice will blot out the past with its failures and disappointments and give you a new beginning.

The Passover sacrifice was for *all.* "Speak ye unto *all* the congregation of Israel, saying, In the tenth day of this month they shall take to them *every man* a lamb."[11] Here we see the all-inclusiveness of our Lord's sacrificial death. A very important question presents itself in connection with Christ's sacrificing Himself: Was the sacrifice of Christ designed to provide deliverance for certain individuals who were chosen by the Father and given to Him; or was it intended to render possible the redemption of the whole race alike? We are making no at-

---

[6] John 3:3
[7] Ephesians 2:1
[8] 2 Corinthians 5:17
[9] John 3:36
[10] John 5:24
[11] Exodus 12:3

tempt here to answer either for or against the claims of Calvinism or Arminianism, but we stand firmly against limiting the atonement in its value or in its power. The message of the gospel is that "God so loved the *world*, that He gave His only begotten Son, that *whosoever* believeth in Him should not perish, but have everlasting life." [12] Jesus said to His disciples: "Go ye into all the world, and preach the gospel to every *creature*." [13] The Apostle Paul writes: "He died for *all*." [14] In the first Epistle that bears his name, the Apostle John says: "He is the propitiation for our sins: and not for our's only, but also for the sins of *the whole world*." [15] And in the Revelation he sees the four and twenty elders around the throne singing: "Thou art worthy to take the book, and to open the seals thereof: for Thou wast slain, and hast redeemed us to God by Thy blood out of every kindred, and tongue, and people, and nation." [16] From these passages we are clearly taught that Jesus Christ was sacrificed in order that God would have a ground upon which He could pass over and save *all* who would believe in His Son.

The Passover sacrifice had to be without blemish—"Your lamb shall be without blemish." [17] So rigid was this law that the Jews examined with care every sacrifice that was selected for the altar. After our Lord had lived among all classes of men for thirty-three years, it was agreed upon by all that He was a spotless Lamb. Isaiah depicts God's Sacrifice going to His death in unresisting innocency.[18] Peter assures the saints: "Ye were not redeemed with corruptible things, as silver and gold, from your vain conversation received by tradition from your fathers; But with the precious blood of Christ, as of *a lamb without blemish and without spot*." [19] Christ is the Lamb whom

[12] John 3:16
[15] 1 John 2:2
[18] Isaiah 53:7
[13] Mark 16:15
[16] Revelation 5:9
[19] 1 Peter 1:18,19
[14] 2 Corinthians 5:15
[17] Exodus 12:5

John called "worthy." [20] He "knew no sin." [21] He "did no sin." [22] "In Him is no sin." [23] If one blemish had been discovered in Jesus Christ; He would have been an unfit sacrifice.

Out of the last war there comes the story of a little, frail old man who entered the Red Cross blood donor center in Oakland, California. He stood patiently in line waiting his turn at the reception desk. He wore a pleasant smile and was conspicuous by his immaculate clothing, his cleanliness, and his carefully combed hair. As his turn came the receptionist asked him his age, and smiling, he said: "Eighty."

"I'm sorry," she answered, "but you are too old to give a pint of blood." Disappointment came over the man's face, but before turning away, he said quietly: "I was not going to tell you this if you had accepted me. I knew that I could not survive a blood donation, so I dressed for my funeral. I would have died happy, knowing my death might mean life for some boy somewhere far from home." All blood used for such purposes must meet every requirement of medical science, and the old gentleman could not meet those requirements. But the Lord Jesus Christ, the Antitype of the Old Testament sacrifices, was of acceptable age as well as being physically and morally fit. In the vigor of young manhood He met every righteous requirement of divine justice. He came into this world prepared to die, to offer Himself a ransom for us all. He was the perfect Sacrifice, so perfect that God found satisfaction in His wondrous work in behalf of sinners.

❧

Look, now, at the manner of the slaying of the Passover sacrifice—"The whole assembly of the congregation of Israel shall kill it." [24] Who was responsible for the death of the sacrifice? Answer: The whole assembly. Now ask the question. Who was

[20] Revelation 5:12   [21] 2 Corinthians 5:21   [22] 1 Peter 2:22
[23] 1 John 3:5   [24] Exodus 12:6

responsible for the death of Christ? and the answer comes clear and unmistakable that every person in heaven and on earth had a hand in the bloody sacrifice of God's Lamb on Calvary's Cross. Solomon Zeitlin insists that the Jews did not kill Jesus. He writes: "A superficial reading of the story of the Passion gives the impression that the Jews were responsible for the crucifixion of Jesus. As we analyzed the narrative of the trial and crucifixion against the background of the times, however, it became evident that the Jewish people were not responsible for the death of Jesus. The synoptic Gospels accused the Jews only of rejecting Jesus, but they did not accuse them of His death." Professor Zeitlin's remarks sound good, but they are inconsistent with what the Bible teaches. The Hebrew prophet Zechariah speaks of Israel's guilt in the death of Jesus and her acknowledgment of that guilt when Jesus comes again: "And one shall say unto Him, What are these wounds in Thine hands? Then He shall answer, Those with which I was wounded in the house of My friends." [25]

The Apostle Peter in his first sermon at Pentecost openly and fearlessly charged the Jews with guilt in connection with Christ's crucifixion: "Ye men of Israel, hear these words; Jesus of Nazareth, a man approved of God among you by miracles and wonders and signs . . . Him . . . ye have taken, and by wicked hands have crucified and slain." [26] Nor will the eternal record ever change of that exciting moment when Pontius Pilate sought to release Jesus, and the Jews with one accord cried out: "Let Him be crucified," and again, "Let Him be crucified," and "His blood be on us, and on our children." [27] Indeed the Jews were responsible for the death of Christ.

So also were the Gentiles guilty of crucifying Jesus. David, in the second Psalm, obviously prophesied the hatred and rejection shown by Herod, Pilate, and the Gentiles against Jesus:

[25] Zechariah 13:6   [26] Acts 2:22,23   [27] Matthew 27:21-25

"Why do the heathen rage, and the people imagine a vain thing? The kings of the earth set themselves, and the rulers take counsel together, against the Lord, and against His anointed, saying, Let us break their bands asunder, and cast away their cords from us." [28] They were Gentile soldiers who "stripped Him [Jesus] . . . platted a crown of thorns, . . . put it upon His head . . . and they spit upon Him, and took the reed, and smote Him on the head." [29] For centuries the Gentiles have cried after the Jews, "Christ killers"; but before they continue to flaunt their charges they had better examine their own record. The most generally accepted and widely used creed in churches where Gentiles worship declares that Jesus Christ "suffered under Pontius Pilate." The anti-Semites who show bitter hatred against the Jews and hurl the charge against them are stating only a partial truth. While it is true that Jews cannot be absolved from guilt in Christ's death, neither can the Gentiles; for they must share the guilt. The inscription above the cross witnesses to the fact that man is represented there in his religion (Hebrew), in his wisdom (Greek), and in his power (Latin).

Finally, when we analyze the manner of the slaying of God's Sacrifice, we see that God Himself was responsible. It was Jehovah's command to Israel that they kill the lamb on the night of the Passover. So Isaiah says: "All we like sheep have gone astray; we have turned every one to his own way; and *Jehovah hath laid on Him the iniquity of us all.*" And again: *"It pleased Jehovah to bruise Him."* [30] God's part in the death of His Son is borne out by Peter when he said of Jesus: "Him, being delivered by the determinate counsel and foreknowledge of God" [31] . . . "Who verily was foreordained before the foundation of the world." [32] The sacrifice of Christ was part of the eternal plan of God to redeem fallen humanity to Himself.

❧

[28] Psalm 2:1-3
[31] Acts 2:23
[30] Matthew 27:27-30
[32] 1 Peter 1:20
[30] Isaiah 53:6,10 R.V.

The Passover sacrifice was to be killed in the evening—"The whole assembly of the congregation of Israel shall kill it in the evening." [33] The margin of the Authorized Version says: "between the two evenings." A. J. Kligerman writes: "Jesus our Paschal Lamb, died 'between the evenings.' The suffering began at the third hour, 9 A.M.,[34] and when the sixth hour came, 12 noon, darkness covered the whole land till the ninth hour, 3 P.M., the very hour of Israel's sacrificing the Passover lamb." David Baron says: "From the contemporary testimony of Josephus, and from Talmudical authorities, there cannot be a doubt that, at the time of our Lord, it was regarded as the interval between the sun's commencing to decline and its actual disappearance."

The blood of the Passover sacrifice had to be applied according to divine instruction—"They shall take of the blood, and strike it on the two side posts and on the upper door posts of the houses." [35] "And ye shall take a bunch of hyssop, and dip it in the blood that is in the bason, and strike the lintel and the two side posts with the blood that is in the bason." [36] It was not enough that the lamb be without blemish and that it be slain; it was necessary that the blood be properly sprinkled. They were to take the blood and strike it on the two side posts and on the upper door posts of the houses. Notice the use of the word "strike" in these passages. The Hebrew word is *nathan,* and it is translated "give." When we read the verses using the word "give" instead of "strike," it changes the meaning entirely, throwing an altogether different light upon the act. August Van Ryn points out the beautiful and striking contrast—*"take* and *give."* In our sinful and lost condition we have nothing that can satisfy the righteous demands of God. His

[33] Exodus 12:6   [34] Mark 15:25   [35] Exodus 12:7
[36] Exodus 12:22

hatred and judgment against sin leaves the sinner without any shelter from the wrath to come. But God in grace and in mercy has offered His Son as a sacrifice, a substitute for us. First, we take (or receive) the blood of Christ as the cleansing from our sins and the shelter from God's judgment. Then we present the blood to God as our only hope and plea.

> "For my pardon, this I see—
> Nothing but the Blood of Jesus;
> For my cleansing, this my plea—
> Nothing but the Blood of Jesus."

It was not sufficient that the lamb be perfect and that its blood be shed, but it was essential that the blood be *taken* and then *applied* (or *given*). Here we see a clear and simple foreshadowing of God's plan of redemption. The Lamb of God was slain, and He shed His precious blood in order that men might be cleansed from every sin and be eternally saved. But have *you* accepted His blood? Have you received it as your only hope of forgiveness and cleansing? If you have not, your case is hopeless until you do accept the atoning work of the Son of God. Without the divine application of His blood to our hearts, we could never hope to live eternally in His presence, for man's access into the holiest is "by the blood of Jesus." [37]

❧

The blood of the passover sacrifice was to be applied by using a bunch of hyssop—"And ye shall take a bunch of hyssop, and dip it in the blood that is in the bason, and strike the lintel and the two side posts with the blood that is in the bason." [38] Hyssop was a small plant bearing little clusters of blue flowers, and it was well known in the regions round about Palestine and Egypt. It was such a common plant that it was easily accessible

[37] Hebrews 10:19   [38] Exodus 12:22

to all. In this the hyssop speaks of faith, for the Scriptures teach plainly that the sacrificial work of Christ is to be taken hold of by faith.

Faith is a virtue that is found everywhere. If a man refuses to lay hold of Jesus Christ by faith, it is not because he does not have access to that faith. It is seen and used every day in almost everything we do. By faith we eat canned foods, accept checks, and board trolleys and buses. Now faith is not merely believing Jesus. Some people believe Him to the extent that they accept as truth the words which He spoke. They give intellectual assent to His statements, but they never have taken Him seriously enough so as to surrender their lives to His will and commit themselves to Him for eternal life. They believe Him but they do not believe in Him. They do not cling to Him as their stay in life and their hope for eternity. They claim to have confidence in Him, but in a certain sense faith and confidence are not the same.

If a man is naturally optimistic and hopeful he may have confidence that everything will turn out all right, and even though he feels that he has faith, he has only confidence. Faith is taking God at His Word and believing that "He can because He is omnipotent, and He will because He promised." Says Bob Jones, Jr.: "Faith is superior to confidence as divine omnipotence is superior to moral weakness. Confidence may enable a man to climb a mountain whose lofty peak challenges his efforts. Faith removes the mountain. Confidence helps a mariner to sail his boat safely through a stormy sea, but only faith can enable a man to walk on the waves. Faith has this foundation—the Word of God—and 'the foundation [Word] of God standeth sure.'" Have you exercised faith thus in God's Word? Have you laid hold of God's sacrifice on the Cross to save you from the grave and hell? "Believe on the Lord Jesus Christ, and thou shalt be saved." [39]

[39] Acts 16:31

HE'S THE ONE

Is there anyone can help us,
    One who understands our hearts,
When the thorns of life have pierced them till they bleed;
One who sympathizes with us,
    Who in wondrous love imparts
Just the very, very blessing that we need?

Is there anyone can help us
    When the load is hard to bear,
And we faint and fall beneath it in alarm;
Who in tenderness will lift us,
    And the heavy burden share,
And support us with an everlasting arm?

Is there anyone can help us,
    Who can give a sinner peace,
When his heart is burdened down with pain and woe;
Who can speak the word of pardon
    That affords a sweet release,
And whose blood can wash and make us white as snow?

Is there anyone can help us
    When the end is drawing near,
Who will go through death's dark waters by our side;
Who will light the way before us,
    And dispel all doubt and fear,
And will bear our spirits safely o'er the tide?

Yes, there's One, only One,
The blessed, blessed Jesus, He's the One;
When afflictions press the soul,
When waves of trouble roll,
And you need a friend to help you,
                    He's the One.

                                        J. B. MACKAY

HIS SYMPATHY

"Touched with the feeling of our infirmities." [1]

As the doctor lays his instrument to the heart and listens, lay your ear on the heart of the universe and detect the surging restlessness and feverishness in it. Whether in the busy city streets or in the quiet country valleys, one is sure to find suffering. To some it is the pain and privation of the body. To others it is the ache and anguish of a broken heart. To still others it is a troubled and tormented mind. The act of one man's disobedience has left an open sore upon the hearts of men which no human sympathy can heal.

Must men live and die with a broken heart? Since all humanity is engulfed in a vortex of sorrow must we all spin helplessly and hopelessly, each to his own fate? We purpose in this message to show that the Lord Jesus Christ is the only perfect balm for broken and sorrowing hearts, and that without Him men will search in vain for sympathy and succor for their ills and pains. Creation is indifferent and nature severe. Society may often comfort, but it is regretfully limited. How strengthening to turn to the Lord Jesus who can sustain us as we bend under our burdens in the dark moments of life!

> "The great Physician now is near,
>   The sympathizing Jesus;
> He speaks the drooping heart to cheer,
>   Oh, hear the voice of Jesus."

[1] Hebrews 4:15

Sympathy and compassion are synonymous terms denoting a fellow-feeling. One cannot have compassion until one feels in consequence what the person feels who is in need of sympathy. The most genuine sympathizers have at some time been great sufferers, for God does not work through us that which He has not first worked in us. In his second Epistle to the Corinthians, the Apostle Paul speaks of the Lord as "The God of all comfort; Who comforteth us in all our tribulation, that we may be able to comfort them which are in any trouble, by the comfort wherewith we ourselves are comforted of God. For as the sufferings of Christ abound in us, so our consolation also aboundeth by Christ." [2] We need to turn to the risen Lord, for in Him "we have not an high priest which cannot be touched with the feeling of our infirmities; but was in all points tempted like as we are, yet without sin." [3] The Greek word which is translated "touched with the feeling of" is *sympatheia,* and from it comes our word *sympathy.* The same word occurs at least once more in the New Testament where it is translated *compassion.*[4] When we suffer, Christ can feel *with* us. "In all their afflictions He was afflicted." [5] Truly, we have an High Priest who can be touched with the feeling of our infirmities. He is able to sympathize because He alone can enter intelligently into our distress.

In Hebrews the divine Sympathizer is called our High Priest. Under the Mosaic law the priest and the prophet differed. Prophets were men raised up in the time of crises to meet spiritual emergencies in the life of the nation. They censured sharply, "and they came with a whip for the horse, a bridle for the ass, and a rod for the fool." They rebuked iniquity and raised their voices in protest above the roar of revelry and over the depth of degradation. But the priest did not come as such. He did not censure the sinner nor mete out judgment for

[2] 2 Corinthians 1:3-5   [3] Hebrews 4:15   [4] Hebrews 10:34
[5] Isaiah 63:9

sin. He stood between man and God as a minister of mercy with his hands extended in blessing and benediction. Just so Jesus Christ our High Priest came not to condemn the world but that the world through Him might be saved.[6] Today He occupies the place on the right hand of the Majesty on high, able to save to the uttermost, seeing He ever liveth to make intercession for us. It is folly to ignore Jesus Christ who alone can give beauty for ashes and joy for sorrow.

The prophet Isaiah said: "Surely He hath borne our griefs, and carried our sorrows." [7] Having borne our griefs on the cross, He is well able to bear them now. And since there He carried our sorrows, He is better able to be the carrier of them now. Let the grief-stricken and sorrowing bring all to Jesus, "A man of sorrows, and acquainted with grief," [8] and He will bear them along and care for them until that day when His high priestly ministry is no longer needed, and they shall reign with Him forever.

The whole life and ministry of Jesus was one of sympathy and mercy. His plea was "Come unto Me, all ye that labour and are heavy laden, and I will give you rest." [9] This was not Christ's call to the few but to the multitude. "Come unto Me *all.*" It was His invitation to the unreasonable and unregenerate, the dissatisfied and disconsolate. To all who desire to be rid of the load of sin and sorrow, Jesus offers an invitation to Himself, and He promises rest.

∽

On five different occasions the Gospel writers tell us that our Lord was moved with compassion (or sympathy) to minister to people. In the first of these references we read: "But when He saw the multitudes, He was moved with *compassion* on them, because they fainted, and were scattered abroad, as sheep

6 John 3:17   7 Isaiah 53:4   8 Isaiah 53:3
9 Matthew 11:28

having no shepherd." [10] The sympathy of Jesus is poured out first upon the ignorant, helpless, dying multitudes who are unfit to die. The sight of the masses, lost and scattered as sheep having no shepherd, moved our Lord to deep pity. *"He was moved with compassion!"* There always has been deep pity in the heart of Jesus for those who were lost and dying in their sins. Oh, the magnitude of our Saviour's love! There never has been anything in man that God should sympathize with him and save him, for "we are all as an unclean thing, and all our righteousnesses are as filthy rags.[11] The only cause of God's care for sinners is that the deepest attribute of the being of God is love and compassion.

Dr. G. Campbell Morgan has pointed out that we are not to look at this word *compassion* as if it meant pity merely. We can pity people and stand by helpless while they die in misery. But the sympathy of Jesus was comradeship in sorrow, fellowship in agony. Jesus Christ came so intimately in touch with human life that its pain was His pain. If it were sickness, Christ identified Himself with the sickness. If it were grief, He identified Himself with the grief. When He saw the multitude lost in sin, He identified Himself with the very issues of their sin. That is compassion. Such sympathy is never passive but always active. He was *moved*. The inmost seat of His tenderest affections and most violent passion compelled Him to act in behalf of this distressed and scattered multitude. His love reached to all, even to the vilest. One often hears: "I have no sympathy for so-and-so." Our Lord never allowed prejudice or personality to keep Him from sympathizing with anyone and, personally, I am thankful that He did not.

The very condition of this multitude was a call for compassion—"They fainted, and were scattered abroad, as sheep having no shepherd."

The Bible speaks of men as lost and shepherdless:

[10] Matthew 9:36   [11] Isaiah 64:6

He "made His own people to go forth like sheep, and guided them in the wilderness like a flock." [12]

"All we like sheep have gone astray." [13]

"My people hath been lost sheep: their shepherds have caused them to go astray, they have turned them away on the mountains: they have gone from mountain to hill, they have forgotten their resting place." [14]

"Israel is a scattered sheep." [15]

"But go rather to the lost sheep of the house of Israel." [16]

"We are accounted as sheep for the slaughter." [17]

"For ye were as sheep going astray; but are now returned unto the Shepherd and Bishop of your souls." [18]

Can you tell of any more pitiful sight than a field of bewildered, helpless, distressed sheep set upon by wolves? Yet this is how Jesus saw men and women. To Him they were lost, lacerated sheep, dying from the wounds of sin and straying without a shepherd.

"The Lord is my shepherd." [19]

"Give ear, O Shepherd of Israel." [20]

"He shall feed His flock like a shepherd: He shall gather the lambs with His arm, and carry them in His bosom, and shall gently lead those that are with young." [21]

"I am the good shepherd: the good shepherd giveth His life for the sheep. . . . I am the good shepherd, and know My sheep, and am known of Mine." [22]

"Now the God of peace, that brought again from the dead our Lord Jesus, that great shepherd of the sheep, through the blood of the everlasting covenant." [23]

"And when the chief Shepherd shall appear, ye shall receive a crown of glory that fadeth not away." [24]

[12] Psalm 78:52   [13] Isaiah 53:6   [14] Jeremiah 50:6
[15] Jeremiah 50:17   [16] Matthew 10:6   [17] Romans 8:36
[18] 1 Peter 2:25   [19] Psalm 23:1   [20] Psalm 80:1
[21] Isaiah 40:11   [22] John 10:11,14   [23] Hebrews 13:20
[24] 1 Peter 5:4

Christ became all things to all men. To the hungry, He was the "Bread of Life"; to the blind He was the "Light of the World"; to the dead He was the "Resurrection and the Life"; to the ignorant and unwise He was the "Wisdom of God"; to the lost He was the "Way"; to the sick He was the "Great Physician"; and to the lost and straying sheep Christ was the "Good Shepherd." Thank God, the sympathizing Saviour is "the same yesterday, and today, and for ever!" [25] In pity the Lord Jesus, the Shepherd of souls, is seeking the lost sheep that are wandering from the fold of God.

> "And although the road be rough and steep,
> I go to the desert to find My sheep."

> "And Jesus went forth, and saw a great multitude, and was moved with compassion toward them, and He healed their sick." [26]

On one occasion when the Pharisees challenged our Lord's right to forgive sins, Jesus defended His ministry as a healer of souls by comparing Himself with a healer of men's bodies. He said: "They that be whole need not a physician, but they that are sick." [27] Our Lord was a true physician in every respect, and all true physicians will go where they are needed, whether a clean city hospital or a malaria-infested jungle. Besides, the true physician is sympathetic.

When Jesus came down from the mountain, there came to Him a wretched leper so utterly contaminated with the loathsome disease that he had almost lost his sense of being human. "And Jesus, moved with *compassion,* put forth His hand, and touched him." [28] While all others put distance between themselves and the leper, expressing their pity in shallow words,

[25] Hebrews 13:8   [26] Matthew 14:14   [27] Matthew 9:12
[28] Mark 1:41

Jesus, the Sympathizer, extended His touch of compassion to the poor outcast.

There is the maniac of Gadara from whom everyone turned in terror. He too needed a physician, but men fled frightened from his presence. Can Jesus help this poor demented, demon-controlled man? The story is full of interest.[29] He went to where the man was and healed him completely. Witnesses came and found the man "sitting, and clothed, and in his right mind: and they were afraid."[30] Such is our Saviour's sympathy for man and His sovereignty over Satan. Those who are wounded mentally and held in fear by the devil can look with confidence to the Lord Jesus Christ for deliverance. Mark tells how the sympathy of Jesus led Him to many such persons: the daughter of the Syrophenician woman,[31] the boy at the foot of the mountain,[32] and Mary Magdalene out of whom he cast seven devils.[33] After the maniac of Gadara had been healed, Jesus said to him: "Go home to thy friends, and tell them how great things the Lord hath done for thee, and hath had *compassion* on thee."[34] What Jesus did for this man He can and will do for any and all who will put their trust in Him.

❧

We are shown the sympathy of Jesus in His lesson on forgiveness. Peter came to Him, and said: "Lord, how oft shall my brother sin against me, and I forgive him? till seven times? Jesus saith unto him, I say not unto thee, Until seven times: but, Until seventy times seven."[35]

Then Jesus gave a parabolic illustration of the servant who owed his master ten thousand talents. When the lord of that servant began to exact his demands upon his subject, "The servant therefore fell down, and worshipped him, saying, Lord,

---

[29] Mark 5:1-19 [30] Mark 5:15 [31] Mark 7:24-30
[32] Mark 9:17-29 [33] Mark 16:9 [34] Mark 5:19
[35] Matthew 18:21,22

have patience with me, and I will pay thee all. Then the lord of that servant was moved with *compassion,* and loosed him, and forgave him the debt." [36]

The story does not end here. In fact, it has a sorry sequel. However, verse twenty-seven sets forth clearly the compassion of Christ in forgiveness. Note the difference between human forgiveness and divine forgiveness. Human forgiveness is limited to the remission of the penalty, but divine forgiveness always follows the exaction of the penalty. We are forgiven because our sins have been dealt with on the Cross of Calvary. There can be no forgiveness of sins without first the shedding of blood, and the shedding of Christ's blood means the exaction of the penalty for our sins—"Without shedding of blood is no remission." [37] The *medium* of forgiveness is the blood of Christ—"In whom we have redemption through His blood, even the forgiveness of sins." [38] The *measure* of forgiveness is infinite and boundless—"In whom we have redemption through His blood, the forgiveness of sins, *according to the riches of His grace.*" [39]

In sympathy Jesus looks upon man in his sin and in his helplessness to obtain forgiveness. The first petition that Jesus uttered from His cross was "Father, forgive them." [40] How all-inclusive is the sympathy of the Saviour! Forgive them! Whom? Forgive these soldiers who, with cruel hearts and wicked hands drove the nails into His body? Yes, forgive them. Forgive them—Pontius Pilate, who lacked the courage of his convictions? Yes, forgive him. Forgive them—Annas and Caiaphas, the crooked and consummate politicians? Yes, forgive them. Forgive them—the Pharisees and Sadducees, false religious rulers and blind leaders of the blind? Yes, forgive them. And in compassion that same prayer is the burden of His heart for you and me. Christ sees our lost and helpless estate. He

---

[36] Matthew 18:26,27   [37] Hebrews 9:22   [38] Colossians 1:14
[39] Ephesians 1:7   [40] Luke 23:34

longs to save each of us. He sacrificed Himself for our forgiveness. Even today He is praying: "Father, forgive them." What limitless compassion!

Are you in sin? Are you sorrowing? Have you been wounded by the maltreatment of others? Is your spirit crushed, your heart troubled? Are you poor and destitute of this world's goods? Are you fearful about the future? Then reach up in faith, as did the woman of old, and touch the hem of Christ's garment. He will show compassion toward you. Here are the lines from one who found Jesus sympathetic—

> "I've tried in vain a thousand ways
> My fears to quell, my hopes to raise;
> But what I need, the Bible says,
>   Is ever, only Jesus.
>
> My soul is night, my heart is steel,—
> I cannot see, I cannot feel;
> For light, for life, I must appeal
>   In simple faith to Jesus.
>
> He died, He lives, He reigns, He pleads;
> There's love in all His words and deeds;
> There's all a guilty sinner needs
>   For evermore in Jesus.
>
> Though some should sneer, and some should blame,
> I'll go with all my guilt and shame,
> I'll go to Him because His Name,
>   Above all names, is Jesus."

Would you know the comfort and consolation of Christ? The living Saviour abiding in our hearts is able to make real in every circumstance the sufficiency of Himself. God's compassion is not too small for you. He will satisfy and meet every need. But be sure you do not mistrust nor wrongly accuse your heavenly Father. When He gives medicine, He never opens the wrong bottle. In your weakness look up to Jesus, and He will strengthen you with might by His Spirit in the inner man.

"Tell it to Jesus, He understands thee,
  Reads all the secret intents of thy heart,
  Foes may misjudge, and friends may mistake thee;
  He will not deal with thee but as thou art."

THE LOST REWARD

I had a vision, and therein I saw
    Great store of rich rewards, unowned, unclaimed,
And questioning my Heavenly Guide of these;
    I heard His answer, silent and ashamed.

"These are the treasures that were meant for thee,—
    This blessing only waited for thy prayer;
Because thou wast not faithful to thy trust
    Here is a crown that thou canst never wear.

"Because when fierce temptation thou didst meet
    Thou didst not call My name and turn and flee,
But in thine own poor strength the fight essayed,
    The overcomer's gifts are lost to thee.

"Because thou hast not used the keys I gave
    Unlocking all the riches of My grace,
So dost thou dwell in poverty of soul
    And mourn the limitations of thy place.

"Because thou hast been slothful in the race,
    Here is a victor's palm thou canst not bear,
Because thou hast not closer walked with Me,
    My heart's deep joy thy heart can never share."

HIS SEVERITY

"I feared thee, because thou art an austere man." [1]

The heart of man is ever responsive to the message that tells of the gentleness and tenderness of God, and tears flow more readily when the love of God is preached than when the wrath of God is declared. God is love. Of this we may be certain, because the Word of God teaches it and Jesus Christ has proved it. All that we know about God is to be found in the Bible, the Written Word, and in Jesus, the Living Word. Whatever a man wants to know about God he must acquire from these two sources. The character of God has been described in His Word and demonstrated in His Son. Man can have a full length portrait of God as he studies the Bible and beholds the Lord Jesus Christ. "No human eye has ever seen God: the only Son, who is in the Father's bosom—He has made Him known." [2] Jesus Himself said: "The Father is in Me, and I in Him." [3] "He that hath seen Me hath seen the Father." [4] By His life and death He showed the world how tender and sympathetic God really is. No doubt the world would be satisfied if it could believe that the nature of God was confined to these lovely graces always displayed in sweetness of disposition. But there is a firmness and a sternness in His character as well. In bringing God into full view of man, our Lord Jesus showed that the divine character is one of severity and austerity.

[1] Luke 19:21   [2] John 1:18 Weymouth   [3] John 10:38
[4] John 14:9

404

For nineteen centuries now the world has looked upon the words of Christ with awe and wonder. All are agreed that "never man spake like this man." [5] Words as comforting and cheerful as His never fell from mortal lips. In the darkest night of grief, the heart takes on new courage in His promises. But not all of His preaching contained words of comfort and condolence. There were times in His ministry when the axe was laid at the root of fruitless trees, when His words lashed out with open frankness. He spoke with a fervor and fire that burned into the innermost recesses of the heart. On several occasions His words, like the piercing thrust of a sharp two-edged sword, cut through to lay bare the secrets of the hearts of men. Never did His sentences contain the spineless, sickly sentimentality that we hear so much in these days. When Jesus spoke there was no compromise. His messages always showed open frankness and demanded exacting requirements.

Some people have found it difficult to reconcile the severity of God with the love of God. But the fact of the matter is the two can never be separated. "Whom the Lord loveth He chasteneth, and scourgeth every son whom He receiveth." [6] In His message to Laodicea He said: "As many as I love, I rebuke and chasten: be zealous therefore, and repent." [7] The stern notes in our Lord's words reveal divine love just as much as do His words of cheer and comfort. "More than that," said a friend, "without these severe tones we should almost completely miss the deeper compassion, the anguish, the cross that was ever in the heart of the Son of God." A father fails if strength does not go along with sweetness. True devotion to children is never without discipline. Along with love there must lie a firmness hard as steel. Christ always said what He meant and meant what He said.

∾

[5] John 7:46   [6] Hebrews 12:6   [7] Revelation 3:19

Jesus was severe in His denunciation of all who neglect the spiritual welfare of children. A more acrimonious statement never fell from His lips than that which follows. Read it carefully: "At the same time came the disciples unto Jesus, saying, Who is the greatest in the kingdom of heaven? And Jesus called a little child unto Him, and set him in the midst of them, And said, Verily I say unto you, Except ye be converted, and become as little children, ye shall not enter into the kingdom of heaven. Whosoever therefore shall humble himself as this little child, the same is greatest in the kingdom of heaven. And whoso shall receive one such little child in my name receiveth Me. But whoso shall offend one of these little ones which believe in Me, it were better for him that a millstone were hanged about his neck, and that he were drowned in the depth of the sea. Woe unto the world because of offences! for it must needs be that offences come; but woe to that man by whom the offence cometh! Wherefore if thy hand or thy foot offend thee, cut them off, and cast them from thee: it is better for thee to enter into life halt or maimed, rather than having two hands or two feet to be cast into everlasting fire. And if thine eye offend thee, pluck it out, and cast it from thee: it is better for thee to enter into life with one eye, rather than having two eyes to be cast into hell fire. Take heed that ye despise not one of these little ones; for I say unto you, That in heaven their angels do always behold the face of My Father which is in heaven. For the Son of man is come to save that which was lost. How think ye? if a man have an hundred sheep, and one of them be gone astray, doth he not leave the ninety and nine, and goeth into the mountains, and seeketh that which is gone astray? And if so be that he find it, verily I say unto you, he rejoiceth more of that sheep, than of the ninety and nine which went not astray. Even so it is not the will of your Father which is in heaven, that one of these little ones should perish." [8]

[8] Matthew 18:1-14

The entire paragraph is scathing. There is keenness and severity in every word of it. Look now at verse six: "But whoso shall offend one of these little ones which believe in Me, it were better for him that a millstone were hanged about his neck, and that he were drowned in the depth of the sea." Have you grasped the seriousness and the importance of these words? The word *offend* means to *cause to stumble,* and Jesus is saying that a sorer punishment than He mentions here awaits any and all who cause a child to stumble.

If we are to understand clearly the solemnity of this warning, let us learn first that every child is potentially lost. Every baby born into the world possesses a sinful nature. Sin is inherent in the whole human race. It is not popular in some circles to preach on the subject of the total depravity of man. Everyone wants to believe that bad men may be saved, but few are willing to acknowledge that good folks may be lost. But God says: "There is none righteous, no, not one." [9] From Adam until this present hour not one baby born into the world has been rightly related to God except Jesus. Any philosophy or religion which teaches that men have attained to a standing of righteousness before God is false. David by the Holy Spirit testifies: "They are corrupt, they have done abominable works, there is none that doeth good." [10] "Behold, I was shapen in iniquity; and in sin did my mother conceive me." [11] "For there is not a just man upon earth, that doeth good, and sinneth not." [12] No sprinkling of water or laying on of hands can change the sinful nature of your baby. The parable of the lost sheep in Matthew 18:12,13 is part of our Lord's sermon on the lostness of a child. The stray sheep in this parable is applied to the lost child. The Christian Church has always held that little children are not willful sinners, but rather creatures of hereditary environment. If they die before reaching the age of accountability they are not lost but safe. But, remember, every baby that grows until he or she can knowingly sin will be lost unless brought to a saving knowledge of the Lord Jesus Christ, because there is none righteous, *no, not one.*

Since there is none righteous, it follows that "there is none that understandeth." [13] Because the nature is distorted the intellect is darkened. Sin has incapacitated the mind so that it has no spiritual discernment. When Jesus gave the parable of the sower, He spoke of a man who "heareth the word of the kingdom, and understandeth it not." [14] Men think that they understand God, but God insists that there is none that understandeth. Men have written prolifically about God, but they have merely scribbled. "The world by wisdom knew not God." [15] An unsaved man may be brilliant and educated, but he is spiritually ignorant, for "the natural [or unregenerate] man receiveth not the things of the Spirit of God: for they are foolishness unto him: neither can he know them, because they are spiritually discerned." [16] No amount of natural ability will furnish a man with spiritual understanding. Because "there is none that understandeth," children need to be taught God's plan of salvation. This is the best time to do it inasmuch as children are willing listeners—teachable and trustful.

To offend a little child, that is, to cause a child to stumble either by failing to teach him God's way of salvation or by teaching him error, is a gross sin in the sight of God. God's dealing with all who neglect the spiritual welfare of children will be in severity. The solemn declarations of Christ are against those persons who are guilty of the offence of failing to evangelize boys and girls. Children are bound by environment and guided by influence so that it is a more serious offence to neglect the winning of a child to Christ than to neglect an adult.

More destructive than the damage done by the atomic bomb,

[13] Romans 3:11   [14] Matthew 13:19   [15] 1 Corinthians 1:21
[16] 1 Corinthians 2:14

more devastating than a hurricane, more to be feared than an epidemic of smallpox, is the evil being done to the youth of America through neglect of Christian training. The intellectual and spiritual leprosy of paganism, the anti-Christian teaching and un-Americanism in our public schools, the moral corruption within our national life, and the moral breakdown of the home are all contributing to the steady increase in juvenile court cases involving boys and girls under sixteen years of age. You parents, preachers, and Sunday school teachers who fail to discharge your solemn responsibility to the children in your care are causing these little ones to stumble, and of each of you Jesus said: *"It were better for him that a millstone were hanged about his neck, and that he were drowned in the depth of the sea . . .* woe to that man by whom the offence cometh."

Jesus was severe in His denunciation of those who desecrated the house of God. Two times in His ministry, one at the commencement and again at the close, He cleansed the Temple. John writes:

> "And the Jews' passover was at hand, and Jesus went up to Jerusalem, And found in the temple those that sold oxen and sheep and doves, and the changers of money sitting: And when He had made a scourge of small cords, He drove them all out of the temple, and the sheep, and the oxen; and poured out the changers' money, and overthrew the tables; And said unto them that sold doves, Take these things hence; make not My Father's house an house of merchandise." [17]

Matthew says:

> "And Jesus went into the temple of God, and cast out all them that sold and bought in the temple, and overthrew

[17] John 2:13-16

the tables of the moneychangers, and the seats of them that sold doves, And said unto them, It is written, My house shall be called the house of prayer; but ye have made it a den of thieves." [18]

Surely it is not insignificant that the Spirit of God should record these two instances of our Lord's anger, both in connection with the same act. What did Jesus find when He came into the Temple? "Those that sold oxen and sheep and doves, and the changers of money." Selling animals and changing coinage were not sinful acts in themselves. Jews, coming to Jerusalem from surrounding countries, would not have the Jewish coins necessary for the temple tax. Then, too, the animals could have been legitimately sold as offerings for a sacrifice. It was a matter not only of convenience but of necessity for these Jews from distant places to be able to purchase their sacrifices in Jerusalem.

How, then, can we account for the severe action of Jesus? W. Graham Scroggie says: "First, because these traffics were being pursued *in a wrong place,* within the temple area. And secondly, because this traffic was being carried on *in a wrong spirit,*" the spirit of greed, commercialism, and fraud. These transactions could have been carried on elsewhere without becoming a money-making scheme, but the priests themselves were supervising their own "racket" and sharing handsomely in the spoils. Such profanation of the house of God stirred Jesus to righteous indignation, so in sovereign majesty and fearless authority He declared Himself against it. The divine record says: *"He drove them all out of the temple."*

What would Jesus find today were He to walk into some of our churches? How much business there is in our churches that does not ascribe praise and honor to the triune God! The spirit of quietness, reverence, and worship has been replaced

[18] Matthew 21:12,13

with hilarity, dancing, theatricals, movies, lodge conventions, etc. All of these things we have witnessed here in Bristol, Pennsylvania. These things are of the world and are not found in a place that is set apart for prayer and the ministry of God's Word. The churches no longer influence the world for righteousness. Many so-called "churches" have reversed their programs in an endeavor to keep up with the world. "He drove them all out." How sad! But what else could He do? He was but insisting upon God's eternal standard; namely, that separation which always has been demanded of His redeemed people. Do you think that Jesus would lower the divine standard were He to walk into some of our so-called Protestant churches today? We fear that the record of their past would have to be identical with what we have found in the Scriptures—"He drove them all out."

The actions of Jesus were the actions of God. He was representing the Godhead. How it must have cut those priests who were in the Temple to hear the Son of God quote the Holy Scriptures in support of what He did. He took them directly to their own writings, those divinely inspired sayings that were penned by the Hebrew prophets, Isaiah and Jeremiah. And He "said unto them, It is written, My house shall be called the house of prayer; but ye have made it a den of thieves." [19] This was a citation from two Old Testament passages: "Mine house shall be called an house of prayer for all people," [20] and "Is this house, which is called by My name, become a den of robbers in your eyes?" [21] How true He was to the Word! They could not deny that He was right. We must admire the fearlessness and the force of the Saviour. He had not ceased to love. He was acting according to heaven's holy standards, and we cannot deny that He got results. Of course Christ was charged with stirring up the people,[22] but they needed it. We could profit by

[19] Matthew 21:13 [20] Isaiah 56:7 [21] Jeremiah 7:11
[22] Luke 23:5

that kind of stirring in the churches today. The modern psychology of *How to Win Friends and Influence People* was not a part of Christ's preaching, particularly when one must compromise on the sound biblical doctrine of "the wrath of the Lamb" and fall into the error of using God's love for license. "Don't be so stern in your preaching," said a modern minister. "You can catch more flies with molasses than you can with vinegar." But the philosophy of fly exterminators finds no application where sin abounds in the hearts of men. We are not dealing with insects but with never-dying souls that must give an account before God. Furthermore, I have seen too many of the soft-pedal type of preacher stuck in their own molasses.

Dr. G. Campbell Morgan has a fine comment on the cleansing of the Temple. "What did He find in the Temple? . . . everything conveniently arranged for in the Temple courts. That is what He found. *Religion made easy.*" People will be satisfied with their "religion made easy" when it has the sanction of their particular church or denomination upon it. We are living in the ease era, the era of progressive paganism, the era of unsoundness. The people have itching ears, and instead of hearing a sound Bible message, they sit at ease in Zion while the minister publicly confesses: "I do not like the word 'damnation' on the lips of Christ, so I always change it to something that sounds softer." *"Religion made easy"* indeed reflects the trend of the times. The sugar-coated suavity of some ministers is but a trick to gain the friendship and the following of the people. But this much must be said of Christ, He would not condone such hypocrisy. Let all professing Christians and church-going men take heed, "For the time is come that judgment must begin at the house of God." [23]

"But woe unto you, scribes and Pharisees, hypocrites! for ye shut up the kingdom of heaven against men: for ye

[23] 1 Peter 4:17

neither go in yourselves, neither suffer ye them that are entering to go in." [24]

"Woe unto you, scribes and Pharisees, hypocrites! for ye devour widows' houses, and for a pretence make long prayer: therefore ye shall receive the greater damnation." [25]

"Woe unto you, scribes and Pharisees, hypocrites! for ye compass sea and land to make one proselyte, and when he is made, ye make him twofold more the child of hell than yourselves." [26]

"Woe unto you, scribes and Pharisees, hypocrites! for ye are like unto whited sepulchres, which indeed appear beautiful outward, but are within full of dead men's bones, and of all uncleanness. Even so ye also outwardly appear righteous unto men, but within ye are full of hypocrisy and iniquity." [27]

"Ye serpents, ye generation of vipers, how can ye escape the damnation of hell?" [28]

❧

Jesus was severe in His denunciation of all who sought to enter heaven falsely. He said: "Verily, verily, I say unto you, He that entereth not by the door into the sheepfold, but climbeth up some other way, *the same is a thief and a robber*." [29]

All thoughtful people are agreed that, despite his remarkable progress, man is bound by limitations. The atomic bomb is man's most recent and most remarkable discovery, but every advancement that he makes merely serves to emphasize more clearly than ever that man lives in a restricted realm. What is true in the physical is likewise true in the spiritual. Science and philosophy have been unsuccessful in their attempt to explore the spiritual realm. The tower of Babel ended only in confusion and showed how muddled man's mind was. God showed us that if ever man was to scale the infinite heights from earth

[24] Matthew 23:13   [25] Matthew 23:14   [26] Matthew 23:15
[27] Matthew 23:27,28   [28] Matthew 23:33   [29] John 10:1

to heaven it would have to be through a divinely-provided way. Jacob did not build the ladder upon which he saw the angels descending and ascending. That ladder was let down from heaven. Furthermore Jacob could never boast that he had any part in it. God made certain of that. He let down the ladder while Jacob lay helplessly sleeping.

Certainly, every path that man is traveling today leads to the rediscovery of human inability to save himself. We have achieved electric lights, but they have not lighted the way into the presence of God. We have mastered refrigeration, but it has not cooled the hot lustful passions of man's heart. We have every available power at our disposal, but man cannot muster together enough power to save a single soul from sin. We have built towering skyscrapers, but they have brought us no nearer to heaven. If there is any quest for God, man in his own strength and wisdom is getting nowhere fast. Sin is responsible for separating man from God, and who ever heard of a nation or international conference to combat sin? We spend millions to explore the poles and the stratosphere, no expense being spared to remove obstacles, but no nation or league of nations has spent one dollar to remove the big black monster that separates man from God.

There is a brand of moralistic preaching, but Jesus said that he who seeks entrance into heaven by simply preaching and practicing morals is a thief and a robber. There are those who maintain that if one does the best he can, surely God will not exclude such a one from heaven, but Jesus brands all such as thieves and robbers. Any attempt on man's part to reconcile himself to God apart from the atoning work of the Lord Jesus Christ at Calvary is a part of that army which has been battling against Jesus Christ and His Church and running its bloody course for nineteen centuries. When will man learn that there is no salvation without Christ? People like to believe that all creeds are good, and that eventually all will lead to the same goal. Jesus said, however: "*I* am the way" [30] and "*I* am the door" [31] and He insists that "He that entereth not by the *door* into the sheepfold, but climbeth up some other way, the same is a thief and a robber." [32]

Man is not what scientists tell us he is, "an accidental bundle of atoms drifting toward oblivion." Man is God's creature, a never-dying soul. He is separated from God because of his own willful sin, and God is seeking to reconcile man unto Himself, but now that man has failed so miserably God will not think of a reconciliation save through the blood of His Son. Do you not sense your need of Jesus Christ? Do not think of need as a sign of weakness. The best test of the genuineness of your desire to be reconciled to God is in the size and amplitude of your need as you yourself see it. God's final decision is one of sternness and austerity—"He that believeth on Him is not condemned: but he that believeth not is condemned already, because he hath not believed in the name of the only begotten Son of God." [33]

[30] John 14:6
[32] John 3:18
[31] John 10:7
[33] John 10:1

SHIPWRECKED ON GOD

Shipwrecked on God! 'Tis not till then we know Him;
'Tis not till then we trust Him to the uttermost;
'Tis not till then we prove Him all sufficient
And feed upon His breast alone.

Shipwrecked on God! O blessed place of safety!
Shipwrecked on God! No greater place of rest.
Shipwrecked on God! All shorelines broke asunder,
With nothing left in all the universe but God.

Shipwrecked on God! Then face to face we see Him,
With naught between to dim the vision of His Love.
'Tis then we learn the secret of Redemption,
When we have nothing left in earth or heaven—but God.

Shipwrecked on God! 'Tis not till then we vanish;
'Tis not till then we find we're hid with Christ in God,
And cease from all our trying and our struggling,
To find at last that Christ is All in All.

Shipwrecked on God! No land in sight to flee to;
Where height and depth cannot be reached,
      nor length nor breadth be spanned,
We sink into the mighty sea of God's own fulness,
To find that nothing else remains—but Him, the Christ of God.

Shipwrecked on God! With naught but Christ remaining,
I've found in Him Life and Breath, Environment—yea All!
I've ceased from all my trying and my toiling,
I've entered into rest to toil no more;
He lives in me His life, while I abide within Him,
And now to me to live is Christ forevermore.

CECILIA M. BARTON

HIS SUFFICIENCY

"Who is sufficient for these things?" [1]
"Our sufficiency is of God." [2]

Sir James Simpson, that noted Edinburgh physician, was once asked the question: "What do you consider the greatest discovery you ever made?" Without one moment's hesitation, he replied: "That I have a Saviour." Obviously the eminent doctor had discovered the all-sufficiency of the Lord Jesus.

The years bring change. In each soul are built many lonely hearthstones; life leaves its empty chairs. Joys which we once felt would remain unequalled vanish into forgetfulness. Streams which once brought glad refreshing to our hearts have dried and no trace of the stream-bed is left. Treasures of wealth, success, and comfort have been interred with the years. Skies once sunlit and bright have oozed out leaden drops of regret. Nothing seems permanent. All is changed. Into such gloom bursts the hallelujah fact, "Thou remainest!"

"Thus through life's days, whoe'er or what may fail me,
    Friends, friendships, joys in small or great degree,
Songs may be mine, no sadness need assail me,
    Lord, *Thou remainest!* Still my heart hath Thee."

All who have trusted in the Son of God have found Him equal to every circumstance and abundantly able to supply every need. C. H. Spurgeon tells of how when he realized the

[1] 2 Corinthians 2:16   [2] 2 Corinthians 3:5

fact that God's grace was sufficient for him, unbelief became absurd. It was as if some little fish, being very thirsty, was troubled about drinking the river dry and Father Thames had said, "Drink away, little fish. My stream is sufficient for thee." Or it was like a man on a lofty mountain saying to himself, "I breathe so many cubic feet of air, I fear I shall exhaust the oxygen in the atmosphere." But the earth would say, "Breathe away, O man. My atmosphere is sufficient for thee." Truly we can say with Philip, "It sufficeth us." [3] Yet how often we fail to recognize His Presence!

One of the greatest mistakes many people make is that of looking to themselves. It is not uncommon to hear people boast that they are "self-sufficient." But we need learn that soul-satisfaction can never be wrought within man himself. The Apostle Paul warns us of this great danger when he says: "Not that we are sufficient of ourselves to think any thing of ourselves." [4] The teaching of Paul in this verse runs parallel with other Bible passages which teach us that man is totally depraved and absolutely insufficient to meet his own soul's need.

Modernists like Dr. Harry Emerson Fosdick and others oppose the teaching of God's Word when they urge man to "know thyself." In a sermon entitled "I Believe in Man," Dr. Fosdick says: "If a man is having trouble endeavoring to say, 'I believe in God,' he may get light starting closer home and endeavoring to say, 'I believe in man.' . . . Jesus' attitude toward human personality can be briefly described as always seeing people in terms of their possibilities. He habitually looked at men in terms of what *they* might become. . . . He saw prodigals in far countries and women taken in adultery, and thought of them in terms of *their* moral possibilities." Such statements as the above quotation cannot be reconciled with what the Bible teaches. The never-dying words of Jesus are: "Without Me ye can do nothing." [5]

---

[3] John 14:8   [4] 2 Corinthians 3:5   [5] John 15:5

It is true that Shakespeare was the son of a bankrupt butcher and of a woman who could not write her name; Beethoven, the son of a consumptive mother and a father who was a confirmed drunkard; Schubert, the son of a peasant father and a mother in domestic service; Michael Faraday, born over a stable, his father an invalid blacksmith, his mother a common drudge, and his education begun by selling newspapers on London's streets. We acknowledge that these men, along with others, have made great strides. But do not think for one moment that the literary accomplishments of a Shakespeare, the musical productions of a Beethoven or a Schubert, or the scientific discoveries of a Michael Faraday have satisfied the soul's quest for God. If the "moral possibilities" in the best of us were realized, we still would be far from God, without Christ, and without hope in the world.

Still others look to the church with the satisfaction that, in itself, the church is sufficient for the spiritual needs of man's soul. How foolish and futile! If the power to save the soul (and be sure your soul needs to be saved) lies within the church, then which church saves? The Protestant Gentile, the Jew, the Catholic, and the various heathen worshipers, all seem to feel that the hope of eternal life lies within their respective groups. By firm conviction my denominational choice is that of Baptist, but I could not recommend that you join my church and pledge yourself to its services and functions in order to be saved. The truth of the matter is *no church saves*. How wonderful and God-honoring it would be if actually there could be only one Church with the hundreds of millions of worshipers the world over bowing down to God Almighty in the Name of His Son the Lord Jesus Christ! How glorious and God-pleasing if there were no Reformed Presbyterians, Bible Presbyterians, Presbyterian Churches of the U.S.A.; no Northern Baptists, Southern Baptists, Free-will Baptists, Two-Seed-in-the-Spirit Baptists, Primitive Baptists, Duck River Baptists, Hard Shell Baptists;

no Protestant Episcopalians, Reformed Episcopalians, Anglicans, Church of England Episcopalians; no Roman Catholics, Greek Catholics, Holy Eastern Orthodox Catholics, Polish National Catholics; no English Methodists, Wesleyan Methodists, Primitive Methodists, Methodist Protestants, Methodist Church of Canada, Methodist Episcopal South, Methodist Episcopal; no Evangelical Lutherans, Reformed Lutherans, Old Lutherans, American Lutherans, Dutch Lutherans, Swedish Lutherans, German Lutherans, Augustana Lutherans, Free Lutherans, Missouri Synod Lutherans; but instead, only one Church, united in faith in one Saviour from sin and hell. The churches in themselves or in their ordinances are as powerless to save as a godless club or secret society.

❧

The purpose of this message is to show the all-sufficiency of Christ. By His death and Resurrection He is man's all-sufficient *Saviour*. When Jesus bore our sins in His own body on the Tree, dying the Just One for the unjust, He opened the way for man to enter into the presence of God. James McKendrick, the Scotch evangelist, used to say: "Christ is an all-sufficient Saviour for an insufficient sinner." This was Brother McKendrick's way of expressing briefly what the Apostle Paul wrote to the Ephesians—"For by grace are ye saved through faith; and that not of yourselves: it is the gift of God: Not of works, lest any man should boast." [6] If you have been looking within yourself, you have erred greatly, and you have a wrong conception of the Christian doctrine.

The modernistic conception recognizes that there is something wrong with man, that he is not what he ought to be, and that man's civilization and culture have been used for his own destruction. However, the modern view of man is that fundamentally he is good, and that if we continue to preach sociology, economics, reform, culture, and democracy, he will

[6] Ephesians 2:8,9

recover himself, build up his character, and improve his environment. But if this program is sufficient, it is needless to say that there is no room for the Bible doctrine of salvation by grace through faith in Jesus Christ. Since modernism admits that there is something wrong with man even after six thousand years of self-effort, it must concede that man has failed, and that in himself and in all that he has produced, he is far from God.

To debate or argue the sufficiency of Christ as the wor'd's Saviour is needless. Those of us who have been delivered from the burden of sin know full well that "He is able also to save them to the uttermost that come unto God by Him." [7] Brilliant infidels may attack the sufficiency of Christ, but "He is able." Unbelieving college professors may direct their sarcasm against our Lord's sufficiency, but "He is able." Higher critics may denounce the Scriptures as untrue, unreliable, and unhistorical, but "He is able." A careful study of the Scriptures will convince you that Jesus is all you need. Many of the great thinkers who thought they were self-sufficient, once they carefully investigated the Bible, were led to acknowledge Jesus Christ as their personal Saviour. Lord Lyttleton, General Lew Wallace, Sir William Ramsey, Lord Rochester, Professor Henry Drummond, Felix Mendelssohn, and many others turned from their self-righteousness to find Christ an all-loving, all-embracing, all-sufficient Saviour. The Atonement of Jesus Christ is unlimited in its power to save. It is *sufficient* for the salvation of the entire human race.

Christ is all-sufficient to sustain us *amidst* trials and sorrows. Nowhere are the followers of Christ promised exemption from the cares and tribulations of this life. Jesus Himself announced to His disciples: "In the world ye shall have tribulation." [8]

[7] Hebrews 7:25   [8] John 16:33

Privation and persecution have fallen repeatedly on the pathway of Christians, and in not a few cases the severest suffering has come to the choicest saints. But in every instance our
Lord has proved more than equal to the occasion. "When thou
passest through the waters, I will be with thee; and through
the rivers, they shall not overflow thee: when thou walkest
through the fire, thou shalt not be burned; neither shall the
flame kindle upon thee." [9] When writing to the Corinthians the
Apostle Paul shared with them one of the deepest experiences
of his life. According to Paul there was given to him "a thorn
in the flesh." [10] Whatever the thorn was it constituted a cause
for discouragement in his labors for Christ. Though a mighty
man in prayer Paul does not hesitate to tell us that he sought
the Lord in prayer on three occasions that He might remove it
from him. Yet Paul's request was refused. God did not remove
it. But Paul's explanation of his great suffering is that God
permitted it lest his self-sufficiency should spoil him for the
great task to which he had been called. Yet the Lord did not
forsake His servant. Divine provision was made to sustain him
in the midst of his affliction. Paul testifies that in the darkest
hour he heard the comforting and assuring word of the Lord—
"My grace is *sufficient* for thee." [11] Just when Paul was becoming aware of his insufficiency, God was making known His
sufficiency. Here is the secret of being triumphant in tribulation
—not trusting ourselves, but casting our burden upon the Lord,
knowing that He will sustain us. As we lean on the all-sufficient
and all-sustaining Saviour, we may be able to testify with Paul:
"Therefore I take pleasure in infirmities, in reproaches, in necessities, in persecutions, in distresses for Christ's sake: for when
I am weak, then am I strong." [12] Troubles on every side bring
out God's sufficiency in a way that the absence of pressure cannot.

❧

[9] Isaiah 43:2   [10] 2 Corinthians 12:7   [11] 2 Corinthians 12:9
[12] 2 Corinthians 12:10

He is all-sufficient for the believer's *security*. The believer in Christ has been delivered from all condemnation. Some Christians live in fear of losing their salvation, but such fear is caused by ignorance of the truth. Jesus said: "He that heareth My word, and believeth on Him that sent Me, hath everlasting life, *and shall not come into condemnation*." [13] Paul taught that "there is therefore now *no condemnation* to them which are in Christ Jesus." [14] In chapter eight of Romans he asks: "Who shall separate us from the love of Christ?" [15] And then the apostle answers this question by the Holy Spirit in a grand finale of the symphony of the gospel. Hear him: "For I am persuaded, that neither death, nor life, nor angels, nor principalities, nor powers, nor things present, nor things to come, Nor height, nor depth, nor any other creature, shall be able to separate us from the love of God, which is in Christ Jesus our Lord." [16] "Who shall impeach those whom God has chosen? . . . Will Christ Jesus, who died, or rather who rose to life again, who is also at the right hand of God, who moreover is interceding for us?" [17] In view of the fact that God has cleared us of all guilt on the ground of Christ's death and Resurrection, the most serious charge of our most violent foes—be that charge true or false—can never cheat us of our redemption and the subsequent inheritance which is ours in the Lord Jesus Christ. "He is able also to save them to the uttermost that come unto God by Him, seeing He ever liveth to make intercession for them." [18] By His death He saved us and by His life He keeps us. It is a cheap boast that claims one is kept by any merit of his own. If one who has been born again can ever be lost, what or who decides when a Christian has lost his salvation? Can such a one ever be saved again? If he can, how often can such foolishness happen in his life? All Christians sin at times in thought and in deed, but remember that Christ died for all of

[13] John 5:24 [14] Romans 8:1 [15] Romans 8:35
[16] Romans 8:38,39 [17] Romans 8:33,34 (Weymouth)
[18] Hebrews 7:25

our sins—past, present and future. "The blood of Jesus Christ His Son cleanseth us from *all sin.*" [19] The mere meditation of the vastness of God's love in His saving and keeping power constrains us to live holy before Him. We will be tempted, to be sure, and we may yield occasionally to temptation, still we "are kept by the power of God." [20] Let us draw near even now to our all-sufficient Saviour in absolute surrender to His perfect will.

In His all-sufficiency Jesus *satisfies.* There are longings of the soul which cannot be satisfied by any other. At the fountain of the water of life there is perennial freshness. Writing on this theme Dr. A. C. Gaebelein has said: "He is the inexhaustible reservoir filled with the supplies of His infinite grace." When He met the woman at the well, He said: "Whosoever drinketh of the water that I shall give him shall never thirst; but the water that I shall give him shall be in him a well of water springing up into everlasting life." [21] Here is water that no man can draw himself. Jesus said it is "the water that *I shall give him.*" On one occasion, He preached to the crowds: "If any man thirst, let him come unto Me, and drink. He that believeth on Me, as the scripture hath said, out of his belly shall flow rivers of living water." [22] The deep-seated thirst for satisfaction lies within every human breast, and man searches in vain when he turns to the beggarly elements of this world to quench that thirst. The broken cisterns of the world only leave us restless and unsatisfied. But so soul-satisfying in quality and so abundant in quantity is the Water of Life that he who comes to Christ and drinks quenches his own thirst and the thirst of others about him. Whenever you meet a Christian out of whom pours forth blessing on other lives, you may be

[19] 1 John 1:7   [20] 1 Peter 1:5   [21] John 4:14
[22] John 7:37-38

certain that he has drunk of the Fountain which never runs dry. "Blessed be the God and Father of our Lord Jesus Christ, who hath blessed us with all spiritual blessings in heavenly places in Christ." [23]

[23] Ephesians 1:3

THE
THIRD
PERSON

THE LORDSHIP OF THE SPIRIT

"Now the Lord is that Spirit." [1]

Who is the Holy Spirit? This question arrested me for the first time in 1938 when a book by that title appeared in print. It was written by the late Henry W. Frost, and I shall ever be grateful for both the inspiration and the instruction that I received from its pages. Too few persons are being challenged by Dr. Frost's question, hence this brief discussion on the Person and work of the Holy Spirit. The need for more Biblical preaching and writing on this subject is evidenced in almost every church group as we see the appalling ignorance concerning the neglected and almost forgotten Third Person of the Holy Trinity.

The Scriptures contain many titles given to the Holy Spirit. We have gleaned but a few, and a careful examination of the contexts in which these titles are found will show clearly that each refers to one and the same Person, the Holy Spirit, the Third Person of the Trinity: the Spirit of God,[2] the Spirit of wisdom and understanding,[3] the Spirit of the Lord God,[4] the Spirit of the Lord,[5] the Spirit of truth,[6] the Spirit of the living God,[7] the Spirit of life,[8] the Spirit of glory,[9] the Holy Spirit,[10] the Spirit of grace and of supplications,[11] the Spirit of Christ.[12]

[1] 2 Corinthians 3:17   [2] Genesis 1:2   [3] Isaiah 11:2
[4] Isaiah 61:1   [5] Luke 4:18   [6] John 14:17
[7] 2 Corinthians 3:3   [8] Romans 8:2   [9] 1 Peter 4:14
[10] Psalm 51:11   [11] Zechariah 12:10   [12] Romans 8:9

429

The very first thing that is absolutely essential in order for any believer to live a full and fruitful life is to know the Holy Spirit and His relation to the Christian. If a believer's mind remains darkened concerning the Spirit's function and ministry in the world, that believer must of necessity limit his own usefulness in the Lord's work and be deprived of the subsequent rewards that are to be apportioned to God's faithful servants.

The Ephesian Christians formed a local church that showed great possibilities in the work of the gospel, but many of them were powerless to accomplish great things for God. The Apostle Paul was used by God to discover the cause of their powerlessness when he asked the question: "Have ye received the Holy Spirit since ye believed?" and they gave the surprising answer: *"We have not so much as heard whether there be any Holy Ghost."* [13] Here lies the root cause of the deadness and the indifference in many churches today. The average Christian knows too little about the Holy Spirit. Even among evangelical Christians there seems to be a tendency to major on minors. Those who engage in hairsplitting debates on the fine points of eschatology are often ignorant of the doctrinal and practical aspects of the Bible's teaching about God the Holy Spirit.

Perhaps you have wondered why some men are used of God and some are not. You have met men who had the advantages of college and seminary training, who had a fine command of words, and who knew the original languages of the Holy Scriptures, yet they seemed to have missed the secret to spiritual power and blessing. We all

[13] Acts 19:2

have met such men. We know them too well. Wherein are they lacking?

Spiritual impotency is due to failure to study the Bible, the only source of truth concerning the Spirit of God. When we earnestly study and sincerely believe what the Scriptures teach about the Holy Spirit, growth in grace and the appropriation of divine power to accomplish great things for God must result.

Many testify to the blessing and power that has come into their lives once they grasped the great truth of the personality and deity of the Holy Spirit. The late Bishop Handley C. G. Moule testified: "Never shall I forget the gain to conscious faith and peace which came into my soul from a more intelligent hold upon the loving and most gracious personality of the Holy Spirit. It was a new contact, as it were, with the inner and eternal movements of redeeming goodness and power."

The statements that follow make up the foundational and fundamental truths about the Spirit that men need to know.

THE HOLY SPIRIT IS A PERSON

It is surprising that, after nineteen hundred years of Christian testimony, men are still asking the question: "Is there such a Person as the Holy Spirit?" One reason why so many people are in doubt and darkness concerning this question is the fact that Christians do not give the Spirit His rightful place. Very frequently we hear believers giving praise to God for the gift of His Son; rarely do we hear a child of God praising God for the gift of His Spirit.

Furthermore, God's Holy Spirit is treated as merely an influence. It is not uncommon to hear Christians referring to the Holy Spirit as "It." Certainly anyone who is ignorant of His Personality cannot love Him as one of the Persons of the Holy Trinity. He is little known because He is seldom recognized by those who claim to be born of Him. Recently someone asked if it mattered whether we believe the Holy Spirit to be the Third Person in the Godhead or merely a divine influence. Yes, it does matter. It makes all the difference between truth and error. Any failure on our part to understand correctly the truth about the personality of the Spirit will rob us of blessing, victory, and fruitfulness in this life as well as eternal benefits in the life to come.

Certain men in religious circles today deny the personality of the Spirit simply because the Holy Spirit does not possess a body. But these departers from the truth are not fair in either interpretation or conclusion. My body is not my *personality*. My body is my *person*. It is my *person* that is visible and not my personality. My person only expresses my personality. When death overtakes a man, it is not the man's personality that dies, but merely his person (his body). The body is the dwelling place of the personality.

The soul part of man is a trinity in unity: by the *mind* he thinks; by the *heart* he loves; by the *will* he acts. These make up man's personality. Now the Holy Spirit possesses a mind.[14] He is the Master Mind that moved and guided men to write the Bible. The Holy Spirit loves. He descended upon our Lord Jesus in the form of a

[14] Romans 8:27

dove,[15] and the dove is a symbol of love. We are told that the dove is the only bird that has no gall. And Paul wrote: "The love of God is shed abroad in our hearts by the Holy Ghost." [16] Also the Holy Spirit possesses a will. It is the Spirit's work to give to every child of God some gift, thus we read of "the selfsame Spirit, dividing to every man severally as He *will*." [17]

Both the Old and the New Testament Scriptures refer to the Holy Spirit as a Person. Always clearly distinguished from the Father and the Son, He is shown to be the infinite and eternal Third Person of the Holy Trinity. While the three Persons of the Trinity are one in being, they are not one in position or function. In essential being, each is one with the other so that there is one God, but their personalities and positions are distinct and different. The following verses will show that the Spirit has His own place in the Trinity and that He has a special work to do which never overlaps the work of the Father or of the Son, although the unity between the three never ceases to exist.

"Go ye therefore, and teach all nations, baptizing them in the name of the Father, and of the Son, and of the Holy Ghost." [18]

"Now there are diversities of gifts, but the same Spirit. And there are differences of administrations, but the same Lord. And there are diversities of operations, but it is the same God which worketh all in all." [19]

"The grace of the Lord Jesus Christ, and the love of

[15] Matthew 3:16   [16] Romans 5:5   [17] 1 Corinthians 12:11
[18] Matthew 28:19   [19] 1 Corinthians 12:4-6

God, and the communion of the Holy Ghost, be with you all. Amen." [20]

"There is one body, and one Spirit, even as ye are called in one hope of your calling; One Lord, one faith, one baptism, One God and Father of all, who is above all, and through all, and in you all." [21]

"Elect according to the foreknowledge of God the Father, through sanctification of the Spirit, unto obedience and sprinkling of the blood of Jesus Christ: Grace unto you, and peace, be multiplied." [22]

"But ye, beloved, building up yourselves on your most holy faith, praying in the Holy Ghost, Keep yourselves in the love of God, looking for the mercy of our Lord Jesus Christ unto eternal life." [23]

Before our Lord's crucifixion He assured His disciples: "I will pray the Father, and He shall give you another Comforter, that He may abide with you for ever; Even the Spirit of truth." [24] The word that sheds light on our subject is the apparently insignificant word "another." There can be only one of two meanings to this word; either it means *another* of a different kind or *another* of the same kind. Here it emphatically teaches that Jesus would send *another* of the same kind. This means that He was going to send one exactly like Himself who would possess the faculties of a Person, One who would think, love, and act like Himself. Dr. G. Campbell Morgan says: "The word 'another' here is of a particular nature and character. It is *allos*, not *heteros;* consequently the word *another* does not indicate a different quality, but a similarity of quality. . . . Under these circumstances He [Jesus] said, 'I will send you *another* Paraclete: Another to stand by your side, Another to take exactly the same place that I have filled in your lives during these past three years.' "

It is both interesting and instructive to read the personal pronoun used by our Lord in many passages as He sought to impress upon the minds of His disciples the important fact that the Holy Spirit was not merely an influence emanating from God but truly a Person. Note particularly the pronouns "He," "Him," and "Whom" in the following passages: "And I will pray the Father, and He shall give you another Comforter, that *He* may abide with you for ever; Even the Spirit of truth; *Whom* the world cannot receive, because it seeth *Him* not, neither knoweth *Him;* but ye know *Him;* for *He* dwelleth with you." [25] "But when the Comforter is come, *Whom* I will send unto you from the Father, even the Spirit of truth . . . *He* shall testify of Me." [26]

The following quotation came to the attention of the writer several years ago, and though its source is unknown, it has been well written that "the use of these pronouns is the more remarkable from the fact that in the Greek language the word for Spirit is a neuter noun, and according to Greek usage, the pronouns that refer to it should be neuter, and yet in many instances a masculine pronoun is used, thus bringing out very strikingly how the Bible idea of the Personality of the Holy Spirit dominates grammatical construction." It is both incorrect and ir-

[25] John 14:16, 17   [26] John 15:26

reverent to make any reference to the Holy Spirit as "It."
He is not an impersonal influence but the Spirit of God,
the Third Person in the Holy Trinity.

We must not be confused at this point. Remember,
there are not three Gods. There is one God, eternal,
omnipotent, omnipresent, and omniscient; and He is able
to manifest Himself to man in three personalities: God
the Father, God the Son, and God the Holy Spirit. The
very first verse in the Bible says: "In the beginning *God*
created the heaven and the earth." [27] This first name of
God in the Scriptures is the Hebrew word "Elohim." The
name Elohim, which is translated "God" in the Bible, is a
plural noun. We know this because the word ends with
"im," and whenever we come across a Hebrew word ending with "im," it denotes plurality just as the letter "s"
denotes plurality when added to a noun in the English
language. Hence the word "God" in the original expresses
the plurality of persons in the Godhead, not more than
one God, but one God in three Persons. This leads us to
our next thought; namely,

THE HOLY SPIRIT IS A DIVINE PERSON

Frequently He is called "Lord." The prophet Isaiah
testifies: "I heard the voice of the *Lord*. . . ." [28] Here
Isaiah is calling the Holy Spirit Lord. This is clearly
understood as we read the words of Paul: "Well spake the
Holy Ghost by Esaias [Isaiah] the prophet. . . ." [29]
Again Isaiah shows us the Lordship of the Spirit when he
says: "The grass withereth, the flower fadeth: because

[27] Genesis 1:1   [28] Isaiah 6:8   [29] Acts 28:25

the Spirit of the Lord bloweth upon it." [30] It is because He is Lord that He can pronounce judgment upon both men and plant life.

David said: "Whither shall I go from Thy Spirit? or whither shall I flee from Thy presence? If I ascend up into heaven, Thou art there: if I make my bed in hell [or the grave], behold, Thou art there." [31] In the words, "Thy presence," the Spirit is spoken of as God, and here also one of the divine attributes, omnipresence, is attributed to Him.

It is impossible to find one spot, however remote, where the Spirit of God is not present. Within every believer, in every corner of the globe, He carries on His gracious work. Go where you will, wherever the redeemed of God are to be found, each enjoys His presence and operations. The Holy Spirit cannot be ignored, nor can we escape Him. He is omnipresent.

"Omni" means "all," and it is His omnipresence, the fact that He is everywhere at the same time, that proves His deity. When Jesus, the Second Person of the Trinity, was here in the flesh, He was bound by the limitations of the flesh. When He was at Nazareth He could not be somewhere else. But such limitations cannot confine the Holy Spirit. In every part of the world, wherever the saints of God are to be found, the Spirit of God is present.

In the New Testament we have many passages that clearly set forth the personality and deity of the Holy Spirit. When Ananias and Sapphira sold a possession and kept back part of the price, Peter said: "Ananias, why

[30] Isaiah 40:7   [31] Psalm 139:7, 8

hath Satan filled thine heart to lie to the Holy Ghost? . . . thou hast not lied unto men, but unto God." [32] Men cannot deceive nor lie to mere influence; therefore Ananias had lied to none other than God, the Holy Spirit.

The divine authority of the Spirit is seen in the separation of Paul and Barnabas unto the service of the Lord. "The Holy Ghost said, Separate Me Barnabas and Saul for the work whereunto I have called them." [33]

Again, the deity of the Holy Spirit is set forth in His display of *omniscience,* an attribute that deity alone can claim—"The Spirit searcheth all things, yea, the deep things of God . . . the things of God knoweth no man, but the Spirit of God." [34] Arthur Way says: "To us did God unveil them by the agency of His Spirit. Yes, the Spirit can explore all things, even the abysmal depths of God's designs." Because He is God, He knoweth all things. Man cannot probe the depths of deity, yet the most intimate counsels are open to the Spirit's careful discernment. E. H. Bickersteth has said: "His knowledge embraces infinity and spans eternity." He is the "Eternal Spirit" according to the Apostle's words in Hebrews 10:14; therefore He is possessed of divine intelligence and understanding.

In his second Epistle to the Corinthians, Paul writes of that day, yet in the future, when the veil shall be taken away from the heart of the Jew, and their heart shall "turn to the Lord." [35] Then in the very next verse he makes it clear just whom he means by the Lord, for he adds: "Now the Lord is that Spirit." [36]

---

[32] Acts 5:1-4   [33] Acts 13:2   [34] 1 Corinthians 2:10, 11
[35] 2 Corinthians 3:16   [36] 2 Corinthians 3:17

In 2 Thessalonians 3:5 the Spirit is seen in His sovereignty, directing the heart of the believer toward the Father and the Son: "The Lord direct your hearts into the love of God, and into the patient waiting for Christ." Here one Person of the Trinity is directing us to the other two Persons of the Trinity. The Lord who directs the heart of the child of God is none other than the Spirit Himself. These are but a few of the many references in the Word of God that establish the irrefutable fact of the personality and deity of the Holy Spirit. In the succeeding chapter we will see from time to time many evidences of this great truth, such as the Spirit possesses life,[37] the Spirit thinks,[38] the Spirit possesses individuality,[39] the Spirit speaks,[40] the Spirit prays,[41] the Spirit teaches,[42] the Spirit loves,[43] the Spirit curses,[44] the Spirit guides,[45] the Spirit hinders.[46]

THE PROMISE OF THE SPIRIT

When Jesus was here upon earth, it was obvious that His disciples were constantly dependent upon Him. He had established His deity, proving beyond the shadow of a doubt that He was God. He forgave sin in its loathsomeness and enfeeblement. He demonstrated His authority over the natural and the spiritual realms, and by so doing won the admiration and respect of His followers. But Christ's disciples never understood fully the meaning and the manner of His life's work. Once they were certain that our Lord was the promised Messiah, the idea of His

---

[37] Galatians 6:8
[38] Romans 8:16
[39] John 16:7-11
[40] Acts 8:29
[41] Romans 8:26, 27
[42] John 16:14
[43] Romans 15:30
[44] Isaiah 40:7
[45] John 16:13
[46] Acts 16:6; 2 Thessalonians 2:7

leaving them was never a part of their thinking. During His earthly life they looked for Him to set up the kingdom of God upon earth at that time, and even the plainest teaching from His own lips had not been able to disabuse them of that thought. He told them clearly "how that He must go unto Jerusalem, and suffer many things of the elders and chief priests and scribes, and be killed," but Peter took Him and openly rebuked Him, saying: "Be it far from Thee, Lord: this shall not be unto Thee." [47] He taught them openly of His Resurrection and return to the Father, but they could not grasp His teaching. He would utter statements such as: "I go to prepare a place for you," and "I go unto My Father," but they never fully comprehended the intent of those words. Yet we cannot imagine that they all ignored completely the idea of His leaving them. Some of them must have given serious thought to the messages He gave them on His going away, for ample space is given in the Scriptures to His discourse on the One whom He would send to act with divine authority after He would ascend to the Father. But before we consider the promise of the Spirit as it came from Jesus Himself, we shall think together upon two Old Testament passages as they relate to this subject.

The Promise of the Spirit in Type. The promise of the Spirit is seen in type when we study the Feasts of Jehovah as recorded in Leviticus, chapter 23. The *first* of these great occasions is the Passover which answers spiritually to the sacrificial death of our Lord Jesus Christ. This first feast, in its spiritual application, is symbolic of God's

[47] Matthew 16:21, 22

provision for sinners in the death of His Son at Calvary. There can be no question as to the application of this type, for we have the words of the Apostle Paul: "Christ our passover is sacrificed for us." [48]

The *second* of the feasts was called the Feast of Unleavened Bread.[49] It was to be of seven days' duration, from the fourteenth day of the first month until the one and twentieth day of that same month at even.[50] The outstanding characteristic of this feast was the rigid exclusion of leaven from their houses. Now leaven, in both the Old and the New Testament, is emblematic of evil and never of good. The Feast of Unleavened Bread refers to the walk of all those who have appropriated Christ's death. Paul says: "Therefore let us keep the feast, not with old leaven, neither with the leaven of malice and wickedness; but with the unleavened bread of sincerity and truth." [51] The Christian Church also commences its week on the "first day," the Lord's Day, and for seven days, or throughout the entire week, the Christian shuns all evil (leaven), and lives wholly unto God.

Inseparably and intimately connected with the Passover and the Feast of Unleavened Bread is the *third* of these great celebrations, called the Feast of Firstfruits.[52] The children of Israel were to bring the firstfruits of the harvest. The firstfruits was a sheaf that was to be waved before the Lord as a pledge of the greater harvest that was to follow. The type is clear and unmistakable. The Lord Jesus Christ in His Resurrection from the dead is the firstfruits or the guarantee of a greater resurrection

[48] 1 Corinthians 5:7   [49] Leviticus 23:6-8   [50] Exodus 12:18
[51] 1 Corinthians 5:8   [52] Leviticus 23:9-14

which is to follow. Again it is Paul who writes: "But now is Christ risen from the dead, and become the firstfruits of them that slept." [53] "Christ the firstfruits; afterward they that are Christ's at His coming." [54] Our Lord is the firstfruits of that great harvest of the redeemed that shall be raised from the dead at His coming.[55]

So far, we have looked at three great feasts in the life and worship of Israel. They typify for us the death of Christ in the Passover, the separated life of the believer in the Feast of Unleavened Bread, and the Resurrection of our Lord in the Feast of Firstfruits. We come now to the *fourth* of these important occasions, and we are to observe the continued progression in type and fulfillment. This feast is called the Feast of Weeks, so designated in Deuteronomy 16:9, 10, where we read: "Seven weeks shalt thou number unto thee: begin to number the seven weeks from such time as thou beginnest to put the sickle to the corn. And thou shalt keep the feast of weeks unto the Lord thy God . . . ." This occasion is sometimes called the Feast of Pentecost, for it speaks to us of Pentecost when the Holy Spirit came down to abide in the midst of the believers. Notice how we arrive at the name:

"And ye shall count unto you from the morrow after the sabbath, from the day that ye brought the sheaf of the wave offering; seven sabbaths shall be complete: Even unto the morrow after the seventh sabbath shall ye number fifty days; and ye shall offer a new meat offering unto the Lord." [56]

[53] 1 Corinthians 15:20   [54] 1 Corinthians 15:23
[55] 1 Thessalonians 4:13-18   [56] Leviticus 23:15, 16

The Feast of Weeks (or Pentecost) was to be observed exactly fifty days after the Feast of Firstfruits. The Greek word *Pentecost* means "fiftieth," and the fulfillment of the type took place on the Day of Pentecost,[57] on the fiftieth day from the Resurrection of our Lord Jesus Christ. About fifteen hundred years before Christ was born, God gave the promise of the coming of the Holy Spirit, and we know from the New Testament that His coming took place on the Day of Pentecost. On that day the Spirit came to indwell the Church of Christ as a whole, as well as to indwell every true believer. Later in this volume we shall study more closely His coming when He formed into one body all who believed on Christ, "For by one Spirit are we all baptized into one body."[58]

The Promise of the Spirit in Prophecy. There is a well-known and significant passage in Joel, chapter 2, in which the Holy Spirit is promised. The prophet says: "And it shall come to pass afterward, that I will pour out My Spirit upon all flesh; and your sons and your daughters shall prophesy, your old men shall dream dreams, your young men shall see visions: And also upon the servants and upon the handmaids in those days will I pour out My Spirit."[59] On the day of Pentecost, Peter said: "This is that which was spoken by the prophet Joel."[60] Peter is not saying that the day of Pentecost is the complete fulfillment of what is written by Joel. The apostle is merely stating that something like that great event which took place on the day of Pentecost had been prophesied by Joel. He was seeking to enlighten the Jews

[57] Acts 2 [58] 1 Corinthians 12:13 [59] Joel 2:28, 29
[60] Acts 2:16

from the message of their own prophets that this sudden outpouring of the Holy Spirit was foretold.

Joel's prophecy cannot be completely accomplished until Israel has been restored to God. It is a promise of the Holy Spirit to be poured out upon Israel as a nation, and as yet this has never come to pass. The fulfillment began on Pentecost, and it has been a continual process from that day until our own. Now we look for the completion and consummation of the fulfillment which will take place just before our Lord returns in His power and glory. In another place God gives the same promise to Israel: "Yet now hear, O Jacob my servant; and Israel, whom I have chosen. . . . I will pour My Spirit upon thy seed, and My blessing upon thine offspring." [61] Israel is God's chosen people under His special care, and they are yet to repent as a nation and accept the Messiah. In that day, when they turn to God in obedience, the Holy Spirit will be poured out upon them even as the promise was given to the prophets.

The Son's Promise of the Spirit.

"And I will pray the Father, and He shall give you another Comforter, that He may abide with you for ever." [62]

"But the Comforter, which is the Holy Ghost, whom the Father will send in My name, He shall teach you all things, and bring all things to your remembrance, whatsoever I have said unto you." [63]

"But when the Comforter is come, whom I will send

[61] Isaiah 44:1, 3   [62] John 14:16   [63] John 14:26

unto you from the Father, even the Spirit of truth, which proceedeth from the Father, He shall testify of Me." [64]

"Nevertheless I tell you the truth; It is expedient for you that I go away: for if I go not away, the Comforter will not come unto you; but if I depart, I will send Him unto you." [65]

"Howbeit when He, the Spirit of truth, is come, He will guide you into all truth: for He shall not speak of Himself; but whatsoever He shall hear, that shall He speak: and He will shew you things to come. He shall glorify Me: for He shall receive of Mine, and shall shew it unto you." [66]

"And, behold, I send the promise of My Father upon you; but tarry ye in the city of Jerusalem, until ye be endued with power from on high." [67]

"And, being assembled together with them, commanded them that they should not depart from Jerusalem, but wait for the promise of the Father, which, saith He, ye have heard of Me." [68]

"But ye shall receive power, after that the Holy Ghost is come upon you: and ye shall be witnesses unto Me both in Jerusalem, and in all Judaea, and in Samaria, and unto the uttermost part of the earth." [69]

THE PRESENCE OF THE SPIRIT

This discussion on the Lordship of the Spirit would not be complete if we failed to consider the actual appearing

[64] John 15:26   [65] John 16:7   [66] John 16:13, 14
[67] Luke 24:49   [68] Acts 1:4   [69] Acts 1:8

of the Holy Spirit among men. If He is merely the object of controversy, One who is talked about, but who never puts in His appearance, then we have not arrived at a successful conclusion. After listening to a message on the personality and deity of the Holy Spirit, a gentleman approached the preacher and asked: "Excuse me, sir, but just where is this Holy Spirit?" It was a good question, for if the Holy Spirit is a divine Person (and He is), then the unbeliever must come under the influence of His personality and power.

While Jesus was yet with His disciples, the meaning of His life and work had not become clear to them. They looked for Him to be a political deliverer, and they themselves had hoped to share in the spoils. So when He spoke to them of His forthcoming sufferings and death, they imagined Him to be mistaken. Their blindness naturally plunged them into an abyss of despondency upon Christ's arrest and crucifixion. After His death they became the disillusioned group. Recovering from the first shock of His crucifixion, they must have thought much about His promises concerning the other Comforter whom He said He would send. After His Resurrection from the grave, our Lord appeared to His own and assured them: "Behold, I send the promise of My Father upon you: but tarry ye in the city of Jerusalem, until ye be endued with power from on high." [70] The question arises: "Did the Holy Spirit come?" Certainly the disciples knew that He had, for His coming made every difference in their lives and ministry. Without Him they could not have carried on but would have given up in despair.

[70] Luke 24:49

As the disciples were gathered at the national Feast of Pentecost, fifty days after our Lord's Resurrection, the Lordship of the Spirit was made blessedly real to them. They knew that Christ had risen from the dead, but that fact in itself did not increase the number of their company. But on the fiftieth day after His Resurrection, three thousand souls believed on Jesus Christ and were saved.

What changed the fear and defeat of the disciples into a glorious victory? It was the sudden arrival of their new Commander in Chief. The Spirit had come even as Jesus had promised. A new day had dawned in human history. "When the day of Pentecost was fully come, they were all with one accord in one place. And suddenly there came a sound from heaven as of a rushing mighty wind, and it filled all the house where they were sitting. And there appeared unto them cloven tongues like as of fire, and it sat upon each of them. And they were all filled with the Holy Ghost." [71]

There is not the slightest inference in the preceding statement that the Spirit ever had been absent from the affairs of men since the beginning of creation. On the very first page of the Bible we see Him bring cosmos out of chaos. Over and over again we read of the Holy Spirit's coming upon men in Old Testament times, taking possession of them in order to accomplish some mighty deed through them. But what is before us here is something different. Man never witnessed anything like it in the past. In every age there were occasions when He came *upon* men, but now it is His coming *into* men.

[71] Acts 2:1-4

When the Holy Spirit came on Pentecost to declare His sovereignty and Lordship, two signs were given which were the symbols of Himself. They were wind and fire. These were not the Spirit, but the Spirit's coming was *like* wind and fire. Jesus himself used the symbol of the wind when He spoke to Nicodemus concerning the working of the Holy Spirit in regeneration. He said: "The wind bloweth where it listeth, and thou hearest the sound thereof, but canst not tell whence it cometh, and whither it goeth: so is every one that is born of the Spirit." [72] We all concede that there is much about the wind that is mysterious and inexplainable. The wind is not visible to the eye, yet no one denies either its existence or power. So it is with the operation of the Spirit in man's regeneration. The rushing wind filling the house was the first sign of the Spirit's advent. Those who are untaught have said that such symbolic teaching is arrived at only by a stretch of imagination. However, the English word *spirit* is translated from the Hebrew word *rush* in the Old Testament and from the Greek *pneuma* in the New Testament, and both words mean literally *breath* or *wind*. Jesus was telling Nicodemus that it was the Spirit, the Breath, who comes to breathe divine life into dead sinners.

The second symbol of the Holy Spirit which was given at His coming was that of fire. As far as the Jews were concerned, the Divine Presence always had been symbolized by fire. When God called Moses to deliver Israel out of Egypt, He appeared to Moses "in a flame of fire out of the midst of a bush: and he looked, and, behold, the bush burned with fire, and the bush was not consumed." [73]

[72] John 3:8   [73] Exodus 3:2

Again, when Moses and Aaron appeared before the presence of the Lord in the Tabernacle, "there came a fire out from before the Lord." [74] When God called Moses up into the Mount to give him the Ten Commandments, we read that "the Lord descended upon it in fire." [75] Later, Moses referred to that incident by reminding the people: "The Lord talked with you face to face in the mount out of the midst of the fire." [76] Elijah was acquainted with fire as a symbol of God's presence when he challenged the people: "Call ye on the name of your gods, and I will call on the name of the LORD: and the God that answereth by fire, Let Him be God." [77] The Holy Spirit is called "the Spirit of burning," [78] "a consuming fire." [79] Of Him the prophet wrote: "He is like a refiner's fire . . . and He shall sit as a refiner and purifier of silver." [80] John the Baptist testified of our Lord: "He shall baptize you with the Holy Ghost, and with fire." [81]

Certainly no more suitable symbols could be found to make plain to man the great truth that the Spirit of God had come. Furthermore, no other symbols could as adequately reveal to us the regenerating, illuminating, purifying power of the Holy Spirit as wind and fire. Those disciples who were gathered together on the day of Pentecost were convinced by sound and by sight that the promised Third Person of the Holy Trinity had at last descended.

How sad that in our hymnology there is scarcely a recognition of the presence of the Holy Spirit. Think of

[74] Leviticus 9:24
[75] Exodus 19:18
[76] Deuteronomy 5:4
[77] 1 Kings 18:24
[78] Isaiah 4:4
[79] Hebrews 12:29
[80] Malachi 3:2, 3
[81] Matthew 3:11

some of the many hymns that begin by invoking the Spirit of God to "come," as though He were not already here but afar off:

> "Come, Holy Comforter . . .
> Spirit of holiness, On us descend." [82]

> "O send Thy Spirit, Lord,
> Now unto me." [83]

> "Come, Holy Spirit, heavenly Dove." [84]

> "Holy Spirit, all divine,
> Dwell within this heart of mine." [85]

When the believer in ignorance or forgetfulness asks for the Holy Spirit, he "unconsciously unchristianizes himself," for it is written: "If any man have not the Spirit of Christ, he is none of His." [86]

The Holy Spirit has come. He is here now, indwelling all who have been born again. "Because ye are sons, God hath sent forth the Spirit of His Son into your hearts, crying, Abba, Father." [87] Stop right now, and humbly thank God for the gift of His Spirit.

[82] "Come Thou Almighty King"   [83] "Break Thou the Bread of Life"
[84] "Come, Holy Spirit, Heavenly Dove"
[85] "Holy Ghost, with Light Divine"
[86] Romans 8:9   [87] Galatians 4:6

THE LIFE OF THE SPIRIT

". . . The Spirit is Life . . ." [1]

The Holy Spirit is the Spirit of life. Paul wrote: "For the law of *the Spirit of life* in Christ Jesus hath made me free from the law of sin and death." [2] Now the Spirit, who is life, is actively engaged in imparting His life to men. Remember, the Spirit is God; therefore the life of the Spirit is divine life. In contrast to the Spirit of God being life, the spirit of man is death. He is under the law of sin and death. Paul, looking back to the preconverted days of those who have been regenerated, says: "And you hath He quickened [or made alive], *who were dead* in trespasses and sins." [3] "Dead in trespasses and sins" is God's way of describing the condition of all men who have not been born again. They are the unsaved and are under the control of "the spirit that now worketh in the children of disobedience." [4]

THE WORK OF THE SPIRIT IN REGENERATION

In his lost condition, man needs to be saved, and this he cannot be apart from God. "Salvation is of the Lord." [5] God said: "I, even I, am the Lord; and beside me there is no saviour." [6] In our thinking of God as Saviour, we must

[1] Romans 8:10
[4] Ephesians 2:2
[2] Romans 8:2
[5] Jonah 2:9
[3] Ephesians 2:1
[6] Isaiah 43:11

451

keep in mind the Trinity. The Father is Saviour in His demonstration of love for the world when "He gave His only begotten Son." [7] The Son is the Saviour because He came to die as the Sacrifice for sin. Because He was born to die, it was written of Him at His birth: "Unto you is born this day in the city of David a Saviour, which is Christ the Lord." [8] But the Spirit is the Saviour also, and it is our purpose in this chapter to show how He operates in the regeneration of the unsaved. A special work of the Spirit is wrought in a man before and after he is born again, and when this ministry in regeneration is recognized by Christian workers, greater results in soul-winning will be accomplished.

Let there be no misunderstanding concerning the Spirit's qualification to operate in man. Someone has suggested that, in a peculiar sense, the Spirit of God is the Spirit of Man, not of men in general, but the Spirit of the God-Man, Jesus Christ. The Holy Spirit was the active agency in the birth of the Son of Man. God had said to Joseph: "Fear not to take unto thee Mary thy wife: for that which is conceived in her is of the Holy Ghost." [9] When our Lord was baptized just prior to His public ministry, the Spirit of God descended upon Him with a special anointing for the work. [10] Then as the Saviour died upon the Cross, He offered Himself "through the eternal Spirit," [11] so we can say with certainty that "He knoweth our frame; He remembereth that we are dust." Rightly so is He called "the Spirit of Christ" because He dwelt in the Son of Man. Therefore He knows

[7] John 3:16
[10] Matthew 3:16
[8] Luke 2:11
[11] Hebrews 9:14
[9] Matthew 1:20

the impulses and weaknesses of human flesh. He is the Spirit of the Man Christ Jesus, and as such He is acquainted with all our ways.

The work of the Holy Spirit in regeneration commences with the conviction of sin. Before our Lord Jesus Christ went to the Cross, He told His disciples that after He departed from them to go back to the Father, He would send the Comforter (meaning the Holy Spirit). Then He added: "And when He is come, He will reprove the world of sin." [12] The word "reprove" means *to convict,* and the passage is teaching us that the work of the Spirit, so far as the world is concerned, is the conviction of sin.

When Jesus was here He spoke openly against sin and brought conviction to men's hearts, but after He went away the Holy Spirit was sent to carry on that same work of conviction. We are thinking now in terms of His blessed ministry among those yet in their sins. It is a work of *conviction,* and not a work of *conversion.* There is a vast difference between the two. Conviction is that state of the heart and mind in which a man is convinced of certain facts. Conversion is the response of the heart and mind to the conviction. Now it is the Spirit's work to convict, but He never forces the person who is convicted to respond to conversion against his own will.

Man is a free moral agent. He has the precious heritage of liberty, a gift from God, and the Holy Spirit of God respects that right. The destiny of man is not arbitrarily decided by God, therefore the Holy Spirit never presses man against his will. When He, the Third Person of the Trinity, begins His work in one's heart, the decision, as

[12] John 16:8

to whether or not one acts upon the conviction, must come from the individual. He will not coerce our wills. When men are convicted of their sin and need of a Saviour, that has been the special ministry of the Spirit. He is inviting them to be saved. "The Spirit and the bride say, Come. And let him that heareth say, Come. And let him that is athirst come. And whosoever will, let him take the water of life freely." [13] This is His invitation, and we can but sound the warning that our Lord sent to the seven churches in Asia: "He that hath an ear, let him hear what the Spirit saith." [14]

In pressing this truth still further, let it be said that no man can be born again apart from the work of the Holy Spirit. A man may be convinced in his mind as well as be stirred emotionally to tears and sorrow, but the new and never-ending life that God alone gives is imparted by His Spirit. We are not implying that a soul is saved by the Holy Spirit apart from the finished work of Jesus Christ on Calvary's cross. Such teaching would be opposed to the whole plan of salvation revealed in God's Word. Apart from the work of Christ on the cross the Holy Spirit could be only a condemning agent. But what the Spirit does is to convict the lost soul of the sin of unbelief, and point him to the Lamb of God Which taketh away the sin of the world. When we read the account of our Lord's interview with Nicodemus, we hear Him say emphatically: "Except a man be born again he cannot see the kingdom of God," and then He goes on to say:

[13] Revelation 22:17   [14] Revelation chapters 2 and 3

"Except a man be born of water *and of the Spirit*, he cannot enter into the kingdom of God." [15]

First, let it be understood that the water spoken of in the preceding verse does not mean baptism. Nowhere in all Holy Writ do we ever read of anyone receiving the new birth by water baptism. In the Bible baptism is a figure of death and not of life. Paul said: "Know ye not, that so many . . . as were baptized into Jesus Christ were baptized into His *death?* Therefore we are buried with Him by baptism into death." [16]

The figurative use of the word *water* in the following verses found in the New Testament cannot apply to baptism. Rather is it a symbol which denotes the *Word of God*. When Jesus said: "Whosoever drinketh of the water that I shall give him shall never thirst," [17] He was not speaking of literal water nor of baptism, but the *Word of God*. The Apostle Peter clarifies this in his first Epistle where he says: "Being born again, not of corruptible seed, but of incorruptible, by the *Word of God,* which liveth and abideth for ever." [18] Being born again and receiving divine life is not dependent upon water baptism. It is, rather, brought about through the Word of God being pressed and impressed upon our hearts by the power of the Holy Spirit working in us.

Someone has asked if all men brought under conviction of sin by the Holy Spirit become saved. The answer is an emphatic "No." We have two Biblical illustrations of this, one in the Old Testament and the other in the New.

[15] John 3:3-5   [16] Romans 6:3, 4   [17] John 4:14
[18] 1 Peter 1:23 (See also Eph. 5:26)

When God saw the wickedness in the days of Noah, He said: "My Spirit shall not always strive with man." [19] We admit a difficulty in the interpretation of this verse, some scholars teaching that the Hebrew word rendered "strive" would be better expressed by the word "dwell." But however the word "strive" is translated, we have here a solemn warning of the limitation of God's mercy. The Holy Spirit convicts of sin; but where a man willfully or blindly persists in continuing in sin, the Spirit of God will one day cease to strive with that man.

The New Testament illustration occurs in the defense of Stephen before the council. After Stephen had related the stubbornness characterizing the Jews, he said: "Ye stiffnecked and uncircumcised in heart and ears, ye do always resist the Holy Ghost." [20] With such rebellion and resistance, God was withdrawing His offer to the Jew. Dr. Morgan says that "the peril of resisting the Spirit is that of those who are not born again." If any who read these lines have not experienced the regenerating power of the Holy Spirit, do not resist Him any longer. Regeneration is "not by works of righteousness" but by the "renewing of the Holy Ghost." [21] The Holy Spirit is the agent in regeneration, convicting men of sin and causing them to be born again. He brings the gift of eternal life and the impartation of the divine nature.

THE SPIRIT'S QUALIFICATION

Many passages in both the Old and New Testaments reveal the Spirit's ability to impart and sustain life. Active in creation, He manifests His life-giving and life-sustain-

[19] Genesis 6:3   [20] Acts 7:51   [21] Titus 3:5

ing power. "The origin and the preservation of everything in nature are spiritual," says Dr. Morgan. We read: "And the earth was without form, and void; and darkness was upon the face of the deep. And *the Spirit of God* moved upon the face of the waters." [22] Here the Holy Spirit moved upon, or brooded over, the desolation, confusion, and emptiness, thus bringing cosmos out of chaos.

C. H. Mackintosh describes it thus: "He sat brooding over the scenes of His future operations. He alone could enlighten the darkness, cause life to spring up, substitute order for chaos, open an expanse between the waters, where life might display itself without fear of death. These were operations worthy of God." So, then, the very first mention of any Person of the Godhead in re-creation is that of the Holy Spirit. And in the original creation also, the Third Person of the Godhead was active. Job testifies: "By His Spirit He hath garnished the heavens." [23] Speaking of all creation, both animate and inanimate, the Psalmist wrote: "Thou sendest forth Thy Spirit, they are created." [24] These are mighty statements not wholly clear to our finite minds, but by faith we accept them as facts. We are creatures living in the midst of a created earth; and in that creation the Holy Spirit shared with the Father and the Son.

In the Biblical account of the creation of man, we find the Spirit mysteriously but distinctly revealed—"And the LORD God formed man of the dust of the ground, and *breathed* into his nostrils the *breath* of life; and man became a living soul." [25] Here we have God's ideal man

[22] Genesis 1:2   [23] Job 26:13   [24] Psalm 104:30
[25] Genesis 2:7

"created in His [God's] own image." [26] The material man was first formed from the dust of the earth, but in that material form alone, man was void of self-consciousness. Then, as the result of the inbreathing of the Breath of the Almighty, man became a living soul. Apart from the life-giving and life-sustaining power of the Spirit of God, man could not have entered into his new environment nor his new relationship with God. The body is not the man. We read: "Man became a living soul," and that by the Breath (or the Spirit) of God. In the book of Job we have a clear statement that ascribes the creation of man to the Holy Spirit: "The Spirit of God hath made me, and the breath of the Almighty hath given me life." [27] Indeed, the Holy Spirit is the Spirit of Life. Being the Third Person of the Godhead and the Creator of life, He is well able to give eternal life to those who will cease resisting Him.

Again the Holy Spirit becomes the life-giver in the Incarnation of our Lord Jesus Christ. Born of the Virgin Mary, our Lord had no earthly Father; yet he had a natural birth and possessed a human body which Jesus Himself said was prepared by the Father.[28] With regard to the Son's part in the Incarnation we read: "Forasmuch then as the children are partakers of flesh and blood, He also Himself likewise took part of the same." [29]

The actual conception of our Lord's body in the womb of the Virgin Mary is ascribed to the agency of the Holy Spirit. Hear the testimony in the divine records when Mary questioned the angel as to her possibility of conceiving and bringing forth a son: "The Holy Ghost shall come upon thee, and the power of the Highest shall overshadow thee." [30] By the inspiration of the Almighty, Matthew wrote: "Now the birth of Jesus Christ was on this wise: When as His mother Mary was espoused to Joseph, before they came together, she was found with child of the Holy Ghost." [31] Then when Joseph became troubled at Mary's condition, "the angel of the Lord appeared unto him in a dream, saying, Joseph, thou son of David, fear not to take unto thee Mary thy wife: for that which is conceived in her is of the Holy Ghost." [32]

To all of us, the conception by the Holy Spirit is the mystery of mysteries. Even the Apostle Paul says: "Without controversy great is the mystery of godliness." [33] Under the secret glory of it all, our hearts bow with humility and faith in adoration of the Spirit of God and His holy operation in the Incarnation of our Lord. Most surely He has met the requirements for impartation of life.

Our Lord's virgin birth by the Holy Spirit is a type of the sinner's new birth by the same Spirit. Just as Mary surrendered her body to the Holy Spirit in order that Jesus might be formed in her, so the sinner, by yielding to the wooing of the Spirit, experiences the forming of Christ in him so that he can testify with Paul: "Christ liveth in me." [34]

However, our Lord did not retain His physical life. Upon the Cross He died, and His life was taken from Him, but the Spirit of Life, who was the divine agency

[30] Luke 1:35   [31] Matthew 1:18   [32] Matthew 1:20
[33] 1 Timothy 3:16   [34] Galatians 2:20

when Jesus was conceived in the virgin, was present at
Calvary when our Saviour gave Himself in death, so that
we read of Him "who through the *eternal Spirit* offered
Himself without spot to God."[35] As the life of our Lord
left His body, the Holy Spirit was present guarding that
for which He was responsible. Jesus died as He was born,
overshadowed by the Holy Spirit, the Spirit of Life.

We are not surprised, therefore, to read of the close
association and active part of the Spirit in our Lord's
victorious resurrection from death. The rising again of
Christ from death and the grave is just as indissolubly
linked with the agency and power of the Holy Spirit as
was His virgin birth. The Apostle Paul certifies: "But if
the Spirit of Him that raised up Jesus from the dead
dwell in you, He that raised up Christ from the dead
shall also quicken your mortal bodies by His Spirit that
dwelleth in you."[36]

As the Spirit of Life, the Holy Spirit has power over
death, and He demonstrated that power when He raised
our Lord Jesus Christ from among the dead. Peter also
speaks of our Lord as "being put to death in the flesh, but
quickened [or made alive] by the Spirit."[37] The Lord
Jesus, the spotless Lamb of God, suffered death for us.
When His body was nailed to the tree He died physically,
but that same body, by the power of the Holy Spirit, was
given life again. In that Spirit-given life He appeared to
His disciples and to others, so that He, through the Holy
Ghost, gave commandments unto the apostles whom He
had chosen.[38] The risen Christ, raised by the Spirit of

[35] Hebrews 9:14   [36] Romans 8:11   [37] 1 Peter 3:18
[38] Acts 1:2

Life, spoke and acted by the Spirit in His glorified body
as He did in the days of His humiliation.

What glorious truth is revealed in the foregoing Scriptures! Here are divine certainties that prove the Spirit's
qualifications to impart and sustain life. He is the channel
by whom those dead in trespasses and sins are made
alive in Christ Jesus. The Holy Spirit in regeneration
is the enabling power that causes us to realize that we
have been born anew. Indwelling the believer, the Holy
Spirit Himself bears witness with our human spirit that
we are the children of God.[39] It is the operation of the
Spirit that makes a man a Christian. It is impossible to
possess eternal life, to know one is saved, and yet have
not the Holy Spirit; for "if any man have not the Spirit
of Christ, he is none of His." [40]

WHAT HAPPENS WHEN WE BELIEVE?

When a sinner, convicted of sin by the Holy Spirit,
responds to that conviction and receives Jesus Christ as
personal Saviour, he is born again immediately. He becomes a partaker of the divine nature with a life altogether
different from that of the unregenerate man. All this has
come about by the aid of the Holy Spirit. When the decision was made to accept Jesus Christ as Saviour and Lord,
it was not in his own strength, but by the Spirit's power,
for "No man can say that Jesus is the Lord, but by the
Holy Ghost." [41] Any true confession of the Saviourhood
and Lordship of Jesus Christ is possible only by the
Spirit of God. With the new birth, then, there commences
a new relationship with the Holy Spirit that we could not

[39] Romans 8:16   [40] Romans 8:9   [41] 1 Corinthians 12:3

know heretofore. We shall seek to explain this new relationship in the following paragraphs.

The Spirit's Incoming. We quote once again the apostle's words wherein he declares: "If any man have not the Spirit of Christ, he is none of His." [42] There is a widespread unscriptural teaching which asserts that the Holy Spirit does not enter *into* every believer at the time of conversion, but that He enters the heart as a second work, or second blessing, some time after conversion. Such teaching is false, and a study of the following Scriptures will show that the Holy Spirit does not enter into a few favored believers, but that He comes into the heart of every true believer in Christ immediately upon conversion.

Let us look first at some of the verses which false teachers use as a basis for their belief that a believer must continually ask for the gift of the Holy Spirit before he can receive Him.

At first glance at Luke 11:13 it would seem that one could be saved but not receive the Holy Spirit until he had been prayed for. Our Lord said: "If ye then, being evil, know how to give good gifts unto your children: how much more shall your heavenly Father give the Holy Spirit to them that ask Him?" [43] We dare never lose sight of the fact that, even though all Scripture is profitable, there is a dispensational interpretation and application of the Scriptures. Rightly understood, no verse in the Bible contradicts the fact that the Holy Spirit enters when He saves.

Concerning the above verse in the Gospel according

[42] Romans 8:9   [43] Luke 11:13

to Luke, Dr. Lewis Sperry Chafer says: "The relation of the Spirit to men during the earth ministry of Christ was progressive . . . and the statement from Christ that the Spirit might be had by asking was so new to them that, so far as the record goes, they never asked." Dr. Chafer is correct, for the Scriptures do not say that they ever did pray for the Holy Spirit. But suppose now that they would have prayed for the Spirit's coming. It would have been an intelligent prayer because the Spirit was not yet given. But now that He has come, there is no sense in praying for His coming. Before our Lord ascended to the Father, He promised that He would come back again, so we sometimes include in our prayers: "Even so, come, Lord Jesus." [44] Certainly not one of us will pray for His coming after He is here.

Now a final word concerning what Jesus said about praying for the Holy Spirit. We cannot be dogmatic in saying that our Lord was teaching His disciples to pray for the Spirit Himself rather than His power. If we link verse thirteen with what follows, it becomes clear that He was speaking in the context about the power of the Spirit. He had just finished casting a demon out of a man, and some who were standing by accused Him of casting out the demon by the power of Beelzebub, the chief of demons. Then Jesus answered that He had not cast out the demon by a diabolical power but by the finger of God, or as Matthew states, "by the Spirit of God." [45] He was performing miracles by the power of the Holy Spirit, and that same power was available to the disciples for their asking. The doctrine of the Spirit's incoming being a

[44] Revelation 22:20   [45] Matthew 12:28

second work of grace after regeneration and conditioned upon the believer's asking fails in the light of Luke 11:13. "Ye have received the Spirit of adoption [or son-placing], whereby we cry, Abba, Father" [46] includes every believer and not a select few who have "prayed through" until they got "it."

Peter makes another statement that confuses some: "And we are witnesses of these things; and so is also the Holy Ghost, whom God hath given to them that obey Him." [47] The false idea that is taken from this verse is that the Holy Spirit's coming is dependent upon a life of obedience after one is saved. The fact of the matter is that Peter is not speaking to believers at all, but to the unsaved, and it is an appeal to the unsaved for "the obedience of faith." [48] The context is clear and understandable; the Spirit is given to those who obey God by trusting His Son as their Saviour. It has to do with the obedience of sinners unto salvation. When an unsaved man obeys the gospel, he becomes saved and receives the gift of the Spirit. On the other hand, there is the sad and bitter end "of them that obey not the gospel of God." [49] Have you obeyed the gospel by acknowledging Jesus Christ as Saviour? If you have, then you are a child of God, "And because ye are sons [not because ye are *obedient sons*], God hath sent forth the Spirit of His Son into your hearts, crying, Abba, Father." [50]

Another difficult passage that some have used, upon which to build an erroneous doctrine, is recorded by Luke in the Book of the Acts. "Now when the apostles

[46] Romans 8:15　　[47] Acts 5:32　　[48] Romans 16:26
[49] 1 Peter 4:17　　[50] Galatians 4:6

which were at Jerusalem heard that Samaria had received the Word of God, they sent unto them Peter and John: Who, when they were come down, prayed for them, that they might receive the Holy Ghost: (For as yet He was fallen upon none of them: only they were baptized in the name of the Lord Jesus.)" [51] There are those who teach from this incident that the laying on of hands is necessary today to the receiving of the Holy Spirit.

We cannot escape the fact that we have in this passage in the inhabitants of Samaria a group of believers who were baptized in the name, or by the authority, of the Lord Jesus, but who had not yet received the Holy Spirit. There is no denying that this is so. But why did not these Samaritans receive the Holy Spirit immediately upon their confession of faith in the Lord Jesus Christ? This order did not repeat itself when Peter preached a little later on in the house of Cornelius. We are told that while Peter preached the Word of God, "the Holy Ghost fell on all them which heard the Word." [52]

The answer to this apparent discrepancy rests with the fact that from Pentecost until Peter's visit to Cornelius, the gospel was preached to Jews only. Now we know that the Jews had no dealings with the Samaritans. [53] For many years there existed a rivalry between them, the Jews in the south believing that the temple at Jerusalem was the place where God was worshiped, and the Samaritans in the north claiming that the temple at Mt. Gerizim was the place where God was worshiped. [54]

It is not hard to understand that if the Holy Spirit had

[51] Acts 8:14-17   [52] Acts 10:44   [53] John 4:9
[54] John 4:20

been given to both the Jews and the Samaritans immediately upon receiving the Word, there would have been a faction in the Church right from the start. Both groups would have claimed that they were the true Church, and the strife may have continued down through the centuries. God foresaw the difficulty, and made provision for it by withholding the Holy Spirit from the Samaritans until the apostles had arrived to identify themselves with their new brethren in Christ. When God gave the Holy Spirit to the Samaritan believers through the prayers and the laying on of the hands of the Jewish apostles, immediately there was an open recognition that they were one. This human rite cannot be set up as a system, nor can we build a doctrine upon any one single incident or text. When the Samaritans received the Holy Spirit, there burst upon them new light, the truth that the "Church which is His body" is God's only living organism on earth, and that "by one Spirit are we all baptized into one body." How blessed to know and rest in the truth that all believers, whether faulty like the Corinthians, to whom Paul addressed this precious truth, or fully yielded, "whether we [believers] be Jews or Gentiles, whether we be bond or free; . . . have been all made to drink into one Spirit." [55]

We have one further passage in the Book of Acts that calls for prayerful observation: Paul came to Ephesus where Apollos had been, "and finding certain disciples, He said unto them, Have ye received the Holy Ghost since ye believed? And they said unto him, We have not so much as heard whether there be any Holy Ghost. And

[55] 1 Corinthians 12:13

he said unto them, Unto what then were ye baptized? And they said, Unto John's baptism. Then said Paul, John verily baptized with the baptism of repentance, saying unto the people, that they should believe on Him which should come after him, that is, on Christ Jesus. When they heard this, they were baptized in the name of the Lord Jesus. And when Paul had laid his hands upon them, the Holy Ghost came on them; and they spake with tongues, and prophesied." [56]

Two thoughts must be taken into consideration in order to understand the context of the preceding quotation. First, the word "since." We quote a helpful and enlightening paragraph by Dr. G. Campbell Morgan:

"The word 'since' creates an entire misrepresentation of the question he asked. That is something to be stated emphatically, because it is on the presence of that word, that the misrepresentation of this passage has been based. The tense of the verbs 'receive' and 'believe' is the same, so that it may be rendered, 'Received ye the Holy Spirit when ye believed?' Not have ye received since; as though there were a belief at some time, and a subsequent reception of the Spirit; which in the terminology of our own day is described as a 'second blessing.' Paul asked no such question."

Secondly, a fact overlooked by well-meaning brethren is that these disciples that Paul found at Ephesus were not Christians but disciples of John the Baptist. By reasoning that these were Christians, they conclude that a man may be born again and not have the Holy Spirit. These Jewish disciples had been instructed by Apollos,

[56] Acts 19:1-6

but Apollos had only a limited knowedge of the gospel, "knowing only the baptism of John," for when Aquilla and Priscilla heard him preach in the synagogue, "they took him unto them, and expounded unto him the way of God more perfectly." [57] Obviously Paul was impressed by the absence of any evidence of salvation; and so to prove the genuineness of their faith in the Lord Jesus Christ as personal Saviour, he asked them if, upon believing, they received the Holy Spirit. Their answer was sufficient evidence that they had not been born again. After Paul had given them the full truth of salvation through faith in the finished work of Christ, the Holy Spirit came unto them.

Finally, let us look at one more passage that has been misinterpreted to teach that some who believe do not have the Spirit. Paul writes: "In whom ye also trusted, after that ye heard the word of truth, the gospel of your salvation: in whom also after that ye believed, ye were sealed with that Holy Spirit of Promise." [58] There are those who teach that the *believing* and the *sealing* are successive but not simultaneous. However, a correct rendering of the text dispels the faintest suggestion that between our believing in Christ and the sealing with the Spirit there is any intervention of time. The text should read: "Having believed, ye *were* sealed." The sealing is a figurative expression denoting a finished transaction and divine ownership. The Spirit Himself is the Seal, and nowhere in all the Bible are we taught to seek the sealing with the Spirit, for "having believed, ye were sealed," and

[57] Acts 18:25, 26   [58] Ephesians 1:13

it is His presence which assures us of both salvation and security.

The Spirit's Indwelling. The believers at Corinth were doubtless ignorant of the Spirit's indwelling, for Paul asks: "Know ye not that ye are the temple of God, and that the Spirit of God *dwelleth* in you?" [59] This means more than the Spirit's incoming; it indicates permanency of residence. When the Spirit made His advent into this world, He came to abide in the world throughout the entire dispensation of grace. The Spirit is present in the world *indwelling* every true child of God, and not one word of God's Word does He ever withdraw. When Jesus promised the Spirit to His own, it was that He might abide with us forever.[60]

In the Old Testament He was not known as the abiding Spirit because He merely came upon men for awhile and then left them. David, burdened by his great sin, prayed: "Take not Thy Holy Spirit from me," [61] but such a prayer cannot reasonably be prayed today, for when Christ died He provided full and complete redemption.

Because of the immutable value of the work of Christ, the Spirit has no occasion to leave the believer. Besides, the permanency of the Spirit is necessary if the work of Christ for us is to avail before God. Samuel Ridout says: "It would drag Christ from His throne in glory, if the Spirit could depart from a believer." By disregarding the Spirit's indwelling as God's provision for daily victory, we slip back into our old habits and ways of living, for the Spirit's indwelling overcomes sin in us. The Spirit

[59] 1 Corinthians 3:16   [60] John 14:16   [61] Psalm 51:11

is never said to leave the Christian, for once we have been born from above He comes into our hearts to stay. We are sealed with the Holy Spirit "unto the day of redemption." [62] O blessed truth!

[62] Ephesians 4:30

THE LEADING OF THE SPIRIT

"For as many as are led by the Spirit of God, they are the sons of God." [1]

An honest and humble Christian recognizes at once his need of divine leadership. No Christian can afford to be ignorant of the greatness of this need. Our Heavenly Father anticipated it, and in the Person of the Holy Spirit, He has met it fully. Believers are not at home in the world. Strangers and pilgrims, we dare not look to the world or its leaders for guidance. Jesus saw how much the disciples would need to be directed, so He promised them: "When He, the Spirit of truth, is come, He will guide you into all truth." [2] Just as we are warned not to enter densely wooded areas without a guide, so this world is a howling wilderness, and the Christian who does not seek the guidance of the Holy Spirit will wear himself down wandering aimlessly.

The normal Christian experience is a desire to know and to do the will of God. How to find His will is something too few of us know much about. Under the dispensation of law, Israel had a written code that governed their national life, social life, and religious worship. But one of the remarkable realities and precious privileges of this age of grace is to be led by the Holy Spirit. Paul says:

[1] Romans 8:14   [2] John 16:13

471

"If ye be led of the Spirit, ye are not under the law." [8] Those who have a long list of self-made rules saying "thou shalt" and "thou shalt not" cannot say that this is God's method of leading His children. God intended that His children should be led by a living Person, and that Person is none other than the Holy Spirit. Only as we submit to His leading are we delivered from bondage and from the power of a legal mind.

Some Christians are abnormal in that the leading of the Spirit is not experienced by them. The abnormal Christian who does not enjoy the Spirit's leading often has a desire to understand more fully how he may know the will of God. To aid all such who have this holy desire, we give ourselves to the study of how a believer can ascertain divine guidance in his life. A knowledge of His Person and work is absolutely essential to a correct understanding of God's will for His children. No personal understanding of the divine will is possible apart from the Holy Spirit, for it is His function to bring men into conformity with the plan and purposes of God.

RECOGNIZING THE HOLY SPIRIT

Before the child of God submits himself to the leading of a spirit, he should make certain that he is yielding to the Holy Spirit. This is important because the Holy Spirit is not the only spirit in the world. Made in the image of God, man is a trinity in unity: spirit, soul, and body. It is easy to yield to the spirit of man instead of the Spirit of God. Paul warns believers when he speaks of the days before their conversion in which they walked

[8] Galatians 5:18

"according to the prince of the power of the air, the *spirit* that now worketh in the children of disobedience." [4] The spirits are *working*. The Spirit of God *"worketh"* in the believer "both to will and to do of His good pleasure," [5] and the spirit of Satan "worketh in the children of disobedience." Both are contending for the domination and the directorship of men's lives.

The Christian must have a sure means of trying the spirits, for not every spirit that speaks to him will be the voice of the Holy Spirit. An impulse, a desire, or an urge to do some seemingly worth-while thing may be the suggestion of an evil spirit. The Bible distinguishes clearly between "the Spirit of truth, and the spirit of error." [6] Hence we are warned: "Beloved, believe not every spirit, but try the spirits whether they are of God." [7] It is essential that one recognize and clearly identify the Holy Spirit before hearkening to Him. God, in His Word, has set forth His marks of identification whereby His children may be certain before they yield allegiance to any spirit. The voices contending for power and authority are so numerous that we need to recognize the voice of the Holy Spirit.

The Holy Spirit may be recognized by His consistency with the teachings of Christ. Jesus said: "He shall teach you all things, and bring all things to your remembrance, whatsoever I have said unto you." [8] The Holy Spirit will never lead you to do anything contrary to what our Lord taught. Some Christians seek to justify their wrong deeds by arguing that they *feel* they are doing right. I am re-

[4] Ephesians 2:2   [5] Philippians 2:13   [6] 1 John 4:6
[7] 1 John 4:1   [8] John 14:26

minded of a young Christian girl who sought to convince me that she could remain true to her Lord, even though she should marry an unbeliever with whom she claimed to be in love. Such was the leading of an evil spirit and not the Spirit of God, for the young man had purchased a divorce from his first wife without any Biblical grounds, and Jesus taught clearly that such a remarriage would be adultery.[9] The Holy Spirit will never lead you to do anything that is contrary to that which our Lord taught.

The Holy Spirit may be recognized by His agreement with the whole of God's Word. If this were not so, He could not be trusted but would have to be labeled as being inconsistent, for He is the Author of the Word. "Holy men of God spake as they were moved by the Holy Ghost." [10] When one is seeking the leading of the Spirit, he must never disregard the Word.

Christians who neglect the study of the Word of God will have difficulty in knowing the mind of the Spirit. I have become wary of all persons who boast of knowing the will of God but slight His Word. I am not discounting the testimony of those who claim to have received direct and personal communication from the Lord Himself, but I have met some who boasted of such an experience, and, at the same time, have been led into questionable pursuits and practices. The Holy Spirit cannot lead any person contrary to that which is written in the Word of God.

How it must grieve God as He looks upon the numerous false and fanciful interpretations of the prophetic Scriptures! It is obvious that men have sought to become

[9] Matthew 5:32; 19:9 [10] 2 Peter 1:21

prophets instead of allowing the Holy Spirit to guide them. Jesus promised: "He will shew you things to come." [11] Many brethren in the ministry have set dates for the return of Christ and have "revealed" who the antichrist was, only to find from bitter experience how easy it is to be led by a false spirit when interpreting Scripture.

The Holy Spirit may be recognized by His unity. Paul contrasted the unity of the Holy Spirit with the confusion of other spirits in his first Epistle to the Corinthians. He wrote: "The spirits of the prophets are subject to the prophets," and then he adds: "God is not the author of confusion." [12] Ten men, each guided by his own human spirit, can have pandemonium, but ten men all guided by the Holy Spirit will be in unity. Later Paul exhorted believers "to keep the unity of the Spirit in the bond of peace." [13]

The coming of the Holy Spirit at Pentecost witnessed among the brethren a unity conspicuous by its absence today. We read that "they were all with *one accord* in one place," [14] and that "continuing daily with one accord . . . the Lord added to the church daily." [15] When the disciples daily did their part (continued with one accord), God daily kept His part of the agreement (added to the Church). I was asked to preside over the meeting of a certain congregation which had met to call a new pastor. The names of two candidates were submitted to the congregation, and a secret ballot was taken. The members were split on their views as to which man should become the church's next pastor. Only the Lord Himself pre-

[11] John 16:13
[14] Acts 2:1
[12] 1 Corinthians 14:32, 33
[15] Acts 2:46, 47
[13] Ephesians 4:3

vented a near riot, for both groups contended that they were led of the Holy Spirit in the matter of voting. But the results of their voting proved that such was not the case. This church in Pennsylvania needed what that small band of disciples had in Jerusalem: "These all continued with *one accord* in prayer." [16]

Where there is contention, strife, and disagreement among brethren, we may be certain that the Holy Spirit is not leading. D. L. Moody once said: "Strife is Satan's strategy. There is one thing I have noticed as I have traveled in different countries: I have never known the Spirit of the Lord to work where the people are divided. There is one thing that we must have if we are to have the Holy Spirit of God work in our midst, and that is unity."

The Holy Spirit may be recognized by the way He exalts Christ. Jesus said that when the Spirit should come, "He shall testify of Me," [17] and again, "He shall glorify Me." [18] The Spirit always attracts men to Christ, never to Himself. We can always be sure that anything to which we are drawn that is not Christocentric is not the leading of the Spirit. By this standard every church should measure its program and every believer should judge his actions. The spirit of man seeks to exalt man, but the spirit of God exalts the Son of God. It is possible for men to be led by Satan and at the same time think they render God a service.[19] "Hereby know we the Spirit of truth, and the spirit of error." [20] "Every spirit that confesseth that Jesus Christ is come in the flesh is of God: And every spirit that confesseth not that Jesus Christ is come in the flesh is not

[16] Acts 1:14
[19] John 16:2
[17] John 15:26
[20] 1 John 4:6
[18] John 16:14

of God." [21] A modernist publicly denied the virgin birth of our Lord, and then he defended himself by claiming that he was led of God. This man certainly did not try the spirits. The Holy Spirit, acting in conformity with the Word of God, will always glorify the Lord Jesus Christ.

So far we have mentioned three spirits: the Spirit of God, the spirit of man, and the spirit of Satan. The Apostle Paul mentions another when he says: "Now we have received, not the spirit of the world." [22] (The Holy Spirit may be recognized by His opposition to the world and to all that is worldly.) The word "world" in 1 Corinthians 2:12 is the word *kosmos,* and it means the world system. Anything that is according to the world system is worldly, and all worldliness is harmful to the cause of Christ. The spirit of this world is enmity against the Spirit of God. Jesus said: "The Father . . . shall give you another Comforter . . . even the Spirit of truth; whom the world cannot receive, because it seeth Him not, neither knoweth Him." [23] A Christian minister, in order to get back the crowds that were gradually leaving his church, introduced a worldly program into the church. He sought to defend his action by saying that God leads different men in different ways, and that he believed he was led by the Holy Spirit to start this "worldly" program in order to win back his people. But all the Biblical evidence was against the dear brother's action, for the Holy Spirit never condones worldliness.

The Spirit of God will always agree with the Word but never with the world. Worldliness and the will of God are diametrically opposed to each other. We can see the op-

[21] 1 John 4:2, 3   [22] 1 Corinthians 2:12   [23] John 14:16, 17

position expressed in the first Epistle of John where we read: "The world passeth away . . . but he that doeth the will of God abideth for ever." [24] There is that subtle attraction of the world that has misled many Christians; therefore we need to keep our lives pure and keep our hearts in tune with God, so that we can discern the voice of the Holy Spirit from the voice of the spirit of the world.

If we are to be led by the Spirit, it is not enough to know how we may recognize Him; but it is essential that we know Him personally and intimately. Our secondhand knowledge of the Holy Spirit is one big reason for our sometimes being led in the wrong direction. We may know all about Him from the testimony of others, but it is not the same as knowing Him in a personal way so as to commune with Him at all times. The fact that we are acquainted with His Works does not mean that we know Him.

I have been richly blessed by the writings of certain men in the gospel ministry. I know something of their careers. But until I am introduced to them, shake hands with them, and fellowship with them, I cannot say that I know them. O that men would have a consciousness of the Holy Spirit's blessed presence in their lives! I like what Daniel Steele said in his book, *The Gospel of the Comforter:* "Unconscious regeneration in water-baptism and unconscious reception of the Holy Spirit through a bishop's hands in confirmation are doctrines lacking Biblical proof, the only proof possible after the exclusion of consciousness. If a human person enters my library and addresses me while writing these words, I know it. Shall

[24] 1 John 2:17

I not know it if a divine Person knocks at the door of my heart and, at my invitation, enters?" Now declares Christ: "Ye know Him, for He abideth with you, and shall be in you."

THE HOLY SPIRIT LEADING THE EARLY CHURCH

The Book of Acts contains the historical account of the Spirit's leading even as our Lord had promised. The Holy Spirit is mentioned in the Acts more than fifty times, so that we have here a series of practical illustrations of His leading. Knowing that He had come for the express purpose of guiding them, the apostles were ready to submit to whatever He told them to do.

The Holy Spirit was recognized as the administrator of the Church, when the first Church officers were chosen. When the number of the disciples was rapidly multiplying, the twelve called the multitude of the disciples, and said: ". . . Look ye out among you seven men of honest report, *full of the Holy Ghost* . . . and they chose Stephen, a man full of faith and of *the Holy Ghost* . . . and Stephen . . . did great wonders and miracles among the people. . . . And they were not able to resist the wisdom and the Spirit by which he spake." [25] The twelve knew that if the Church was to carry out her mission, her leaders would have to be Spirit-filled and Spirit-led men. Jesus had taught them that.

The sovereign leading of the Spirit is the Church's great need today. If a man's pockets are filled with money, he is made a deacon or an elder, and no one cares whether or not he is filled with the Spirit. Folks say that "money

* Acts 6:1-10

talks," and in their eagerness to feel its influence, the voice of the Spirit is not heard and His power is not felt. The Spirit of God is given no consideration while men try to guide the affairs of God in the energy of their flesh.

When John Robinson, the pastor of a congregation of refugee Puritans at Leyden, was bidding farewell to that party of exiles leaving for New England on the Mayflower, he said: "I charge you, that you follow me no farther than you have seen me follow the Lord Jesus Christ."

Let us cease to be followers of men, for the influence of Christ's Church will be felt in the world only as the Holy Spirit is leading her believing members. Men may be filled with satanic hatred against us, but when we, like Stephen, are filled with the Holy Spirit and guided by Him, our enemies will not be able to resist the Spirit by which we are led.

Another of the seven deacons chosen was Philip, the lay-evangelist. Philip was in the midst of a mighty revival in Samaria.[26] Crowds were believing, "and there was great joy in that city," says Luke. Then God removed Philip from the scene of the revival, where apparently he was much needed, and sent him to Gaza, a deserted fortress in the extreme south of Palestine. With the success that Philip was having, he might have settled down to strengthen the new converts; but God had other plans for His servant. As he walked obediently on his way, chariots passed now and then. Perhaps Philip wondered why he must leave the large crowds at Samaria to travel in the midst of these few passing chariots. But Philip was filled with the Holy Spirit, and being willing to be led by the Spirit of

[26] Acts 8:1-8

God, He trustfully and obediently continued on his way as the chariots passed by.

Suddenly he saw a chariot with a single black man as its occupant. "Then the Spirit said unto Philip, Go near, and join thyself to this chariot." [27]

We are not to be surprised at the Spirit's speaking to Philip, but it is cause for much joy to note how Philip at once recognized and knew Him. The voice was known to Philip; therefore he had no difficulty in distinguishing the spirits. Moreover, there was an eagerness on Philip's part to do his Master's bidding, for we are told that "Philip ran." Little wonder that God does not use us all in the same way!

Spirit-led Christians are never misled. Philip was guided to a man who himself was seeking guidance. When Philip asked him: "Understandest thou what thou readest?" the eunuch answered: "How can I, except some man should guide me?" This black man was actually looking for someone to guide him in the way.

How blessed it is indeed to be so led by the Holy Spirit that we ourselves can lead others without difficulty! As one of God's undershepherds, I feel quite keenly my responsibility of leadership. How dreadful to have to stand before the Lord and be judged with those religious teachers whom Jesus labeled "blind guides"! [28] "Let them alone," He said; "They be blind leaders of the blind. And if the blind lead the blind, both shall fall into the ditch." [29] O how we need to walk in close communion with our blessed Lord so that we do not lead others in the wrong direction!

[27] Acts 8:29   [28] Matthew 23:16   [29] Matthew 15:14

After Philip had led the eunuch to a saving knowledge of the Lord Jesus Christ, then to the water of baptism, we read that "the Spirit of the Lord caught away Philip, that the eunuch saw him no more. . . . But Philip was found at Azotus." [30] We are not going to discuss here whether the catching away of Philip was "some undefinable spiritual catching away" or a physical bodily transferring of His servant by God. Personally, I believe it was a physical experience, and it involves no problem at all in my mind. It is sufficient to know that Philip was walking near enough to his Lord to be led by the Spirit in every detail of his life.

In the thrilling account of the gospel witness extended to the Gentiles, we see a definite and direct leading of the Spirit. While Peter was sleeping on the housetop of Simon the tanner at Joppa, a vision was given to him. He saw heaven opened and a great sheet let down by the four corners. The sheet contained all kind of animals, both clean and unclean according to the Jewish mind. Then came a voice to him saying: "Rise, Peter; kill, and eat." [31] But Peter protested that he never had eaten anything common or unclean, for to the Jew the eating of an unclean animal was a gross sin.

God had a purpose in the vision. The vessel typified the Church, and the four corners spoke of the four corners of the world. The clean animals represented the Jew, and the unclean, the Gentile. But God saw them all in the same light—clean; for He said to Peter: "What God hath cleansed, that call not thou common." [32]

The ultimate purpose of the vision was to lead Peter to

[30] Acts 8:39, 40   [31] Acts 10:13   [32] Acts 10:15

the house of Cornelius where the Gentiles might have an equal opportunity with the Jew to hear and believe the gospel of Christ. Peter was not yet fully convinced that this was right, and "while Peter thought on the vision, *the Spirit said unto him,* Behold, three men seek thee. Arise therefore, and get thee down, and go with them, doubting nothing: *for I have sent them.* Then Peter went down to the men which were sent unto him from Cornelius." [33] Even though Peter was slow in understanding the meaning of the vision because of his Jewish prejudice, he did not mistake the direct leading of the Holy Spirit in the matter. The Spirit led him to see the great truth, "That the Gentiles should be fellowheirs, and of the same body, and partakers of His promise in Christ by the gospel." [34]

No man today who claims to be a Christian and who hates the Jews can say that he is led of God. Where the Spirit is leading, as He did in the case of Peter, the believer will be made to see that God is not yet finished dealing in love with His chosen people. The Abrahamic and Davidic covenants never were revoked by God. Today, His promise to bless them that bless the Jew and to curse them that curse the Jew still holds good. Our attitude toward the Jew will determine which of the spirits is leading us.

Let us turn now to Acts, chapter thirteen. It is a very important part of the book, containing the account of the beginning of the Church's mighty missionary movement. One might expect to read of a committee banquet or a convention to lay the plans for evangelizing the world, but such was not the case. These men were gathered at the

[33] Acts 10:19-21   [34] Ephesians 3:6

church in Antioch waiting for the Spirit to guide them, and "as they ministered to the Lord, and fasted, the Holy Ghost said, Separate Me Barnabas and Saul for the work whereunto I have called them." [35] This was not a "pep" meeting to raise money and choose men to be sent forth on some missionary enterprise.

The choice of personality and place of ministry was not left to the wisdom of men—"As they ministered to the Lord, and fasted, the Holy Spirit said. . . ." What did He say? "He said: *"Separate Me."* These men were to have the consciousness that the Spirit had called them, and under His authority and in His liberty they were to go forth. No individual or group of people has any right to make such a move unless that move be under the impulse and guidance of the Holy Spirit. All true Christian ministry is the exercise of spiritual gifts which are of the Holy Spirit, and not by the might and genius of men.

Is the Spirit of God able to make known His will perfectly to an individual or to an assembly? Are men able to distinguish His voice from other voices and to know that He is leading? Unquestionably the answer is "yes." "So they, being sent forth by the Holy Spirit, departed . . ." and the missionary triumphs which followed prove the possibility of the same triumphs today if only men will be willing to be led by Him.

When the Holy Spirit calls men and sends them forth to do a special work, those men can count upon guidance to the places where they should visit. The Spirit, knowing when and where to send the servant of the Lord, will not

[35] Acts 13:2

allow him to travel the path of his own choosing, provided he is a ready and willing listener to the divine voice.

A helpful illustration of the restraining of the Spirit in service is given to us in the case of Paul and Silas. Paul decided that he would take the gospel into Asia, but he was "forbidden of the Holy Ghost to preach the Word in Asia." [36] Then he endeavoured to carry the witness into Bithynia, "but the Spirit suffered them not." [37] Here is another kind of guidance, being restrained by the Spirit.

The Holy One had blocked the way into certain fields, for He reserves that right for Himself. There is no land unknown to Him. There is not a condition with which He is not familiar. He foresees every problem and can never be taken by surprise. If only we will not faint when He closes doors but wait and pray, He will lead us in another direction.

When I first read the foregoing incident in the Scriptures a number of years ago, I wondered why the Holy Spirit protested Paul's plan. That large province of Asia with its prosperous cities surely needed the gospel. But I now feel satisfied that it was only a matter of *time*. The Macedonian need was the greater at that moment, and the Holy Spirit knew it. Later Paul was privileged to spend three years in Ephesus, the capital of the province of Asia, and as far as we know, all Asia heard the gospel.

Let us not grow discouraged and faint when the leading of the Spirit conflicts with our own desires and plans. How glorious to be able to look back on past experiences and thank God that we were prevented from going our

[36] Acts 16:6   [37] Acts 16:7

own way and were guided in the path of His choosing!

Beloved, the Spirit guides, perhaps not always in the way we think He should, but remember, He guides, "not by flaming visions always, not by words articulate in human ears; but by circumstances, by commonplace things, by difficult things, by dark things, by disappointing things. The Spirit guides. If we make up our minds that the way of guidance is the way of flaming vision, and rolling thunder, and an articulate voice, and a lifting to a height of ecstasy, then we may never be guided." Let us seek to know more of this humble dependence upon the leading of the Spirit. The age is evil. The servants of the Lord are just as much in need of divine guidance today as were the apostles in the early Church.

LET GOD LEAD YOUR LIFE

The Holy Spirit longs to lead God's children today just as He led them in the early Church. His leading assured them of victory. Our failure to follow Him is the reason why we are so often defeated. You and I have known altogether too much of this defeat, and unless we are ready and willing to listen to and to obey Him, then we shall continue to live our own lives apart from the divine will. All that God wants to do now is to make us willing.

Someone has said: "God is able to speak loud enough to make a willing soul hear." Have you surrendered yourself to do as God may choose? I spoke recently with a young man who appeared unsettled and unhappy in his Christian experience. Such a state is oftentimes a sign that the person is not in the will of God, so I said to my young friend: "Have you honestly sought to know and to do the will of God?" The answer that he gave me revealed the cause of his misery. He said: "I want to know and do God's will, but I'll never be a missionary." Personally I do not think that God will ever call him to become a missionary, but his unwillingness to commit himself to do whatever God chooses stood in the way of his knowing just what the will of God was. Unless you are willing right now to say "Yes" to every command of God, and that without any mental reservation whatever, you might just as well not talk about the will of God. You are deceiving yourself.

Are you conscious of being subject to His will? The Lord Jesus could say: "I came not to do My own will, but the will of Him that sent Me." Our two boys at home would never realize our plans for them if they should stubbornly rebel against yielding to the will of their parents. God wants to work in us "that which is well-pleasing in His sight," [38] and we may be assured that His will is always "good," "acceptable," and "perfect." [39] When we yield to His leading, we find too that it is good, acceptable, and perfect.

Let the Holy Spirit lead you through prayer. He has a very definite and an active part in the prayer life of all believers. He enters into prayer-fellowship with us every time we pray. The Holy Spirit understands the will of God for us, and if we are not praying in the Spirit, our prayers are not accepted of God nor are they answered. Paul writes: "Likewise the Spirit also helpeth our infirmities: for we know not what we should pray for as

[38] Hebrews 13:21   [39] Romans 12:2

we ought: but the Spirit Himself maketh intercession for us with groanings which cannot be uttered." [40]

There are times in our lives when we are at a loss to know which way to turn and it seems that there is no language or utterance with which to make our needs known: "We know not what we should pray for as we ought." We enter the region of the inconceivable and un-utterable, the place of the divine plan and purpose where the human mind can neither ask nor receive. That is when we need the Holy Spirit to lead us. O how well acquainted we are with our infirmity and our weakness when we try to pray! So the Holy Spirit "helpeth our infirmities." We need help when we pray, so He takes hold of our weakness. The practice of prayer calls for spiritual assistance, and right here we are assured of the Spirit's help. "He maketh intercession for us with groanings which cannot be ut-tered." The Son is our Intercessor in Heaven,[41] while the Spirit is our Intercessor on earth.

Jude says: "But ye, beloved, building up yourselves on your most holy faith, *praying in the Holy Spirit*, keep yourselves in the love of God." [42] Praying is not easy. It is a warfare against principalities and powers, therefore we must pray "in the Spirit." [43] As you seek the will of God in prayer enter into communion with your divine Prayer-Partner, the blessed Holy Spirit.

Let the Holy Spirit lead you through faith. When we pray in the Spirit we are praying according to God's will, and "If we ask anything according to His will, He heareth us." Knowing that we have God's attention and that our

---

[40] Romans 8:26   [41] Romans 8:34   [42] Jude 20
[43] Ephesians 6:18

praying has been in "the communion of the Holy Ghost," we may have faith to believe that we shall receive that for which we have asked.

Andrew Murray has said: "The leading of the Spirit must very specially be a thing of faith, and that in two senses. The beginning of the leading will come when we learn in holy fear to cultivate and act upon the confidence: The Holy Spirit is in me, and is doing His work. . . . In the Holy Spirit is the most intimate communication of the Divine Life; here faith may not judge by what it feels or understands, but simply submits to God to let Him do what He has said. . . . Faith has also to be exercised in regard to each part of the leading."

We start on the path of following the Spirit's leading by believing, and so we continue in that same exercise of faith. Most Christians ask God to lead them, but they are afraid to step out in faith. If your prayer is in the Spirit, then why do you doubt? If you are sure that He is leading, you do not have to see ahead. "Faith walks without seeing, but the faith that walks will see."

Lord Bolingbroke once asked Lady Huntingdon how she reconciled prayer to God for particular blessing with absolute resignation to the divine will. "Very easy," answered her ladyship; "just as if I were to offer a petition to a monarch, of whose kindness and wisdom I have the highest opinion. In such case my language would be, 'I wish you to bestow on me such a favor; but your majesty knows better than I how far it would be agreeable to you, or right in itself, to grant my desire. I therefore content myself with humbly presenting my petition, and leave the event of it entirely to you.' " This is confidence in

God, and without it we stand still when God would lead us on. Much of our not being led is due to our unwillingness to walk by faith.

"But are we not in danger of being led away by the imaginings of our own hearts, and counting as leading of the Spirit what proves to be a delusion of the flesh?" asks someone. Our answer is in the affirmative. In answer to this query, we refer our readers to the tests given earlier in this chapter. We may be certain of divine guidance if the leading is in agreement with the Word of God as taught by the Spirit of God, if it brings unity and not strife, if it exalts the Lord Jesus Christ, and if it is in opposition to the world and all that is worldly. May it please God to quicken our faith in the consciousness and certainty of the leading of His Holy Spirit.

THE LIBERTY OF THE SPIRIT

"Where the Spirit is Lord, there is liberty."[1]

A false idea has pervaded the minds of unbelievers causing them to feel that becoming a Christian places one under rules and regulations that rob life of its liberties. When a man becomes a Christian, the world looks upon him with sympathy as though he were being put behind prison bars, and now life for him is stripped of its fullness and freedom. Certainly this is one of the sharpest and most effective weapons of the enemy, and never has there been a worse perversion of the truth. Contrary to this Satanic delusion, the new birth introduces the sinner into a new experience of freedom. Until we are born of the Spirit, there is a slavery and servitude from which there is no release. But after we have believed and have been born again, we enter into a freedom that is more important and more precious than any civil or religious liberty. It is that inner liberty of the Holy Spirit.

FREE FROM THE CURSE OF THE LAW

In the Bible the believer's liberty is spoken of in several ways. First of all, the Apostle Paul tells us that "the law of the Spirit of life in Christ Jesus hath made me free

[1] 2 Corinthians 3:17—Free translation suggested by the author

from the law of sin and death." [2] Here the power of the law of the Spirit is set in contrast to the power of the Mosaic Law. At Sinai Israel was placed under law. The people realized that they were in bondage to sin, and, try as they would, there was no release. Then God sent the law by Moses, and when the people saw it, they were very optimistic and self-confident. They said that all that the Lord had spoken they would do. But Israel did not realize her utter impotence and inability to keep the law.

In itself the law was unable to free the people from the power of sin. This was what "the law could not do, in that it was weak through the flesh." [3] The law demanded righteousness, but it could not provide the power to attain unto it. Now there was nothing wrong with the law if it were upheld and honored. It is "holy, and just, and good." [4] The whole source of trouble was in the flesh which manifested desires contrary to the law. Israel admitted that the law was spiritual and its requirements righteous, but the people were powerless to make their lives measure up to it.

The giving of the law was one of the outstanding events in human history, and it began a new dispensation in the life of the nation Israel. It was never intended to be in force permanently. The Mosaic law was merely a temporary covenant given for temporary purposes "till the Seed [Christ] should come to whom the promise was made." [5] Yet all the while that the law was in force, it exacted a penalty from all violators and transgressors. "Now we know that what things soever the law saith, it

---

[2] Romans 8:2 [3] Romans 8:3 [4] Romans 7:12
[5] Galatians 3:19

saith to them who are under the law: that every mouth may be stopped, and all the world may become guilty before God." [6]

Let us understand clearly the purpose of the law. It was not given to justify men in the eyes of God, for "by the deeds of the law there shall no flesh be justified in His sight." [7] Many people who have fixed "religious" convictions find this truth extremely difficult to accept. They ask: "If keeping God's law avails me nothing for righteousness in His sight, *why did He give it?*" Paul gives the answer when he says: "By the law is the knowledge of sin."

Man is proud and boastful and needs to be humbled. The law intensifies the knowledge of sin and causes man to become speechless before God. It was not the function of the law to save. Man cannot be saved by it, simply because he cannot measure up to it. What people need to see is how exceedingly sinful they actually are, and this is exactly what God does through the law. Nothing worse could happen to any one of us than to go through life blinded to our sinful state before God, and then have to spend eternity in hell never having tasted of God's salvation. But no one ever will be able to say that he did not know he was a sinner, "for by the law is the knowledge of sin." [8] How loving and kind on God's part to bring us to a knowledge of our sin and guilt!

The law, then, does not make righteous. It merely incriminates and establishes the guilt of the lawless. He who violates the law finds that he is both convicted and condemned by the law. One single transgression results in the

[6] Romans 3:19   [7] Romans 3:20   [8] Romans 3:20

penalty of the broken law, "For whosoever shall keep the whole law, and yet offend in one point, he is guilty of all." [9]

In Paul's day the Judaizers insisted that their knowledge of the law entitled them to the blessings which belonged to the sons of Abraham. However, they were not aware of what was involved when one submitted to the law of Moses. They failed to see the wide scope of the demands of the law and that it must be punctiliously observed and carried out to the very letter.

If I begin to conform to any law, I must continue on in obedience to that law with a perfect, flawless record. But just as soon as I violate it in one place, I become guilty and must be charged with the penalty of breaking that law. Immediately upon my transgression I have come under the curse of the law.

It is clear that salvation through such a method is utterly impossible, for no man who is imperfect can keep a perfect law. The law does not ask us to do the best we can. It does not offer a premium for keeping *part* of it, but it does impose a penalty for not keeping *all* of it. Therefore the law has become "the ministration of death" and "the ministration of condemnation," [10] so that we speak of the curse of the broken law. Paul says: "For as many as are of the works of the law are under the curse: for it is written, Cursed is every one that continueth not in all things which are written in the book of the law to do them." [11]

Inasmuch as not one of us has kept the law, we all come under its curse of death, which is eternal banishment

[9] James 2:10   [10] 2 Corinthians 3:7, 9   [11] Galatians 3:10

from God. Those who go about seeking to establish their own righteousness by the work of the law are making that very law to become a yoke around their necks to keep them in bondage.

One of the major effects of the Spirit's work is to free men from the bondage of the law's condemnation and curse. Just as soon as we put faith in Jesus Christ, who is "the end of the law for righteousness to every one that believeth," [12] the Holy Spirit takes up His abode in the believing heart, freeing him from the curse of the law. This is being free indeed! This glorious liberty into which we are led by the Spirit is the heritage of all saints. We are now delivered from the fear and dread of the penalty of the law, for the Spirit has freed us from both its penalty and its power to slay us. Seeing that the law cannot condemn us, no longer do we fear it. Now we love both the Lawgiver and the law. This great truth has been well expressed in a much used hymn:

> Free from the law, O happy condition!
> Jesus hath bled and there is remission.
> Cursed by the law and bruised by the fall,
> Christ hath redeemed us, once for all!

> Now we are free; there's no condemnation;
> Jesus provides a perfect salvation;
> Come unto Me, O hear His sweet call,
> Come, and He saves us, once for all.

This is the glorious liberty in which the Apostle Paul bids us stand. "Stand fast therefore in the liberty wherewith Christ hath made us free, and be not entangled again

[12] Romans 10:4

with the yoke of bondage." [13] This liberty or freedom was gained for us by our Lord's death and resurrection, and "If the Son therefore shall make you free, ye shall be free indeed." [14]

Under law a person has no freedom of self-determination or decision, but the believer in Christ has every liberty in living his life by his dependence upon the indwelling Holy Spirit. By swinging over to the law, the Judaizers were stultifying their actions, losing that freedom of decision and flexibility of self-will. Having escaped the former slavery, they were in danger of becoming entangled in the old legalistic Judaism.[15]

Emancipation from the law does not mean that one becomes lawless. Contrariwise, he has freedom now to do right and not to do wrong. When Peter testified before the first Church council, he said: "Why tempt ye God, to put a yoke upon the neck of the disciples, which neither our fathers nor we were able to bear?" [16] Peter contends that God should not be tempted by refusing His guidance. The disciples of Christ should not be bound again by the law, but should be allowed to enjoy their new liberty of being guided by the Spirit; for God, "giving them the Holy Ghost," [17] would surely guide them. The test of regeneration by the power of the Holy Spirit lies in its standing and staying power, "For we are made partakers of Christ, if we hold the beginning of our confidence stedfast unto the end." [18] As we obey the voice of the Spirit and follow His leading, we continue in His glorious liberty.

[13] Galatians 5:1   [14] John 8:36   [15] Galatians 4:31
[16] Acts 15:10   [17] Acts 15:8   [18] Hebrews 3:14

FREE FROM THE POWER OF SIN

Just as soon as we yield to the Holy Spirit in regeneration, we discover that there are enemies struggling against us. Our foes are three in number: the world, the flesh, and the devil. Each member of the Holy Trinity has a peculiar power over one of these enemies. The world is the *external* foe[19] and is conquered by the *Father*.[20] Satan is the *infernal* foe[21] and is defeated by the *Son*.[22] The flesh is the *internal* enemy[23] and is overcome by the *Spirit*.[24] While it is true that we have three enemies to face, it is glorious to know that we have the Triune God —Father, Son, and Holy Spirit—to overpower them.

The world is both attractive and alluring; Satan is subtle; but the flesh is the believer's worst enemy. If we are honest, we will admit that most of our difficulties are with ourselves. When we are not victorious over the world and the devil, it is because we are being defeated on the battleground of our own personality. By His indwelling presence, the Holy Spirit seeks to free us from ourselves. This is the second liberty that the Spirit bids us stand fast in, freedom from self. A chaplain said: "The greatest enemy we face aboard our ships is not Jap planes or subs, but rust. Today we scrape, tomorrow we paint so the next day we can scrape again." He went on to say that though the enemies of battle rested from their attacks on certain days, the vicious enemy of rust never rested. We have

[19] James 1:27; 4:4   [20] 1 John 2:15-17
[21] Ephesians 6:11, 12; 1 Peter 5:8   [22] Hebrews 2:14; 1 John 3:8
[23] John 3:6; Romans 7:18   [24] Galatians 5:16, 17

found it even so with ourselves. There are days when the world holds no attraction for us and the devil seems to be miles away from us, but there is never a day that we are not troubled with the capital "I."

The source of sin is the sin nature, and there is abundant testimony in the Bible to the fact that the old nature is a part of the believer so long as he remains in this earthly body. The use of the word "flesh" is not confined to the physical body, but it has a moral or ethical meaning which applies to the unregenerate nature of man. When we are born again, we become partakers of the divine nature, to be certain, but we have not completely ridden ourselves of the old nature. In each individual child of God there is the presence of the two opposing natures. Paul says: "The flesh lusteth against the Spirit, and the Spirit against the flesh: and these are contrary the one to the other." [25] We speak rather glibly about "consecration" and "full surrender," but I fear we use these terms rather carelessly. As long as we are seeking our own interests, there is little use of our speaking about these things. And yet we must confess that our experiential knowledge of full surrender is little indeed. And why is there so much defeat within? It is simply because the Spirit of God is not having His way in our lives. He longs to free us from the power of sin, but we will not let Him.

The sinful nature of man, which is the result of the Fall, has a propensity for evil. All of us know too well that there have been times when we desired to do wrong. Every wrong thought and act is sinful, and sin brings the

* Galatians 5:17

soul into bondage. Whether it is prayerlessness, unbelief, hatred, jealousy, it is sin that binds us.

All Christians have been delivered from the penalty of sin, but not all are daily being delivered from the power of sin. Many are in bondage today as they never have been before. True, there are not the dark dungeons, clanking chains, and torturing taskmasters; but there is the slavery of sin. Souls are in bondage whether men realize it or not. The Israelites were God's people, but as long as they dwelt among the Egyptians, "they made their lives bitter with hard bondage." [26] Paul exhorts believers to "be not entangled again with the yoke of bondage." [27]

Every child of God can and should experience an unfettered freedom from sin, "For, brethren, ye have been called unto liberty; only use not liberty for an occasion to the flesh." [28] All false religions and sects promise their dupes liberty and license, but "While they promise them liberty, they themselves are the servants of corruption: for of whom a man is overcome, of the same is he brought in bondage." [29] No false and evil teacher who is enslaved by the sins of legality and professionalism can promise liberty to those who follow him.

He who is truly born again must be guided by the Spirit; he cannot yield to the flesh. The flesh is weak, sick, and diseased. Paul says: "I speak after the manner of men because of *the infirmity of your flesh*." [30] It is sinful [31] and unclean; [32] therefore we must confess with the apostle: "I know that in me (that is, in my flesh,) dwel-

---

[26] Exodus 1:14
[29] 2 Peter 2:19
[32] Galatians 5:19
[27] Galatians 5:1
[30] Romans 6:19
[28] Galatians 5:13
[31] Romans 8:3

leth no good thing." [33] "We are debtors, not to the flesh," [34] and should therefore "make not provision for the flesh." [35] "This I say then, Walk in the Spirit, and ye shall not fulfil the lust of the flesh." [36]

The Christian lives by a law, but it is the law of liberty. James says: "Whoso looketh into the perfect law of liberty, and continueth therein, he being not a forgetful hearer, but a doer of the work, this man shall be blessed in his deed." [37] And then he continued: "So speak ye, and so do, as they that shall be judged by the law of liberty." [38] May we repeat that true freedom, which is the freedom of the Spirit, is not freedom to do wrong; it is freedom to do right.

Dr. D. G. Barnhouse once said: "The Christian is in the position of a prisoner who has been sitting in his prison cell and who is handed a pardon and the key to his cell. If he will turn the lock he may walk out in perfect freedom. Christianity would not be the glorious thing that it is were there nothing but a pardon provided. There must be deliverance as well as pardon."

How sad to find Christians who, having been freed from the power of sin, are willing to leave the place of freedom that has been provided, take the key, open the cell, and go back from time to time into the atmosphere of the cell! We should recognize clearly that the taste for the life of the former prison cell is a corrupt and a depraved taste. And every time we turn from fellowship with God to return to the beggarly elements of this world, we are walking in the flesh and not in the Spirit. Let us

[33] Romans 7:18   [34] Romans 8:12   [35] Romans 13:14
[36] Galatians 5:16 ·   [37] James 1:25   [38] James 2:12

therefore, present our bodies living sacrifices, holy, and acceptable unto Him, and let us walk in the Spirit so that we will not fulfill the lusts of the flesh. Ours is "the glorious liberty of the children of God." [39] "Ye have been called unto liberty; only use not liberty for an occasion to the flesh, but by love serve one another." [40]

FREEDOM OF SPEECH

Shameful silence is one of the sins of saints. Before His ascension into Heaven our Lord said to His disciples: "Ye shall receive power, after that the Holy Ghost is come upon you: and ye shall be witnesses unto Me." [41] Jesus knew from past experience with His disciples that they lacked the freedom of speech, and so He instructed them that the Spirit's coming would give them holy boldness and wisdom in speaking His message. No sooner had the Spirit descended upon them at Pentecost than they discovered that both power and wisdom of speech was theirs. Luke says: "The Spirit gave them utterance." [42]

The Holy Spirit not only imparted a new life but a new liberty also. Cowards who were shamefully speechless were now made bold heralds of the gospel. No doubt the disciples were startled and fearful when Christ commissioned them to go forth into all the world and preach the gospel. But our Lord anticipated their fear and weakness and strengthened their spirits by assuring them that the Spirit's coming would give them power and utterance.

One of the first qualifications to be a spokesman for God is courage. We must admit that in some respects the

[39] Romans 8:21   [40] Galatians 5:13   [41] Acts 1:8
[42] Acts 2:4

disciples were not cowards. They engaged themselves in the hard and dangerous occupation of fishing in the Galilean waters. The continuance of their task helped to toughen their physical fibers. On more than one occasion they displayed a daring to do the difficult. James and John pitilessly would have called down fire from heaven to destroy an entire village of Samaritans.[43] Peter displayed aggressive fearlessness when he "stretched out his hand, and drew his sword, and struck a servant of the high priest's, and smote off his ear." [44] Again he boasted of fearlessness when he said: "Lord, I am ready to go with Thee, both into prison, and to death." [45] Henry W. Frost says: "Such men were no poltroons and they would have manifested this if the Lord had led them forth to physical battles. But, in spite of such equipment, they lacked a vital element to make them prepared for the hidden and undramatic conflict to which Christ had called them, for, all the while, they were moral cowards." Poor Peter stood outside the judgment hall trembling, and when the damsel asked if he were Christ's disciple, his moral cowardice shone forth, as he answered: "I am not." [46]

But how glorious the change when the Spirit came! These same men who were victims of fear and cowardice in the presence of their enemies suddenly become mighty victors, speaking with boldness the things of Christ. Yes, it was Peter who delivered that first great sermon on the day of Pentecost. "Peter, standing up with the eleven, lifted up his voice" [47] . . . "and the same day there were added unto them about three thousand souls." [48]

[43] Luke 9:51-54   [44] Matthew 26:51   [45] Luke 22:33
[46] John 18:16, 17   [47] Acts 2:14   [48] Acts 2:41

The devil will not allow a mighty victory for Christ to go unchallenged. When the Sadducees and the Sanhedrin saw the boldness of the disciples, "they commanded them not to speak at all nor teach in the name of Jesus." But Peter and John came right back at them, and said: "Whether it be right in the sight of God to hearken unto you more than unto God, judge ye. For we cannot but speak the things which we have seen and heard." [49] Silencing and shaming God's children is an effective weapon of the enemy. Only as we present ourselves to the Spirit is He free to do His work through us. Liberty and power in witnessing is the birthright of every believer. Sometimes I wonder if Christians say so little for Christ because their lives are inconsistent. Of course, the more we witness the more will be expected of us. If we say little for Christ, we are free to go along with the world. Speaking for Christ requires separation. There are believers who, like Peter, follow their Lord "afar off." They are "worshiping at a safe distance." I am not implying that it is easy to declare one's self on Christ's side. It is extremely difficult. Truly we need the energizing power of the Holy Spirit to make us courageous and bold. Our age needs more burdened Christians who will get out on the street corner and go into rescue missions, hospitals, and jails with the gospel of Christ. How often and earnestly do you distribute gospel tracts and write soul-winning letters to your friends and loved ones? Certainly confession calls for consecration. Let the Spirit of God control you, and He will give you freedom of utterance.

The liberty of the Spirit is essential in the public

[49] Acts 4:13, 19, 20

preaching of God's Word. If the man in the pulpit has not the utterance of the Holy Spirit, he has no message. Too little emphasis is placed upon the preaching, and yet it is a vitally important factor in the work of the ministry. Of our Lord's first recorded sermon we read that He said: "The Spirit of the Lord is upon Me, because He hath anointed Me to preach the gospel." [50] The Son of God was conscious of the Spirit's unction. As a minister, I know that the clergy like to hide behind the excuse that theirs is a "hard field" and that the Church is laboring in "difficult times." But is any field of Christian service easy? Did the Church ever have an easy time of it? The early apostles died martyrs' deaths for preaching the gospel. But when they preached, something happened. The secret to the apostles' success is given by Peter where he says that they "preached the gospel unto you with the Holy Ghost sent down from Heaven." [51] Paul was never at a loss for words. He could testify: "My speech and my preaching was not with enticing words of man's wisdom, but in demonstration of the Spirit and of power." [52] Later he wrote: "Our gospel came not unto you in word only, but also in power, and in the Holy Ghost, and in much assurance." [53] The Word prospered at Thessalonica because it was received as it was preached: "with joy of the Holy Ghost." [54]

A. J. Gordon says: "The true preacher does not simply use the Spirit; he is used by the Spirit." The time has come when all of us preachers might profitably make a survey of our prayer life and pulpit preparation. Great

[50] Luke 4:18   [51] 1 Peter 1:12   [52] 1 Corinthians 2:4
[53] 1 Thessalonians 1:5   [54] 1 Thessalonians 1:6

preaching that moves men toward God comes from men who are Spirit-filled. We live in a day of shallow preaching, and so we are not to be surprised at the shallow conversions and the shallow living. The besetting sins of some preachers are prayerlessness and laziness. The result is that the Holy Spirit is not in the preaching, hence it is powerless and nothing ever happens. The spiritual success of the preacher's work is not measured by the energy expended nor the crowds which gather, but by the empowering presence of the Holy Spirit. Daniel Steele has said: "There can be no substitute for a personal presence endowed with the gift of speech and with the subtle magnetism of an earnest soul fully surrendered to the Holy Spirit as an organ of His suasive power."

But not all powerless preaching can be blamed wholly on the preacher. Some congregations worry the pastor with many insignificant trivialities. Some pastors are expected to be a "Jack-of-all-trades," everyone's errand boy, church janitor.

The early Church was quick to see the importance of Spirit-filled preachers. The apostles refused to neglect the Word of God and prayer. When a multiplicity of duties would have crowded out their private devotion, "Then the twelve called the multitude of the disciples unto them, and said, It is not reason that we should leave the Word of God, and serve tables. Wherefore, brethren, look ye out among you seven men of honest report, full of the Holy Ghost and wisdom, whom we may appoint over this business. But we will give ourselves continually to prayer, and to the ministry of the Word." [55]

[55] Acts 6:2-4

Paul knew something of the difficulty in preaching to a prayerless audience, so he exhorted the Christians to pray "always with all prayer and supplication in the Spirit . . . for me, that utterance may be given unto me, that I may open my mouth boldly, to make known the mystery of the gospel." [56] The Holy Spirit is needed no less in the pew than in the pulpit. The officers and members of the church and Sunday-school must be well acquainted with the Person and operations of the Third Person in the Holy Trinity if our churches are to gain victories. When the Holy Spirit empowers those of you who occupy the pews in your church, you may expect a spiritual awakening such as you have never witnessed. David M. Dawson has said that the silent pew is the curse and blight of Christianity today. Will you allow your church to languish and die for the lack of Spirit-filled men and women in the pews? God forbid.

FREEDOM OF WORSHIP

We enter now upon a phase of the Spirit's liberty that is disesteemed and disregarded in not a few churches. The writer has preached in hundreds of churches, but he must confess that the vast majority of them knew little or nothing of the true meaning of worship. It would almost seem that the average churchgoer has not learned how to worship.

Do we know what worship is? Worship is the exercise of the whole man—heart, mind, will, person, and possessions —in confession, adoration, praise, and prayer to God.

[56] Ephesians 6:18, 19

There can be no true worship apart from unbounded admiration and adoration. Mere outward forms and ceremonies are not worship. Jesus said: "God is a Spirit: and they that worship Him must worship Him in spirit and in truth." [57] Before a man can worship God, truth in the spirit, in the inward parts, is required of him.

A brief word should be said as to *the time of worship.* We speak now, not of individual worship but of that corporate worship of an assembly which is part of the Body of Christ. Certainly the worship of believers in the early Church was not confined to a once-a-week affair. Yet in order to have that corporate worship of all of the local assembly, they came together regularly on the first day of the week. "And upon the first day of the week, when the disciples came together to break bread, Paul preached unto them." [58]

The first day of the week had a peculiar significance to the New Testament Christians,[59] and it is probable that the Apostle John meant the first day of the week when he wrote: "I was in the Spirit on the Lord's day." [60] This does not mean that the Sabbath was changed from Saturday to Sunday, for the word *Sabbath,* as it is used in Scripture to refer to one particular day of the week, always means Saturday, the seventh day of the week. Christians do not observe the Sabbath, for Sunday is not the so-called "Christian Sabbath." The legalistic idea of Sunday that some Christians have, calling it the Sabbath, is wrong. Christian businessmen ought to make it possible for other Christians to assemble on the first day of the

[57] John 4:24   [58] Acts 20:7   [59] 1 Corinthians 16:2
[60] Revelation 1:10

week to worship God.[61] It is a sin to give over this day
and opportunity to pleasure, travel, and frivolity.

Looking into our subject further, we find that there is
a place for worship. We are not implying here that an
individual cannot worship God alone or that a family
cannot worship God at home. Contrariwise, where individual and family worship are neglected, there can be no
growth in grace and in the knowledge of our Lord and
Saviour Jesus Christ. But surely there is nothing that can
take the place of the corporate worship, for "we, being
many, are one body in Christ, and every one members one
of another," [62] "who worship by the Spirit of God," [63]
"Endeavoring to keep the unity of the Spirit in the bond
of peace." [64]

Positionally, there is the unity of the Body of Christ,[65]
but where there is not the unity of the Spirit in worship
there cannot be the liberty of the Spirit. "Now I beseech
you, brethren, by the name of our Lord Jesus Christ, that
ye all speak the same thing, and that there be no divisions
among you; but that ye be perfectly joined together in
the same mind and in the same judgment." [66] There is
then the occasion for the worship of the local church in
the unity of the Spirit. The first day of the week they
"came together," [67] and so should we, "not forsaking the
assembling of ourselves together." [68]

We need the fellowship of saints. It is that blessed communion that is reserved for the household of faith. Those

[61] For a fuller discussion of this subject see the author's work, *Sinai to
Calvary* (*A Dispensationalist Views the Ten Commandments*)
[62] Romans 12:5   [63] Philippians 3:3 R.V.   [64] Ephesians 4:3
[65] Ephesians 5:30   [66] 1 Corinthians 1:10   [67] Acts 20:7
[68] Hebrews 10:25

who seek the house of God once or twice annually—Easter or Christmas—are losing out on one of the sweetest privileges of Christians this side of Heaven. One writer says that "both from experience and observation, the spirit of worship is associated with assembling. No individual will ever sing with the same enthusiasm and the same exultant sentiment that sweeps the heart when a great choir or a great assembly sing together; and no man, in the solitude of the closet, will ever pray with the same enthusiasm and expectation that he feels when his prayers are 'amened' in the hearts of hundreds of others praying with him." When the disciples "were all with one accord in one place . . . they were all filled with the Holy Ghost." [69] This is the glorious liberty of the Spirit when there is oneness of place and purpose. We may not all have the same opinions, but amidst difference of views, there may be that blessed union and unity of the Spirit. More than this, if we are to have the liberty of the Spirit in worship, there must be the unity of the Spirit, "For through Him we both have access by one Spirit unto the Father." [70] "I was glad when they said unto me, Let us go into the house of the Lord." [71]

Pursuing our subject still further we hasten to consider *the atmosphere for worship*. Many church congregations could do with some teaching on this subject. Irreverence and disrespect are shown in the joking, laughter, and unnecessary noises in the house of God. I have noticed with what quiet and solemnness men and women enter an undertaker's parlor to pay respects to the dead. How much more we should be silenced as we enter to worship the living God!

[69] Acts 2:1, 4   [70] Ephesians 2:18   [71] Psalm 122:1

The prophet said: "The Lord is in His holy temple: let all the earth keep silence before Him." [72] Certainly the atmosphere of any local church has a definite reaction upon the life and spirit of its members, for the local Church body is made up of the composite life of its members. When the atmosphere of the church is one of noisy irreverence, the Holy Spirit is grieved and those in attendance cannot possibly derive the benefit that comes to those who worship where there is the liberty of the Spirit.

Unless we are unavoidably detained, we should be in our seats a few minutes before the service begins, to wait prayerfully upon God. Do not rob your church of a wholesome atmosphere for worship by entering with unconfessed sin in your life, holding a grudge against another person, worrying about finances, or domestic difficulties. Satan will see to it that there will be no worship in the freedom of the Spirit unless we are careful to help create the proper atmosphere. Many a Christian has come to God's house and gone away without worshiping the Lord. Let us learn that they that worship God "must worship Him in spirit and in truth." [73]

The question often is asked: *How can God be worshiped?*" Apparently there is much ignorance on this important subject. A full discussion of the subject of worship came from the lips of our Lord as He talked with the Samaritan woman at the well. She had descended from a long line of worshipers, yet Jesus said to Her: "Ye worship ye know not what." [74] She was unable to state satisfactorily the object of her worship.

[72] Habakkuk 2:20   [73] John 4:24   [74] John 4:22

Whom do men worship today? A careful study of the religions of the world show that "every nation made gods of their own." [75] When Paul went to Athens his spirit was stirred when he saw the city wholly given to idolatry. Immediately he gave himself to preaching the gospel, for he preached unto them Jesus and the Resurrection. Certain religious philosophers of the Epicureans and Stoics, upon hearing Paul's message, said: "He seemeth to be a setter forth of strange gods." [76] Now the Athenians themselves were worshipers, for Paul found their city full of idols and altars. One altar in particular arrested his attention. Of this he spoke openly: "As I passed by, and beheld your devotions, I found an altar with this inscription, TO THE UNKNOWN GOD. Whom therefore ye ignorantly worship, Him declare I unto you." [77]

We in America are far from Athens, and yet how near! Dr. G. Campbell Morgan has said: "Philosophy has been permeated with the conceptions of Christ, and is now inclined to ignore Him. We are largely living in the past, and our cities are as full of idols as was Athens. We are still idolaters. The Epicurean is with us still, indifferent. The Stoic is here still, gathered into so-called ethical societies." All true worship has as its object the Triune God: Father, Son, and Holy Spirit. The first of the Ten Commandments says: "Thou shalt have no other gods before Me." [78] Our Lord Jesus confirmed the Father's command when He said to Satan: "It is written, Thou shalt worship the Lord thy God, and Him only shalt thou serve." [79]

[75] 2 Kings 17:29 [76] Acts 17:18 [77] Acts 17:23
[78] Exodus 20:3 [79] Matthew 4:10

When Peter came to the house of Cornelius, we are told that "Cornelius met him, and fell down at his feet, and worshipped him. But Peter took him up, saying, Stand up; I myself also am a man." [80] Our Romanist friends would profit greatly by reading this passage. Only God is to be worshiped, and that through our Lord Jesus Christ. Even angels refuse to be worshiped, and we are not to worship them.[81] "Worship God," said the angel to John, for worship belongs to deity alone. When Christ was born in Bethlehem, they called "His name Emmanuel, which being interpreted is, God with us." [82]

The Christ Child of the manger is the God of Christianity. When the wise men from the distant Orient came to Jerusalem, they sought out the infant Son of God, saying: "Where is He that is born King of the Jews? for we have seen His star in the east, *and are come to worship Him.*" [83] They traveled a great distance, gave months of their time, and overcame national pride to worship the Son of God. May that deep-rooted, burning desire to acclaim the Lord Jesus Christ in worship possess us even as it did the wise men of old until it shall be said: "In His temple doth every one speak of *His* glory." [84]

God Can Be Worshiped in Music. We are aware that some of our brethren in Christ will take exception to what is about to be said. Certain assemblies have ruled music out of their gatherings. While traveling on a train a few years ago, I occupied a seat beside a young man. We were riding but a short distance when a conversation was opened. Soon we began to enjoy mutual fellowship when

[80] Acts 10:25, 26
[81] Colossians 2:18; Revelation 19:10; 22:8, 9
[82] Matthew 1:23
[83] Matthew 2:1, 2
[84] Psalm 29:9

it was known that we both were ministers of the gospel of Jesus Christ. But the sweetness of that fellowship was short-lived when my new friend found out that we use musical instruments in the church where I serve as pastor. He insisted that ours is not a true New Testament Church because nowhere in the New Testament are we told that the early Church used music in the worship service. When he sought to press an argument on the method of baptism, I felt sorry for the poor fellow, for he reminded me of one who strained at a drizzle and swallowed a downpour. Certainly many of God's children have been drawn closer to the Lord Jesus through the sweet strains of a gospel hymn.

Music speaks a language that cannot be expressed by word of mouth. How empty our worship service would be if we had no way of expressing our love to God, and surely songs and music have been excellent outlets for expressing one's self. When we gather to lift up our hearts in Easter praise, we turn to Charles Wesley's beautiful hymn of the Resurrection, "Christ, the Lord, is Risen Today." From the earliest times Christians saluted each other on Easter morning with the phrase, "Alleluia, the Lord is risen," and then the reply, "He is risen indeed." Certainly the glad "Alleluia" at the end of each line of Wesley's hymn is most appropriate on Easter Day. Wesley discovered that many hearts that never could be reached through preaching were touched and won to Christ through music.

Congregational singing, as we know it in our church today, and the use of musical instruments, came with the Protestant Reformation in Europe. Martin Luther, who was an excellent singer and competent player on the flute and the lute, said that music was a gift and a grace of God that could drive out the devil and make men forget all wrath. His famous hymn, "A Mighty Fortress is Our God," has been the instrument of comfort and strength to many a fainting heart.

No life has more admirably illustrated the value of hymnology than the life of Fanny Crosby. She was only six weeks old when her vision was accidentally destroyed. This was a grievous affliction, but Miss Crosby would not allow it to handicap her for life. Yielding her life to God, she was able to hurdle the obstacle of blindness. She refused to permit her affliction to sour her disposition or to dim her spiritual vision. She voiced her cheerful optimism and thereby brought comfort and cheer to millions through the hundreds of her beautiful hymns that have been published, played, and sung all over the world. Who among us has not been blessed by the well-known and best-loved "Sweet Hour of Prayer," "Pass Me Not, O Gentle Saviour," "Safe in the Arms of Jesus," "All the Way My Saviour Leads Me," "Rescue the Perishing," and "Some Day the Silver Cord Will Break"?

Christians should give careful attention to the musical part of the worship program. Christianity has been called "the singing religion." None of the pagan religions had inspiring music. The Hebrews used music, but their choirs and orchestras of stringed instruments were all trained and employed for the temple worship. Only Christianity has a vital and inspiring song in the hearts of all its followers. The saving grace of our Lord Jesus Christ has changed the minor dirge of uncertainty and gloom to the major symphony of hope, joy, and courage.

Good singing aids in making a strong congregation, leading the people into the right mental and spiritual preparation for the Bible message. T. DeWitt Talmage has said: "In a live church all the people take part in the exercises. A stranger can tell by the way the first hymn starts whether it is a live church. It is a sad thing when the music comes down in a cold drizzle and freezes on the heads of the silent people beneath. It is an awful thing for a hymn to start and then find itself lonely and unbefriended, wandering about, after a while lost amid the arches. That is not melody to the Lord. In Heaven they' all sing. A church that can sing can do anything that ought to be done. In this great battle for God let us take the Bible in one hand and the hymnbook in the other, on the way to triumphs without end, and to pleasures that never die. Sing!" Singing that is inspired by the Holy Spirit pleases God and moves men to Jesus Christ.

A. J. Gordon has said: "The service of song in the House of the Lord is another element of worship whose relation to the Spirit needs to be strongly emphasized." When the Apostle Paul, by the Spirit, commanded believers to "be filled with the Spirit," he added: "Speaking to yourselves in psalms and hymns and spiritual songs, singing and making melody in your heart to the Lord." [85]

When we gather for worship and sing praises to our Lord, we are "teaching and admonishing one another in psalms and hymns and spiritual songs." [86] Dr. F. B.

[85] Ephesians 5:18, 19   [86] Colossians 3:16

Meyer wrote an excellent homily, taking as his text the three words hidden away in an Old Testament genealogy, "Heman a singer." [87] He says: "This is a very brief record to put on a man's grave, but a very expressive one. To decipher that epitaph about Heman is to learn a good deal about him. From this clue we might almost construct his entire personality and character. And it would be well if it could be said of us that we had ministered with song before the tabernacle of the Lord. . . . Sing on, dear heart, sing on. There is nothing that scares off the Devil so quickly as a hymn. . . . There is nothing that brings so much of Heaven into the heart. Singing makes every movement rhythmic, every service praise, every act thanksgiving. Sing when times are dark, you will make them bright; sing when the house of life is lonely, it will become peopled with unseen choristers; go down into the valley of shadow with a song, and you will find yourself singing the new song of Moses and the Lamb when you awake on the other side."

God Can Be Worshiped in Giving. Few people look upon the offering in the church service as a vital part of the worship program. However, giving is both a duty and a privilege enjoined upon all believers when they come together in the house of God. When Paul wrote to the Corinthian church, he did not hesitate to say, "Now concerning the collection. . . . Upon the first day of the week let every one of you lay by him in store, as God hath prospered him." [88] From this passage we are to take it that from the very beginning the early Church had set aside gifts which the people presented when they gathered on

[87] 1 Chronicles 6:33   [88] 1 Corinthians 16:1, 2

the Lord's Day. Christianity is very practical indeed, and is never confined to mere lip service.

Giving is both the duty and privilege of us all. "Let *everyone of you* lay by him in store," says the apostle. This Christian duty and privilege is to be withheld from none. All are included. Furthermore, no true child of God would want to be excluded from this blessed act of worship.

The Christian is not only exhorted to give, but to give *regularly,* "Upon the first day of the week." Important events usually take place at stated times. If not, they may be neglected or forgotten. Christians who worship God in the Spirit would no more think of giving to Him spasmodically or irregularly than they would think of neglecting their house rent or allowing a bill to go unpaid. Those who get the deepest satisfaction from their Christian life are the regular givers to the cause of Christ. If a stingy Christian attends the church and robs God, he himself is hindered in worshiping the Lord. "It is required in stewards, that a man be found faithful." [89]

The true worshiper gives proportionately, "as God hath prospered him." We are to learn from this that we are expected to give according to our means. Jesus said: "Unto whomsoever much is given, of him shall be much required." [90] How much freedom have you in giving of your means for the support of the gospel? He who gives proportionately as God has prospered him finds great joy in giving, and "God loveth a cheerful giver." [91] Those saints who were members of the churches of Macedonia

---

[89] 1 Corinthians 4:2　　[90] Luke 12:48　　[91] 2 Corinthians 9:7

enjoyed "the glorious liberty of the children of God," [92] for though they had undergone "a great trial of affliction . . . their deep poverty abounded unto the riches of their liberality." [93] Christian giving that is in the liberty of the Spirit is always cheerful, purposeful, and bountiful.

Praying and preaching in the power of the Holy Spirit are a definite part of the worship service also, but we have reserved these for a discussion elsewhere in this volume.

[92] Romans 8:21   [93] 2 Corinthians 8:2

THE LOVE OF THE SPIRIT

"For the Lord Jesus Christ's sake, and for the love of the Spirit." [1]

We are approaching one of the most precious and popular themes in all the Bible. Though we live in a changing world, here is an abiding value that we can never lose. Death nor drought, fire nor flood, privation nor poverty can ever wrest it from our hands and hearts. Here, then, is a treasure that endures. It is as eternal as God Himself. "And now abideth faith, hope, *love*, these three; but the greatest of these is *love*." [2]

GOD IS LOVE

The first assuring truth of the gospel is that "God is love." We live in a day when men question the love of God. But we can expect doubt from the unregenerate heart and the unrenewed mind. The great truth that "God is love" has been revealed to man in the Word of God, and unless a man is willing to accept the Bible as God's Word, he may encounter great difficulty in accepting so sublime a truth. The words "God is love" are probably the greatest words that ever have been written. [3]

We are to learn first that love has no origin. Since God is eternal and has no origin, love is eternal and has no

[1] Romans 15:30   [2] 1 Corinthians 13:13   [3] 1 John 4:8, 16

origin, for God is love. I have just finished reading a score of definitions and explanations of love, but each definition needs to be defined and each explanation needs to be explained. There was a time when my parents commenced to love me just as there was a time when I commenced to love our two boys. But there never was a time when God commenced to love us. God has loved us ever since He was God, and He always has been God from all eternity. He says: "I have loved thee with an everlasting love." [4]

We never can say that the love of God was called forth by our love to Him. His love came first. A mother was heard telling her little daughter: "If you obey Mother, God will love you; but if you disobey, God will not love you." What sheer nonsense! How false! The truth of the matter is that God always has and always will love us. He cannot do otherwise, for God is love. If He could cease to love, He would cease to be God.

When the human mind has gone back to the first records of sacred and secular history, it is no nearer the beginning of God's love than it is now. To say that God's love towers like a mountain or descends beyond the depth of the deepest sea beggars description. That which is eternal can never be measured by the things of time.

> He loved me, ere one ray of light
> Had flashed itself across the boundless sky,
> When all was solitude and starless night,
> He loved me then; and shall it ever die?
>
> Ah, no, that love shall onward, onward roll,
> Increasing in its flow, till like the sea,

[4] Jeremiah 31:3

It breaks in thrills of rapture on the soul,
And spends itself through all eternity.

"God is love." Do you believe it? This truth will transform any life and make it anew. R. A. Torrey relates the following story: "When Mr. Moody built his tabernacle in Chicago, he was so anxious that every one that came there should learn one truth, namely, that 'God is love,' and so fearful that some day some preacher might stand in the pulpit and forget to tell the people that God is love, that he had these three words put into gas jets over the pulpit. So every night when the gas was lighted, there it blazed away over the preacher's head, 'God is love.' Whether the preacher told it to the people or not, they could see it for themselves in letters of fire. One night the tabernacle was lighted, but the people had not yet gathered for the evening service. A poor drunkard coming up the street saw the door a little ajar and saw the light, and then stumbled up the steps hoping to find warmth and cheer within. As he pushed the door a little wider, his attention was directed to the sentence in the letters of fire above the pulpit: 'God is love.' He turned away, pulled the door to, went down the steps and went up the street muttering, 'It is not so. That is not true. God is not love. If God were love, He would love me, and God does not love a miserable wretch like me. It is not true.' But all the time, the words were burning down into his soul, 'God is love. God is love.' After a while he turned about and retraced his steps, entered the church again, and took a seat behind the stove over in the corner. Mr. Moody's quick eye caught sight of him, and at the close of the service he hurried to him and sat down beside him. 'What are you crying about, my friend?' he said gently. 'What was it in the sermon that touched you?' The man replied, 'There was nothing in the sermon that touched me. I did not hear a word of your sermon.' 'Well, what was it then that touched you?' asked Mr. Moody. 'That sentence,' pointing to the words in fire, 'that sentence, "God is love." ' Mr. Moody opened his Bible and showed the man from the Bible how God loved him, and how Jesus was an all-sufficient Saviour for all who take Him. The man listened and accepted Christ, and went away that night a saved man."

Yes, "God is love," and it makes us repeat what Robert G. Lee has so beautifully written: "God's love is above and beyond all love as a river is beyond a rill in reach, as the sun is beyond a tallow dip in brightness, as a tree is beyond a twig in fruit bearing, as the wings of an eagle are beyond the feet of a snail in swiftness, as an ocean is beyond a mud-hole in depth, as a mountain is beyond a cave in lofty grandeur, as the perfume of flowers is beyond the odors of a garbage can, as the glories of a dawn are beyond the gaudy stage lights. What depths beyond all fathoming is His love! What heights beyond all climbing is His love! What expanse beyond all measuring is His love! What beauty beyond all describing, what sweetness beyond all absorbing is His love!" But after we have exhausted our vocabulary in an endeavor to describe the love of God, we have merely uttered words.

God proved that He loved us when He sent His Son to die in our stead. "But God commendeth His love toward

us, in that, while we were yet sinners, Christ died for us." [5]
Look within you. Gaze upon the blackness and corruption
of your own heart. Then look away to the Cross and fix
your eyes upon the Substitute who died for you, and you
too will say with the apostle: "We have known and believed the love that God hath to us. God is love." [6] The
priceless evidence of God's love toward the sinner is in
his possession of eternal life received through the Holy
Spirit who is given unto him. Man might die for a loved
one or a dear friend, but only God would die for His
enemies. God hated with bitter hatred man's sin, but He
loved with a great and a yearning heart the sinner. Let us
never forget the first sign of love came from God, not from
us. "Not that we loved God, but that He loved us, and
sent His Son to be the propitiation for our sins." [7] Love is
spiritual. It chooses its object with decision and determination and thus it becomes self-denying. Such is the
love of God. God is love.

GOD'S LOVE IS FOUR-DIMENSIONAL

Love is impossible of definition. This is so because the
love of God reaches far back into eternity past. One of
the great revelations of the Bible is the mutual love of the
Father and the Son. Jesus Himself referred to this great
love when He said: "Thou lovedst Me before the foundation of the world." [8] Of our Lord, we read: "Having loved
His own which were in the world, He loved them unto the
end." [9] Even now He "loveth us." [10] He never ceases to
love. He goes on loving us.

[5] Romans 5:8   [6] 1 John 4:16   [7] 1 John 4:10
[8] John 17:24   [9] John 13:1   [10] Revelation 1:5

The Apostle Paul, by the Holy Spirit and the use of his sanctified, daring imagination, gives us the fourfold dimension of the love of God—"the breadth, and length, and depth, and height." [11]

God's Love Is Broad. D. L. Moody was accused by the modernists of his day as being narrow, because he constantly preached the love of God. But Jesus said that "God so loved the world." Now, you will agree that this is not narrow. God's love is broad enough to include all men, everywhere. God's love embraces the fierce, bloodthirsty, degraded, miserable, and most wretched beings who have ever lived. God's love embraces the most unlovely and the most unattractive so that "whosoever" will may come. From the remote corners of the globe resounds the echo of a universal, inclusive, extensive, impartial love, the love of the Father that sent the Son to be the Saviour of the world. The love of God—oh! so broad! Only by the Spirit's strengthening can we come to comprehend the knowledge of the breadth of such love.

God's Love Is Long. "*And length,*" adds Paul. How long is the love of God? It is not merely as long as a dispensation, or a decade, or a generation. God's love is as long as eternity. In the mind of God, from before the foundation of the world, God loved us, yet uncreated. The Bible tells us that Jesus Christ was as a Lamb slain before the foundation of the world.[12] When this great truth is believed we see the love of God in action, removing our sins from us as far as the east is from the west. Truly, His love is long.

One day we were driving along the Lincoln Highway,

[11] Ephesians 3:18   [12] Revelation 13:8

parallel to the Pennsylvania Railroad. A long string of freight cars caught the eyes of our boys. They could see freight cars as far as visibility permitted in both directions. Our younger boy was the first to speak: "That's the longest thing in the whole world!" Perhaps what he said was true in his own little world. But when we come to see the blackness of our sin and then, in contrast, view the love of God in Christ, we exclaim in rapturous tones, "That's the longest thing in the world!" But only by the enlightenment of the Holy Spirit are we able to come to a knowledge of the length of God's love.

God's Love Is Deep. By the Holy Spirit the apostle continues his description of this four-dimensional love by adding the words: *"and depth."* Can the human mind fathom the depth of His wonderful love? The Scriptures declare that Jesus "is able to save them to the uttermost that come unto God by Him." [13] The statement is tremendous. By it is meant that He saves from the uttermost depths of sin and degradation. "He brought me up also out of an horrible pit, out of the miry clay." This was the testimony of the Psalmist.[14] His fathomless love is deep enough to reach down into the depths of a poor sinner's need. Isaiah said: "He led them through the deep." [15] No man is sunk so deep in sin that Christ cannot save him, for "In His hand are the deep places." [16] The wonder of such a love is too deep for the finite mind to lay hold of, "But God hath revealed [it] unto us by His Spirit: for the Spirit searcheth all things, yea, the deep things of God." [17]

[13] Hebrews 7:25   [14] Psalm 40:2   [15] Isaiah 63:13
[16] Psalm 95:4   [17] 1 Corinthians 2:10

God's Love Is High. And how high is His love? It is higher tnan our thoughts. "It is high, I cannot attain unto it." [18] But God has made it possible for us to know His love. We need not go higher than Mount Calvary, for there on Golgotha's brow His Son was lifted up to die, and thank God, He was not lifted up above the view of man. His love reaches to the heights of the most cultured members of society, yet not too high for the unlearned and ignorant.

> O wide-embracing, wondrous love,
> We read thee in the sky above;
> We read thee in the earth below,
> In seas that swell, and streams that flow.
>
> We read thee best in Him who came
> To bear for us the Cross of shame,
> Sent by the Father from on high,
> Our life to live, our death to die.
>
> O love of God, our shield and stay
> Through all the perils of our way;
> Eternal love, in Thee we rest,
> Forever safe, forever blest.
>
> HORATIUS BONAR

It is essential that we have in our minds this mathematical framework of the fourfold conception of the love of God—*breadth, length, depth,* and *height.* Love is a glorious thing, and there is nothing in Heaven or in earth more glorious than the love of God as it was manifested in Christ at Calvary. Annie Johnson Flint has put into verse this great text of the fourfold conception of divine love.

[18] Psalm 139:6

How broad is His love? Oh, as broad as man's trespasses,
  As wide as the need of the world can be;
And yet to the need of one soul it can narrow—
  He came to the world and He came to me.

How long is His love? Without end or beginning,
  Eternal as Christ and His life it must be,
For to everlasting as from everlasting
  He loveth the world and He loveth me.

How deep is His love? Oh, as deep as man's sinning,
  As low as that uttermost vileness can be;
In the fathomless gulf of the Father's forsaking
  He died for the world and He died for me.

How high is His love? It is high as the heavens,
  As high as the throne of His glory must be;
And yet from that height He hath stooped to redeem us
  He so loved the world and He so loved me.

How great is His love? Oh, it passeth all knowledge,
  No man's comprehension its measure can be;
It filleth the world, yet each heart may contain it—
  He so loves the world and He so loves me.

ANNIE JOHNSON FLINT

This is the love of the Spirit. God is a Spirit; God is love. When we are regenerated by the Spirit, then it is that we enter into our first lessons of this mighty subject. Love is mysterious and undefinable to those who have not the Spirit, but to the believer it becomes the glorious revelation of the heart of God. His compassion He expressed to the prophet Hosea: "My heart is turned within Me, My compassions are kindled together." [19]

[19] Hosea 11:8 R.V.

THE HOLY SPIRIT IMPARTS HIS LOVE

The Apostle Paul wrote: "The love of God is shed abroad in our hearts by the Holy Ghost which is given unto us." [20] Man is naturally selfish. In each of us there is the urge to advance our own interest, enlarge our own prestige, defend our own rights, promote our own prosperity. The strain of self-love runs in us all. In some, it is the dominant strain, while in others it is the understrain. There is that branch of science called sociology, or the science of living together. Those who occupy the highest chairs in this field tell us that the intelligent man is interested not only in his own welfare, but in the welfare of others. And we must admit that there is in the world a measure of philanthropy and humanitarianism. However, an honest sociologist, when investigating the laws and forces which regulate human society, will acknowledge that this branch of science has not found as yet the solution to the international unrest and hatred, the labor difficulties which have resulted in bloodshed, and the domestic problems which keep the divorce courts active.

There is something lacking in the hearts of men like the Russian Czars who let four and one-half million peasants starve in order to force millions more to submit to their rule. Where is the advancement of the science of sociology in Nazi Germany where millions of Jews were tortured and slain? The Bataan "death march" proves beyond a shadow of a doubt that the Japanese who were educated in American schools and colleges did not find the science of sociology sufficient to subdue their passion for power,

[20] Romans 5:5

their ambition to acquire, and their uncontrolled mania to murder in cold blood.

In his description of this age, the Apostle Paul says that "men shall be lovers of their own selves." [21] Here self is seen taking the place of God. Calvin says: "He who loveth himself claims a superiority in everything, despises all others, is cruel." How true this statement has proved to be during recent years! The Nazi and Japanese soldiers cared for nothing but themselves, their power, their career; hence their ruthless and brutal treatment of the conquered peoples. This love of self is unchristian, and only proves that he who seeks his own interest and loves self first is the enemy of God. True love "seeketh not her own." [22]

Our Lord Jesus Christ made a positive contribution to sociology. He loved with an unchanging and unchangeable love, and then He commanded His followers to go and do likewise. His own selfless love was always in the interest of others. The First Commandment is that we should love the Lord our God with our whole being, heart, soul, mind, and strength. The Second Commandment follows with the teaching that we should love our neighbor as ourselves. Paul tells us that "all the law is fulfilled in one word, even in this; Thou shalt love thy neighbor as thyself." [23] Adding his divinely inspired comment, James says: "If ye fulfill the royal law according to the Scripture, Thou shalt love thy neighbor as thyself, ye do well." [24] The whole legal system was a denunciation of selfishness and an urge to brotherly love. Now we are not

[21] 2 Timothy 3:2   [22] 1 Corinthians 13:5   [23] Galatians 5:14
[24] James 2:8

under the law, but under grace, and only as we are saved by grace and stand in grace are we able to obey the injunction to love. The moment a man is born again, the Holy Spirit sheds abroad in his heart the love of God. Love is the Spirit's fruit[25] which is poured forth from the great loving heart of the Father.

"LOVEST THOU ME?"

God's love imparted to us by His Spirit should motivate our love. It should cause us to love Him. John writes: "We love Him, because He first loved us." [26] His love came first; ours follows. If the love of God has been shed abroad in our hearts by the Holy Spirit, then it follows that we will love Him, and "He that loveth not knoweth not God." [27]

Our salvation cost God the blood of His own dear Son. What does our salvation cost us? God is not a merchant seeking to sell salvation to sinners. God did not barter Heaven's treasure for some earthly commodity. But since His love for us compelled Him to offer Jesus Christ for our redemption, He asks that we love Him in return. We are His creatures, and His Father-heart longs for our affection.

We must know Him to love Him, and to know Him is to love Him. Why does God love all people everywhere? F. W. Boreham says: "God loves them because He knows them. We always love people if we know them. It is always safe to conclude that if we do not love a man, it is because we do not know him. We do not know the world, and therefore we do not love the world. But God knows

[25] Galatians 5:22   [26] 1 John 4:19   [27] 1 John 4:8

the world and therefore 'God so loved the world.' " Now
let us ask ourselves whether we love God; if we do not, it
is because we do not know Him.

God does not call upon the unconverted to love Him,
for said Jesus: "I know you, that ye have not the love of
God in you." [28] First, the Father wants men to receive the
gift of His love, the Lord Jesus Christ. We cannot share
with others what we ourselves do not possess. There is a
close relation between the Spirit and the love of God, and
when the Spirit enters our hearts, His love enters to possess us. True Christian love is not merely human love;
it is definitely a manifestation of divine love operating
through the human heart. It is the answer to our Lord's
prayer: "That the love wherewith Thou hast loved Me
may be in them." [29] Where there is no love, there is no
life.

There is both an interesting and instructive passage in
the closing portion of the Gospel according to John. It is
one of our Lord's postresurrection appearances to His
disciples. After their tiring night of fruitless angling, the
Saviour appeared to them in the mists of early morning.
It never occurred to the disciples that it might be Jesus.
At first they did not recognize Him, but then He made
Himself known. Their misfortune and physical discomfort
were at once recognized by Him. He filled their nets, fed
their bodies, and furnished them with a warm fire; for
they were drenched and chilled.

Then He asked a question. Three times He propounded
it straight at the heart of Peter: "So when they had dined,
Jesus saith to Simon Peter, Simon, son of Jonas, lovest

[28] John 5:42   [29] John 17:26

thou Me more than these?" [30] The question is one of
contrast and comparison, and exactly what Jesus meant
by "these" we cannot tell. Jesus may have meant the
disciples, for these were Peter's pleasure, his pastime, his
profit. But whatever the Saviour meant, I am inclined to
believe that He was thinking of anything and everything
that bids for our affection. Jesus was about to leave this
earth, but before He ascended He must leave His holy
work with the disciples. Therefore He had a right to ask
them how much they loved Him. They were going to serve
Him, and any measure of success in His service is dependent upon our devotion to Him. Before our Lord assigns
any task to us to perform, He asks for our love. Jesus
knows that when we have love we are quick to obey and
willing to sacrifice.

Hence our Lord's thrice-asked question to Peter at
the sea of Galilee. Why three times? Certainly it was
not because Jesus doubted Peter's answer or affection, but
because Peter had denied his Lord three times, and must
three times openly avow his love and loyalty to the
Saviour. How considerate on the part of our Lord! He
did not expose Peter's sin and put him to shame by making an open show of his failures, yet how deftly He
probed the heart of Simon. Every act and word was a
reminder to Peter of his past failings. It was while he
stood around "a fire of coals" [31] that Peter denied any
knowledge of Christ. Here again there is a fire of coals,
and Peter cannot escape the past. Jesus even called him
"Simon," carrying Peter's mind back to the day when
the Master had first called him by that name. By this time

[30] John 21:15   [31] John 18:18

Peter knew that Christ wanted his love before anything else.

The qualifications for effective service is that of love for the Lord. This application suits us all, for the debtorship of love is binding upon all. Does God have a right to ask for our affections? Indeed so! Wherever there is fidelity and faithfulness, love's obligation is never shirked or shifted. Can you not hear the risen Lord asking you even now: "Lovest thou Me?"

Not many days after that memorable meeting on the shore of the lake, Peter and the rest of the disciples received a baptism of love that they never had experienced before. The occasion was the day of Pentecost when the Holy Spirit descended and the love of God was shed abroad in their hearts. It was a new Peter who delivered that first great address at Pentecost. The love he expressed for his Lord and the compassion he showed for lost souls after Pentecost is nowhere revealed in the Gospel records. The Book of Acts shows that the same was true of the rest of the disciples. They were possessed by a love that was possible only through the operative power of the Holy Spirit. The Apostle Peter had scarcely gotten through the introduction to his first Epistle when he penned the words: "Whom having not seen, ye love." [32] How can we love anyone whom we have not seen? How can we love Him who died and rose for us if we have not seen Him? How can we love the dark-skinned natives in the jungles if we have not seen them? The answer is given us in the Word of God, and it is the whole burden of this chapter: "The love of God is shed abroad in our hearts

[32] 1 Peter 1:8

by the Holy Spirit which is given unto us." If we love Him, it is through the Spirit's imparting and impulse. It could not be otherwise.

CONSTRAINING LOVE

Love Produces Service. The Apostle Paul could testify: "For the love of Christ constraineth us." [33] That was Paul's testimony, and he wished the same for us all. In reading the Epistles of this mighty apostle, we cannot escape his oft-repeated reference to himself: "I serve." [34] Service is a virtue by which Paul lived and died, and whether he lived or died for his Lord, it was to him a "reasonable service." Now not all service is the product of love, but whenever the love of Christ is constraining us, we are serving Him. Love's constraint has no room for idleness. Idle hands are loveless hands.

The presence of the love of God in our hearts will lead us into a reasonable service for Him. We are saved to serve. There is no place for idlers in the Church of the living God. Even in this world, there is no place for people who refuse to work. When Jesus stood face to face with the man born blind, He saw one who needed help. Seeing the need, our Lord was moved to pity. Human need always stirred Him to action. Can you stand face to face with human need and do nothing about it? When in the history of the world have so many people needed help? All about us there is economic insecurity, industrial uncertainty, mental confusion, and spiritual wandering. Do these conditions move you to compassion and action? Seeing the need of the blind man, Jesus said: "I must work the

[33] 2 Corinthians 5:14   [34] Acts 27:23; Romans 1:9; 2 Timothy 1:3, etc.

works of Him that sent Me." [35] Meeting human need was a must with the Son of God. Is it so with you, with me? The fruit of the Spirit is love, and when He is allowed to live and love through us, then we will be constrained to serve.

Our day is witnessing in the Church a restraining from service instead of the constraining to service. We know that God loves us and that the love of God is in our hearts. Knowing our own hearts as we do, this great truth would be almost unbelievable if we did not see it with our own eyes in the Word of God. Think of it! The very love of God is shed abroad in my little, sin-scarred, self-possessed heart! Of this love, then, we are representatives of God to this unlovely and loveless mass of humanity. The Apostle Paul argues the necessity of earnest enthusiasm in Christ's service on the ground that the Saviour's constraining love will carry us along with the impetuosity of a driving torrent. Love is the most powerful motive to devoted service to Jesus Christ. The crying need of this and every generation is the heroic demonstration of what we say we believe. If we are to be identified with Christ in this life, then it follows that ours must be a course of action. Jesus lived on the plane of spiritual, self-sacrificing service. So must we, for it is the love of Christ which constrains us.

When we are constrained by the love of God, we are serving our friends. Jesus said: "Greater love hath no man than this, that a man lay down his life for his friends." [36] This is exactly what our Lord did for His friends. And why? In order that He might bring us to

[35] John 9:4   [36] John 15:13

God. Friends are those with whom we share our secrets, and Jesus would not have been a Friend to sinners if He had withheld God's plan of salvation from us. But His love would not permit Him to remain silent and indifferent about the need of the soul.

How would you feel toward a Christian who was your close friend for twenty years, but yet made no effort to influence you to Christ? I once read of two such men. One day Jim, the unsaved man, said to his friend: "John, how long have we been friends?"

"About twenty years," came John's reply.

"We have never had any differences, have we, to speak of?"

"No, Jim, we have been pretty good buddies. We have hunted, fished, camped, and lived together with scarcely a ripple of unpleasantness."

"John, how long have you been a Christian?"

"I guess around thirty years," John answered.

"Well, John, I must say I don't believe much in your brand of Christianity. If it is the real thing, it must teach you to love people, and you don't love me a particle, and I am your best friend."

John began to defend himself, but Jim pressed on in his conversation and continued: "You have been a Christian for thirty years, and my friend for twenty years, and in all those years you have never opened your lips to me about your Saviour, or the need of my own soul."

Oh, Christian, where is the love that we confess with our lips? Have we spoken to our friends about their relation to our Lord Jesus Christ? The friend and watcher of lost souls is on the alert to witness because the love of the

Spirit possesses him, that early love of the soul when it first fell in love with the Lord. The highest human love at its best is a weak and sentimental thing, but the heart that is fired by the love of Christ is brave and bold and burning with a desire to see its friends saved.

When we are constrained by the love of Christ, we are serving our enemies. Paul reminds us that it was *"while we were yet sinners,* Christ died for us" and that "when we were enemies, we were reconciled to God by the death of His Son." [37] "And you, that were sometime alienated and enemies in your mind by wicked works, yet now hath He reconciled." [38] Jesus could say: "Love ye your enemies, and do good, and lend, hoping for nothing again; and your reward shall be great, and ye shall be the children of the Highest: for He is kind unto the unthankful and to the evil." [39]

When we set out to love those who are opposed to us, our assignment is not easy. We know, further, that the highest human love could never accomplish this task. Only by the Spirit's presence in one's life can any of us love our enemies. The talk of the liberal that human love and divine love are one and the same thing is far from the truth. We can love our enemies—yes—but only as the love of Christ constraineth us. Of course, the extent of our service to our enemies is dependent upon the measure of our love to Christ.

We can serve our enemies under a power other than love. Men sometimes practice obedience and render acts of service under the influence of fear or under a conviction of duty, "like an honest Pharisee of the olden time, to

[37] Romans 5:8, 10   [38] Colossians 1:21   [39] Luke 6:27, 35

observe rigidly the enactments of the law; but there will be no heart in his obedience, and no holy passion in his soul. But let the love of God be shed abroad in his heart by the Holy Ghost given unto him, let there be a perception of love in God, let there be sight of the Crucified as well as of the Cross, and there will be at once a passion filling the whole soul with vehemence of absorbing desire."

During the early part of World War II, Hitler had hundreds of thousands serving him, but that service was given under force and fear. None of Hitler's prisoners could ever say: "The love of Hitler constrains me." They feared his hatred, and so they served him to spare their own lives. We all would do the same. But no Christian serves the enemies of Christ and ministers to their need under the powers of fear or force. His love has won our hearts, and it is that divine love that constrains me to identify myself with Jesus Christ in His interests in other people. His love in me directs me to be as kind to others as He has been to me.

Love Prompts Sacrifice. When the love of Christ is constraining us, we do not stop to count the cost. The highest human love will often prompt sacrifice, but only Christ's love in us and through us is able to make Christlike men of us. A pig grovels in the mud satisfying its selfish desires because that is the pig's nature. The pig will never fly to the heights of the eagle, simply because by nature it knows nothing of the desires and the possibilities which the eagle possesses. To change a pig in the mud to an eagle soaring high in the sun, the pig's nature must be exchanged for that of the eagle. And until such an exchange were made, if it could be, the pig would remain a pig in its slime.

So it is concerning the sacrifice of Christ and man. Being selfish and sinful by nature, man will continue to grovel selfishly in his own slime until the love of Christ is substituted for the old selfish life. When His love is having its way, sacrifice is substituted for selfishness. His love in us obliterates the old degrading desires, and we pay the price, whatever it is, so that others may see Christ in us. Self-enthronement is never prompted by the love of Christ. "The deepest affection in the believing heart will always be the love of Jesus. The love of home, the love of friends, the love of letters, the love of rest, the love of travel, and all else, are contracted by the side of this master passion." So said Pushon. Love is never guided by gold, fed by the passion of fame, pressed into service for popularity, nor bound by law. Even if we were to engage ourselves in sacrificial service which was not moved by the love of Christ, it all would be cold and heartless.

In one of his brilliant esays, F. W. Boreham tells of receiving an interesting letter concerning one of Europe's most eminent pianists. His recitals were crowding the most spacious auditoriums in Europe with ecstatic admirers. But a kind critic had this to say about the famed artist: "He was a lonely, taciturn man, and a certain coldness and aloofness stole into his play." However, one day a famous woman pianist, older in years and experience, laid her hand on the shoulder of the brilliant young performer, and said: "Will you let me tell you, my boy, that your playing lacks one thing? So far you have missed the greatest thing in the world. And, *unless you fall in love,* there will always be a certain cold perfection about your music. Unless you come to love another human being passionately and unselfishly, you will never touch human hearts as deeply as you might."

Lift the application of this story over into the realm of the spiritual. Unless we are impelled by divine love, there is something cold and unspiritual about our service and our sacrifice. Certainly I must say with assurance that my human best, minus the love of Christ is unprofitable, for "though I bestow all my goods to feed the poor, and though I give my body to be burned, and have not love, it profiteth me nothing." [40] Yet, to be controlled and constrained by His love will plunge me madly into a Spirit-guided mission for Him. When in the dungeon at Aberdeen, Rutherford said: "Oh, my Lord, if there were a broad hell betwixt me and Thee, if I could not get at Thee except by wading through it, I would not think twice but I would plunge through it all, if I might embrace Thee." Rutherford was constrained by divine love, and we believe that he meant what he said. Love will unite our hearts to the Saviour in unbroken fellowship, but it will also bind us to the lost and brokenhearted.

The moment the Holy Spirit comes into the heart, bringing with Him the love of God, we are drawn away from those things that are against love for Him. There may be times when our desires are driven in two directions, but if the Holy Spirit is in control, we may be sure that the love of Christ will constrain us. Paul had such

[40] 1 Corinthians 13:3

an experience when he said: "I am in a strait betwixt two, having a desire to depart, and to be with Christ; which is far better: Nevertheless to abide in the flesh is more needful for you." [41] There was a strong pressure being exerted from two sides, but Paul would turn neither to the right nor to the left for any selfish purpose. His whole life was mastered and motivated by the love of Christ through the Spirit who dwelt within him. Can we say the same of ourselves? This is love's way. God desires to use you and me as instruments through which He can keep on loving the world.

How essential that the love of the Spirit be magnified in us! I could not seek for a true interpretation of life on either side of the grave from a loveless soul. I would never go to a blind person who never saw a sunset to describe to me the beauty of a sunset. Nor could I seek for knowledge about the love of God and eternal life from one who has not the love of God in him. It takes more than a great mind to convey the love of God; it takes a great heart.

The Apostle Paul was changed from a hater to a lover. When he breathed out threatening and slaughter against the Church, men fled from him. He was a character to be shunned and avoided. But then he was mastered by love, the love of God in Christ, and that love drove him into the very presence of God and then out to win men to Jesus Christ. And those who knew him were quick to notice the change. Men, women, and children no longer fled from him; they were drawn to Christ through him. Paul was loving souls to Jesus, and they could not resist

[41] Philippians 1:23, 24

the passion and power by which he labored to bring them the light of the gospel. Sacrifice prompted by the constraining love of Christ had accomplished through Paul the mighty purposes of God. Beloved, let love reign in your mortal body by the Holy Spirit which is in you. It is the one power by which a life of obedient service and sacrifice can be lived.

Love Prevents Schism. I have just read for the first time Professor E. H. Klotsche's *Christian Symbolics.* The author states that his purpose in preparing the volume was to acquaint students, pastors, and laymen with the distinctive characteristics "of all Christian denominations and sects represented in this country." The book is most enlightening and revealing, but when I laid it down, I was conscious of a terrible awakening in my own heart. I cried: "O, God, why all this strife and division within the household of faith?" In the ranks of fundamentalism there is a vociferous insistence upon doctrinal correctness and dispensational exactness that has brought about a verbal and literary warfare among Christ's own. While men are striving for doctrinal orthodoxy, there is relatively little concern about the obvious heterodoxy of life. The rancor and jealousy among brethren is frightful. While we take pride in the correctness of our theology, many look with scorn and even laughter at the incorrectness of our lives. A creed that does not change our conduct is powerless.

This poor showing among the saints is proof that there is something wrong with our belief. In the doctrinal statements of evangelical Christians there is included the important ministry of the Holy Spirit. The Bible teaches us that as we permit the Spirit to have His sovereign way in our lives, He will produce in us the fruit of love. However successful a Christian becomes in the eyes of men, he has the approval of God upon his efforts only so far as he permits the Holy Spirit to produce the love of God through his life. The love of the Spirit will not permit a schism but will prevent it. One may be a popular preacher of God's meekness, patience, longsuffering, and the like; but if that one engages in the dissipating sins of criticism, contention, and contesting, his ministry cannot be in the power and demonstration of the Holy Spirit. It is a shameful sin to subscribe to the first principles of divine revelation while refusing to submit to the mind and mastery of the Holy Spirit.

The Apostle Paul wrote: "I therefore, the prisoner of the Lord, beseech you that ye walk worthy of the vocation wherewith ye are called, With all lowliness and meekness, with longsuffering, *forbearing one another in love;* Endeavouring to keep the unity of the Spirit in the bond of peace." [42] With these words, Paul commences that portion of the Epistle that revolves around some essential issues of the practical side of the Christian life. At once we are to observe the large place that is given to the subject of maintaining unity.

As a requisite to *forbearance in love,* without which there can be no unity, we must be humble, meek, and patient. For such unity our Saviour prayed: "That they all may be one . . . that the world may believe." [43] The Holy Spirit is one divine Person, who by the divine attribute of omnipresence indwells every believer everywhere.

[42] Ephesians 4:1-3   [43] John 17:21

If we welcome His continued presence and do not grieve Him, quench Him, nor resist Him, He will bring us together in unity. If we are proud, arrogant, impatient, and hasty, the Spirit is not having His way in our lives, and such actions cause a schism in the Body of Christ. Too often it has been with a shock of surprise and disappointment that we have met with strife and division among members of the family of God.

Forbearing one another in love—how little we know about it! Yet this is true Christ-likeness. In the Colossian Epistle we read: "Forbearing one another, and forgiving one another, if any man have a quarrel against any: even as Christ forgave you, so also do ye." [44] Are we Christ's? Russel Jones has said: "Successful Christian loving is inseparably bound to Christ. Christian love is not merely the imitation of Christ's example. Christian love is the appropriation of Christ's experience." So Paul adds: "Above all, put on love." As we are clothed upon with this garment of the believer, we will *forbear*, which is *to put up with*. This is not always the easy thing to do, but we may be sure that it is the right thing.

The eyes of love will see good in others and the mouth of love will speak good of them. The Apostle Peter wrote: "Above all things be fervent in your love among yourselves; for love covereth a multitude of sins." [45] The King James Version speaks of charity, and it is literally *love in action*. Are we zealous in demonstrating our love toward our brethren? Hatred causes us to see the faults in others, but those same faults will be covered when love is operative in us by the Holy Spirit.

[44] Colossians 3:13   [45] 1 Peter 4:8 R.V.

Once an ancient artist was commissioned to paint a portrait of Alexander the Great. Noticing that Alexander was disfigured by a scar on his forehead, the result of a powerful blow of an enemy, the artist became greatly embarrassed. The artist knew that if he painted the scar as it appeared, he would hurt the pride of the great general. On the other hand, if he did not show the scar, the portrait would not be true. After thinking the matter through, he decided to paint Alexander with his forehead resting in his hand, so that the scar was covered by the hand. Even we, also, by the hand of love can cover the scars of our brethren in Christ.

In one of his books of sermons, Dr. Robert G. Lee tells a true and touching story about Dr. Orlando P. Scott, a well-known surgeon of Chicago. In an automobile accident, Dr. Scott's wife was seriously and painfully injured, great pieces of flesh being torn from her leg. As gangrene set in, skin grafting was necessary in order to save the limb. The noted surgeon chose to operate upon his own wife. Furthermore, the skin for the grafting process the doctor decided must be cut from his own flesh. Since he was operating on himself, a general anesthetic could not be used. Time after time he drove the knife into his own flesh without showing any sign of pain. The writer says: "So touching was the heroism and the marvelous fortitude under such inevitable suffering that frequent sobs were heard among the nurses who observed the operation." Then he continued: "The brave surgeon was relieved by something more than an anaesthetic. He was under the influence of a power that can make even pain to possess pleasure. In his mind there was no sacrifice.

It would have been harder not to do what he did—because he loved."

It cost Dr. Scott something to cover the ugly infection of the one he loved; but because he loved, he found himself powerless to do otherwise. It is not uncommon to meet brethren who are "overtaken in a fault." What course of action should we pursue when sin casts its ugly blight upon another member of the body of Christ? Paul says: "Ye which are spiritual, restore such an one in the spirit of meekness." [46] Here on the one hand, we have a man who is detected in a transgression. On the other hand, we see the spiritual Christian, one in whom the Spirit rules, who, because of the Spirit's sovereignty in his life, can do nothing other than love and restore the weaker brother. When we were born again into God's family we lost, in a certain sense, our individuality. We are no longer units, but a unity, members of one body, one in Christ by the Holy Spirit. Maybe we shall have difficulty in understanding each other, but let us make certain that others feel the love of the Spirit that beats in our hearts.

[46] Galatians 6:1

THE LIMITING OF THE SPIRIT

"Grieve not . . . . Quench not."[1]

In our studies so far we have considered the Lordship, the Life, the Leading, the Liberty, and the Love of the Holy Spirit. It has been our aim to see God work in a twofold way: first, in the salvation of the lost; secondly, in the creation of a desire in a true believer to let God move his life. Upon every Christian God has bestowed a wondrous gift, that of His Holy Spirit to guide our affairs and to lead us to do His will. God has a deep personal interest in each of His children. He is concerned about us as individuals. So in order to assure us of victory He sent His Holy Spirit, the omnipresent One, to occupy each life and to have the unhindered use of our whole being. Into each regenerate life the Holy Spirit comes to dwell. The Lord knew that man could not keep His holy law by mere human effort, so He said: *"I will put My Spirit within you, and cause you to walk in My statutes, and ye shall keep My judgments, and do them."* [2] By the power of His indwelling Spirit, God would "cause" us to do what He would have us do.

Before the Holy Spirit can dwell anywhere there must of necessity be a cleansing process. The Spirit of God is a holy Spirit and He cannot dwell where there is sin and

[1] Ephesians 4:30; 1 Thessalonians 5:19   [2] Ezekiel 36:27

defilement. Before He takes up His abode in any man a mighty inward change must first be wrought. His holiness will permit Him to dwell only in a holy place, so "God, which knoweth the hearts . . . giving them the Holy Ghost . . . purifying their hearts by faith." [3] Having complete knowledge of the deceitfulness and vileness of the human heart, God had to create in man a clean heart before His Spirit could enter.

When God created Adam He created him in His own image. In this human body He took up His abode when He breathed into man's nostrils the breath of life. But when this temple in which God dwelt became defiled, God moved out, and it became subject to death and decay. Then four thousand years later God sent forth His Son, and for thirty-three years He tabernacled among us in the Person of Jesus Christ. John says: "And the Word was made flesh, and dwelt [or tabernacled] among us." [4]

Just as the first temple (Adam) was destroyed because of sin, likewise this last temple (Christ) had to be destroyed because of sin. It was not His sin but the sin of the world that brought destruction to the temple of His body. Jesus had said: "Destroy this temple [speaking of the temple of His body], and in three days I will raise it up." [5] As He said He would, our Lord arose again in three days, and forty days after His Resurrection He ascended into Heaven and sat down on the right hand of the Father. Once again this left the earth without any temple in which God could dwell. But ten days after Christ's ascension, God the Holy Spirit came down on the day of Pentecost to indwell every member of the Body, the Church. Since

[3] Acts 15:8, 9   [4] John 1:14   [5] John 2:19, 21

that hour every believer in the Lord Jesus Christ has become the temple of the Holy Ghost, God's dwelling place. Paul says: "What? know ye not that your body is the temple of the Holy Ghost which is in you, which ye have of God, and ye are not your own? For ye are bought with a price: therefore glorify God in your body, and in your spirit, which are God's." [6]

DEFILING THE TEMPLE OF THE HOLY SPIRIT

While it has pleased God to dwell in the believer as His temple, that dwelling must be kept clean. Adam enjoyed communion with God until he defiled the body, and just as soon as sin entered, the communion with God was broken. Now it behooves us as Christians to turn over to God completely this house with all of its contents. Paul writes: "I beseech you therefore, brethren, by the mercies of God, that ye present your bodies a living sacrifice, holy, acceptable unto God, which is your reasonable service." [7] When God redeemed us, He purchased and paid for us, spirit, soul, and body. The apostle says: "I pray God your whole spirit and soul *and body* be preserved blameless unto the coming of our Lord Jesus Christ." [8] God wants the body of the believer preserved from every defilement. We need to yield our "members servants to righteousness unto holiness," [9] "that the life also of Jesus might be made manifest in our body." [10] Heaven's Holy Guest is grieved when He must dwell in an unclean temple. Every defilement of the body limits the operations of the Holy Spirit in and through the believer.

[6] 1 Corinthians 6:19, 20   [7] Romans 12:1   [8] 1 Thessalonians 5:23
[9] Romans 6:19   [10] 2 Corinthians 4:10

Christians need to study the Bible on this subject of the body and get God's thoughts on the matter, for we are limiting the Spirit of God by our abuse and misuse of the body. Let us not forget that our Lord wrought our redemption through His body, "Who His own self bare our sins in His own body on the tree." [11] He kept His body pure that He might present it a sacrifice for us, and now He asks us to keep our bodies clean that we should present them a living sacrifice to Him.

The word "present" contains the idea of sacrifice and it was used in connection with the offering of Jewish sacrifices in the Old Testament. When the Jew would bring his lamb or bullock to the tabernacle he would present it to the priest to be offered to God. This sacrificial offering, after having passed inspection, would be presented to God on the altar, so that God could say: "Whatsoever toucheth the altar shall be holy." [12] In contrast to those dead sacrifices that Israel offered, God is asking His children to turn their bodies over to Him, to present themselves upon the altar a living sacrifice.

It is worldly to cater to the body. The world advertises the body today more than it has ever done. It is exposed, exploited, and appealed to on billboards, in magazines, and in newspapers. The body is being subjected to a slow but sure suicide, poisoned by alcohol, nicotine, abuse from wrong eating, improper rest, and improper exercise.

Speaking of the last days preceding His Coming, our Lord said: "For as in the days that were before the flood they were eating and drinking, marrying and giving in marriage, until the day that Noah entered into the ark,

[11] 1 Peter 2:24   [12] Exodus 29:37

And knew not until the flood came, and took them all away; so shall also the coming of the Son of man be." [18] In Noah's day the people were slaves of bodily appetites and voluptuous desires. Certainly history is repeating itself. Men and women today are ruled by their bodies.

How few Christians regard the body as the instrument for the dwelling of the Spirit of God! No wonder the Lord has so little use for many of His children! He is limited by our unwillingness to give back to Him that for which He holds the purchase price. I have been asked often whether or not smoking or drinking the social glass of wine is wrong. I once replied: "Would you smoke or drink in the church auditorium?" The answer came immediately: "Indeed not! This is the house of God." Well, so is the Christian's body the perpetual dwelling place of the Holy Spirit. Dare we so much as give thought to keeping it less clean and free from defilement than we would a building of wood, brick, or stone made with hands? God forbid. The body is the vehicle of expression, therefore a yielded body is the practical test of genuine conversion.

The mercies of God reached us through the body of Jesus. Now my body, indwelt by His Spirit, must translate those mercies for the salvation of others. Many young people through dancing, petting, and caressing have broken down modesty and natural inhibitions of purity. God is grieved. The Holy One is limited in His operations through the bodies of believers.

Our Lord knew how the appeal of the body would limit His disciples in service, so He cautioned them: "Take no thought for your life, what ye shall eat, or what ye shall

[18] Matthew 24:37-39

drink; nor yet for your body, what ye shall put on. Is not the life more than meat, and the body than raiment?" [14] Jesus is not inferring for one moment that His followers are to be careless or improvident. Contrariwise, He encourages them to put first things first. "Seek ye first the kingdom of God, and His righteousness; and all these things shall be added unto you." [15] "Behold the fowls of the air . . . your heavenly Father feedeth them. . . . Consider the lilies of the field, how they grow; they toil not, neither do they spin. . . . Wherefore, if God so clothe the grass of the field . . . shall He not much more clothe you? . . . Your heavenly Father knoweth that ye have need of all these things." [16]

If we sacrifice our bodies to do His will He has promised to supply every need.[17] "Let not sin . . . reign in your mortal body." [18] "Mortify the deeds of the body." [19] "The body is not for fornication, but for the Lord; and the Lord for the body." [20] Paul could say: "I keep under my body, and bring it into subjection: lest that by any means, when I have preached to others, I myself should be a castaway." [21] "Temperate in all things" was the standard Paul used for his body.

Women take pride in painting and marking their bodies. Such actions are worldly and superficial. There are marks to be borne in the body of the believer, but they are the marks the world hates. Says the mighty apostle: "I bear in my body the marks of the Lord Jesus." [22] The word "marks" is from the word "stigma." It was used in

---

[14] Matthew 6:25
[15] Matthew 6:33
[16] Matthew 6:26-30
[17] Philippians 4:19
[18] Romans 6:12
[19] Romans 8:13
[20] 1 Corinthians 6:13
[21] 1 Corinthians 9:27
[22] Galatians 6:17

connection with the slaves in the Phrygian temples. These slaves gave themselves for life to the service of the temple and were therefore branded with the name of some deity. The body of the believer should bear his relationship to the Holy Spirit who dwells within him. "The religious devotee branded himself with the peculiar mark of the god whose cult he affected; so was Paul branded with the marks of his devotion to the Lord Jesus."

Dear Christian, offer your body freely to the Holy Spirit. It belongs to Him. Put your body under His control. It is His dwelling place, and if we misuse our feet, hands, tongues, eyes, ears, stomachs, or any other part of our body we grieve Him sorely and thus we limit our usefulness to Him. Once I heard a Christian say to another believer that if he went into a taproom or to a movie, the Holy Spirit would not go with him. This is wrong; the Holy Spirit goes wherever the child of God goes. The body is His home. And when we defile the body, we not only limit Him but we bring judgment upon ourselves. We are warned: "If any man defile the temple of God, him shall God destroy; for the temple of God is holy, which temple ye are." [23] How solemn is this warning! We are taught here that Christians die prematurely for defiling the temple of the Holy Spirit. Even some in that church at Corinth had died because of this sin.[24] O, let us not delay one moment in presenting our bodies to Him!

GRIEVING THE HOLY SPIRIT

The Bible issues some plain commands to Christians relative to their relationship with the Holy Spirit. The first

[23] 1 Corinthians 3:17   [24] 1 Corinthians 11:29, 30

of these that we will mention comes from the pen of the Apostle Paul. He writes: *"And grieve not the Holy Spirit of God, whereby ye are sealed unto the day of redemption."* [25] The word "grieve" here carries with it the idea of *causing pain.* Believers are expressly forbidden to do or say anything that might cause the Spirit of God to become grieved. Consider the fact which is clearly emphasized in the text, namely, that the Spirit possesses personality. It is not possible to grieve that which does not possess personality. This text defeats the false theory that the Spirit is merely some sort of emanation from God. A mere influence could not suffer pain or pleasure. But the Spirit of God, the Third Person of the Trinity, is deeply sensitive to all that is not right in the eyes of God.

Before we consider the main idea of the text more fully, notice how it testifies clearly to the Spirit's deep concern for us. If He is grieved because of our misconduct, then it stands that He loves us. We are grieved mainly by the conduct and experiences of those whom we love most. So it is with the Holy Spirit. If He is caused pain because of the sins and unbelief in the world, how much greater is that pain when He must look upon those same sins and unbelief in the hearts of Christians?

Have you ever stopped to consider that it is a matter of great importance to the Spirit of God what you do? The thought is challenging, and it is a mighty incentive to a holy walk. As a boy I was tempted, as most boys are, to do some rather mischievous things. One reason why I did not do all that I was tempted to do was the fact that I knew certain actions on my part would cause my mother

* Ephesians 4:30

grief and tears. But the grief that Mother felt because of her boy's behavior could not be compared with the grief that the Spirit feels. If only we realized the extent of His sorrow and pain, how much we would despise ourselves! How careful we would be before we speak or act!

The only mention of grieving the Spirit in the New Testament is found in Ephesians 4:30. The immediate reference, as shown by the context, has to do with the speech of Christians. "Let no corrupt communication proceed out of your mouth. . . . And grieve not the Holy Spirit of God. . . . Let all . . . evil speaking be put away from you." [26] Certainly the speech is one way in which we show what is in the heart, "for of the abundance of the heart his mouth speaketh." [27] Conversation reveals our true selves. All conversation unbefitting and unbecoming to a child of God causes the Holy Spirit great pain. Our communications and conversations are to be "good to the use of edifying, that it might minister grace unto the hearers." Therefore we are exhorted: "Let your speech be alway with grace, seasoned with salt, that ye may know how ye ought to answer every man." [28] The Spirit of God is sensitive to any misuse of the tongue, and when we so grieve Him we limit His operations through us.

The Spirit is grieved and thereby limited when we speak falsely. "Wherefore putting away lying; speak every man truth with his neighbor: for we are members one of another." [29] Lying and truth are exact opposites, and appear here as such: *"Putting away lying—speak truth."* Ruth Paxson says: "Within its range comes de-

[26] Ephesians 4:29-31   [27] Luke 6:45   [28] Colossians 4:6
[29] Ephesians 4:25

ception, hypocrisy, misrepresentation, artificiality, shams, half-truths, and unreality. We have here limited lying to speech; but we can lie by our deeds, and by our false pretensions and professions." God desires "truth in the inward parts," [30] for when our hearts are controlled by the Holy Spirit we can be expected to be truthful with others. All lies—white, gray, and black—are satanic; for there is no truth in Satan. "He is a liar, and the father of it." [31]

The Christian is called to be honest in so-called "little things." We are never to exaggerate nor overstate facts. When God first set down in writing what the relationships and walk of His people should be, He said: "Ye shall not steal, neither deal falsely, neither lie one to another." [32]

Among the things that God hates is "a lying tongue . . . a false witness that speaketh lies." [33] It is written further: "Lying lips are abomination to the Lord: but they that deal truly are His delight." [34] God hears and answers prayer, but never the prayer of the liar; "He will not hear," said the prophet, "for your lips have spoken lies, your tongue hath muttered perverseness." [35] Lying is one of the filthy garments of the old man and must be put off if the Holy Spirit is to work through us unhindered.

The Spirit is grieved and thereby limited when we speak unkindly of others. You may know something concerning someone else, but to repeat it to another can be both unkind and unnecessary. Words are oftentimes offensive, and when we offend we grieve the Spirit. "If any

[30] Psalm 51:6 [31] John 8:44 [32] Leviticus 19:11
[33] Proverbs 6:16-19 [34] Proverbs 12:22 [35] Isaiah 59:2, 3

man offend not in word, the same is a perfect man." [36] The tongue is but a little member, but it can be "a world of iniquity . . . that it defileth the whole body," and when the temple is defiled the Spirit is grieved. God cannot use a filthy vessel, and indeed it is defiling to say the least when the tongue is used to spread rumors that reveal sin and limit the usefulness of God's children. Oftentimes the rumors we hear about other people are unfounded and unwarranted and never should have been passed along to someone else. "Who is a wise man and endued with knowledge among you? let him shew out of a good conversation his words with meekness of wisdom." [37]

Whenever a mud slinger engages in his favorite pastime, he cannot escape getting some of that mud on himself. We speak harshly, critically, and maliciously about someone; but we carry defilement away on ourselves. It is impossible to please God while our tongues run loose. A man's religion is vain when he "bridleth not his tongue."

I remember visiting with some friends one evening. Unfortunately the conversation turned to persons and personalities not present. Another Christian's name was mentioned, and before we knew it we were all engaged in speaking disparagingly about our brother in Christ who was not there to defend himself. I went home that night feeling that all had had a good time, but when I tried to pray I found I was unable. My pillow turned to stone. By misusing my tongue I had defiled the temple of the Holy Spirit, and He was grieved.

Talebearing is a sin that is repeatedly rebuked in the

[36] James 3:2   [37] James 3:13

Bible. "The words of a talebearer are as wounds." [38] God commanded His people: "Thou shalt not go up and down as a talebearer." [39] We become meddling fools when we speak unkindly and unnecessarily about others. "Let none of you suffer . . . as a busybody in other men's matters." [40] Some Christians enjoy maligning men whom God is using, but playing loose with the good names of others is a dangerous sport. No one is ever built up by tearing someone else down. This is a filthy evil in the sight of God, and when committed by a member of the body of Christ it grieves and pains the Holy Spirit.

The Old Testament word for "grieve" is "vex." It appears once only—"But they rebelled, and vexed [or grieved] His Holy Spirit: therefore He was turned to be their enemy, and He fought against them." [41] In the verse preceding this the prophet presents us with a most graphic view of God's love for Israel: "In all their affliction He was afflicted, and the angel of His presence saved them: in His love and in His pity He redeemed them; and He bare them, and carried them all the days of old." They cried by reason of their bondage and God delivered them from the hand of the enemy. But there came a day when the compassion and forbearance of God was exhausted. He did not cease to love them, but they themselves had limited Him by grieving His Spirit. Instead of using their voices to praise God, they murmured and complained until they so vexed the Spirit of God that He was compelled to fill their lives with hardship in order to break their rebellious and complaining spirits. And if Christians, who

[38] Proverbs 18:8   [39] Leviticus 19:16
[40] 1 Peter 4:15 (see also 1 Timothy 5:13)   [41] Isaiah 63:10

should be praising God and testifying to others about Him, fall into the sin of criticizing and complaining, God's Spirit will become so vexed that we, too, will have to repent and confess our sin before He can ever use us again.

Have you grieved Him? Are you guilty of misusing your tongue? What kind of communication comes from your lips? Is it corrupt, critical, unkind, complaining? Meet a man who so grieved the Spirit of God that he resolved to control his tongue. He said: "I will take heed to my ways, that I sin not with my tongue." [42] Then he adds: "I will keep my mouth with a bridle." O Christian, bury the refuse and rubbish of the tongue, and out of the rubbish heap the Spirit of God will bring revival. We are appointed to live every moment of our lives with the Holy Spirit of God.

Says L. S. Chafer: "A child of God lives either with a grieved or an ungrieved Spirit." *Any and all sin grieves Him*. What is His attitude toward your life just now? Confess every known sin immediately, and you will have removed the hindrance that is limiting the Spirit in you.

"And grieve not the Holy Spirit of God, whereby ye are sealed unto the day of redemption."

QUENCHING THE HOLY SPIRIT

"Quench not the Spirit." [43] Usually we associate the word "quench" with thirst and fire. Here it undoubtedly refers to fire; but note the comment by George Matheson: "There is a thirst which ought not to be quenched—the thirst for God. It is like no other thirst in the world. Other

[42] Psalm 39.1   [43] 1 Thessalonians 5:19

thirsts are quenched when they meet their object, but the thirst for God will be quenched if it does *not* meet its object. When the hart pants after the waterbrooks its panting is allayed by tasting of the waterbrooks, but the panting of my soul for God is kept alive by tasting of God. If I do not taste of God I shall cease to thirst for Him; the Spirit will be quenched. To quench that thirst is to sink into a pauper's grave." It is the Holy Spirit who creates a desire for holy things. He keeps alive the thirst of our souls for God. When we will not be drawn by His wooing and leading, then it is that we quench Him. Hence the command: "Quench not the Spirit."

Now let us look at the text in the light of the context comparing it with other Bible passages. The word *quench* takes us back to the reference of the presence of the Spirit of God as fire. When He came at Pentecost, "there appeared unto them cloven tongues like as of fire, and it sat upon each of them." [44] To speak of quenching the Spirit is to use a metaphor meaning to put out a fire.

The exhortation to Christ's followers is: "Let your light so shine before men, that they may see your good works, and glorify your Father which is in heaven." When the light is shining so as to glorify God, we may be assured that the Holy Spirit is not quenched, for He is both the oil and the flame. In the parable of the virgins, there were five foolish who took their lamps with them but no oil. Hence at the midnight hour there was no light. Why? Because their lamps were not filled with oil.

Christians are to be shining lights in the world, but without the filling of the Holy Spirit, there is no light. He

[44] Acts 2:3

is called "the Spirit of burning" to purify and to empower for service. Wherever the believer resists the efforts of the Spirit to cleanse and use him, he quenches the Spirit. The Spirit does not withdraw from the believer, for we can never quench Him out of our lives; but He does restrain His power.

The Spirit is quenched when we are unthankful and do not praise God for everything. Paul says: "In every thing give thanks. . . . Quench not the Spirit." [45] How often the Spirit is quenched by our forgetfulness and indifference to the goodness and mercy of the Lord! It is the Holy Spirit who warms the heart to praise and thanksgiving. If we neglect praise, forget to be thankful, and fail to worship the Lord, then the fire dies down. Quenching the Spirit dims the light that reveals the grace of God in Jesus Christ. Do you "sit by a fireless hearth trying to warm yourself by human embers that refuse to flame and by ashes that give no warmth"?

Real gratitude is seldom born of circumstances. Only as I realize that God loved me as an individual and sent His Son to die for me am I reminded to be grateful. Your salvation and mine were not a chance meeting with God. By His love He sought, by His blood He bought, by His grace He brought us to Himself. Can we be so ungrateful as to fail to render praise and thanksgiving to Him for all His benefits? When I was first saved, I was really grateful. At first, everyone was seeing in me a demonstration and expression of gratitude. The fire really burned in those first days after my conversion. Then I became so absorbed in the gift that I forgot the Giver. I frowned

[45] 1 Thessalonians 5:18, 19

upon those who were not saved and boasted of my assurance of Heaven. I missed a few days in coming humbly to thank Him and gradually the fire died down. I had quenched the Spirit. My ingratitude made it impossible for Him to bestow upon me the more abundant blessing that He was able and eager to give. "How sharper than a serpent's tooth it is to have a thankless child!"

It is apparent that the injunction, "Quench not the Spirit," is related to the idea of Christian service. The manifestation of the Spirit in "prophesyings" [46] was not to be quenched. We quench the Spirit when we are disloyal to His call to service, when we refuse to do His bidding. It is the Holy Spirit who bestows gifts for service, and only those whose gifts are being used are enjoying the revival fires burning in them. Men perpetually quench the Spirit by saying "no" to serving the Lord. God has a work to do in this age, and that work is being done by men and women who are indwelt by His Spirit. The Spirit, working according to divine plan, is quenched when we refuse to do our part. We have seen water quench fire and discouragement quench enthusiasm; just so does rebellion on the part of a Christian quench the Holy Spirit's leading in His life. When He calls us and we offer alibis and excuses instead of following His every command, we limit His activity and operations in and through us.

The story was told about Mendelssohn, that famous musician and composer, that he once visited a cathedral which had in it one of the most valuable organs in all Europe. He listened for a while as the organist played;

[46] 1 Thessalonians 5:20

then he ascended the steps to the organ loft and asked the organist for permission to play it.

"I do not know you," replied the organist, "and we do not allow any chance stranger to play upon this organ."

The famous musician waited patiently, and at last he persuaded the man to let him play. Mendelssohn sat down at the organ, his fingers glided over the keys, his feet touched the pedals, and the mighty cathedral was filled with music such as the organist had never heard before. And then with tears in his eyes he laid his hand on Mendelssohn's shoulder.

"Who are you?" he asked.

"Mendelssohn," came the brief reply.

As the organist composed himself, he said: "To think that an old fool like myself nearly forbade Mendelssohn to play upon our organ."

My dear Christian, the Holy Spirit within you desires to touch the cords of your life and make them vibrate with the praises of God and the testimony of His grace. He will produce melody such as you have never known before if only you will allow His hand to touch the keys. If you refuse Him His right and privilege you will quench Him, and your life will know only those limitations of the flesh. "Quench not the Spirit."

THE LUXURIES OF THE SPIRIT

". . . God giveth to all liberally. . . ." [1]

The life of the Christian as planned and provided by God is the life of Christ in its fullest measure. It is the abundant life, not only for a few believers, but for all. When our Lord said: "I am come that they might have life, and that they might have it more abundantly," [2] He was speaking of every sheep within His fold. He had no thought whatever of a dispensational breach. All who would ever come to Him were included. Writing to all the saints at Colosse, Paul states it thus: "In Him ye are made full." [3]

Before He went away, Jesus Christ promised to send the Holy Spirit who would perfect in the believer, that is, bring to full growth and maturity, the abundant life. Obviously all Christians do not live on the same spiritual plane. To some we minister as "unto spiritual" while to others we minister as "unto carnal." [4] Now the "carnal" Christian is no less organically united with the Lord Jesus Christ than the spiritual. Furthermore, the Holy Spirit indwells every Christian no matter what the spiritual condition of the Christian might be. However, we all are acquainted with the difference in the quality of the daily life and walk of Christians.

[1] James 1:5   [2] John 10:10   [3] Colossians 2:10 R.V.
[4] 1 Corinthians 3:1

565

Undoubtedly we all desire to improve ourselves. We know that there are higher heights to be reached and more of God's glory to behold. These are the luxuries of the Spirit, two in number: *the fullness of the Spirit* and *the fruit of the Spirit*.

THE FULLNESS OF THE SPIRIT

This subject has not received the attention that might be given to it. The fullness of the Spirit does not mean the baptism in the Spirit. Two words explain two important phases of the ministry of the Holy Spirit. These words are *baptism* and *filling*. Too much confusion exists among Christians on this subject, and oftentimes one term is used when another is meant. It is not possible to know the mind of God unless we know the Holy Spirit's use of words in the Holy Scriptures. Dr. W. Graham Scroggie has said: "If we believe in the full inspiration of the Bible, we must acknowledge that its words are inspired, that they are employed always with discrimination, and that the truth on any given subject may be discovered by a close examination of the use of words which have five differing shades of meaning. If *our* thoughts are conveyed by the words we employ, how otherwise are God's?"

Baptism or Filling? The baptism with the Spirit differs in several ways from the filling with the Spirit. The first essential difference between the two is of great importance. It has to do with our seeking. No person who is truly Christian needs to seek after the baptism with the Spirit. Some teach that the baptism with the Holy Spirit "is a supernatural enduement for which each Christian should seek, an experience subsequent to conversion, and quite distinct from the experience of being born of the Spirit when one accepts Christ as Saviour." This teaching is not in accord with what the Bible has to say, as we understand the Word of God. Most leaders who believe in the Spirit's baptism as a subsequent experience after one is born again teach also that some other supernatural sign or gift, such as speaking in tongues, the gift of healing, or the gift of prophecy accompany the baptism. Of course, such teaching is based upon experience and not upon the Word of God. We are not looking askance upon those who testify of their experiences, but we are insisting that the right understanding of this subject must be obtained from the Word of God before any conclusions can be drawn from experience.

In order to understand what the New Testament means when it refers to the baptism with the Holy Spirit, let us turn to verses pertaining to this subject. The teaching is confined to a few passages. In the Gospels when John the Baptist is the spokesman, the announcement, "He shall baptize you with the Holy Ghost," [5] is prophetic of an event that heretofore had never taken place. These passages point forward, we believe, to Pentecost, and it was that about which the risen Lord Jesus was speaking when He said: "For John truly baptized with water; but ye shall be baptized with the Holy Ghost not many days hence." [6] Now we believe that the baptism with the Holy Spirit was the Spirit's coming at Pentecost, when all who believed were baptized into the mystical Body of Christ.

The Apostle Paul says: "In one Spirit were we all

[5] Matthew 3:11; Mark 1:8, Luke 3:16; John 1:26, 33
[6] Acts 1:5

baptized into one body." [7] The baptism with the Spirit has nothing to do with power for Christian service, but it relates directly to the forming of the Body of Christ, uniting vitally and organically all who are born again into the family of God. The baptism with (or *in*) the Spirit is always the work of the Lord Jesus Christ. He alone is the Baptizer. We never read of anyone being baptized *by* the Spirit. Of a truth every believer has been baptized by our Lord in the Spirit. When we are saved, we become a vital part of the already-baptized body of Jesus Christ. The baptism took place at Pentecost, and it is the first operation that is applied to the believing heart.

The Apostle Paul speaks of "one body, and one Spirit . . . one Lord, one faith, *one baptism,* one God and Father of all." [8] It is in the one Spirit that we all (believers) have been baptized into one Body,[9] so that the Christian need never seek after the baptism with the Spirit. Jesus saw to that. All that we need to do is to accept the fact that the transaction is finished once for all. As far as we understand the Scriptures, the believer's baptism with the Spirit has to do with our *standing* as a vital and integral part of the mystical Body of Christ, and not with our *state*. We can find nothing in the New Testament which teaches that some Christians have "never received the baptism of the Holy Spirit" and that all such should seek "it" until "it" is found. Dr. Scroggie says that "this error is due perhaps, to the confusing of the fullness of the Spirit with the baptism." Let us learn, then, that the baptism with the Spirit, insofar as the believer is concerned, is a finished transaction, a foundation fact.

[7] 1 Corinthians 12:13 R.V.   [8] Ephesians 4:4, 5   [9] 1 Corinthians 12:13

The apostolic experiences as recorded in the Book of Acts are not necessarily model experiences for all Christians today. The New Testament Epistles contain not so much as one single exhortation to believers to seek the baptism with the Spirit.

The use of the word "baptism" usually marks an initial experience. It is so when one is regenerated. Immediately upon acceptance of the Lord Jesus Christ as personal Saviour, the newly-saved sinner is baptized into the Body of Christ. He need never seek the baptism as a "second work of grace," for such teaching is not derived from the New Testament. The four instances in the Acts which speak of the baptism with the Spirit belong to the transition period. Dr. McQuilkin has said: "We must see clearly the distinction between the New Testament days and the ages that have followed. . . . The New Testament writers and teachers were not simply preaching the gospel. They were making the gospel to be preached, or rather the Holy Spirit was completing through them the revelation of the truth which constituted the faith once for all delivered to the saints. We must, therefore, beware of drawing false conclusions from the glorious truth that Christ is the same yesterday, today, and forever. He is the same, but He is not obliged to do in our day all the things that were done in the days when the gospel was in the making."

The Need. But does this truth justify the complacent attitude that there is no need for a manifestation of the Spirit's power in the lives of God's children today? Certainly it does not! We are to expect evidences of the Holy Spirit's presence and power. We have a right to look for a mighty demonstration in this day. But tongues, visions, shakings, anointing of handkerchiefs or aprons, authoritative acts such as the death of Ananias and Sapphira, or the opening of prison doors were not intended to be continued throughout this age. They belong to that transition period when the dispensation of the Holy Spirit was being inaugurated, and there is not the slightest indication in the Epistles that we have any right to insist upon their permanence.

From personal experience and observation we all are ready to admit that our expressions do not always become the child of God. Too often we find ourselves falling short of a God-honoring life. Not enough of us are concerned about a daily life of power and victory. We know the doctrinal difference between the carnal and the spiritual man but not always do we enjoy the blessings of the Spirit-filled life. Being filled with the Spirit is the larger manifestation of His presence and power in the life, and this we believe to be the need of the hour. Hence we shall devote a few pages to the consideration of God's command in Ephesians 5:18: "Be filled with the Spirit."

The filling of the Spirit is the divine enablement for every believer to live a life of victory, a day-by-day deliverance from the attractions of the *world*, the appetites of the *flesh*, and the snares of the *Devil*. The abundant enabling power of the Holy Spirit is available to all Christians so that none need to experience an impotent and defeated life. It is both possible and practical to live a life in the will of God, and this we can do as we allow the Holy Spirit to dominate us and have complete right of way. Ruth Paxson has written: "As the refusal of life in

Christ is the greatest sin of the unbeliever so the refusal of life more abundant in the Holy Spirit's fullness is the greatest sin of the believer. To be filled with the Spirit is not the privilege of a few but it is the prerogative of all believers." We are expected to be filled with the Spirit, and anything less than His fullness is below normal.

Three times in the New Testament strong drink and its effect are set over against the filling with the Spirit and its effect. It was predicted of John the Baptist: "He shall be great in the sight of the Lord, and shall drink neither wine nor strong drink; and he shall be filled with the Holy Ghost." [10] We are told that on the day of Pentecost when the disciples "were all filled with the Holy Ghost," the unbelievers mocked them saying: "These men are full of new wine." [11] Finally, Paul adds: "And be not drunk with wine, wherein is excess; but be filled with the Spirit." [12] Under the power of strong drink men are influenced to say and do things that otherwise they would not. Usually they turn to it for a stimulant in some hour of difficulty, or for the ecstatic results which it produces. But the child of God finds his delight and source of sufficiency in the Holy Spirit. The Spirit-filled life is not one of defeat and dejection.

Divine Provision for the Spirit's Filling. To be filled with the Spirit is the blessed privilege that every child of God may claim. And yet, we admit that we have not shared in the privilege as we ought. Why is it that we do not have the infinite, unfathomable fullness of the Spirit? Why is it that He does not possess us and work through us mightily to convict others of sin and bring them to Christ?

[10] Luke 1:15   [11] Acts 2:12-17   [12] Ephesians 5:18

The infilling of the Holy Spirit demands the emptying of the life. Andrew Murray has said: "The first condition of all filling is emptiness." One may study all about this aspect of the Spirit's work and then seek it continuously, but until this first condition of emptiness is met, there can be no filling. No life is truly Spirit-filled before this emptying process has taken place. This is probably the greatest hindrance to being filled with the Spirit. Could it be that right here you are asking where one must begin the emptying process in order to be filled? If you are, the question is a good one and one which we shall seek to answer. Let us approach the problem by giving consideration to the nature of the Holy Spirit as it is revealed in His names and titles.

He Is the Spirit of Life. "The Spirit of life," [13] "The Spirit is life," [14] "The Spirit giveth life." [15] As we sought to point out in chapter two, the Holy Spirit is the Author of life and therefore is grieved when there enters into our lives those things that savor of death. The Spirit will not even stand to see our bodies remain dead in the grave, for, says Paul: "If the Spirit of Him that raised up Jesus from the dead dwell in you, He that raised up Christ from the dead shall also quicken your mortal bodies by His Spirit that dwelleth in you." [16] The Spirit of God knows nothing of death, for all death grieves Him. The believers in the Sardis Church were not Spirit-filled. The Apostle John wrote of them: "Thou hast a name that thou livest, and art dead." [17] When Christians defile their garments with the stench of those who are spiritually dead, that is,

---

[13] Romans 8:2   [14] Romans 8:10   [15] 2 Corinthians 3:6
[16] Romans 8:11   [17] Revelation 3:1

when believers insist upon finding their fellowship with unbelievers, they cannot be filled with the Spirit. The Spirit warreth against the flesh because all flesh has the mark of death upon it. So then let us give ourselves to our God and to His Word, for these shall never perish. When we are yielded completely to the Giver and Sustainer of Life, then it is that He will fill us.

He Is the Spirit of Faith. Paul says: "We having the same Spirit of faith." [18] Since He is the Spirit of faith, He is grieved when we doubt, distrust, or disbelieve. Behind all the worry, anxiety, and fretfulness of God's children, there is the heart of unbelief. All the blessings of salvation have come to us through simple faith in our Lord Jesus Christ and in the written Word. So all the blessings and victories of the Spirit-filled life hang upon the same simple faith in God and His Word.

Our Lord warned His own against unbelief assuring them that faith was the answer to their daily material needs: "Wherefore, if God so clothe the grass of the field, which to day is, and to morrow is cast into the oven, shall He not much more clothe you, *O ye of little faith?*" [19] The second time our Lord used the phrase, "O ye of little faith," He taught the alarmed disciples that faith is the answer to fear: "And He saith unto them, Why are ye fearful, *O ye of little faith?*" [20] The third time, our Lord spoke directly to Peter. As long as Peter kept his eyes on Jesus, he could walk the waves, but just as soon as Peter got his eyes off the Lord, he sank. Too often we are like Peter. When we should, by faith, seize the opportunity in the impossibility, we are fearful of the impossibility in the

[18] 2 Corinthians 4:13   [19] Matthew 6:30   [20] Matthew 8:26

opportunity, so that Jesus must say: *"O thou of little faith,* wherefore didst thou doubt?" [21]

Finally, our Lord had to rebuke the disciples when they became so preoccupied about their material needs that they missed His teaching. He was warning them against false teaching and they misinterpreted Him. Why did they misinterpret Him? Because they were more concerned about the material than the spiritual. Then He chided them for their lack of faith: *"O ye of little faith,* why reason ye among yourselves, because ye have brought no bread?" [22] Such unbelief grieves the Holy Spirit in this age no less than it did the Lord Jesus when He was here on earth. The answer to every Christian need and problem is faith, and when we are not trusting, we are not filled with the Spirit. Hence faith is a prerequisite to a Spirit-filled life.

He Is the Spirit of Truth. "Even the Spirit of truth." [23] Anything in our lives that is deceitful or false will keep us from being Spirit-filled since all untruth grieves the Holy Spirit. So strongly opposed is He to all that is false that He struck dead Ananias and Sapphira because of a secret sin in their hearts. When they brought their possessions, they pretended that part of it was all of it, and the Holy Spirit was grieved. If we would know the blessing and conquest of a life filled with the Spirit, then we must confess and clean out of our lives all that is deceitful and hypocritical. There is no power where deceit and hypocrisy exist. Certainly we are not deceiving God but ourselves, and self-deception is dangerous. Christians sometimes deceive and lie to each other. Lying is an

[21] Matthew 14:31   [22] Matthew 16:8   [23] John 14:17

abomination to God,[24] a hindrance to prayer,[25] and the path to hatred.[26] Every lie shall be detected by God[27] and is punishable. Would you be filled with the Spirit? Then be truthful.

He Is the Spirit of Grace. "The Spirit of grace."[28] No ungracious Christian is filled with the Spirit. Occasionally we hear of a believer who is unkind, unlovely, unforgiving, or thankless. A Spirit-filled child of God is controlled by the Spirit, and he will always display those characteristics that are true of Him. Three times in the Old Testament we read of God as being "gracious and merciful, slow to anger, and of great kindness."[29] Now when the Spirit fills us, He brings into our lives these divine virtues. Paul, by the Spirit, writes: "Be ye kind one to another, tender-hearted, forgiving one another, even as God for Christ's sake hath forgiven you."[30]

"Should a Christian forgive his or her enemies?" a young lady once asked. Another asked: "Must I keep on forgiving over and over again?" The standard for Christians in this matter of forgiveness is to be found in our blessed Lord. You are to forgive "even as God for Christ's sake hath forgiven you." Certainly no one has ever hurt you as much as you have hurt God, and yet He has shown His kindness to you. The only reason for our unkindness is that we are not filled with the Spirit.

The garments of the Spirit-filled Christian are listed in Colossians 3:12-17: "Put on therefore, as the elect of God, holy and beloved, bowels of mercies, *kindness,*

---

[24] Proverbs 12:22   [25] Isaiah 59:2, 3   [26] Proverbs 26:28
[27] Proverbs 12:19   [28] Hebrews 10:29
[29] Nehemiah 9:17; Joel 2:13, Jonah 4:2   [30] Ephesians 4:32

humbleness of mind, meekness, longsuffering." **Kindness**
is thoughtfulness of others, selflessness. We cannot see
how it is possible for a believer to be filled with the Spirit
and not show the kindness of God toward others. Kindness is one of the garments of the spiritual life, and is a
gracious characteristic of the Spirit of grace. To be filled
with the Spirit necessitates the emptying of all that is not
gracious.

He Is the Spirit of Wisdom. "Making mention of you in
my prayers; That the God of our Lord Jesus Christ, the
Father of glory, may give unto you the Spirit of wisdom." [31] Now the wisdom of the Spirit is both desirable
and necessary if we are to make a success of the Christian
life. Wisdom is a combination of the possession and right
use of knowledge.

Let us distinguish between the wisdom of this world
and the wisdom of God. Only the true believer has access
to the mind of the Lord. And yet, not all believers know
and understand some of the slightly deeper truths of
God's Word. They have not gone beyond their acceptance
of Christ as Saviour. There is no growth in the knowledge
of the things of God. Does this mean that all believers
have not received the Spirit? Indeed not! When Paul
prayed that God might give to the Ephesian Christians
"the Spirit of wisdom and revelation in the knowledge of
Him," he did not mean that they had not received the
Spirit, or that they could possibly receive Him in some
new way. It was a prayer for the Spirit to have His way
in opening to them the truth of God and in giving them a
deeper insight into the Word.

[31] Ephesians 1:16, 17

Many Christians admit that their reading of the Bible has given them no further understanding of the will of God. When you meditate upon the Word of God, do you hear His voice interpreting eternal truth and guiding you in His way? This is as it should be. The deep things of God are revealed by His Spirit,[32] and not until we yield ourselves to Him will He fill us and impart divine wisdom. It is then that He has the liberty to act in our behalf as the Spirit of wisdom and revelation.

He Is the Spirit of Holiness. Our Lord Jesus Christ is declared to be the Son of God with power, "according to the Spirit of holiness." [33] His full title is "the Holy Spirit." God has a standard of holiness for His children, and anything less than that standard is sin. The Holy Spirit is sensitive to all that is worldly, unclean, or defiling, and when any such thing comes into our lives, it cannot be said that we are Spirit-filled.

William Kelly has said: "That same energy of the Holy Ghost which was displayed in Jesus when He walked in holiness here below, was demonstrated in resurrection; and not merely in His own rising from the dead, but in raising the dead at any time." And to this remark we would like to add that the same power of the Holy Spirit which Jesus displayed when He walked in holiness on earth is available to all those who, through faith in Him, have been born into God's family.

Be not afraid of this term "holiness." It is simply the equivalent of being filled with the Spirit. Personalities exchange places: self abdicates and the Spirit moves in. We surrender, and the Spirit takes possession. We yield to

[32] 1 Corinthians 2:10   [33] Romans 1:4

Him; He takes control. Let us pray that God will empty us of self and fill us with Himself, allowing Him to will and to do of His good pleasure. Beloved, we have not yet attained, but we must press on, seeking to do only those things that please Him. This is the normal Christian experience.

He Is the Spirit of Power. "For God hath not given us the spirit of fear; but of power, and of love, and of a sound mind." [34] There is no impotency with the blessed Holy Spirit. To be filled with the Spirit is to possess the plenitude of His power. In both the Old and the New Testaments we have examples of those who are described as being filled with the Spirit. And in each instance it is to be noted that the filling with the Spirit was the enabling power for accomplishing some mighty task. These Biblical examples of the Spirit-filled life must not be overlooked.

From the standpoint of both wisdom and power, the building of the Tabernacle in the wildnerness was a human impossibility. God knew the limitations of His people, so He said: "See, I have called by name Bezaleel the son of Uri, the son of Hur, of the tribe of Judah: And I have filled him with the Spirit of God, in wisdom, and in understanding, and in knowledge, and in all manner of workmanship." [35] Later on Moses testified to the people that the secret of the wisdom and power in erecting the Tabernacle was in the Spirit-filled leadership of Bezaleel.[36] So it must be today in the building of the Church of the Lord Jesus Christ. Our Lord Himself is the Builder; but we are His workmen, and as we are filled with the Holy

[34] 2 Timothy 1:7   [35] Exodus 31:2, 3   [36] Exodus 35:30, 31

Spirit, we are empowered to take great strides in this holy task.

Joshua was a mighty leader, and we have marveled at his accomplishments for God, but let us not forget that when God laid hands on him, he "was full of the Spirit." [37] We have rejoiced in the power and prophecies of Micah, but we need to know that he was a man "full of power by the Spirit of the Lord." [38]

Thus we have in the old dispensation concrete examples of Spirit-filled men who were endued with skill, wisdom, and power to do God's work. These examples looked forward to the Spirit's coming at Pentecost when His greater fullness would be available to every member of the Body of Christ.

Even in the Gospels, before the Pentecostal experience, there are several references to men and women who were filled with the Spirit. These were persons who were anticipating the coming of the Messiah. They formed a little company, few in number, but strong in the hope of the Saviour's appearing. Of the parents of John the Baptist we read: "Elisabeth was filled with the Holy Ghost," [39] "And his father Zacharias was filled with the Holy Ghost." [40] Before John was born, the angel of the Lord predicted that he would be filled with the Holy Spirit. [41]

According to the New Testament records, John the Baptist was the pioneer soul-winner, introducing the Saviour of whom the prophets had spoken. In his proclamation of "the Lamb of God," John preached the

[37] Deuteronomy 34:9   [38] Micah 3:8   [39] Luke 1:41
[40] Luke 1:67   [41] Luke 1:15

doctrine of substitution, how that the Messiah had come to offer Himself as a sacrifice for sin. The doctrine was hated in the Baptist's day even as it is in ours. Preaching it cost John his life; but before the enemies of Christ beheaded him, he had won converts to Jesus Christ. No man could have lived such a life and died such a death as John the Baptist apart from a special enduement of divine power.

Men, like John, who are filled with the Spirit, will not be popular with all classes, but they are bound to attract others to Jesus. John was merely a voice, but the voice was that of the Spirit of God speaking through him. What God did through John the Baptist, He can still do in our modern age if only we will give ourselves over to the Holy Spirit for the full display of His power in us.

We find more examples in the Book of the Acts of people being filled with the Spirit than in any other book in the Bible. At least ten times Luke records the names and occasions. On the Day of Pentecost when the disciples were all filled with the Holy Ghost, there were added to them about three thousand souls. This was not merely drawing three thousand souls to the meeting in the energy of the flesh, but the mighty demonstration of the Holy Spirit in conversion. These Spirit-filled disciples formed the effective Body with the adequate spiritual resources to carry on the work of the Lord Jesus Christ. There could have been no substitute at Pentecost to take the place of the practical power of the Holy Spirit. When He filled the disciples, God was at work through them.

It is clear that the filling with the Spirit was not a once-for-all transaction. The experience was repeated. The record lists such names as Peter (Acts 4:8), who certainly was with the group at Pentecost; a group of disciples (4:31); Stephen (6:5, 7:55); the first deacons of the early church (6:3); Paul (9:17; 13:9); Barnabas (11:24); and the disciples at Antioch (13:52). It was through these that the work of Christ was being carried on. And the unbelievers, including the authorities of the day, knew that the work was not of man, for they asked: "By what power?" [42] We know that it was the promised power of the Holy Spirit, and it is that necessary and adequate power which is needed today for God's great evangelistic program.

New Testament evangelism can be carried on by no human effort apart from the Spirit of God. The results must come by miraculous means, by the supernatural power of the Holy Spirit as He possesses and equips men to do this supernatural work. And when we are Spirit-filled, there is no power of demons, or men, or whatever there be, to resist the Word of God when it is preached in the power and demonstration of the Holy Spirit.

THE FRUIT OF THE SPIRIT

It appears quite clear from the teaching of our Lord that He has chosen and called us for the direct purpose of bearing fruit. He said to His disciples: "Ye have not chosen Me, but I have chosen you, and ordained you, that ye should go and bring forth fruit, and that your fruit should remain." [43] The issue in the fifteenth chapter of the Gospel according to John is fruit. "Herein is my Father glorified, that ye bear much fruit; so shall ye be my dis-

[42] Acts 4:7   [43] John 15:16

ciples." [44] The whole passage is beautiful indeed, but the parable of the vine and the branches is intended to teach us the wonderful and solemn thought that the Lord is depending upon us to bear fruit. The Apostle Paul calls it "the fruit of the Spirit," [45] the ninefold excellency of our Lord Jesus Christ which is to appear in every believer.

Let us not confuse the fruit of the Spirit with the much activity of some churches. Just as fruit in the natural sense is the product of an inherent energy of a living organism, so the fruit of the Spirit is the product of the Holy Spirit's power operating through those who have been brought into living union with Christ. Not all religious work is fruit-bearing. A tree bears fruit after its kind. When our Lord warned of false prophets which come in sheep's clothing, He said: "Ye shall know them by their fruits." Then He added: "Every good tree bringeth forth good fruit; but a corrupt tree bringeth forth evil fruit. A good tree cannot bring forth evil fruit, neither can a corrupt tree bring forth good fruit . . . Wherefore by their fruits ye shall know them." [46] The character of the fruit gives evidence of the character of the power that produces it. The work of the Holy Spirit in the believer is to make fruitful, and when He is in absolute control, we are bearing fruit. While it is true the Holy Spirit indwells every believer, the operation of the Spirit in the believer demands the co-operation of the believer himself. The fruit of the Spirit cannot be borne in anyone who refuses to be controlled and led by the Holy Spirit.

We do not know whether anything visible, such as the vineyard on the way to Gethsemane or the vine carved

[44] John 15:8   [45] Galatians 5:22, 23   [46] Matthew 7:15-20

over the great door of the temple, suggested to our Lord the parable of the vine and the branches. We do know, however, that the great privilege and responsibility of bearing fruit rests with the followers of Jesus Christ and it was this lesson that the parable was intended to teach.

All students of the Word of God know that at one time fruitbearing was Israel's calling, so that the figure of speech in itself was perfectly familiar to the disciples when they heard it. In Jotham's parable, Israel is referred to as "the olive tree . . . the fig tree . . . the vine." [47] Of these three symbols of Israel, the vine emerges in Biblical literature as the most familiar. Israel was Jehovah's vine. In a song of Asaph, we read: "Thou hast brought a vine out of Egypt." [48]

Now the purpose of a vine is not to spread branches but to bear fruit. Israel failed, so that Hosea wrote: "Israel is an empty vine, he bringeth forth fruit unto himself." [49] Under the parable of a vineyard, the prophet Isaiah depicts Israel's unfruitful condition and Jehovah's subsequent judgment.[50] Jeremiah added a further word when he penned the words of God, saying: "Yet I had planted thee a noble vine, wholly a right seed: how then art thou turned into the degenerate plant of a strange vine unto me?" [51] All of this points to the fact that Israel, as the vine, had completely failed to bear fruit according to the purpose of God.

Now when our Lord spoke His parable, He said: "I am the *true* vine." [52] Israel had been cut off, as is clearly seen in our Lord's parable of the wicked husbandman; for

[47] Judges 9:7-15
[50] Isaiah 5:1-7
[48] Psalm 80:8
[51] Jeremiah 2:21
[49] Hosea 10:1
[52] John 15:1

He declared: "The kingdom of God shall be taken from you, and given to a nation bringing forth the fruits thereof." [53] If Israel had failed, God had not! Though God had brought forth Israel to bear fruit, He would not abandon His plans simply because the nation had failed. Thus, in a few words, He told His disciples that He and those associated with Him would take up the privileges and responsibilities where Israel would not. But even Him the Hebrew people cast out of the vineyard and killed.[54] Seeing the inescapable Cross just ahead of Him, our Lord committed to His followers the sacred and solemn privilege of bearing fruit according to God's purpose. Israel would not bear fruit, and the True Vine they rejected, so now those who are in vital union with the Lord Jesus Christ shall have the glorious privilege of bringing forth fruit. The fruit is borne by the power of the indwelling Holy Spirit, and it is called His fruit. It is not within the power of man to produce the fruit of the Spirit. The nine graces that make up the beautiful cluster of fruit as mentioned in Galatians 5:22 and 23 are developed by the Holy Spirit as we allow Him to control us.

Union and communion with Christ make fruitfulness. Jesus said: "The branch cannot bear fruit of itself, except it abide in the vine; no more can ye, except ye abide in Me." [55] And then He added these words: "I am the vine, ye are the branches: He that abideth in Me, and I in him, the same bringeth forth much fruit: for without Me ye can do nothing." [56] In these verses it is plainly taught that fruitbearing is conditioned upon communion or fellow-

[53] Matthew 21:43   [54] Matthew 21:39   [55] John 15:4
[56] John 15:5

ship with the Lord. Jesus is the Vine, and while the Vine is up yonder in Heaven, we are vitally linked with Him through the blessed Holy Spirit. If we have trusted the Lord Jesus as Saviour, we are branches in the living Vine, placed in this world to bear fruit; but the fruit is borne only as we walk in unbroken communion with our Lord.

Do we realize the value of this new union with Christ? Are we aware of the unlimited possibilities of Christian character and service as we walk in Him? F. B. Meyer has said: "The vine-root is not enough in itself, it must have branches to carry its rich juices to the cluster, so that these may hang free of each other in the sun and air. Christ must have branches—long lines of saved souls extending down the centuries—through which to communicate Himself to men." How necessary we are to the Lord Jesus! He has chosen us and cannot do without us. Through us He achieves His eternal purpose of gathering fruit unto Himself.

The Word of God makes fruitful. We have this lesson clearly taught in our Lord's parable of the Sower, the seed, and the soils. In the parable itself,[57] He told them that the seed was the Word, and that when it was sown, it fell upon four different kinds of soil: the way side, stony ground, thorns, and good ground. There was that which "yielded no fruit,"[58] and that which "did yield fruit."[59] In each case and in each of the four kinds of soil, the same seed was sown; but only one of the soils, the "good ground," yielded fruit. Three degrees of fruitbearing are suggested in the terms thirtyfold, sixtyfold, and an hundredfold,[59] which is in keeping with the fruit, more

[57] Matthew 13:3-9; Mark 4:3-9, Luke 8:4-8   [58] Mark 4:7   [59] Mark 4:8

fruit, and much fruit in the parable of the Vine and the branches.[60]

If we would be fruitful, we dare not neglect our reading and study of God's Word. To do so is a serious error which will keep the life barren and unfruitful. Most Christians who suffer a lapse in their spiritual life admit inconsistency in their use of the Bible. The Word of God grows in human hearts, and there it produces its fruit, so that the Psalmist said: "Thy Word have I hid in mine heart." [61] Paul referred to the Word as "the Word of God, which effectually worketh also in you that believe." [62] When we hear and heed the truth, it finds lodgment in the heart and there it works to produce fruit unto God. The unbelieving Jews could not bear fruit, for to them the Lord Jesus said: "Ye have not His Word abiding in you." [63] To the saints at Colosse, Paul wrote of "the Word of the truth of the gospel; Which is come unto you, as it is in all the world; and *bringeth forth fruit,* as it doth also in you, since the day ye heard of it, and knew the grace of God in truth." [64] Since the Word of God is a divinely-ordained means of producing fruit in the believer's life, we can only exhort our readers in the words of the great apostle: "Let the Word of Christ dwell in you richly." [65]

As we abide in Him and His words abide in us, the Holy Spirit produces His fruit in us. Notice Paul's choice of the Word *fruit* in contrast to the word *works.* The Christian experience is the product of the power of the

[60] John 15:2-5
[63] John 5:38
[61] Psalm 119:11
[64] Colossians 1:5, 6
[62] 1 Thessalonians 2:13
[65] Colossians 3:16

indwelling Spirit of God. This the apostle calls fruit, and it is set forth in the following words:

Love. God is love, and in the heart of the man who puts his trust in Jesus Christ, divine love is shed abroad by the Holy Spirit. Paul says: "The love of God is shed abroad in our hearts by the Holy Ghost which is given unto us." [66] Love is the queen of the graces and it is the Christian's new *constraint,* "for the love of Christ constraineth us." [67] Love is likewise the Christian's new *covering* for the weaknesses of our brethren, "for love shall cover the multitude of sins" [68] because love "rejoiceth not in iniquity." [69] A proverb says: "Hatred stirreth up strifes: but love covereth all sins." [70] Finally, love is the believer's new *commandment.* Jesus said: "A new commandment I give unto you, That ye love one another." [71] True faith and obedience expresses itself in love. This is the fruit of the Spirit.

Joy. The joy which is the fruit of the Spirit must, like love,[72] have a spiritual basis. Paul calls it the "joy of the Holy Ghost." [73] It is the Spirit's fruit; hence it can never be possessed by one who is not possessed of Him.

Happiness depends upon happenings, but the joy of the Holy Ghost is the fruit of the Spirit's control. It enters into a sphere where the violence of man can never reach. When the disciples faced persecution for preaching the Word, they "were filled with joy, and with the Holy Ghost." [74] Jesus had told them that when men would revile

[66] Romans 5:5
[69] 1 Corinthians 13:6
[72] Romans 5:5
[67] 2 Corinthians 5:14
[70] Proverbs 10:12
[73] 1 Thessalonians 1:6
[68] 1 Peter 4:8
[71] John 13:34
[74] Acts 13:50-52

and persecute them, they should "rejoice."[75] On another occasion, he said to them: "Ye shall be sorrowful, but your sorrow shall be turned into joy . . . and your joy no man taketh from you."[76] The joy of the Spirit is independent of circumstances, manifesting itself even under severe trial.[77] The grounds for Christian joy are the *preaching* of the Gospel,[78] the *power* of the gospel in salvation,[79] the *prosperity* of other believers,[80] and the future *prospect* of our reward.[81] As we yield ourselves daily to the blessed Holy Spirit, we shall find as Nehemiah found and expressed to God's people in the face of bitter opposition, that the joy of the Lord is our strength.[82]

Peace. The Bible teaches us that "God is not the author of confusion [tumult or unquietness], but of peace."[83] He is called "the God of peace,"[84] and "The Prince of peace."[85] Since there is no peace in the heart of the natural man, it is the Holy Spirit's work to bring peace with Him when He comes to each of us in regenerating power. After one has been saved, it is to be expected that the fruit of peace will be in evidence in that one's life. The word is *eirene* and in its verb form it means "to bind together."

The fruit of the Spirit is a *harmonized relationship between God and man,* accomplished for us by Christ in His death, and made vital in us by the coming of the Holy

[75] Matthew 5:10-12   [76] John 16:20-22

[77] James 1:2; 2 Corinthians 7:4; 8:2; 1 Thessalonians 1:6

[78] Philippians 1:18   [79] John 4:36; Acts 15:3; Luke 15:6, 7

[80] Romans 12:15; 2 Corinthians 7:13; 1 Corinthians 12:26

[81] Matthew 5:12; Luke 6:22, 23   [82] Nehemiah 8:10

[83] 1 Corinthians 14:33

[84] Romans 15:33; 16:20; 2 Corinthians 13:11; 1 Thessalonians 5:23; Hebrews 13:20; Philippians 4:9   [85] Isaiah 9:6

Spirit. The Apostle Paul declared, in Ephesians 2:16 and 17, that Jesus Christ died, "that He might reconcile both [Jew and Gentile] unto God in one body by the cross, having slain the enmity thereby: And came and preached peace to you which were afar off." The sinner is alienated from God, at enmity with Him, but by his acceptance of Christ's work upon the Cross, which work was the work of peace,[86] he is bound together in a harmonized relationship with the Lord. When one is born again, he ceases to fight God, for the armistice between God and him has been declared. This very thought formed a part of apostolic preaching.[87]

In the next place, the fruit of peace is *a harmonized relationship between men*. The Apostle Paul said by the Spirit: "The kingdom of God is . . . peace . . . in the Holy Ghost." [88] The Bible does not allow for Christians being at variance. The exhortation is to "be at peace among yourselves," [89] and: "If it be possible, as much as lieth in you, live peaceably with all men." [90] Our Lord exalted His disciples to "have peace one with another." [91] Christians are bound together to God and also to each other.

Finally, the fruit of peace is *a state of rest in the believer's heart* ruling the inner man so that there is calm and quietness. This state of inward rest is not objective such as the peace with God which comes to us when we are justified,[92] but it is subjective, a tranquility and quiet within. Paul says: "The peace of God, which passeth all

---

[86] Colossians 1:20

[87] Acts 10:36

[88] Romans 14:17

[89] 1 Thessalonians 5:13

[90] Romans 12:18

[91] Mark 9:50

[92] Romans 5:1

understanding, shall keep your hearts and minds through Christ Jesus." [93] "Let the peace of God rule in your hearts." [94]

Longsuffering. The word "longsuffering" has been translated "long-tempered," "patience toward others." It has been defined as that quality of self-restraint in the face of provocation which does not hastily retaliate nor promptly punish. We know far too little in our personal experiences of the steadfastness of the soul under trial. Too few of us know how to forbear under ill-treatment, without anger or thought of revenge. Only the Spirit-filled child of God suffers long, refusing to surrender to circumstances. Someone has suggested that all these graces that make up the fruit of the Spirit are but varied expressions of love, and that joy is love exulting; peace is love in repose; longsuffering is love on trial. Paul wrote: "Love suffereth long." [95] In His early communications to man, God revealed Himself to Moses as "The Lord God, merciful and gracious, longsuffering." [96] The Apostle Peter speaks of the time "when once the longsuffering of God waited in the days of Noah." [97] Even today the longsuffering of God waits patiently over vessels of clay that deserve His wrath.[98] The longsuffering of God has been misused and abused. Instead of leading men to repentance and godliness, it is being taken advantage of. Yet God patiently invites the sinner to come and be saved. The fruit of the Spirit is longsuffering, patient endurance, even among those who wrongfully use us. Longsuffering characterizes all labor that is motivated by love.

[93] Philippians 4:7 [94] Colossians 3:15 [95] 1 Corinthians 13:4
[96] Exodus 34:6 [97] 1 Peter 3:20 [98] Romans 2:4

Gentleness. The word gentle means not rough, harsh, or severe. When the Holy Spirit mellows in us all that is harsh and austere, we are bringing forth His fruit. Writing to the Thessalonians, the Apostle Paul said: "We were gentle [mild] among you." [99] Paul could exhort Timothy to "be gentle unto all," [100] and to Titus he wrote: "Be no brawler, but gentle, shewing all meekness unto all men." [101] Too often we become sharp and bitter instead of mild and soft-spoken. A gentle Christian does not find it difficult to get along with one who is froward.

Goodness. Here the Apostle Paul is referring to that quality in a man that aims at what is good. We are not to confuse this word with the word "gentle." The same idea is not intended in both words. Sometimes we can do good to others, not necessarily by gentle means, but by a display of sterner qualities. When Paul denounced all uncleanliness, he added: "For the fruit of the Spirit is in all goodness." [102] By his stern denunciation he did them good. When a man whose life is ruled by the good, points out to us the worth of moral goodness, then he does us good. When our Lord drove the buyers and sellers out of the temple,[103] He was doing them good. Goodness is love in action, desiring and procuring the welfare of others.

Faith. We naturally think of this word "faith" in the sense of trust in God for salvation. While the idea of a firm conviction that what God says is correct is contained in the word "faith," the Greek word here is *pistis,* and it means the faithfulness and fidelity that are produced in the life yielded to the Holy Spirit. Faithfulness in my life

[99] 1 Thessalonians 2:7   [100] 2 Timothy 2:24   [101] Titus 3:2
[102] Ephesians 5:3-9   [103] Matthew 21:12, 13

insures loyalty to others and obedience to God. The Christian in whose life the Spirit is bringing forth His fruit will be true to his promises and faithful to his task.

God is faithful.[104] Even though there are those who will not believe in His Son, their unbelief shall not make the faithfulness of God without effect, for God is true.[105] If only a few should confess their sins in Jesus' name, *God is faithful* (to His Son) and just to forgive them and cleanse them from all unrighteousness.[106] When you are called upon to suffer or to doubt, count on the faithfulness of God; for "God is faithful, who will not suffer you to be tempted above that ye are able; but will with the temptation also make a way to escape, that ye may be able to bear it." [107]

It was on the ground of the faithfulness of God that the prophet encouraged Israel.[108] It was on the basis of the faithfulness of God that Paul assured the saints at Thessalonica of the redemption of their bodies, for, said he: "Faithful is He that calleth you, who also will do it." [109] While we wait for that day, the enemy will continue to attack us, "But the Lord is faithful, who shall establish you, and keep you from evil." [110] Our Saviour is "a merciful and faithful High Priest." [111] One thing, above all others, that God requires of us is that we be "found faithful." [112]

Meekness. When we use this word, it often suggests weakness and pusillanimity, but no such meaning is attached to it here. Hogg and Vine say: "The common as-

---

[104] 1 Corinthians 1:9   [105] Romans 3:3, 4   [106] 1 John 1:9
[107] 1 Corinthians 10:13   [108] Isaiah 49:7   [109] 1 Thessalonians 5:24
[110] 2 Thessalonians 3:3   [111] Hebrews 2:17   [112] 1 Corinthians 4:2

sumption is that when a man is meek, it is because he cannot help himself; but the Lord was meek because he had the infinite resources of God at His command. The believer is to cultivate meekness for the same reason." Meekness does not suggest in the least a low conception of one's own abilities. Meekness requires courage and faith.

The Lord Jesus was a meek man;[113] that is, He was possessed of a mild and humble spirit both when He was being rejected and when He was being applauded. He was never occupied with self. All believers should be adorned with the garment of meekness,[114] and when this fruit is not in our lives, we should pursue it. "Follow after . . . meekness."[115] James exhorteth us to "receive with meekness the engrafted Word." [116] We may well seek to imitate the meekness of our Lord Jesus Christ.

Temperance. The word is literally self-control. It means possessing power, having mastery over one's self. In modern times temperance (self-control) has been limited chiefly to strong drink, but the Scripture idea is self-control in all things. It is a virtue too lightly considered in our day, and its absence from the lives of many Christians has rendered them impotent in the service of the Lord. There is great need of rational restraint of all our natural impulses and desires, for we can abuse as well as use the powers with which God has endowed us. If we are to use these powers rightly, the will of man must be exercised in self-control. In the words of the Apostle Peter

[113] Zechariah 9:9 *cf.* Matthew 21:5; Matthew 11:29
[114] Colossians 3:12   [115] 1 Timothy 6:11   [116] James 1:21

"self-control" follows knowledge,[117] so that the believer is responsible to practice what he knows.

Now while this is the fruit of the Spirit, we must keep in mind that the Holy Spirit operates in us as we co-operate with Him. If we refuse to yield to Him, His fruit cannot be borne in us. When Paul used the figure of a race to illustrate the life of Christian service, he made it plain that the winner "is temperate in all things." [118] Rigid self-denial over a period of time was necessary in order to compete in a contest that might last but a few minutes, and then the prize was merely temporal. How willing a Christian should be to subject himself to self-control, discipline, and self-denial in order that he might serve his Lord in an acceptable manner! If there is to be victory for us, it can be only as we allow the Holy Spirit to rule our human spirit.

Oh, are we satisfied to live a negative life that is unfruitful? Let us heed God's Word so that it does not become unfruitful in our lives.[119] Let us give diligence to the truth that we "shall neither be barren nor unfruitful in the knowledge of our Lord Jesus Christ." [120] If we are living in sham or pretense, we are "trees . . . without fruit." [121] When we tamper with this world, there can be no fruit;[122] therefore "have no fellowship with the unfruitful works of darkness." [123] Christians are to keep occupied in the holy things of God, "to maintain good works for necessary uses, that they be not unfruitful." [124] Yield yourself to the Holy Spirit's leading and He will bring forth His fruit in you.

[117] 2 Peter 1:5, 6
[120] 2 Peter 1:8
[123] Ephesians 5:11
[118] 1 Corinthians 9:25
[121] Jude 12
[124] Titus 3:14
[119] Mark 4:19
[122] Romans 6:21

BIBLIOGRAPHY

and

INDEX OF
SCRIPTURE TEXTS

BIBLIOGRAPHY

ROY L. ALDRICH. "Who Was Responsible for the Death of Christ?" *Revelation*. April 1945.

SIR ROBERT ANDERSON. *The Lord From Heaven*.

HYMAN J. APPELMAN. *Power Through the Holy Spirit*. Grand Rapids: Zondervan, 1945.

HAROLD P. BARKER. *The Vicar of Christ*. Chicago: Good News Publishers, 1947.

DAVID BARON. *The Servant of Jehovah*. New York: Doran, 1922.

_____. *Types, Psalms and Prophecies*. New York: American Board of Missions to the Jews, 1948.

PETER BAYNE. *The Testimony of Christ to Christianity*. New York: Sheldon, 1862.

E. H. BICKERSTETH. *The Spirit of Life*. New York: Robert Carter and Bros., 1870.

JAMES MACDOUGALL BLACK. *The Dilemmas of Jesus*. New York: Revell, 1925.

LORAINE BOETTNER. *The Person of Christ*. Grand Rapids: Eerdmans, 1943.

WICK BROOMALL. *The Holy Spirit*. New York: American Tract Society, 1940.

C. GORDON BROWNVILLE. *Symbols of the Holy Spirit*. New York: Revell, 1945.

LEWIS SPERRY CHAFER. *Systematic Theology*. Volumes I and II.

WILLIAM G. COLTMAN. *The Holy Spirit Our Helper*. Findlay, OH: Fundamental Truth Publishers, 1946.

RAYMOND L. CRAMER. *The Master Key*. Los Angeles: Cowman Publications, 1951.

JAMES ELDER CUMMING. *Through the Eternal Spirit*. New York: Revell, 1896.

W. E. DENHAM. *The Comforter.* New York: Revell, 1935.

D. H. DOLMAN. *Simple Talks on the Holy Spirit.* Atlantic City, NJ: The World Wide Revival Prayer Movement, 1939.

E. SCHUYLER ENGLISH. "The Impeccability of Our Lord," *Our Hope.* July 1944.

―――. *Things Surely to Be Believed.* New York: Our Hope Press, 1946.

WILLIAM EVANS. *The Great Doctrines of the Bible.* Chicago: The Bible Institute Colportage Association, 1912.

F. W. FARR. *The Christ You'll Have to Know.* Los Angeles: American Prophetic League, 1939.

HENRY W. FROST. *Who Is the Holy Spirit?* New York: Revell, 1938.

A. C. GAEBELEIN. *The Christ We Know.* Chicago: Bible Institute Colportage Association, 1927.

―――. *The Holy Spirit in the New Testament.* New York: Our Hope.

A. J. GORDON. *The Ministry of the Spirit.* New York: Revell, 1935.

JAMES R. GRAHAM, JR. *Spirit, Soul, Body.*

J. HAROLD GWYNNE. *One Thing Needful.* Grand Rapids: Eerdmans, 1941.

HARRY A. IRONSIDE. *Holiness, the False and the True.* Neptune, NJ: Loizeaux Brothers, 1912.

WIL R. JOHNSON. *Why Believe?* Grand Rapids: Zondervan, 1942.

BOB JONES, JR. *As the Small Rain.* Grand Rapids: Zondervan, 1945.

JOHN B. KENYON. *The Bible Revelation of the Holy Spirit.* Grand Rapids: Zondervan, 1939.

AARON J. KLIGERMAN. *Feasts and Fasts of Israel.* Baltimore: Emmanuel Neighborhood House, 1931.

HAROLD SAMUEL LAIRD. *Portraits of Christ in the Gospel of John.* Chicago: Bible Colportage Association, 1936.

ROBERT G. LEE. *Glory Today for Conquest Tomorrow.* Grand Rapids: Zondervan, 1941.

JOHN LINTON. *The Devil's Bird Cage.* Philadelphia: Westbrook, 1943.

HERBERT LOCKYER. *The Heritage of Saints.* London: Pickering and Inglis.

_____. *The Breath of God.* Cleveland: Union Gospel Press, 1949.

S. FRANKLIN LOGSDON. *Lest Ye Faint.* Toronto: Evangelical Publishers, 1949.

J. GRESHAM MACHEN. *The Christian Faith in a Modern World.* New York: Macmillan, 1936.

WALTER A. MAIER. *Victory Through Christ.* St. Louis: Concordia, 1943.

F. E. MARSH. *Emblems of the Holy Spirit.* New York: Alliance Press Co., 1911.

J. C. MASSEE. *Christ and Human Personality.* New York: Revell, 1941.

_____. *The Holy Spirit in Scripture and Experience.* Cleveland: Union Gospel Press, 1917.

GEORGE MATHESON. *Voices of the Spirit.* New York: A. C. Armstrong and Son, 1892.

JAMES G. McCONKEY. *The Three-fold Secret of the Holy Spirit.* Pittsburgh: Silver Publishing Company, 1897.

G. CAMPBELL MORGAN. *The Teaching of Christ.* New York: Revell, 1913.

HANDLEY C. G. MOULE. *Veni Creator.* London: Pickering and Inglis.

ANDREW MURRAY. *Like Christ.* Philadelphia: Altemus, 1895.

_____. *The Spirit of Christ.* London: Nisbet and Company, Ltd., 1888.

J. W. H. NICHOLS. *The Feasts of the Lord.* Neptune, NJ: Loizeaux Brothers, 1938.

GUSTAVE F. OEHLER. *Theology of the Old Testament.* Grand Rapids: Zondervan, 1883.

GEORGE P. PARDINGTON. *Outline Studies in Christian Doctrine.* Harrisburg: Christian Publications, 1926.

J. M. PENDLETON. *Christian Doctrines.* Philadelphia: The Judson Press, 1878.

ARTHUR T. PIERSON. *The Bible and Spiritual Life.* Los Angeles: The Biola Book Room, 1923.

JOHN R. RICE. *The Power of Pentecost.* Wheaton: Sword of the Lord Publications, 1949.

———. *We Can Have Revival Now!* Wheaton: Sword of the Lord Publications, 1950.

SAMUEL RIDOUT. *The Person and Work of the Holy Spirit.* Neptune, NJ: Loizeaux Brothers, 1899.

WILLIAM B. RILEY. *Seven New Testament Soul-Winners.* Grand Rapids: Eerdmans, 1939.

FREDERICK W. ROBERTSON. *Sermons.* 3 volumes, New York: Dutton, 1906-1909.

PHILIP SCHAFF. *The Person of Christ.* New York: American Tract Society, 1913.

KLAAS SCHILDER. *Christ Crucified.* Grand Rapids: Eerdmans, 1940.

———. *Christ in His Suffering.* Grand Rapids: Eerdmans, 1938.
———. *Christ on Trial.* Grand Rapids: Eerdmans, 1939.

W. GRAHAM SCROGGIE. *The Baptism of the Spirit.* Edinburgh: Marshall, Morgan, and Scott.

OSWALD J. SMITH. *The Spirit Is Working.* Grand Rapids: Zondervan, 1939.

GEORGE SOLTAU. *Four Portraits of the Lord Jesus Christ.* New York: Charles C. Cook, 1905.

———. *Person and Mission of the Holy Spirit.* New York: Charles C. Cook.

JAMES STALKER. *The Christology of Jesus*. New York: A.C. Armstrong and Son, 1899.

H. C. THIESSEN. "Did Our Lord Partake of the Humanity of Mary?" *Our Hope*. September 1940.

AUGUST VAN RYN. *His Appointments*. Neptune, NJ: Loizeaux Brothers, 1944.

EDWARD WHITE. *Life in Christ*.

WALTER L. WILSON. *Ye Know Him*. Kansas City, MO: The W and M Publications, 1939.

W. T. P. WOLSTON. *Another Comforter*. Edinburgh: Lowland and Border Book Depot, 1892.

SOLOMON ZEITLIN. *Who Crucified Jesus?* New York: Harper, 1947.

SAMUEL ZWEMER. *Evangelism Today*. New York: Revell, 1944.

INDEX OF SCRIPTURE TEXTS

EXODUS

PSALMS

MARK

LUKE

JOHN

ACTS

ROMANS

1 CORINTHIANS